May

Rec'd
Summer '55

MEMOIRS
OF
HENRY VILLARD

IN TWO VOLUMES
VOLUME I

MEMOIRS

OF

HENRY VILLARD

Journalist and Financier

1835–1900

IN TWO VOLUMES

VOL. I, 1835–1862

BOSTON AND NEW YORK
HOUGHTON, MIFFLIN AND COMPANY
The Riverside Press, Cambridge
1904

COPYRIGHT 1904
BY FANNY GARRISON VILLARD
ALL RIGHTS RESERVED

Published March 1904

PREFACE

THE circumstances of the composition of this Autobiography of the late Henry Villard are set forth in his own words on page 373 of Volume II. The events of his youth in his native land before coming to the United States he chose to describe in his mother tongue. This portion of his memoirs his family edited and published for private distribution two years after his death, under the title, "Heinrich Hilgard-Villard: Jugend-Erinnerungen, 1835–1853" (New York, 1902). A brief abstract of this charming and highly interesting narrative constitutes the Introduction of the present volumes.

Seven of the eight books written in English are in the first person. Unable, by reason of his rapidly failing health, to finish the memoirs upon the scale of the ante-bellum period, Mr. Villard devoted his last summer to a compendium of the period from 1863 to 1900 written in the third person (Book VIII). He originally intended to make a record for his family, with possible publicity that others might profit by the lessons of his life. As he proceeded and arrived at his experiences in the Civil War, he began, as he explains, to feel the ardor of the historian, and, using the Official Records of both sides in the greatest of American conflicts, he described the various campaigns in which he took part, or was especially interested, with great elaboration and obviously for the public eye. The importance of his observations in the field and of his laborious researches determined the inclusion of these studies, notwithstanding their bulk, in the present publication. A detailed exhibition of his relations to the development of the far Northwestern States may some day also find its way into print.

A work occupying so many years in preparation amid frequent and protracted interruptions — conceived, moreover, and expressed in two languages together with a change of person — must needs be lacking in unity and proportion, but is not, it is believed, correspondingly deficient in interest. Great pains have been taken to control facts, names, and dates; yet there must be errors and inconsistencies which have been overlooked in so wide and populous a tract of human action.

No revision of the text herewith published could remove all traces of the author's German origin; nor could such editing have been warranted. The man speaks for himself. His character shines through his manifold large undertakings, his achievements and disappointments, as also in his love of his native and adopted countries, his championship of every cause which made for political and social uplifting, and his delight in doing good. But his philanthropy is only faintly portrayed by his own hand; of its full extent he alone was aware.

THORWOOD, November, 1903.

TABLE OF CONTENTS

VOLUME I

	PAGE
INTRODUCTION (1835-1853)	1

BOOK I.—FIRST EXPERIENCES IN AMERICA

CHAPTER I.—NEW YORK AND WESTWARD HO (1853-1854)	11
CHAPTER II.—WITH KINSFOLK IN ILLINOIS (1854-1855)	28
CHAPTER III.—LEGAL EXPERIMENTS (1855-1856)	36
CHAPTER IV.—THROUGH POLITICS TO JOURNALISM (1856-1857)	48
CHAPTER V.—CORRESPONDENT AND SCHOOL-TEACHER (1857-1858)	68

BOOK II.—IN CIVIL-WAR TIME: BULL RUN

CHAPTER VI.—THE LINCOLN-DOUGLAS DEBATES (1858)	89
CHAPTER VII.—THE PIKE'S PEAK GOLD FEVER (1858-1859)	98
CHAPTER VIII.—AT CHERRY CREEK (1859)	115
CHAPTER IX.—FROM THE ROCKIES TO THE MIDDLE WEST (1859-1860)	127
CHAPTER X.—WITH LINCOLN AT SPRINGFIELD (1860-1861)	140
CHAPTER XI.—AT WASHINGTON IN SUMTER DAYS (1861)	153
CHAPTER XII.—FORMATION OF THE FEDERAL ARMY (1861)	176
CHAPTER XIII.—BLACKBURN'S FORD AND BULL RUN (1861)	183

BOOK III.—IN CIVIL-WAR TIME: SHILOH

| CHAPTER XIV.—KENTUCKY IN THE SUMMER AND FALL OF 1861 | 203 |
| CHAPTER XV.—THE OCCUPATION OF NASHVILLE (1862) | 218 |

CONTENTS

	PAGE
CHAPTER XVI.—The Battle of Shiloh (1862)	235
CHAPTER XVII.—The Siege of Corinth (1862)	263
CHAPTER XVIII.—Buell's Retreat to the Ohio (1862)	282
CHAPTER XIX.—The Perryville Campaign (1862)	306

BOOK IV.—IN CIVIL-WAR TIME: FREDERICKSBURG

CHAPTER XX.—In Washington Once More (1862)	335
CHAPTER XXI.—With Burnside before Fredericksburg (1862)	344
CHAPTER XXII.—The Battle of Fredericksburg (1862)	353
CHAPTER XXIII.—Carrying the News to Washington (1862)	385

ILLUSTRATIONS

Henry Villard, aged 51 .... *Frontispiece*
   From a photograph by W. Höffert, Berlin.

Henry Villard, aged about 13 .... *to face* page 6
   From a daguerreotype. (He stands at the left of the group, which includes also his mother, his sister Emma, and his uncle, Robert Hilgard.)

MAPS

The Rheinpfalz (Palatinate) .... *to face* page 1
First Battle of Bull Run .... *to face* page 183
Pittsburg Landing and Shiloh .... *to face* page 235
Perryville .... *to face* page 311
Fredericksburg .... *to face* page 353

CHRONOLOGY OF HENRY VILLARD

1835. April 10. Born at Speyer, Rhenish Bavaria.
1839. Home in Zweibrücken.
1849-50. At school in Phalsbourg, Lorraine.
1850-52. At the gymnasium in Speyer.
1852-53. Studies at Munich and Würzburg.
1853. August (September ?). Sails from Hamburg for America.— October 18. Lands in New York.—November 18. Western wanderings begun.
1854. Christmas. At Belleville, Illinois.
1855. At Belleville and Peoria, Illinois.
1856-57. Edits *Volksblatt* at Racine, Wisconsin.
1857-58. Teaches a district school at Jonestown, Lebanon County, Pennsylvania.
1858. Reports Lincoln-Douglas debates in Illinois.
1859. Visits Denver and Cherry Creek, Colorado.
1860-61. Reporter for the Associated Press at Springfield, Illinois.
1861. February. Accompanies Lincoln and Presidential party to New York.— Founds news syndicate in Washington, and becomes telegraphic correspondent there of the New York *Herald*.— July 21. Witnesses first battle of Bull Run.— Sent by the *Herald* to Kentucky.
1862. Visits Fort Donelson immediately after its capture by General Grant (February 16).— Enters Nashville before General Buell.— Reaches Pittsburg Landing at close of first day's fighting, April 6; witnesses that of the second day, and the subsequent occupation of Corinth, May 30.—Witnesses Perryville campaign and battle, October 8.— Becomes Washington war correspondent of the N. Y. *Tribune*.—Witnesses battle of Fredericksburg, December 13, and brings the first tidings to Washington.
1863. Sent to Port Royal by the *Tribune*, and witnesses Dupont's engagement of the Charleston forts from on board the *New Ironsides*, April 7.—First visit to Boston.— Sent to Murfreesboro' by the *Tribune* to report Rosecrans's operations.— Disabled by fever, and misses the battle of Chickamauga (September 19, 20).
1864. Organizes news agency in Washington, and joins Grant's army in the Wilderness in May, and brings to Washington the first tidings of the battles there.— Witnesses explosion of the mine at Petersburg, July 30.—To Europe; reunion with his father.—Winter in Munich.

1865. April 15. Lands in Boston.—Becomes Washington correspondent of the Chicago *Tribune*.
1866. January 3. Marries Fanny Garrison.—To Europe in July, as correspondent of the New York *Tribune* in the Franco-Prussian War.— Winter in Munich.
1867. In March to Paris as correspondent of the Chicago *Tribune* at the World's Fair.
1868-70. Home in Boston.—Secretary of the American Social Science Association.
1870-71. To Germany, with mortgage-bank plan.
1871-72. First employment as expert in American railroad affairs.
1872-73. Serious illness in Heidelberg.
1873. Joins committees of bondholders of Oregon & California R. R. Co. and of Kansas Pacific R. R. Co.
1874. Their delegate to the United States.
1875. Opens Oregon immigration bureau in New York.
1876. First visit to Oregon.—President of Oregon & California R. R. Co. and of Oregon Steamship Co.—A receiver of the Kansas Pacific.
1877. Desperate illness in San Francisco.
1878. Dislodged by Jay Gould from Kansas Pacific receivership.
1879. Victorious over Gould.—Buys out creditors of the Oregon Steamship Co. and the Oregon Steam Navigation Co.—Conceives the Oregon Railway & Navigation Co.
1880. Contract for division of traffic with Northern Pacific R. R. Co.— Founds Oregon Improvement Co.— Buys the two Oregon railroads.
1881. Gains control of the Northern Pacific R. R. by the "blind pool."—Elected its president, and founds the Oregon & Transcontinental Co.—Buys the New York *Evening Post* and *Nation*.
1882-83. Extends the main line of Northern Pacific and builds branches.
1883. Organizes St. Paul & Northern Pacific Co.— Builds St. Paul & Manitoba R. R.— Procures the writing of a 'History of the Northern Pacific Railroad.'— Leads international excursion to witness completion of the Northern Pacific.—Involved in collapse of the road.—Resigns presidency of the Oregon & Transcontinental, Oregon Railway & Navigation Co., and Northern Pacific.
1884-86. To Germany.
1885. Resigns presidency of the Oregon & California R. R.
1886. To New York as representative of the Deutsche Bank.—Saves the Oregon & Transcontinental.
1887-88. Re-enters the Northern Pacific board.
1889. Founds Edison General Electric Co.—Final retirement from Oregon Railway & Navigation Co.—Chairman of finance committee of the Northern Pacific.
1890. Founds the North American Co. to absorb the Oregon & Trans-

continental.— Loses his son Hilgard.— To Germany.— Interview with Chancellor Caprivi.— Visit to Bismarck.
1891. Last official tour of the Northern Pacific.
1893. Retires from the Northern Pacific and North American boards.
1893-94. Tour of the Mediterranean and sojourn in Europe.
1898. To Europe for the last time.
1899. Last tour over the Northern Pacific.— Visit to Alaska.
1900. Dies November 12.

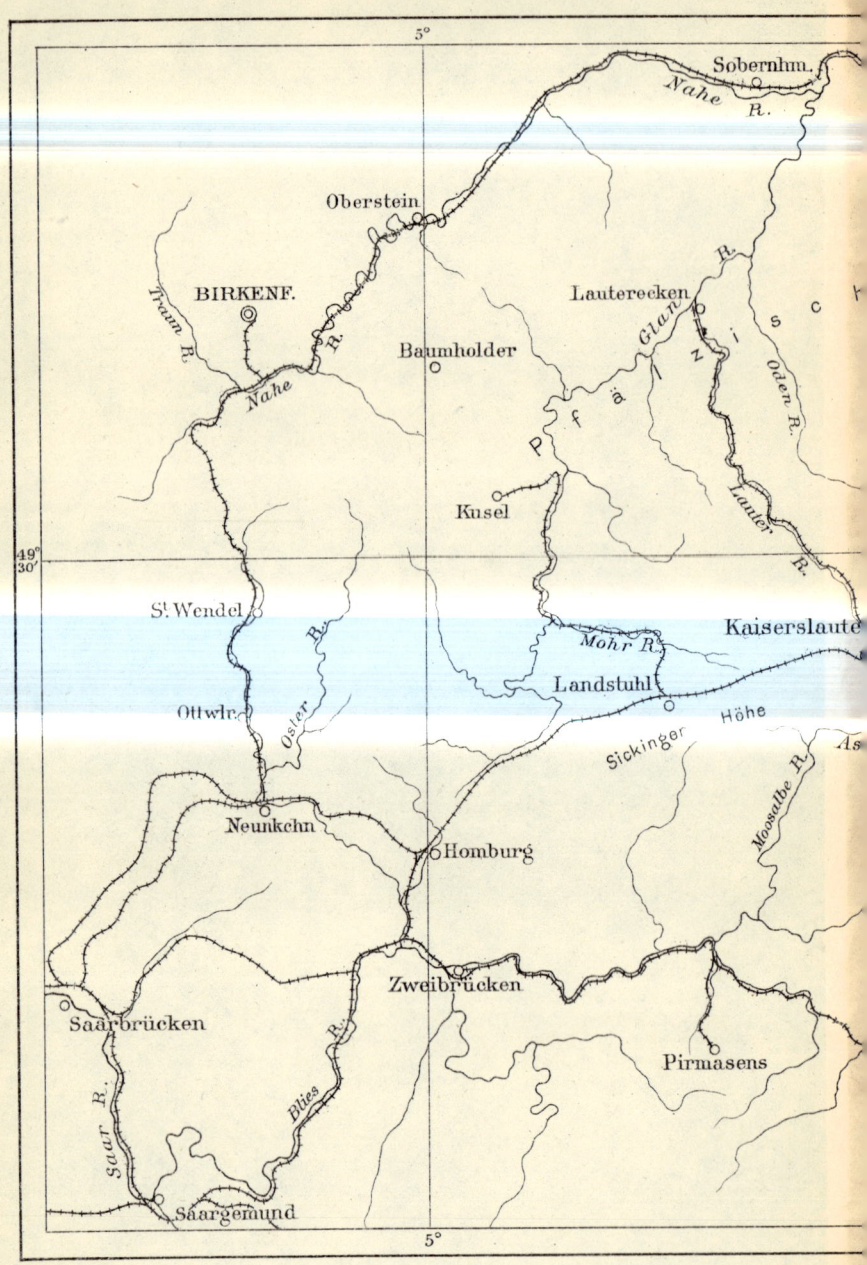

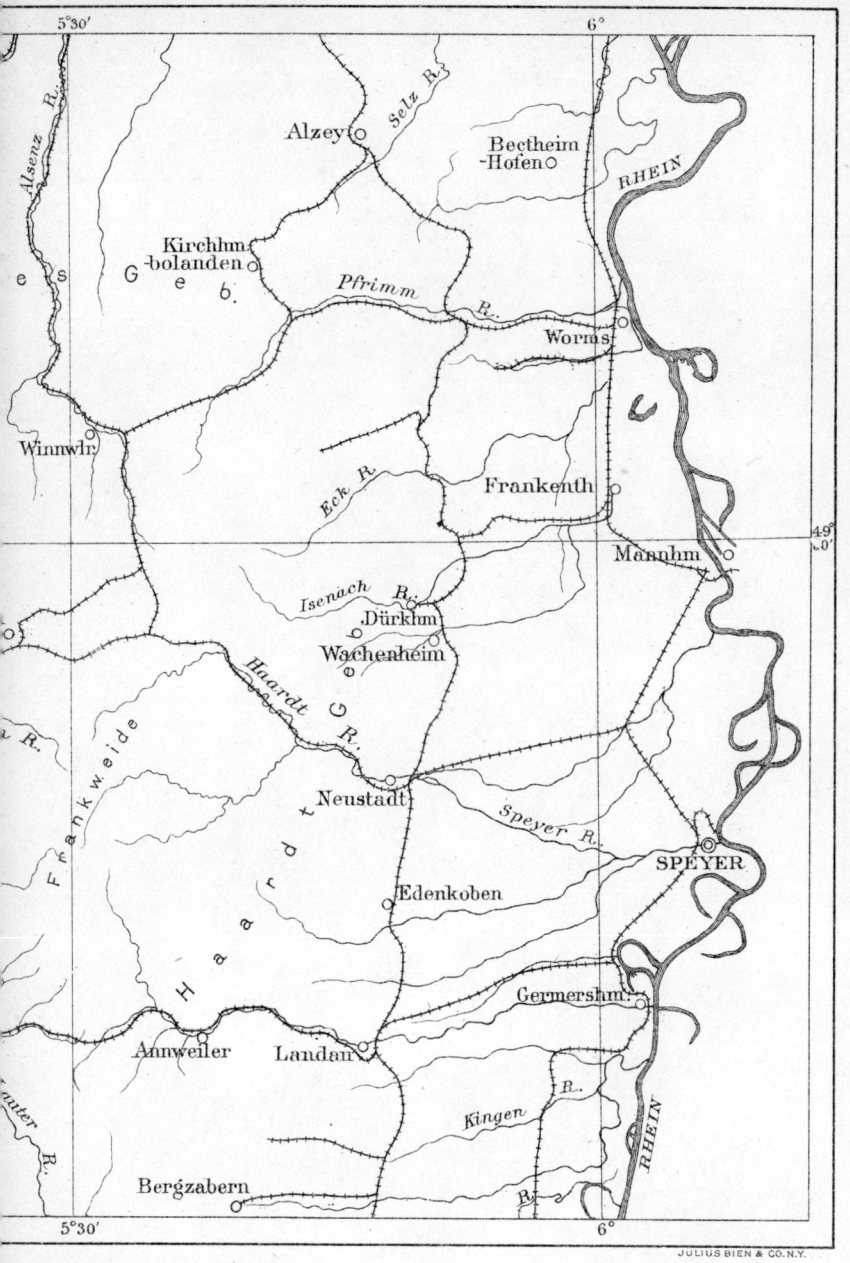

INTRODUCTION

ANCESTRY: EARLY YOUTH IN GERMANY.—1835–1853

HENRY VILLARD was born on April 10, 1835, in Speyer, Rhenish Bavaria, in the home of his maternal grandparents, which now bears a municipal tablet commemorating the event. His baptismal name was Ferdinand Heinrich Gustav Hilgard. His branch of the Hilgard family, whose surname occurs widely in South German village nomenclature, was of Nassau stock.[1] His first known ancestor, Johann Hilgard, was a landowner and a member of the Reformed Church. His descendants of the fourth, fifth, and sixth generations filled pastorates in various parts of what is now Rhenish Prussia. One of them, Gerhard Samuel Hilgard, wrote in 1792 'A Defence of the Revealed Christian Religion,' which he dedicated and presented to King Frederick William II. His son, Jacob Hilgard, was tutor to the heir of the Prince of Nassau-Weilburg, and afterwards associate pastor at Bacharach on the Rhine, where he married a daughter of the pastor, Theodor Erasmus Engelmann, a

---

[1] The line, briefly tabulated, is as follows:

Johann[1] Hilgard (deceased before 1626) and Doris Zwenk.

Philipp[2] Hilgard (1603–1634) and Christine Caesar; married in 1626.

Johann Gottfried[3] Hilgard (born in 1628) and Anna Katharina Caps; married in 1654.

Johann Heinrich[4] Hilgard (born in 1669) and Luise Margarete Mauel; married in 1701.

Gerhard Samuel[5] Hilgard (1717–1810).

Jacob[6] Hilgard (1752–1813) and Maria Dorothea Engelmann (1760–1845); married in 1782.

Georg Friedrich (Fritz)[7] Hilgard (1784–1859) and Lotte Henrich (1780–1818); married in 1806.

Gustav Leonhard[8] Hilgard (1807–1867) and Lisette Pfeiffer (1811–1859), parents of "Henry Villard"; married June 11, 1833.

recluse, but a man of great learning. After Jacob's marriage, the Prince of Nassau-Weilburg gave him the pastorate of Marnheim, a village on the military road to Mainz. At the time of his occupancy this was considered a very lucrative charge, but the exposed position of Marnheim led to its being plundered freely by both contestants in the wars growing out of the French Revolution. Both Jacob Hilgard and his wife believed in the doctrines of the Revolution, and he was so outspoken in favor of them that he was driven by mob violence into exile for four years.

Henry Villard's grandfather was Jacob's son Friedrich. His education suffered considerably because of the unrest of the times and the consequent impoverishment of the family. An uncle sent him to the gymnasium at Idstein in Nassau, and helped him to become a notary in Nancy. Later he was made burgomaster in Kirchheimbolanden, a village near Marnheim, mayor of Speyer, and incumbent of other important Government offices. A man of very solid character and of unusual beauty of person, he was first married to Charlotte Henrich, the daughter of a rich banker whose descendants still carry on his banking business in Neustadt on the Haardt.

Their first-born was Gustav Leonhard Hilgard, who in turn became father of Henry Villard. Gustav, the most talented of the five sons born to Friedrich Hilgard by his first marriage, was somewhat hot-blooded and masterful, with beautiful light-blue eyes and curly, dark-brown hair. Educated at the gymnasium in Speyer, he afterwards studied at the universities of Munich, Heidelberg and Würzburg, at all of which an inheritance received from his mother, who died in 1818, enabled him to live handsomely and to lend a helping hand to needy fellow-students. In 1828 he passed a brilliant examination, and went with his brother Theodor to Paris to attend law lectures at the Collège de France. Returning to the Palatinate, he was appointed to a small legal position at Zweibrücken, and later was transferred to Frankenthal, where he filled a somewhat higher position. Early an admirer of Katharina Antonia Elisabeth (commonly called Lisette) Pfeiffer, he formally asked for her hand in 1830. The marriage was delayed for nearly three and one-half years because of the difference in religion of the pair, Lisette being a Catholic. Finally the consent of the Church was obtained and the home was set up in Frankenthal. Lisette, a charming personality with blue eyes, blond hair and delicate features, was the daughter of a veteran—Franz Pfeiffer—of the wars against France from 1790 until 1801, during which time he fought in the army of the Prince of Condé. For his services, and in recognition of three serious wounds, he was invested in 1816 with the order of St. Louis, which ennobled him and entitled him to a pension. When his military career ended, Franz Pfeiffer entered the civil service, becoming in 1817 director of the Government salt monopoly in Speyer. He married in 1809 Marie Anna Berchtold. As Henry Villard spent most of his boyhood in Pfeiffer's house, this genial, extraordinarily handsome, and kind-hearted grandfather played an important part in the boy's life.

Gustav Hilgard experienced the usual changes of station which then came frequently to those in the legal employ of the Government. In 1839 he settled in Zweibrücken, and remained there until 1856, when he was appointed a justice of the Supreme Court of the kingdom of Bavaria at Munich. Zweibrücken was therefore the true scene of Henry Villard's boyhood, although he made many visits—sometimes staying a year—to his grandparents in Speyer. The boy early proved himself a natural leader in games and in the broils between the children of the city's aristocracy and those of the working classes. His remarkable imagination early displayed itself, as did a thirst for knightly romance, for puppet theatres and theatricals. He soon showed, despite his aristocratic tendencies, that he shared the republican instincts which manifested themselves throughout the Hilgard family, except in the case of his father. Indeed, a large political family migration had taken place in 1833 and 1835 to Belleville, Illinois, a town a few miles from St. Louis, embracing his great-uncle Theodor Erasmus Hilgard, who resigned a judgeship, because he "deemed it a priceless advantage to make my [his] children freemen."

In 1848 the French Revolution upset the whole of South Germany, and incidentally had a marked influence upon the career of Henry Hilgard, although he was then but thirteen years of age. The expectation of an immediate invasion by the forces of the new French Republic threw the entire town of Zweibrücken, like the rest of Rhenish Bavaria, into a state of feverish excitement. In the gymnasium, which Henry had entered with difficulty, and prematurely, as soon turned out, studies could hardly be thought of, and politics was the sole theme of conversation. The right of public meeting was soon granted by the monarchy to the people, and the addresses of the Revolutionary orators, together with the recruiting of a militia force of five hundred men, furnished the youth of the town with endless excitement. The proceedings of the Frankfort Parliament interested Henry so greatly that he finally obtained his father's permission to visit Robert C. Hilgard, a step-uncle (but little older than himself), then entering mercantile life in Frankfort. He spent a week with this young relative, seeing the sights of the city and listening to the speakers at the sessions of the Parliament. By this time Henry's political sympathies were profoundly democratic, and, with boyish enthusiasm, he returned to his home wearing a "Hecker hat" with a red feather. The rector of the gymnasium was so incensed at this as to give him, on his return, a choice between the hat and expulsion. This incident did not improve Henry's relations with his father, who continued to be loyal to the Government and bitterly hostile to the Revolutionary movement with which his brothers sympathized most keenly. The demoralization of Henry's studies, for which he was plainly not ripe, led to parental threats of apprenticing him to a trade.

In May, 1849, the Revolution began in earnest with the establishment of a provisional government for Rhenish Bavaria at the town of Kaiserslautern. Since it demanded the adhesion of all officials, Henry's father went into a brief exile. By June the gymnasium was at a standstill, and Henry was free to roam the streets and watch the beginnings of war. Before this occurred, he and his classmates conspired to omit, in the repetition of the customary daily prayer, the passage about the welfare of "His in-Christ-anointed Majesty, our most gracious Lord and King." As fortune would have it, the city pastor, Dr. Krieger, who was the religious instructor, called upon Henry when the class next assembled. The latter repeated the prayer without reference to the King. Taken sharply to task, the boy still refused to pray for the sovereign, saying that it would be disloyal to the rightful provisional Government. His classmates stood by him. "This," cried the pastor, "is open rebellion and contempt of religion, of his Majesty the King and of myself. I will instruct you no longer." And he flung out of the room, never to return.

A Prussian army under the command of Prince William of Prussia, afterwards Emperor William of Germany, speedily ended the existence of the new republic. The youngsters of Zweibrücken, Henry among them, had no more thrilling adventure than the spending of a night on a reconnoissance with the militia of the town. This body, much decreased in numbers, later saw brief active service, in which one of the older students of the gymnasium lost his life. With the restoration of the old order, the gymnasium was reopened. The head of the school, the rector, at once sentenced Henry Hilgard for insubordination and rebellion. The punishment was a refusal to advance him with his class, which meant the loss of a year's studies. This added greatly to his father's dissatisfaction, and led to a renewal of the threat of an apprenticeship.

As a compromise, Henry succeeded, with the aid of his mother, in obtaining his father's consent to his spending a year at a French semi-military college in Phalsbourg in Lorraine, to which sons of prominent families were frequently sent. In order to obtain some knowledge of French he went to Phalsbourg in September, 1849, a month in advance of the opening of the school. Here he was fortunate in obtaining daily tuition from no less a personage than Alexandre Chatrian, already a story-writer, but not yet famous. When the school began, the life was found to be very rigorous, the study hours long, those for recreation few, the food insufficient, and the morale of the boys as a whole poor. Despite the fact that he found only one or two congenial friends, Henry enjoyed the life and profited by it, especially physically, growing a foot in height and changing from a weakling to a handsome, vigorous and shapely lad. A visit to his home at Easter in 1850 impressed his parents with his improvement so favorably that his father decided to send him in the fall to Speyer to his grandmother's (Franz Pfeiffer had died suddenly in 1847, almost in Henry's presence), in order to allow him to complete his schooling at the gymnasium in that city.

In September, 1850, Henry passed a brilliant examination at Phalsbourg, visited his mother in Switzerland, and was settled in Speyer in his new home, in which he continued to live until his graduation in 1852. As a scholar he took no high rank, but by this time a strong taste for German literature asserted itself, and a desire to write, which became more and more pronounced as time went on. As a boy he was devoted to dancing and horseback riding. He was much in company with his classmates, and, belonging to a forbidden students' society, became involved in several escapades, one of which was punished with a day's arrest and confinement on bread and water.

This sentence increased his popularity with those of his own age, and evoked nothing more than a cutting reprimand from his father.

A serious difference with his father was brought about by Henry's career at the universities of Munich and Würzburg, at which he studied in 1852 and 1853. Letters and art were uppermost in his mind when it came to the choice of a profession, but his father failed to see that, as the Germans put it, "the desire of the heart is the voice of fate," and advocated a technical training. He accompanied his son to Munich and had him matriculated at the Polytechnicum. After two months of hard work Henry found his tasks there positively repugnant. Instead of advising his father, he then made the mistake of having himself transferred to the University, and devoted himself to lectures by the poet Geibel and by the æsthete and critic Moritz Carriere. The expense of this change of studies, as well as membership in the Franconia, a fashionable student corps, soon ran him into debt, while the corps life itself, with all its attractions, such as duelling, balls, and "Kneip-Abende," cost him many valuable hours that should have been devoted to his university work. When his father discovered, by accident, the change in his son's mode of life and studies, he ordered him home at once. After much cogitation and much warranted anger, he sent his penitent son to the quieter University of Würzburg, and committed him to a study of the law. Here the subject of this sketch lived quietly and worked hard for some months, but again the old desire for literature and æsthetics, for the study of which he could never gain his father's consent, revived. Gradually the law became more and more distasteful, and his situation was made the more difficult by the necessity of paying off his Munich creditors, who were so ready to trust him when he was a member of the Franconia.

In this emergency he bethought himself of well-to-do relatives at Wachenheim on the Haardt, who loaned him the sum of several hundred gulden, but informed him that they would not keep the loan a secret from his father. Rather than proceed to Zweibrücken and throw himself upon the clemency of a parent who had never treated him otherwise than sternly, and who had insisted upon forcing his son into impossible grooves, Henry decided upon migration to a foreign country. It was his intention to work hard there and to show his parents and sisters that he could make an honorable career for himself by his own endeavors, and this he later thought could be furthered by a change of name. How well he succeeded in his efforts is set forth in the following chapters from his own hand. After trying to obtain temporary employment in Dresden and Hamburg, and declining an opportunity to become an officer in the Austrian army, he took passage on the bark *Nordamerika* for New York, sailing from Hamburg. He landed in America on October 18, 1853, after a tedious and stormy voyage, with but a scanty wardrobe and an empty purse, ignorant of the English language, and without a friend to turn to in the American metropolis.

MEMOIRS OF HENRY VILLARD

BOOK ONE

FIRST EXPERIENCES IN AMERICA

CHAPTER I

New York and Westward Ho.—1853–4

MY landing upon American soil took place under anything but auspicious circumstances. I was utterly destitute of money, had but a limited supply of wearing apparel, and that not suited to the approaching cold season, and I literally did not know a single person in New York or elsewhere in the Eastern States to whom I could apply for help and counsel. To crown all, I could not speak a word of English.

It was natural that this consciousness of my condition should weigh upon my spirits. I felt, indeed, greatly oppressed, and spent the first day in gloomy thoughts at the Hotel Constanz. A travelling companion who had tried to persuade me to accompany him to California noticed my depression, and guessed its cause from what he had drawn out of me on the voyage about my antecedents and plans. He generously offered to lend me twenty dollars, which I accepted, of course, with joy. As my weekly board-bill was to be only five dollars, I felt quite relieved from immediate anxiety, and sufficiently at ease in mind to look the future straight in the face. I resolved to seek some sort of employment without delay, but, at the same time, I could not feel at all sure of success, and determined to make an appeal for help to my relatives in the West. At home I had become acquainted with several of them— my great-uncle, Theodor Adolf Engelmann, the brother of my step-grandmother, and Johann Scheel, who married one of her sisters. But I did not remember their addresses. I knew, however, that another distant relative, Dr. George Engelmann, was a physician in good practice in St. Louis, and so I ventured to address a letter to him, enclosing another for my father's brother Theodor, with a request to forward it. Next I took counsel with the landlord regarding employment, got a number of addresses, including that of the Bavarian consul and the German Emigrant Aid Society, from him and from advertisements in the two German daily papers for help in various occupations, and, thus equipped, began my search for something to do by which I could earn my daily bread.

In the pursuit of my object I saw much of New York. The city had then only about three hundred thousand inhabitants, but, unless my memory deceives me, its leading business streets presented as striking and stunning a picture of intense commercial activity as to-day. The sidewalks on Broadway were certainly very crowded with people, and the street proper jammed full of vehicles of every description. But, of course, the city had comparatively small dimensions. Fourteenth Street was the limit of animated street-life. Beyond it the rows of buildings began to thin out, and above Twenty-third Street things still had an open-country appearance. The Fifth Avenue Hotel was not then built. Between the City Hall and Canal Street there were still whole streets exclusively occupied by private residences. The best and most frequented hotels seemed to be located south of Canal Street. I remember very clearly being struck with astonishment at the sight of the lounging habits of their guests, visible through the great windows of the reading- and smoking-rooms on the ground floor. Whole rows of elevated legs were presented to the passers-by on Broadway. The black servants in several of them astonished me also.

The most renowned hotel was then the Astor House. Several of my fellow-boarders had, like myself, read at home descriptions of its grandeur, and we were all very anxious to see it, as one of the wonders of the age. So we agreed to take a meal there for that purpose, as it was only a few minutes' walk from our own hotel. No one of us knew any English, but that did not deter us, as we supposed that in such an establishment of world-wide fame all the languages of Europe would naturally be spoken. We made our way up-stairs to the office and boldly made our wishes known in our native tongue, but discovered promptly that we were not understood. One of us then tried French, saying: "Nous voulons dîner." The last word was understood by the official in charge, who called a boy and motioned to us to follow him, which we did. We were taken into the dining-room, which did not, however, as far as either size or decoration was concerned, much impress those of us who had seen large Continental hotels. After we had taken seats at a table, each of us was handed a bill-of-fare; but, being English, it was no clearer than Sanskrit to us. We tried both German and French with the waiter, without making the least impression. The head waiter was attracted by our loud efforts to make ourselves understood, and, although equally ignorant of our language, managed to comprehend the situation and, by signs, let us know that we should be taken care of. We were duly served, but, instead of having one course after another, according to the Continental practice, a medley of dishes was put before us, consisting of several kinds of meat and as many vegetables, all at once, followed by a miscellaneous assortment of pudding, pies, cakes, fruit, nuts, cheese, and other things. We were so taken aback that we did not enjoy anything, but were glad, under circumstances so embarrassing, to finish the novel repast at the earliest possible moment. We withdrew in disgust, paid seventy-five cents each, and made our exit from the great building as hungry as we had entered it.

Our landlord was Max Weber, an ex-officer of the Baden army, who had emigrated in consequence of his participation in the revolutionary outbreak of 1849. He afterwards rose to prominence in the War of the Rebellion. Among his regular boarders were several political exiles. These two circumstances made the "Constanzer Hof" a favorite resort of the German refugees then still numerous in New York. Almost every evening there was a gathering of them in the tap-room, where there were noisy political discussions in true German beer-house style. They dwelt upon the Fatherland as well as the United States, and I listened to them with intense interest. That the talk about Germany was very bitter and angry was not surprising to me, in view of the high tide of reaction that had set in; but it astonished and puzzled me to hear likewise violent denunciations of the United States as a sham land of liberty, of its institutions as republican only in form, of the material attractions for European immigrants as a humbug—with other like expressions of grievous disappointment. Among the loudest declaimers in this strain was an individual called Professor Boehm, who supported himself as a writer for the local German press, and who spoke with a deep, gruff voice and snappish sort of delivery. He seemed surcharged with bitterness against the American Republic, and broke out into roaring diatribes against it on the slightest provocation. His prejudices amounted to a kind of monomania, and they were known all over New York. It was considered an amusement to hear him hold forth, and devices were resorted to, such as purposely opposing his views, in order to provoke outbursts on his part. This man did not know a single American, hardly ever saw anything of New York beyond the two or three streets through which his daily round took him, had never been outside of the city, and yet railed continually against everything American. This was an extreme case, but the minds of nearly all the refugees whom I heard express themselves were affected the same way. I need hardly say that, not knowing any better, I was much discouraged by their unfavorable judgment of the country. It acted as a damper to my sanguine expectations of a rapid and highly successful career.

The northern part of William Street, in which the Hotel Constanz was situated, was, in those days, a succession of hotels, boarding-houses, and beer-houses, and hence a centre of attraction for my countrymen. At the upper end of the street stood the Hotel Shakspere, then kept by one Fickler, a fat, jovial Boniface, who had, however, followed at home the more honorable profession of barrister and politician. He had taken a leading part in the Baden revolt, as a member of the revolutionary executive committee. His hostelry was much larger than ours, and was also a popular rendezvous for South Germans, who crowded it on Sundays to overflowing. But the character of the house was low, and it harbored adventurers of both sexes and of all nationalities. Some of the other William Street places represented a still lower grade of entertainment, being nothing less than vulgar concert-halls with suspicious-looking female attendants. Among the inmates of our house, too, some unsavory scandals broke out, and I began to feel decidedly uncomfortable in such surroundings and longed to get away from them. For two weeks I followed eagerly and faithfully every clew in my hunt for employment, but without the least result. The Bavarian consul had an average of twenty applicants for each of the few positions he heard of in the course of a year. I could have had a clerkship with mercantile wholesale and retail firms if I had had a commercial training and known English. My inability, too, to give references prevented me from getting the unfilled places from employers upon whom my earnest appeals and readiness to do any work made an impression. My disqualifications narrowed the circle of possibilities around me every day. Under the impulse of the rapid decrease of my small fund, I tried to get a place as helper in a drug-store or restaurant, and finally even as a waiter in a beer-hall. But my "greenness" or recent arrival in the country, and maybe my perhaps too genteel appearance, were against me. I received, indeed, my first lesson in the advantages which immigrants accustomed to manual labor enjoy over all classes in this country.

While I did not feel at all sure of being made welcome by my relatives, I still had a faint hope of an encouraging reply to my letter. But it had nearly become extinguished when, one evening in the third week of my stay, on entering the hotel in a very discouraged mood, the office-clerk handed me a letter post-marked Belleville, Illinois. It was the expected answer. For some time I did not dare to open it, lest its contents should prove disappointing. It turned out to be a letter from my great-uncle Theodor, couched in cautious language, and telling me, in response to the intimation of my intention to visit Belleville, that my relatives did not desire to see me until they clearly understood the reason why I came to America. As an offset to this rebuff, I unfolded from the letter a draft for fifty dollars.

The next day I made up my mind what to do. Having repaid the twenty dollars I had borrowed, I resolved to try and reach the West with the remainder. As it was already the latter part of November, and as I had nothing but an overcoat in the way of winter clothing, I invested one-third of the balance in a cheap, but warm suit. Thus equipped, I left New York on November 19, with eighteen dollars in my pocket and all my other possessions in a large hand-bag. I had decided to go via Philadelphia and Pittsburg to Cincinnati. My reason for choosing this city as my destination was solely the fact, gathered from my guide-book, that it had a large German population, including a considerable percentage of Bavarians.

There was no direct railway connection between New York and Philadelphia at that time. I took the principal route of travel, by boat to Perth Amboy and thence by rail to Camden on the Delaware, opposite Philadelphia. The boat and train were crowded with emigrants, among them many Germans. We reached Camden after dark, and found the ferry-boat literally swarming with emigrant-runners, who at once beset us with their solicitations. Knowing the risk one was exposed to in trusting them, I felt called upon to warn the ignorant peasants among my countrymen against them. This made me at once the target for their foul abuse and threats. Nothing daunted, I tried, after landing on the other side, to save a party of South Germans from being carried off by three of the ruffians. They seized the baggage and loaded it without permission on their wagons, so as to compel the owners of it to follow. As the runners were Germans, I boldly denounced them before the crowd and called on them to desist. Thereupon all three suddenly fell upon me, swearing loudly, and, before I could defend myself, I was knocked down and probably should have fared very badly but for the intervention of a German-speaking official. My assailants, however, got away with their prey. The official kindly showed me the way to the inn where I intended to spend a day before continuing my journey West.

I wished to stop at this inn for a special reason. I had learned in New York that it was kept by a refugee, formerly a lawyer in my native town, a classmate of my father's, and a friend of long standing of all our family. He had been a member of the German Parliament, and the head of the provisional government that ruled over Rhenish Bavaria for two months in the summer of 1849, and was under sentence of death for that offence. I remembered him as a very good-natured and witty fellow, rather too much given to conviviality, but a gentleman withal. I expected to receive a hearty welcome and to have a good time with him. A disagreeable surprise awaited me. I found him entirely changed. He received me in a cold and indifferent manner, showing no astonishment at my appearance before him, as I naturally expected he would. His face wore a stolid expression and disclosed a reddish hue, the sure sign of the habitual toper. I soon satisfied myself that the man had sunk low in every way, so that I was glad to be turned over to the solitary waiter. The inn was of a third-class character, small and insignificant in all its appointments. Under the circumstances, I was glad to be again under way the next day, having seen as much as my time permitted of the City of Brotherly Love.

The condition of my purse compelled me to travel again by an emigrant-train, as I had done from New York. The sight that greeted my eyes on entering the cars was anything but comforting. The cars were low, narrow, and only half as long as the present ones. The interior, including the seats, was of plain wood. The passengers consisted of a number of families, more or less numerous and dirty, with children of all ages. Each had brought hand-baggage, cooking-utensils and bedding, and was trying to occupy as much room as possible, which led to angry disputes among them. Before starting, the cars reeked with tobacco-smoke and bad odors. I went through all the cars in search of the familiar sound of my native tongue, but I listened in vain, and found myself in the embarrassing predicament of not being able to converse with a single one of my travelling companions, who seemed to consist of native Americans and Irish immigrants.

We moved slower even than freight trains, out of whose way we had to get time and again, and it took us fully a day and a half to reach Pittsburg. At that time the passage of the Alleghany Mountains was still made, on what is now the main line of the Pennsylvania, by means of stationary engines, placed at intervals in the mountains, from which one car after another was pulled up by means of wire ropes. I think that in this way it took us over twelve hours to cross the range. I had to share a narrow seat with another person, so no comfort was to be had in the daytime and no rest at night. A still greater trial, however, was to be obliged to go almost without food during the long journey. We passed the larger towns on the route during the night, when my inability to speak English made me afraid to leave the car, especially as I could not find out the length of the stops. For the same reason, I was afraid to leave the train in search of food in the daytime. Thus I had to depend for sustenance upon the apples and cake that were offered for sale in the cars here and there. Dirty and tired as I was, I greeted our arrival in Pittsburg as a deliverance from much misery.

But I had to fare still worse. I had bought a through ticket to Cincinnati, entitling me to a second-class passage down the Ohio on a certain steamboat-line from Pittsburg. Not knowing the time of the departure of the boats, I made at once for the landing-place. This I managed to find by inquiring my way in stores whose signs indicated the German origin of their owners. There were three boats of the same line loading. I could not find out which would leave first, although I discovered some countrymen among the deck-hands, whom I questioned on the subject. "Whichever will be loaded full first," was the reply. So I felt obliged to spend all day waiting and watching in one of the low German lodging and beer-houses frequented by the deck-hands who crowded the levee. Being no wiser by evening, I thought it best to spend the night there, repulsive as it was. I was given a bed in a room with two others, lay down with my clothes on and slept soundly. In the morning I was told that one of the boats had a sign up that it would leave at noon. After breakfast, I went on board in order to see what accommodations I should have as a second-class passenger. This I soon found out with the aid of a German deck-hand. To my great disgust, I ascertained that my ticket only permitted me to claim a place on the lower deck-quarter occupied by the deck-hands, including a sooty, bare, rough bunk. Made wise by my railroad experience, I laid in a good supply of bread and meat, and betook myself and my bag, with anything but a light heart, to the boat.

We steamed down the river promptly at the appointed time. It was a beautiful Indian summer day, warm and slightly hazy. The bluffs were still bright with the autumn hues of the foliage. The broad, winding river was alive with steam- and other craft. Farm-houses, hamlets and villages were constantly in sight. We stopped at several towns in the course of the afternoon, discharging and receiving passengers and freight. I sat all the afternoon and long after dark on deck near the bow of the boat, beholding and enjoying these varied sights. Finally, I became drowsy and sought the deck-passengers' quarters astern. I found not only all the bunks on both sides occupied by two or more sleepers each, but men, women, and children crowded so closely together on the deck that one could hardly help stepping on them. I tried first to sleep in a sitting position, but after a while I likewise stretched out on the floor with my bag for a pillow, and soon forgot my surroundings. The warmth from the steam-boilers kept those comfortable who, like myself, had no other covering than their overcoats.

I was up again at daybreak, feeling stiff and dirty. I looked about for some washing utensils, but failed to find any. I actually was unable to wash my face and hands during the whole journey, lasting nearly forty-eight hours, owing to the score, more or less, of protracted stops made by the boat. What with my filthy surroundings and the low company, I could not help again feeling much dispirited. Though the weather continued to be fine and the sights along the river even more attractive than the first day, my only thoughts and wishes were for my release from these repulsive experiences. This feeling was intensified by the impossibility of sleeping at all during the second night, owing to the fearful racket made by the landing of piles of freight and filling the empty space with firewood.

It was nearly noon of the second day when the *City of Pittsburg* reached the Cincinnati landing. The levee presented an imposing sight. At least twenty-five boats, stern-

and side-wheelers, were loading and discharging freight, and the bank was crowded with people, vehicles, and goods. Swarms of hotel-runners and omnibuses and carriages were waiting for passengers. Of course, the dirt-begrimed individuals emerging from the deck did not attract the runners. I had the address of a hotel kept by a Rhenish Bavarian whom I had known as a policeman in Zweibrücken, but my appearance seemed so discreditable to me that I was ashamed to go directly there. Moreover, my money was reduced to three dollars, and I had to be satisfied with the cheapest possible quarters. Discovering a number of emigrant boarding-houses on the street along the levee, I selected one kept by an Alsatian, who agreed to furnish me with board and lodging for the even then low price of $2.50 a week. The "Hôtel de Strasbourg" consisted of a bar-room in front, on the first floor, and behind it a room large enough to serve for both cooking and eating purposes. The second floor consisted of a loft, divided by thin board partitions into sleeping quarters. I was assigned to one containing three single beds, of which I happily remained the sole occupant during my whole stay. Altogether, it was the worst-looking tavern I had ever seen, but it at least gave me immediately a chance to clean up, for which I longed, and the food proved to be as good as that I had often had at peasant-houses in the vicinity of Phalsbourg.

Cincinnati even then laid claim to the title of Queen City of the West, and seemed to me to deserve it. It had already over two hundred thousand inhabitants. It occupied as fine a natural site as could well be found, rising gradually from the river to the hills that picturesquely enclosed it like an amphitheatre. It was regularly laid out in streets running parallel with and at right angles to the river. The streets adjoining the Ohio were solidly built up with business edifices, and those farther away with private residences. The buildings were mostly plain, but the whole presented a substantial and comfortable appearance. The upper part of the city was separated from the lower by the Miami Canal, nicknamed the "Rhine" from the fact that the quarter to the north of it was almost exclusively occupied by Germans, who even then formed fully one-third of the inhabitants. My first walk about the city naturally was in that direction.

I had no difficulty in finding the inn kept by the ex-policeman. He welcomed me with real heartiness, as he had served under my father and remembered our whole family well. He at once invited me to take up my abode with him, but, not feeling sure whether he meant to offer me hospitality or to wish to have me as a paying guest, I was afraid to accept. He told me of several Rhenish Bavarians whom I knew by name and who knew my family, and who were in the habit of enjoying a bottle of beer or wine regularly at his house. This was joyful news to me, for I felt sure of finding a suitable position with his and their help. I agreed to call again in the evening, in order to be introduced to my *Landsleute*. I continued my exploration of the city all day, and received such favorable impressions of it that I ardently wished matters would shape themselves so that I could remain there.

As a matter of fact, I stayed only a few days in Cincinnati, as I soon found that my entire ignorance of English and lack of a specific calling made the difficulty of finding employment among the German-Americans in that city very great. In my subsequent wanderings I was obliged to accept whatever work offered, whether light or hard, including manual labor; and altogether had a very trying experience during the winter following, as also during the greater part of 1854. I returned to the Queen City in March of that year, and for several months represented a firm of publishers as canvasser among the German-Americans. I then drifted from Ohio into Indiana, where I had my first experiences as a railroad man as part of the crew of a wood-train on the Indianapolis & Madison Railroad. Every day this train went out into the country for twenty miles or so, loaded up with wood to be used as locomotive fuel, and then ran back to Indianapolis and unloaded in a woodshed. The work was light, the hours were easy, and the pay good, so that I enjoyed the experience (little dreaming what an important part railroads would play in my career) until prostrated by a serious attack of intermittent fever, with which I had already made acquaintance. This confined me to my bed for so long a period that my place on the wood-train was filled before I was able to return to work. After obtaining light employment in Indianapolis until I had fully recovered, I set out for Chicago, and arrived there at the end of October, 1854, a year after my arrival in the United States.

Leaving my trunk at the station, I walked all over the city. Chicago had then a population not exceeding thirty thousand people, though the inhabitants claimed that it was more. Then, as now, the best improved part was south of the Chicago River, while on the north side there were only a few short streets, and still fewer on the west side. Five-sixths of the buildings were cheap wooden structures. Hardly any of the streets were paved, and most of the sidewalks were of wood. Still, there was an air of stir and push about the town that indicated great vitality, and promised a rapid growth in the future. I felt sure that I had come to the right place.

In passing along State Street, even then one of the most important thoroughfares, I noticed under the sign of a boarding- and lodging-house the name Bernhard Norkin, that borne by the elder brother of a playmate of mine in Speyer. Out of curiosity, I entered and inquired for the landlord, and saw, when he appeared, that I was correct in my surmise. As he had left Speyer many years before, he did not recognize me, but welcomed me very heartily, and invited me, on being told that I was a new-comer, to stop at his hotel. I of course gladly agreed to do so, and my trunk was sent for. He introduced me to his wife, a buxom, bright German woman. We had a very well-cooked German dinner together, and I congratulated myself on such an auspicious beginning in Chicago. But this feeling was considerably dampened when I discovered that, after all, I had only got into an ordinary emigrant boarding-house. The keeper of it employed a wagon and two runners, and, by means fair or foul, obtained all his patronage from the emigrant-trains arriving twice daily from the East. I subsequently saw for myself that the runners were not any more truthful or less urgent in their demands than their colleagues in New York. There was but one dining-room, in one corner of which the baggage of the guests was piled up, and a sleeping-hall directly above it, divided into two parts by a thin partition, for men and for women. Each compartment had eight beds, in one of which I had to sleep. Emigrants in those days were no more attractive in respect to cleanliness and otherwise than to-day; hence I was not very happy in my surroundings. But, as the host and hostess were really anxious to do all they could for me, and as I expected the former, who had been in Chicago for some years, to be very helpful to me in getting employment, I concluded to stay in spite of all drawbacks.

Norkin knew a number of Pfälzer, some of whom held influential positions. One of them was one of the publishers, and another one of the editors, of the Illinois *Staats-Zeitung*, at that time and to-day the leading German paper in the city. Another was a successful physician, and still another a wine-merchant. I applied to them all for advice and assistance in finding a suitable occupation, but, though they freely gave me counsel, they proved to be of no real help. I also inserted an advertisement in the *Zeitung*, but received no responses to it. I called daily at various intelligence offices, and, moreover, made personal inquiries for work in all sorts of establishments. But the only openings I found were for waiters in lager-beer saloons, which already abounded in the city, and for drivers of delivery-wagons. My host having assured me that he would board me all winter, if necessary, I did not avail myself of these unsatisfactory chances, although one week after another passed by in involuntary idleness. One morning, when I came down from my sleeping-room, the landlord sang out to me: "Here is some important news for you," and pointed to an advertisement in the *Zeitung*. It was an urgent request to me to send my address immediately to the signer of it, in Belleville, Illinois. The advertiser was Robert Hilgard, my stepuncle and schoolmate. Of course, I felt a great shock of surprise, for it looked as if Robert had come to America on purpose to find me. Norkin had not been told that I was not in communication with my family. He questioned me, and I had to admit the fact, whereupon he urged me to answer the summons immediately. I told him that I had resolved not to make known my whereabouts to my family till I could tell them that I was able to support myself independently; but he insisted that it was my duty to write to Belleville without delay, and he added smilingly that if I did not do so he would. I replied that I would think the matter over for a day or two. Finally, I sat down and wrote Robert briefly where I was, and said that my lot had not been an enjoyable one since landing on this side of the water. I said further that, although I had not been very successful, I was confident of getting along, and that he need not have any anxiety on that account. I begged him also to explain how he happened to be in America, and to give me the fullest possible news of my family.

A week elapsed without bringing an answer to my letter, until, on returning to my lodging-house on the eighth day, a figure rose from a chair, and I recognized at once the tall form and the well-cut, handsome face of Robert himself. He greeted me very cordially, and, without waiting for any questions from me, told me all I wanted to know. He had been away from Belleville for a couple of days when my letter reached there. After reading it, he hesitated whether to write a reply or to make it in person, and advised first with my uncle and other relatives about it; the former authorizing him to offer me a home in his family. He decided finally to come, as he was afraid I might hesitate to accept. His strongest motive, however, was the solemn promise he had given to my mother, who had been a second mother to him, to make every effort to discover my whereabouts and to aid me in my upward struggles. This promise was not, indeed, his main motive in coming to this country a few months before. He had been wishing to go to America ever since he had finished his four years' apprenticeship at Frankfort, believing that his prospects in life would be much better over here. He had visited my parents shortly before leaving Germany, and thus could give the latest news of them and of my sisters. It was such as to move me inexpressibly, and I promised to write home at the earliest possible moment, and open communication with my loved ones after the long interval of more than a year.

Robert then brought up the subject of my immediate future. He urged me to go at once with him to Belleville, assuring me that our relatives were ready to extend a kindly welcome to me. At first I could not look upon his proposal in the same light that he did. At last he appealed to me in the name of my mother, who certainly would not be relieved of her anxieties about me if I continued to lead the precarious life I had led for a year, instead of being under the care and guidance of my relatives. This argument prevailed with me, and we agreed to start together for St. Louis on the following evening. The next day I showed Robert the city. In the evening I took leave of my host and hostess, to whom I expressed my sincere gratitude. We travelled all night, and reached St. Louis the following noon.

We went directly to the house of a maternal aunt of

Robert's, Mrs. Caroline Decker, one of the daughters of my great-great-uncle Friedrich Engelmann, a man already of advanced age when he emigrated with his large family from Rhenish Bavaria. She had married a German-American lawyer in St. Louis, who died, after a few years of happiness, and left her without means, but with a son and daughter to support and bring up. She resolutely started a boarding-house for the better class of Germans, and she was keeping it at the time. She made me feel at home at once. We remained there three days, seeing as much as we could of St. Louis and of some other relatives there. We then went by rail to Belleville, in St. Clair County, Illinois, only fourteen miles distant, stopping over night at the house of John Scheel, whom I knew, as he had visited us in Zweibrücken some years before. He had emigrated with Friedrich Engelmann, having been his assistant in the forestry service, and had married over here his youngest daughter Betty. He was a very active, shrewd man in a business way, and had succeeded in accumulating a moderate competency. He was very popular, and held at the time the lucrative office of Register of Deeds and Clerk of the Probate Court. He lived in a commodious house, enlivened by three small children. This very kind-hearted couple gave me a most cordial welcome, and invited me to remain with them as long as I liked. But Robert and I thought it best to drive to my uncle Theodor Hilgard's farm the next morning.

CHAPTER II

WITH KINSFOLK IN ILLINOIS.—1854-5

THE farm was situated five miles from Belleville in a rolling prairie region, and consisted of about one hundred acres of well-cultivated land. There was a rather small two-story frame house painted white, and with green shutters, with an extension—upon the crown of a hill, in the shade of some lofty trees, and commanding a fine view; also, a large barn and stable combined, and half a dozen other outbuildings used for various purposes. In front of the house was a large vineyard, and behind it a flower- and vegetable-garden. It being winter, the *ensemble* did not look as attractive as in the greenness of summer, yet was altogether pleasing.

My uncle Theodor and aunt, whom I had never seen, were awaiting our coming. The former received me rather stiffly, but the face of the latter fairly beamed upon me with kindness. My uncle was the next youngest of my father's brothers, and was then about forty-six years old. He was a thick-set man, rather under middle stature, with a strong, round head covered with curly hair, and a broad face framed by a full beard. Both hair and beard were already tinged with gray. His face had a set, stern expression in repose, but he had a pleasant smile, which showed that he was really very good-natured. My aunt won my heart at once. She was of good height, and, though already of matronly proportions, still had a graceful figure and movements. The shape of her head was beautiful and her hair still jet-black. Her brilliant, soft black eyes and gentle mouth imparted much light and sweetness to her face (though her features could not be called handsome), and made her very winning. She was, too, just what she seemed to be—clever, vivacious, interested in everything, and overflowing with inexhaustible kindness. I felt attracted to her as to a second mother, and she treated me as a mother would, for which I have always felt profoundly grateful. My uncle was a highly educated man, but was often blunt in his speech and given to ridicule and sarcasm. He was exceedingly well-informed about American as well as European affairs, and was full of progressive and even radical ideas, and not indisposed to talk. It required but little intercourse with him to bring out his absolutely sterling character, which secured him the highest respect of friends and neighbors and the community at large.

The couple were blessed with eight fine, model children —four boys and four girls. The eldest of the boys was named Gustav, after my father; he was a year older than I, and was away studying to be an engineer. The other boys—Carl, Theodor, and Ernst—ranging from fourteen to ten, were sweet-tempered, confiding, lusty fellows, who took at once to their newly arrived cousin. The eldest daughter, Anna, was of my age, a handsome, well-formed girl, with the black hair and bewitching eyes of her mother. The second daughter was a fresh-looking blonde of a very quiet disposition, never happier than when she could serve others. The other two daughters were affectionate, blooming little girls of seven and eight, with whom I quickly established the most cordial relations.

Altogether, I found myself in a family circle again, the equal of which for perfect harmony and mutual affection it would have been hard to find anywhere. I now felt the softening, elevating influences of this sweet home-life, and a sense of inner peace and happiness awoke in me that I had not felt for years. My aunt begged me to do my duty without delay and write to my parents. It was well indeed that I had delayed doing so till I had drawn in the right inspiration from the domestic picture before me. It took me days, however, to compose a letter that satisfied me. When it was done and sent off by mail, I felt the sense of relief that always comes with the final fulfilment of a long-delayed duty. Robert wrote likewise and at length, as I learned only after the lapse of many years; and my uncle and aunt sent letters to my father and mother after I had been a few weeks with them.

My uncle followed the practice of all successful Western farmers in doing every sort of work on his place himself. He had only one regular hand employed to help him, so that if he had not done so from choice, necessity would have compelled him to take a leading part in the farm routine. Though it was winter, there was enough to occupy him more or less, daily. There was also but one female servant in the house, so that much domestic labor devolved upon my aunt and the two eldest daughters in taking care of the large household. Naturally it became irksome to me to be idle while all the grown members of the family were continually busy. Moreover, without anything to do, time came to hang heavily on my hands; so I soon offered my services for any in-door or out-door work, and this offer evidently gave pleasure all round. I helped feed the horses, cattle, and swine. I chopped, sawed, and hauled wood. After snow-falls, I cleared paths all over the place. I assisted in shelling corn, threshing wheat, and even in the annual killing of fat hogs. I performed also a variety of kitchen, dining-room, and yard offices for the ladies. I enjoyed the work, and it was obvious that my willingness to do it strengthened the warm feeling of the whole family toward me. I also had a chance to participate several times in so-called log-raisings, a peculiar custom, brought down from the pioneer days, of mutual assistance among neighbors in setting up dwellings, barns, and stables of logs.

What with these occupations in the daytime, and reading, games, and music in the evening—my aunt and the eldest daughter were very musical—time passed very quickly, and Christmas, 1854, was at hand before we knew it. The observance of it was in true German style, with a great tree which the whole family helped to decorate, and there were presents for everybody. What a contrast my enjoyment of the festival in such a home sphere offered to the loneliness and depression I had experienced during this hallowed season the year before! Until then I had seen none of the relatives but Robert, who stayed at the Engelmann farm about four miles away, and walked over once or twice a week to visit us. On Christmas Day, however, quite a number, old and young, as well as other friends from Belleville, appeared to celebrate the day with the family. The ice was broken for me, and after Christmas I began a round of calls with my uncle and aunt that extended all through January, and introduced me to dozens of pleasant families in the town and country.

My first call was at the Engelmann farm, where my great-great-uncle Friedrich had made his home after his arrival in Illinois. It presented a very modest appearance, consisting as it did of a small one-and-a-half-story frame building with a few outhouses. The farm extended over the slopes of several hills. The soil was not very good, having been chosen, if I remember rightly, mainly for its adaptability to fruit-growing, and on account of its southern exposure and sheltered position from the north winds. The interior of the dwelling was furnished in the simplest possible style, and had but little that could be called comfort. This home was occupied by Friedrich's wife Betty, who had been left a widow at a ripe old age a few years before, with her daughter Josephine and son Adolph. The old lady was a picture of venerableness, was well-preserved for her age, had a clear and active mind, and charming, benignant ways. But she was constantly depressed in spirits by the loss at sea the year before of her son Jacob, who was on his wedding-tour. Adolph I had seen when I visited Zweibrücken six years before. He was a most interesting person then, owing to certain romantic events in his career. When only eighteen, in 1846, he had enlisted for the war between the United States and Mexico, was made a lieutenant for gallantry, and returned with a severe wound that permanently crippled his left arm and secured him a pension for life. Notwithstanding this, he was carried away by youthful enthusiasm when the Schleswig-Holstein war broke out in 1848, while he was in Germany, and he went through it as a private soldier. He was a fine-looking youth, and had kept his striking personality.

It was my uncle's habit to drive into Belleville every Saturday morning and remain till evening. He spent the time in shopping, making calls, dining with relatives, and spending a social hour at one of the numerous beer-saloons, where, according to German custom, a number of his acquaintances met regularly. After the New Year I always went with him, and thus came to know the several families of relatives besides the Scheels. First among them in social position was Gustav Koerner. Trained as a jurist in Germany, and established as an attorney-at-law in Frankfort-on-the-Main, he was compelled to fly in consequence of his participation in the ill-judged political uprising in that city in 1833. He devoted himself to his profession in this country, and was associated with Theodor Engelmann, the oldest son of the *Forstmeister*. He had found it hard at first to obtain a satisfactory practice, but in time became very successful and was one of the best-known lawyers in Southern Illinois. From the beginning, he took a lively interest in politics. He affiliated with the Democratic party, which enjoyed a long ascendancy in Illinois. He rendered valuable service as a party manager and effective speaker both in English and in German, as a reward for which and as a representative of the German element he received much political preferment. He was elected to both houses of the Legislature, made a circuit judge, and subsequently a member of the Supreme Court, and, finally, Lieutenant-Governor and *ex officio* President of the Senate. He was then holding that office. When the proslavery tendencies of his party became so pronounced under Presidents Pierce and Buchanan, he assisted in the formation of the Republican party, and remained one of its leaders till after the Civil War. He was intimately acquainted with Abraham Lincoln, who honored him in 1862 with the mission to Madrid. He was now about forty-five years old, in his prime in every respect. He was a small, slight man, with a strong head, gray hair, and marked features, from whose expression the weakness of his eyes detracted much. He was somewhat distant on first acquaintance, and perhaps a little too self-assertive, but, withal, an amiable man and a very fine conversationalist. With my German conception of the dignity of official position, I looked upon him with awe. He was very happily married to one of the Engelmann daughters, Sophie. They had two sons and three daughters, all very bright and interesting. The elder son Theodor, a cadet at West Point, unfortunately died there during his second year. The two elder daughters, Marie and Augusta, were almost grown up, and promised to be very attractive. The family lived in a comfortable brick mansion, where they dispensed much hospitality.

Theodor Engelmann was no doubt the ablest of the Engelmann sons. With a sufficiency of practical sense to get on in life, he combined strongly idealistic tendencies and very warm feelings, which he preserved till the end of his protracted days. Besides being the law-partner of Koerner, he held the office of Clerk of the Circuit Court, which yielded him a considerable emolument in fees. Another relative was Molly, daughter of Theodor Erasmus Hilgard (then revisiting Germany), who presided over the home which her father had built for himself in West Belleville. She married an American, Sharon Tyndale, of a well-known Philadelphia family, who met with a terrible end. In 1871, while Secretary of State of Illinois and living at Springfield, the capital, he set out one night to take the midnight train to St. Louis, and was found murdered on the street the next morning. No clue was ever obtained to the motive or the perpetrator of the deed, though every effort was made and the State offered a reward of ten thousand dollars. Mrs. Tyndale's three sisters, Rosa, Clara, and Theresa, presented the remarkable case of having married three brothers Tittmann, who, belonging to a distinguished family in Saxony settled in Dresden and Leipzig, went to America from political choice and necessity. Clara, the younger of the two, was a woman of unusual parts, which had, moreover, been carefully developed, and from an early age she was tireless in her endeavor to store her mind with miscellaneous knowledge. Her tastes were strongly linguistic and literary. She was constituted very differently from her sister Rosa, who was quite as intellectual and, at the same time, a picture of sweet womanhood. She must have been beautiful as a young girl.

Besides my relatives, there were a great many nice people living in Belleville and its immediate vicinity. The town had but six or seven thousand inhabitants, and had no special external attractions except that it contained an almost purely German community. I was told that the population included only a few hundred native Americans. We hardly ever heard any English spoken. The business signs were almost exclusively in German. But this very German character of the place and the adjacent settlements made Belleville peculiarly attractive to people of that nationality, of high as well as of low degree. There was a curious representation of the former living in and about the place — quite a sprinkling of noblemen and jurists, doctors, academic teachers, and other professional men, together with merchants of the best type. Most of them had come to America either as political refugees or as victims of the fickleness of fortune; but not a few had, like my uncles, emigrated from choice. All sorts of callings were followed by them in town, and quite a number tried to earn their living as farmers. The latter were known among their own countrymen as "Latin peasants." The most prominent among them was Friedrich Hecker, the well-known exile, who also played no mean political part in this country. He lived about ten miles distant from Belleville. I heard a good deal of him, but never chanced to see him in those days. He and one other among the "Latin peasants" were alone successful as farmers. Even my uncle, as it afterward turned out, failed, notwithstanding the hardest kind of labor, to make both ends meet.

In the latter part of January, to my own great relief and joy as well as that of the others, letters arrived from my father to my uncle, and from my mother and sisters to me. The former expressed his gratitude very warmly to his brother for receiving me into his family, and indicated his willingness to provide for my support to a moderate extent until I could earn a regular living, offering, of course, to reimburse my uncle for any outlay for necessaries that he had incurred for me. I really had no right to expect anything else from him. My mother and sisters wrote in the most loving and encouraging manner. Their letters were full, too, of a great amount of interesting local news. What with the reopened relations with my dear ones and my pleasant surroundings, I felt once more very content and happy.

CHAPTER III

Legal Experiments.—1855-6

THOSE happy days could not last forever. On the contrary, I felt it to be my duty all the time to keep looking about for a suitable position. I consulted with my uncle and my other relatives regularly in regard to my hopes and wishes in that respect, and they were likewise on the lookout. As I could hardly expect anything but ordinary manual employment, I was anxious to find it outside and away from Belleville, as the social position of my relatives would have made it embarrassing to all. Week after week elapsed, however, without my obtaining anything to do. One Saturday, in the latter part of March, 1855, my cousin Scheel informed me that an American acquaintance of his, a Mr. Case, who held in Clinton County, Illinois, the same official position that Theodor Engelmann had—that is, Circuit Court Clerk and Recorder of Deeds—had requested him to find him a clerk to copy deeds in the records. He thought that I might serve the purpose. I had doubts as to my qualifications, inasmuch as, firstly, I had made but little progress in English, owing to my wholly German surroundings, and, secondly, because my handwriting was very bad. But he felt sure that I knew enough to enable me to copy instruments in writing. So we agreed that he should write and inquire about terms. Mr. Case replied that the copying would be paid for at the rate of twenty-five cents a page. I at once made a trial in Theodor Engelmann's office as to the time it would take me to write a page of one of the ponderous record-books, and found that I could write one in less than an hour. After further deliberation, it was decided that

I should accept the offer. Accordingly, on the morning of March 23, I left Belleville for Carlyle, the county-seat of Clinton County, on the Ohio & Mississippi Railroad, about fifty miles eastward, with a letter of introduction from Cousin Scheel to "Zophar Case, Esq.," in my pocket. I need not say that it was with a very heavy heart I left the haven of rest in which I had found a spiritual restoration, and said good-bye to the dear family to which I had become attached almost as to my own.

The train left me in what was more of a village than a town. In fact, there were not more than three dozen buildings in it, and they were scattered over a good deal of space. I was taken to the only hotel in the place, a shabby and even dilapidated-looking frame building, whose interior appointments, including furniture and everything else, were in keeping with the exterior. After dinner, I went to the court-house, a good-sized building in the Grecian-temple style at one time in vogue in the United States, to find my employer. His office was locked, and it was only on my third attempt to enter, after three o'clock, that I found him in. He was seated in an arm-chair, with his feet on the edge of a large coal-stove in the middle of the room. He wore a dirty slouch hat, which did not change its place although I removed mine on entering; likewise, a long, light-blue woollen coat, such as Western farmers are in the habit of wearing, a very dirty shirt without a tie, and vest and trousers of coarse cloth full of grease-spots. The trousers were tucked into the red tops of boots that seemed never to have been blacked.

Such was the appearance of my master to be. He did not utter a word until he had read my letters of introduction, and then only saying, "Oh, it is you," he rose, showing that he was a powerful six-footer, and added, "I will show you your work." He stepped to the large writing-table, pointed to some books standing upright upon it, and opened a large drawer filled with bundles of paper tied with red tape, which he explained were the documents to be copied. I asked whether he wished me to begin at once, and he replied, "The sooner, the better," as the records were very much behindhand. I said that I was ready, whereupon he opened the books and explained in which the different classes of instruments were to be copied. He gave me pen and ink and then resumed his seat, leaving me to begin as best I could. I felt a little embarrassed and nervous, but first went through the book of deeds in order to see the method of copying, and, at the end of an hour, mustered up courage enough to begin writing. In the meantime, several persons came into the office to file instruments and to have a chat with the clerk. At half-past four, the latter left, telling me that I need not stay later than five o'clock, when I must lock the office and take the key with me. He added that the regular office-hours would be from nine till twelve and from one till five, and that he expected me to sweep the office at least three times a week. The last part of his instructions rather surprised me, as he had not referred to such duties in his correspondence about me. As I had long before got over my former prejudices against that kind of service, and knew that it was a very common thing for professional men in the West to sweep out their own offices, I was perfectly willing to comply. The office certainly needed sweeping badly. It really looked as if neither broom nor duster had been used in it for months.

In a few days I became perfectly familiar with my work. It called for no exercise of intelligence, but only careful coöperation between hands and eyes. It was, indeed, the merest mechanical drudgery. The only stimulus I felt was that my daily earnings depended on the number of pages I copied. During the first week I succeeded in copying only a single page in an hour, as it was absolutely necessary to avoid mistakes; corrections not being admissible in records. But I could copy seven pages a day in the second week, and finally even nine in seven hours' work. My master turned out to be an excessively uncouth, but at the same time a very good-natured man, full of that humor that finds vent in the West in anecdotes and stories. He was laziness itself. After I had learned the full routine of the office, which included the reception of instruments for file and record, and of legal papers, and the fees therefor from the attorneys in the suits pending in the Circuit Court, he left everything to me, and he hardly did anything more than talk and joke with the people who called. But he offered me three dollars a week extra for taking charge of everything. The first month I managed to earn about forty dollars, and afterwards between fifty-five and sixty-five dollars a month.

Besides ensuring the means of self-support, my stay in Carlyle had the other great advantage for me that I was compelled to use the English language exclusively. While at my uncle's in Belleville, I hardly ever heard a word of English, for there was not a single American there. Now, with continued practice in speaking and systematic reading in the evening, I made rapid progress. After the lapse of six weeks, I had no difficulty in understanding ordinary conversation and in making myself understood. Having got so far, I made it a point to converse as much as possible, and for that purpose I tried to enter into social relations. There was not much choice in the town in that respect. The population did not exceed two hundred people, and consisted of a few merchants, the county officials, several doctors, not less than a dozen lawyers, who practised in the county circuit courts, and the usual complement of mechanics, with their respective families. The landlord's handsome daughter and two other young ladies constituted the greatest female attractions of the place. The former was very bright in conversation, and took particular pains to help me along in English, so that my calls on her were as good as lessons for me. The social centre of Carlyle was the house of Judge Sidney Breese, formerly United States Senator, then holding the office of Judge of the Supreme Court of the State. There were no young people in his family, but I ventured to call on him, as Mr. Koerner had given me a letter of introduction to him. His manner was rather cold and distant, and I could not get very near to him, though I saw him frequently in the courthouse. He was a man of great natural ability and was considered an eminent jurist. His figure was short and stout, with a large head, short red hair and round face, a good deal like Mr. Case; and he wore large gold spectacles. Upon the advent of warm weather he always wore a blue swallow-tail, brass-buttoned dress-coat, yellow nankeen trousers and vest, and a stove-pipe hat, presenting a truly comical appearance. Like nearly every other man, he had the nasty habit of tobacco-chewing.

I witnessed the monthly sittings of the probate courts and the semi-annual sessions of the Circuit Court, saw some curious illustrations of Western character, and listened for the first time to examples of forensic eloquence. There were among the attending lawyers men of evidently remarkable talent as speakers. I was astonished at the flood of words they managed to pour out. Sometimes the oratorical outbursts seemed to be indulged in on very slight provocation, and hence were rather ludicrous. What struck me particularly was the easy, informal way in which the proceedings were carried on. There was an abandon as regarded manners, too, that could not but shock me, accustomed as I was to the dignified ways of German courts. Several times some of the counsel were in a half-tipsy condition, and became colloquial in their arguments, as if they believed themselves to be in a bar-room. The term of the Circuit Court was held during a very hot spell in June. The judge presided without his coat and with unbuttoned shirt thrown wide open. He sat thus disarrayed, tipped back in his arm-chair, with his legs on the desk before him. The attorneys naturally followed his example and made themselves as cool as possible. One marked incident has remained fixed in my mind. While one of the most loquacious attorneys was making a fiery argument, he was interrupted by the judge, who called out to him: "Jim, you had better keep cool in this hot weather and give me a bite of your tobacco." The pleader stopped, pulled out his plug and carried it to the judge, who took a hasty bite, whereupon the proceedings were resumed.

At the end of three months, my work became very slack. I had worked up the arrearages in recording, extending over nearly six months, and the new filings were so limited that I had only from three to five pages to copy daily. It became, indeed, more and more apparent from day to day that the regular work could yield me only a bare subsistence. I discussed the subject with Mr. Case, and he admitted that this was the fact. The prospect of a necessary change of occupation was thus presented to me. It was delayed for two months by my acting as temporary substitute for another county official who was compelled to go on a long journey. But, after this respite, about the middle of August, with the consent of my uncle, I returned to the farm.

I cannot say that I felt much regret when I turned my back on Carlyle. The life there had, after all, been too monotonous and unattractive, and there certainly was not the remotest chance for any sort of career for me in such a community. I left with sixty dollars in my pocket, my savings after I had provided myself with a modest outfit of summer clothing. I had already learned enough of affairs in this country to know that of all the professions the legal played the most important part, publicly and otherwise. This observation, together with my intimacy with members of the legal profession in Carlyle, made me conceive the notion that the best thing I could do would be to become a lawyer myself. The idea soon took deep root, and I communicated it, shortly after my return, to my uncle Theodor. He at once approved of it, but showed me that my plan could not be carried out without the consent of my father, as he would, of course, have to furnish me with means of support during my study of the law. He kindly offered to write to him in advocacy of my wishes, and it was arranged that I should continue to be his guest until a reply to his letter was received. Accordingly I resumed my former ways, helping all I could on the farm, and varying farm life with visits to relatives and friends.

When my father's answer came, it brought a prompt and favorable acknowledgment of my proposition, and offered to allow me a certain sum annually, for two years, which would enable me to live modestly and devote myself entirely to study. I was overflowing with happiness and enthusiasm because of what I considered an assured and bright future. I saw myself in imagination a successful lawyer and rising politician. The next day we drove to Belleville to consult with Mr. Koerner as to the best course to pursue in preparation for the profession. He at first suggested that I should attend one of the several law schools in this country for a couple of years, and then enter the office of some prominent lawyer to learn the practice. When the question of ways and means was considered—that is, that my father had agreed to provide for me for but two years—it became clear that the only way open to me was the one usually followed in the West up to that time, to begin the study of theory and practice combined, under a practitioner. The conclusion was not satisfactory to me, but I had to accept it. Mr. Koerner offered to give me a desk in his office, but, with reference to my knowledge of English, advised me strongly to try to get a place with a native lawyer. He kindly promised to look about for me among his colleagues in Belleville and St. Louis. A few days later I received a note from him, informing me that he had succeeded in securing my admission into the office of a leading lawyer in Belleville, George Trumbull (a brother of Lyman Trumbull, who afterwards obtained such high distinction as United States Senator from Illinois), and said that I might enter at once. The question of a suitable boarding-place in Belleville was solved by Cousin Scheel's kind invitation to me to become an inmate of his spacious home.

Mr. Trumbull was a descendant of the well-known Connecticut family of that name. In appearance and by nature he was a typical New Englander—keen, nervously active, wholly absorbed in his calling, not even caring for politics, and more reticent than genial. He occupied a small one-story brick building on the public square as an office, having two small front and rear rooms. I was assigned to a desk in the former. At first I had no other duty to perform than to ascertain the wants of callers, if he were out. I was at liberty to devote all the rest of my time to the study of Blackstone, which he placed in my hands and which I attacked vigorously. After a few weeks, the conviction was forced upon me that circumstances worked so much against regularity in that office as to render it very difficult, if not impossible, for me to make much headway in the law. The location was convenient, not only for clients, but for idlers and gossips; Belleville, like most small towns, containing an abundance of them. Altogether too many "dropped in" upon Mr. Trumbull and myself. This annoyance increased steadily as the weather grew cold in the fall and our warm stove became a point of attraction. Then, again, Belleville proved more and more to be a poor place for one so eager as I to perfect myself in the use of the English language. It was as plain as day to me that a mastery of English was the essential condition of success in this country. I had even engaged an American common-school teacher to instruct me in the proper pronunciation of English vowels, consonants, syllables, and words, just as beginners learn spelling, for I saw that most of my employers had failed to acquire it. I labored diligently with the teacher from one to three hours a day, but the benefit I received from his instruction was neutralized by my great want of practice and lack of opportunity to hear or speak English and so get my ear accustomed to it.

Thus, by degrees, I made up my mind to talk with my relatives about the advisability of pursuing my studies at another place, away from the disadvantages referred to.

They consented to the change, after due consideration, and Mr. Koerner again kindly undertook to find what I wanted. About the middle of November it was settled that I should enter the office of a well-known law-firm, Manning & Merriman, in Peoria, Illinois, and I made my arrangements accordingly. I started for Peoria on November 20, and took, in St. Louis, one of the steamboats which regularly ran up the Illinois River. We made such slow progress, owing to numerous stoppages and obstructions because of low water, that we reached our destination only on the third day. Peoria was then, and I believe is now, a beautiful city, rising amphitheatrically from the west bank of the Illinois River, or rather lake into which the river widens at that point. It had about twenty thousand inhabitants in 1855 (over forty thousand now), and was laid out in the usual rectangular way. I stopped over night at a hotel, and next morning presented my letter of introduction to Messrs. Manning & Merriman. I was kindly received, and, after a brief colloquy, assigned to a desk in the office and instructed as to my duties. At first I was simply to copy legal papers drawn up by the principals. I was to receive no compensation, but had the privilege of "reading" in the office when I was not otherwise occupied. I soon got on very good terms with the two partners, and felt entirely at home in their office.

By chance I secured board and lodging in the house of the captain of the boat upon which I had arrived. He was absent most of the time, and his wife, who had the care of several small children, was anything but a good housekeeper, so that I did not fare very well, either as regards regularity or quality of meals. The house, too, was very cold, and, as the winter of 1855–6 was unusually severe, I suffered no little discomfort on that account. There was but one other boarder, a mercantile clerk, a few years my senior, who had recommended the place to me, as he was a relative of the only family in the town to which I had letters of introduction. He was a good-enough fellow, but with very limited mental resources, and was also a strong churchman. He urged me every Sunday to attend divine service with him, but without success. I then first discovered, by a very common experience, that non-church-going is a great social obstacle in this country. From the moment the family to which I presented my letters of introduction found out that I was a free-thinker, they dropped me entirely. I made hardly any other acquaintances than those mentioned. My social isolation made me often feel very lonesome, especially when I thought of the pleasant circle in which I had lived during the previous winter.

Months went by, and the spring approached without my having made much progress in legal lore under the guardianship of Messrs. Manning & Merriman. My one fellow-student, David McCullough, had to confess the same fact as to himself. We agreed, too, entirely, as to the causes of our slow advance. We found the same difficulty that had troubled me in Mr. Trumbull's office: there was not enough privacy for study. Not only clients, but politicians, came to consult with Mr. Manning. It was very entertaining to listen to him, whether he talked law or politics, but also irresistibly diverting from our studies. With the greatest determination, it was impossible to fix one's mind upon the contents of Blackstone, Chitty, and Story, while so much loud talking and joking was going on about us. Thus, McCullough and I daily looked at each other with despair, sighed and then listened perforce, yet often willingly, for the adroit and humorous way in which Mr. Manning answered the questions of the clients as to what he charged for his professional advice, was always very amusing. As day after day passed by with the same discouraging result, the conviction that I could never finish my studies under such circumstances, and that I was, indeed, continually wasting most of my time, gradually forced itself upon me, just as it did in Belleville. McCullough shared this view, and we both arrived at the conclusion that we must make a change.

In the course of the winter, I conceived the idea of writing some letters for publication in the columns of the *Zeitung* that appeared daily and weekly in Belleville. I had retained all along my old faith in my ability to write well. The editor, Dr. Wenzel, a German-Bohemian and political refugee, a man of uncommon talents and acquirements, seemed to take quite a fancy to me, and I felt sure that he would be glad to publish any of my contributions. So I concocted two letters of a partly descriptive and partly philosophic-æsthetic character—at least I considered them such—and sent them to him. They were poor attempts, in imitation of Heine and Boerne, rather stilted and labored. Still, they were printed, and Dr. Wenzel complimented me upon them in his letters of acknowledgment. Unfortunately, I had indulged in some rather sarcastic remarks upon the "German philistinism" that was manifested in a great many ways in Belleville. Letters from my relatives soon informed me that my criticisms had stirred up a good deal of ill-feeling against me. My uncle was particularly sharp in his censure of the license of my pen. I certainly had no deliberate intention to offend anybody, but I had, no doubt, been guilty of a pertness that was unbecoming my years, and decidedly improper in view of the circumstances under which I had gone to Belleville, and the cordiality with which I had been received. This untoward production was my first formal attempt at journalism. To be frank about it, while its effect troubled me in no small degree, the attention it attracted rather flattered my vanity.

This incident helped to mature the resolution that the drawbacks to my law-reading were evolving in me. I reasoned myself into the assumption that it would be futile to expect that such studies as I should be able to pursue in the office would make a good lawyer of me in a short or a long time. Mr. Koerner was right, after all, in his original advice to me to spend two years at a law school, had my father's allowance permitted it. Would it not be creditable, then, I asked myself, to try and earn enough in addition to enable me to go to a law school? Would such a resolute and independent course not also be the best means of dispelling the prejudices that my article had revived against me? Such was my argument, and theoretically I was no doubt right. But the real test would, after all, be the proof of my ability to make the money needed.

While I was casting about in my mind as to ways and means regarding it, I came upon what seemed to be a proper solution. I read in the daily papers long and glowing advertisements of a new work, a 'History [or Encyclopædia] of American Literature.' The value of the work was endorsed strongly by literary men of national reputation. It was to be published in three large volumes for five dollars each, and sold by subscription. The advertising firm, well-known Chicago booksellers, invited enterprising young men of good address to enter into communication with them, and offered to assign certain parts of the country exclusively to persons considered suitable canvassers, and otherwise to make the most liberal arrangements with them.

I thought, here is the right thing for me. Why should it be difficult to sell any number of copies of so well recommended a book, especially when there would be no competition in the sale of it? Why should it not be possible, with a strong will and proper push, to dispose of enough copies in a few months to earn enough to go, perhaps, to the Harvard Law School in the fall? The scheme took complete possession of me. I felt too impatient merely to write to the Chicago firm, and, towards the end of February, 1856, got a week's leave of absence, packed my trunk, and went by train to Chicago.

CHAPTER IV

Through Politics to Journalism.—1856-7

ON applying at the store of the booksellers, at that time the leading firm in the trade in the Northwest, I was taken to the partner in charge of the subscription department. He was a gentleman in speech and manner. He took my measure at once as a youthful enthusiast with a lively imagination and but little judgment. He did not at all urge me on, but spoke very disinterestedly of the uncertainties of the canvassing business; but he failed to sober me. I told him rather proudly that I had been in the business before and knew what special capacities it required, and that I possessed them. He said, finally, that as I insisted upon it, he would be glad to let me make a trial. There would not be much risk in it for me, as I need buy only one copy of the work at a discount. He would assign me to an entirely unexplored and very promising field, the city of Milwaukee. I was to be allowed a commission of thirty-three per cent. on all subscriptions obtained. Being provided with a full equipment of subscription-books and circulars, I lost no time in starting for the scene of my future operations.

Milwaukee has always been an almost German city. In 1856, the preponderance of the German element was even greater than at present; in fact, its Americanization, which has in the meantime progressed very rapidly, had then hardly begun. It was known among German-Americans as "Deutsch-Athen," and, comparatively speaking, deserved the name. There was a large number of educated and accomplished men among my countrymen, and in them the love of music and histrionic art was very marked. Under the leadership of Hans Balatka, who still wields the baton in Chicago, good orchestral and vocal music was more liberally provided for than in any other city in the West. There was also a very good German theatre. Another attraction was the Hotel Weltstein, the best German inn in the United States. It was named after the proprietor, who had belonged to a learned profession in the fatherland, and was a most intelligent, well-informed, and entertaining host, though too fond of a glass of good wine. He was killed twenty-five years afterwards by a fall from a window. He kept his house very neat and clean, furnished an excellent table, and his charges were reasonable.

I obtained quarters there and quickly became acquainted with a number of the leading Germans, who were either regular guests or who had the habit of enjoying a social glass there. I felt at first encouraged by the fact that my work would be mostly among my own countrymen. But I soon found out that it was, on the contrary, a disadvantage, for most of those I approached knew nothing of American literature and did not care much for it. They had not been in the country long enough for that, and, moreover, their purely German surroundings naturally kept their interest in American affairs at a low point. I was made to feel, before long, that they had not become sufficiently emancipated from their feelings of caste not to look down upon me, more or less, as a book-peddler. I strove very hard to obtain subscribers, and regularly set out every morning and devoted all the day to going about from store to store and office to office. I have a lively recollection of a very heavy snow-storm that raged for several days, and was followed by a bitter cold spell which made canvassing very irksome physically. By degrees, the meagre fruits of my efforts caused my sanguine hopes to vanish, and made me uneasy as to the final outcome. At the end of three weeks, I had sold only thirty-five copies in all, twenty-seven to Americans and eight to Germans. I believe that I am correct in saying that only one out of every twelve attempts to sell was successful. I need not mention that that meant all sorts of experiences for me, mostly of a disagreeable character. I had, as a rule, to drink continually of the cup of humiliation. I had the satisfaction of having tried my best, and enjoyed, upon the whole, a good time, socially. Of course, this did not suffice, as I had failed in my real object, which was to make money. The net pecuniary result was that I spent, all in all, five more dollars than I received during the three weeks, though I really had exhausted the field from which I expected so much.

I returned to Chicago much disheartened, and at a loss what to do. I ought to have said ere this that my confidence in the success of the venture had been so great that, before starting for Milwaukee, I had written to Messrs. Manning & Merriman that I had decided to give up the law temporarily, in order to engage in a most promising business that had unexpectedly come in my way.

I was fortunate enough to find what promised to be a suitable place in the office of a firm of real-estate agents, within a few days, by answering a "want" advertisement. The firm name was Staples & Sims, and they had a fine office at the corner of Dearborn and Clark Streets, fronting on Court-House Square. Staples was a retired merchant and capitalist, Sims a Scotch doctor who had not been able to find a satisfactory practice. It was a queer combination and did not last very long, as it turned out. The firm tried to do a commission business—that is, sell other people's real estate on commission. My special function was to attract German customers, and, accordingly, my name appeared under that of the firm, as salesman, in the advertisements in the German papers. My salary was fifty dollars a month and a small interest in the commission business secured by me. There was also a French clerk, as a bait to French buyers and sellers, who besides acted as draughtsman. I was very much set up when I secured the place, and in this hopeful frame of mind I completed my twenty-first year on April 10, 1856.

It was at this time that I received my first lesson in practical politics, so to speak, in this country. I had long before become a regular reader of newspapers, and fully understood the political questions of the day. The deliberate attempts of the Democrats in the South, aided by the bulk of their Northern sympathizers, to secure an extension of the territory open to slavery, in connection with the organization of Kansas as a Territory, was the all-absorbing and all-exciting topic. The formation of a new party out of the elements opposed to the admission of slavery into Kansas and Nebraska had already begun. Free soil was fast becoming a leading issue, not only in national and State, but even in local elections. It was also made the dividing line in the Chicago municipal election that spring. Of course, I had no right to vote, but that did not prevent me from enlisting as a violent partisan on the anti-Democratic side. The contest was fought directly over slavery. The Democratic nominee for Mayor was Thomas Dyer, and the leader of the opposition Frank C. Sherman. The canvass was made by both sides in the usual way, through public meetings, processions, and a most violent newspaper war. I engaged in it with heart and soul. Every evening I attended a meeting, used my voice as loudly as anybody in cheering and shouting, and joined in a torch-light procession. On election day, I acted as ticket-distributor, and had then my first sight of violent scenes and rioting at the polls. The "right" and "wrong" seemed to be so clearly defined that I could not understand how any intelligent mind could be at all in doubt. That the ignorant, priest-ridden Irish should support the Democratic candidates was comprehensible, but it aroused my disgust and indignation that there were Germans on the Democratic ticket, a German newspaper and prominent Germans who actually supported it. I looked upon them as contemptible apostates. I was confident, too, that the unholy combination would be overwhelmingly defeated. My unutterable humiliation and grief may be imagined, therefore, when the Democrats obtained a decisive victory. Influenced by the predictions of the dire, irremediable evils that would befall the country if the Democrats carried the day, I felt wofully depressed in spirit. It seemed to me almost as if the world would come to an end. It took me weeks to forget this grievous disappointment. A certain compensation for it lay in the extensive acquaintance which I secured through my political début.

My connection with Messrs. Staples & Sims continued only till the end of May. They were new to the business, having embarked in it only a few months before they engaged me, and they failed to secure the expected custom. They had also entertained extravagant expectations, which remained unfulfilled, of obtaining German customers through me. At the time mentioned, they proposed to change the terms of my engagement so that I should not be paid a salary, but only be allowed commissions on business secured by me. As I had so far not derived more than twenty-five dollars in this way, I could not possibly accept, and therefore left them.

The loss of my place did not at all trouble me, for I had conceived and was full of a scheme from the realization of which I expected much honor and great profit. It will be remembered that, at that time, both the proslavery and antislavery parties respectively were engaged in promoting with all their might emigration into the disputed Territory of Kansas. In the North as well as in the South, from the New England States to the Mississippi, a lively agitation was going on for the formation of "Kansas emigration societies." Quite a number of such had already been formed and were sending settlers into Kansas. The newspapers announced almost daily the arrival of more or less numerous parties on their way West. My project was nothing less than the forming of a society among the young Germans throughout the Northwest to secure a large tract of land in Kansas and settle the members upon it. The colony was to be, like the other Northern settlements, a vanguard of liberty, and to fight for free soil, if necessary.[1] Of course, I aspired to be the head of the organization. I wrote out a regular plan for it, and, as soon as I was free from office duties, I proceeded to push it. I had no difficulty in interesting in it quite a number of young men, "Turners" and members of political clubs. There was enough enthusiasm among us, but no capital. No one of us could do more than pay a moderate weekly contribution into the treasury. At my suggestion, it was resolved to try and interest local capitalists in our undertaking, and the task devolved upon me. I called upon a number of well-known and wealthy antislavery men, and obtained a dozen subscriptions ranging from fifty to a hundred dollars. Of course, this was not sufficient capital. It then occurred to me that we could far more readily obtain this in the large Eastern cities, which accordingly I persuaded my associates to authorize me to visit for the purpose of soliciting further subscriptions. I made them also instruct me to go to Washington, with a view to getting a donation of land for our purposes from Congress or the Government. I need not say that this feature of the venturesome enterprise was attributable to the fact that I had not the remotest idea of the insuperable difficulties of obtaining any sort of bounty from the Federal authorities.

I went direct from Chicago via Baltimore to the national capital. I had obtained letters of introduction from local political leaders to United States Senators and several members of the House from Illinois. The letters did not endorse my scheme, but said that I would explain what I wanted, simply vouching for my reliability. I devoted one day to sight-seeing before presenting them. Aside from the stately public buildings, Washington presented, thirty years ago, the appearance of a shabby, lifeless Southern town. The former dwarfed the masses of mean buildings

---

[1] He "came very near joining one of the companies of Sharp's riflemen that were being formed all over the North in order to save that Territory to freedom."

around them, making them look shabbier and more insignificant. Intense July heat had set in, and hardly anybody was to be seen on the immense streets. The large colored population, exhibiting characteristics indicative of slavery, was a negatively interesting feature to me. But my general impression of the place was very unsatisfactory.

I had little difficulty in getting at the Illinois Senators, Lyman Trumbull and Stephen A. Douglas, and saw them both. Trumbull was a new member and had not made much of a reputation, while Douglas was at that time the most prominent political character before the American public, owing to his growing opposition to the extreme proslavery demands of his party, so that I considered the chance to see and talk with him quite a feather in my cap. Mr. Trumbull had heard of me as a former student in his brother's office; he knew my relatives, and so gave me a kindly reception. I found him very much like his brother, though of more commanding presence. I submitted our printed colonization plan to him. After reading it through, he asked what he was expected to do about it. Thereupon I dwelt as eloquently as I could upon our wishes for either executive or legislative aid from the Government. I saw a smile steal over his face, which produced a feeling of embarrassment in me; but I went through with my argument. "Young friend," the Senator answered, "I regret that you have incurred the trouble and expense of coming to Washington, for your mission is absolutely hopeless. What you seek is contrary to law and usage, and especially ill-advised in the face of the pending party struggle, in and out of Congress, over Kansas." He could but counsel me to abandon at once all contemplated attempts and to return home. This was a cold-water douche indeed, and I left him very crestfallen.

Nevertheless, during the day, I resolved to try my luck with Senator Douglas. Going to his hotel the next morning, I found more than a dozen callers ahead of me, and it was fully two hours before I stood before the "Little

Giant," as he was already dubbed by his party. The phrase was well suited to him. He was very small, not over four and a half feet high, and there was a noticeable disproportion between the long trunk of his body and his short legs. His chest was broad and indicated great strength of lungs. It took but a glance at his face and head to convince one that they belonged to no ordinary man. No beard hid any part of his remarkable, swarthy features. His mouth, nose, and chin were all large and clearly expressive of much boldness and power of will. The broad, high forehead proclaimed itself the shield of a great brain. The head, covered with an abundance of flowing black hair just beginning to show a tinge of gray, impressed one with its massiveness and leonine expression. His brows were shaggy, his eyes a brilliant black. He glanced at the letters I handed to him, and asked, with his deep, sonorous voice, that never failed to tell upon popular audiences, what he could do for me. I handed him our prospectus, when he remarked: "Can you tell me its substance? My time is so limited that I cannot read it." I tried to explain, but I had hardly alluded to our object when he cut me short, saying: "Never mind, I understand it all, but I can do nothing for you. Similar requests are addressed to me almost daily by societies formed in the interest of the South, and, even if legal difficulties were not in the way, it would never do for me to favor either side in the national controversy, for political reasons." With this brief and emphatic reply I had to be satisfied, and took my leave. It seemed useless to continue my efforts among the members of the House to whom I had recommendations, and hence I took the first train for Philadelphia.

I spent a whole week in the "City of Brotherly Love" in pursuit of my purpose. I had only one letter of introduction, to William D. Kelley, who was even then playing a leading part in the formation of the opposition to the proslavery Democracy into a new party, and who afterwards achieved national distinction as a member of Congress representing the same Philadelphia district for over a generation. He received me very kindly, but did not hold out much encouragement as to local success in my mission. He went so far as to go around with me personally to wealthy political sympathizers. They were nearly all business men; among them was Mr. Drexel, the senior member of the great banking-firm of Drexel & Co. Several of them, and especially Mr. Drexel, examined me closely as to the details of my project, and particularly regarding the precise uses which we proposed to make of the capital I was trying to raise. I was much embarrassed by being unable to answer some of their questions. My plan did not cover the point whether the subscribers would get something like shares in the company in return for their money, or whether they were expected simply to make gifts. The truth was, that my business knowledge had not been sufficient to make me qualified to elaborate the scheme on a joint-stock basis, and that what I really wanted was outright donations. I remember very distinctly how confounded I was by Mr. Drexel's remark: "Supposing that your enterprise were really laudable enough to deserve pecuniary help from me and others, why should you and your associates alone have all the benefits reaped from such assistance?" I got out of the quandary as best I could by stating that the subscribers who desired it could, of course, have their contributions treated by the company as loans. But, as I was utterly unprepared to give any guarantees or to show that the proper legal forms had been provided for in that respect, I not only failed to obtain subscriptions, but evidently became an object of suspicion.

Depressed and humiliated, I proceeded to New York. I put up at the Prescott House, a well-known and well-kept German hotel, mainly patronized by the Germans of the better classes from all parts of the United States and from the old country. One of the first persons I saw among the guests was "Colonel" Blenker, who had acquired considerable notoriety, during the rising in the Palatinate in

1849, as the commander of a so-called "free corps," an independent battalion of young ultra-radicals, who proved, however, more determined in the display of red emblems than on the battle-field. I became acquainted with him at the table d'hôte. He was tall, well-built, with fine manners, but his features, so far as they were not covered by his full beard, had the coloring of a confirmed toper. He was a very loud talker, and, when he did not brag of his martial achievements, could not say enough in denunciation of the United States, where his merits hitherto had not been recognized. I soon found out that the cause of his disgust with the country was the fact that he was obliged to eke out a precarious living as a small market-farmer in Rockland County, New York. He supplied the hotel with vegetables and fruit, and, strange to say, took his pay mostly in dinners and wine. He subsequently played quite a part on the Northern side during the War of the Rebellion.

I had a letter to Dr. Hexamer, a German physician of very high professional and social standing, and also a leader of the local German wing of the newly-formed Republican party. Had he lived, he would doubtless have had a brilliant career, but he was consumptive and had then but a short time to live, as he told me himself. He was one of the kindest and most delightful men in every way that I ever met, ready at once to help my scheme, with which he was much impressed. He introduced me personally to Friedrich Kapp, which proved the beginning of a lifelong intimacy. Kapp was engaged in the practice of law, so he seemed to be just the man I needed to put my project into legal shape. He was very willing, too, to give me the benefit of his advice. He agreed with my Philadelphia critics that I and my associates could not expect the public to place a large sum of money unconditionally in our hands, to be used as we saw fit. He advised me strongly to abandon all efforts to raise money under my original plan, and proposed to me to organize a joint-stock company. However, even a brief discussion of the details of the methods to be followed in acting on his proposition was sufficient, little as I then knew of business affairs, to satisfy me that, in the first place, having no acquaintance, no influence, and no means with which to meet the preliminary expenses, it would be utterly impossible for me to effect such an organization. Secondly, even if I succeeded in forming a company, I could not expect to realize my ambitious dream of controlling it, as I had nothing to contribute towards its capital.

Thus I was compelled to come to the conclusion that my scheme would have to be dropped. I was not inclined, however, to accept it at once, and my mind only gradually worked up to the recognition of that disagreeable necessity. But my reluctance was due as much to lack of conviction as to the recognition of the awkward position in which the miscarriage of my plans would inevitably place me—for had I not collected considerable money in Chicago, which was then spent for travelling expenses?

Meantime, I enjoyed an interesting political experience. Deep excitement over the memorable Presidential election of that year was felt throughout the country. The nomination of John C. Frémont as the candidate for the White House and the opponent of the further extension of slavery had, more than all others, produced intense enthusiasm, in which I shared. Hexamer and Kapp were very active in organizing German Republican clubs in New York and the adjoining cities. I accompanied them regularly to the meetings held for the purpose. Their propaganda was not as widely successful as they thought it would be, for the mass of our countrymen showed a stubborn adhesion (born of ignorance and their traditional voting for the Democratic ticket) to the Democratic party. I was also a regular frequenter of the Republican headquarters, which were established at Clinton Hall on Broadway, nearly opposite Clinton Place. The chairman of the Republican Central Committee was Simeon Draper, a well-known real-estate dealer. I remember well the admiration I felt every time

I saw his commanding figure and heard his stentorian voice. I was also present when a serenade was given to "John and Jessie" (Colonel Frémont's wife, *née* Benton), who occupied a house on Clinton Place, and I had the good fortune to shake hands with them both on that occasion.

I thus loitered in New York for several weeks before returning to Chicago to explain to my associates the reasons for my failure. Most of them were slow to accept my statement that I had tried my best but failed, owing to the nature of our scheme, and criticised my staying in the East longer than was necessary. In settling my account, there was strong opposition to allowing me all that I claimed for travelling expenses, in consideration of which I reduced my claim considerably, though I had charged for only part of my stay in New York. The result of it all was that I resigned and that the "land association" thereupon collapsed.

This sorry ending reduced me again to pecuniary embarrassment. I had not felt justified in drawing the monthly allowance from my father, after leaving Peoria. Thus I found myself with less than thirty dollars in my possession. I had intended to return to New York, feeling sure that, with the aid of my new acquaintances, I could find an acceptable position, but this was now out of the question. At this juncture, I learned accidentally of an opening that seemed to me especially attractive. The Republicans of Racine, Wisconsin, on the direct railroad line between Chicago and Milwaukee, were anxious to win over to their party the large German vote in their city, and for that purpose planned to buy the Democratic German paper and convert it into a Republican organ. They had asked the editors of the Illinois *Staats-Zeitung* to recommend a suitable person to take charge of the concern, and I had heard of the matter through one of them. I was convinced that I was sufficiently familiar with current politics, and that, as for the rest of the needed qualifications, the natural ability which I claimed for myself, together with the energy and enthusiasm that I should bring to the new occupation, would enable me to acquire them speedily. I saw a direct road to literary and political distinction before me. Accordingly, I lost no time in pursuing that great chance. I persuaded my informant to give me a letter of introduction to the Republican Executive Committee of Racine, and took the next train for that place. This was about the end of August, 1856.

Racine was then, and, I am told, still is, a beautiful town. It is situated right on the shore of Lake Michigan, of which it commands a grand view. There was one long, broad street, lined on both sides with business buildings. The residence part consisted of fine shaded avenues intersecting each other at right angles, with numerous attractive homes. The city was the seat of the county authorities, and of a well-frequented college which always enjoyed a good reputation among Western educational institutions. It contained about twelve thousand inhabitants, one-third of whom were Germans. The county population was also largely German. My first impressions of the place were so favorable as to make me doubly anxious to secure the acceptance of my services. The chairman of the Republican Committee, a bright young lawyer, received me with evident pleasure. I felt much relieved on learning from him that I had no competitor. He at once called a meeting of the committee and presented me to them. They asked no questions at all and engaged me on the spot, with expressions of great satisfaction. The committee had a secret option from the publisher of the German paper to buy it at a certain price, and they resolved to proceed at once to raise the necessary money and exercise it. I was to have eighteen dollars a week salary—princely pay, as it seemed to me—and the sole editorial and business management on behalf of the new owners. The chairman at once set out with me to find a suitable boarding-place, and I obtained a very satisfactory one in a genteel private family, for the low price of five dollars a week for a nice room and all my meals. Thus, literally, in less than twenty-four hours after leaving Chicago, I was at anchor in what appeared to be a permanent haven of rest and promise. A feeling of security and hopefulness came over me which I had not experienced to the same degree since I landed on American soil. As it took the committee several days to close the purchase, I had sufficient leisure to see the town and vicinity thoroughly and to make acquaintances. I was charmed with all I saw and heard.

This happiness was somewhat dimmed when the committee had concluded their bargain and I took possession of the weekly *Volksblatt* printing-office for them and ascertained the exact condition of the paper. The man who had sold it was a printer by trade, and had, with one assistant, edited and printed the paper. The supply of type was limited and nearly worn out. There was only an old-style handpress, on which six hundred copies could be printed in a working-day of twelve hours. The appearance of the paper was indeed wretched, and its contents no better. It had been edited mainly with the aid of scissors, but the selections plainly indicated absence of both taste and judgment. There was very little editorial matter, and what there was consisted of commonplace stuff expressed in ungrammatical language. Indeed, the author of it, who was not at all an educated man, confessed that he never had attempted to write out anything, but that it was his regular practice to put such thoughts as he had directly into type. Under the circumstances, it was not to be wondered at that the subscription-list always remained small. There were nominally about three hundred and eighty names on the books, but a close examination proved that many of the rural subscribers had either not paid at all for years, or paid in farming produce—butter, eggs, chickens, potatoes, corn, and the like. Further inquiries also showed that the subscribers were almost entirely made up of shopkeepers, saloon-keepers, mechanics, and farmers, and that two German doctors were the only representatives of the higher education among them. That with such readers there was not much chance for "literary distinction" was plain enough. As the paper was to raise boldly, between two issues, the Republican instead of the Democratic flag in its columns, the effect of this somersault upon the subscribers remained to be seen. It was clear that, as a preventive of numerous desertions among them, the contents of the paper ought to be very much improved; but the poor material equipment rendered this out of the question.

Still, I resolved to try my best. New as I was to the calling, the first weeks were full of hard work and nervous anxiety. I believe that I wrote and re-wrote the editorials in the first number issued under my control half a dozen times, until I could persuade myself that they would pass muster. I worked literally night and day, succeeding, I can say without self-flattery, in producing very respectable papers. There were at the time only three other German Republican papers published in Wisconsin, as against a score of Democratic, but they all complimented my work. The Democratic organs, as was to be expected, raised a great outcry against the political conversion of the *Volksblatt,* and at once began to abuse me as its originator, with much wrath and unanimity of feeling. The change in the politics of the paper provoked also a declaration, by about a score of old subscribers, published in a Milwaukee German paper, that the "treason" of the paper was due to the mercenariness and bad faith of the publisher, who had no right to sell it, as leading Democrats had originally supplied the capital. This added fuel to the flame, and made the war I waged in my columns against political opponents hotter from week to week. More than half of the subscribers stopped their paper; but I did not mind this, as the local managers of the campaign ordered as large an edition as we could print with our facilities, till after the election.

I was not expected to do anything except, through the newspaper, to persuade the local German voters to go with the Republican party. But I was too earnest, and too full of the intense excitement that took possession of the whole Union during the memorable Presidential contest of that year, to confine my activity to writing. I volunteered to organize a German wing of the local Republican club, and, although this was no easy task, owing to the stolid allegiance of my countrymen to the other party, I succeeded in working up a membership of nearly fifty from the smallest beginnings. We held frequent meetings, which gave me the long-desired opportunity to practise public speaking. I readily got over the first embarrassment, common to all beginners in that art, and acquired considerable fluency. I even addressed some gatherings of German voters especially brought together to listen to me. I was so much encouraged that I even ventured on two occasions on the bold experiment of speaking in English before general meetings of the Republican club. I was well prepared, and, as a double precaution against failure, spoke but briefly. It helped me very much to have the opportunity to listen to a number of prominent politicians and fine speakers from other States who came to Racine to address mass-meetings. There were also some very good speakers among the local leaders, whom I heard regularly in the club. The most prominent among them was Judge Doolittle, afterwards United States Senator.

Notwithstanding these political preoccupations, I found time to form a regular connection, as Western political correspondent, with the *Neue Zeit,* a weekly of the highest aspirations, founded by an enterprising German publisher in New York. It numbered among its contributors all the leading German-American writers, as well as eminent literati and journalists in the old country. It was edited with great care, and every number was replete with fine articles on politics, literature, science, music, and other subjects. I had become acquainted with its editors in New York, and had an ambitious longing to be permitted to write for it. Shortly after reaching Racine, I prepared a long letter on the general political situation in the Northwest. I spent much time and labor on it and sent it to the editors at a venture. To my intense joy, there came an answer from them within a week, saying that it was gladly accepted, and that further contributions were desired from me. My compensation was to be five dollars a letter, which was not a liberal allowance, considering the hard work involved in it for me; still, it was adding just so much to my income, and, moreover, I thought it such an honor to write for the *Neue Zeit* that I would gladly have corresponded with it without pay.

I vividly recollect to this hour the feverish anxiety into which I had worked myself by the time of the near approach of the election. I became so restless that even my editorial duties seemed very irksome. I did outside political work from morning till midnight. The night following the elections, I stayed up with the local Republican leaders till the small hours of the morning. The election returns were not encouraging when we finally sought our quarters, but there was no ground for giving up hope. I need hardly say that I felt indescribably woful when it became a cruel certainty on the following day that, instead of achieving a sweeping victory, the Republicans had suffered an overwhelming, humiliating defeat. My inexpressible disgust made me shun the sight of everybody, and it took me nearly a week to recover my balance.

There was enough in the condition of the *Volksblatt* to sober me entirely. As already mentioned, its sudden political conversion had resulted in a considerable melting away of the subscription-list. The election being over, all the campaign subscriptions stopped, of course, and the fact stared me in the face that there remained only about two hundred and fifty names that could be positively relied on for the future. The advertising patronage, too, was slim. The total gross income of the paper from both sources was not more than eighteen hundred dollars. A close calculation showed that it would take nearly twice as much to pay my salary, the wages of two printers, the cost of paper, ink, etc. Moreover, the renewal of type was imperative. During the campaign, the paper had been allowed a subsidy of fifty dollars a week out of the party funds, and, in view of the condition described, it was of vital importance to me to know whether this stipend would be continued. Hence, I naturally communicated without delay with the Republican Committee on the subject, only to discover, however, that all their enthusiasm had evaporated with the lost election. I received, too, my first lesson in that common experience in this and every other free country, that there is the greatest difference between the promises of politicians before an election and their fulfilment after it. I was informed at once that not only had the campaign fund been entirely exhausted, but the committee was still in debt for electioneering expenses, and that hence they could not contribute another dollar towards the *Volksblatt*. Nor was this all. I now learned for the first time that the greater part of the purchase price of the paper was still unpaid—that, indeed, only one-fourth of it had been paid down in cash, and that the balance would become due in six months from the date of purchase and was secured by a mortgage on the whole concern. This revelation was accompanied by the suggestion, which, under the circumstances, sounded a good deal like mockery, that, in view of my zealous services during the campaign, the committee would be willing to waive all claim for the cash payment, and turn the paper over to me, to be dealt with as best I could, upon the sole condition that I should continue to advocate the Republican cause.

The double task was thus to be put upon me of increasing the income of the paper to a living point and making provision within less than four months for the payment of the remaining three-quarters of the purchase price—a decidedly appalling outlook. But my enthusiasm and confidence in myself were greater than my business experience, so, after considering the question for a couple of days, I decided to accept the committee's proposal. I had persuaded myself that, with strong personal efforts, I might succeed in securing considerable additions to the subscription-list. Then I had reason to think that, by adding a job-printing outfit to the establishment, a new source of income might be found. As regarded the unpaid purchase money, I got over the difficulty by assuring myself that, if I was successful in my efforts in other directions and could make a small additional payment, the creditor would probably be willing to grant an extension of time. There remained the necessity of procuring a new lot of type for the paper. I had heard that it was not difficult to obtain credit from type-makers, and that was sufficient to do away with my hesitation on that score.

I can affirm that I left no stone unturned in my subsequent endeavors to establish the *Volksblatt* on a paying basis. I devoted all the time I could spare from my office labors as editor and publisher to a persistent canvass for new subscribers and advertisers. I solicited not only in Racine, but in three other smaller towns in the county. I even visited Milwaukee repeatedly, but at the end of the year I had secured only a hundred and thirty subscribers more and about seven hundred dollars' worth of advertising —about one-third of the amount needed to keep up the paper. A good part of the new receipts, too, I had to use for travelling expenses.

This meagre result brought me to the end of my wits. I had exhausted the whole field in which anything was to be gathered. I might have bought job and ordinary type on credit, if I had made myself personally liable for it, but I was afraid to do so, and did not buy. The inevitable end of my newspaper ownership came early in January, 1857. Unable to pay the wages of the compositors any longer, I advised the chairman of the Republican Committee of my state of stress. He authorized me to turn the concern over to the former owner, who reluctantly accepted it and forthwith changed it back into a Democratic organ. He claimed at the time that the committee, and I myself as its successor in the control of the paper, were liable to him for the balance due, but he had no legal remedy and did not attempt to enforce his claim. Twenty-four years later, when at the height of my prosperity, I received a letter from this same person, saying that he had been ruined by relieving me of the paper and asking for some recognition on my part. I sent him a check for one thousand dollars.

CHAPTER V

Correspondent and School-teacher.—1857-8

I HAD saved enough money to keep me for a few months, and concluded to remain in Racine till spring. Although without any regular employment, I was not idle. I continued my contributions to the *Neue Zeit,* even venturing to alternate letters with brief essays on social and political subjects, which were as readily accepted. I was justified then in believing that I should succeed as a German writer. I also knew that, owing to the limited field open to German journalism and literature in this country, a career as such would hardly be satisfactory as regarded either material profit or reputation. I saw, too, the incomparably wider sphere in both respects of the Anglo-American journalist. I had acquired such familiarity with English that there seemed to be no reason why I should not, with proper diligence, succeed before long in learning to write with sufficient fluency and correctness to enable me to enter that wider arena. I therefore determined to devote myself unremittingly to the task. I practised English composition for several hours every day, unless absent from home. I had to be my own teacher, and I followed a very simple and, as the result proved, effective method. I took a newspaper article or magazine, or a chapter in a novel, or some standard matter, read it over carefully several times, and then tried to reproduce it with pen and paper. Having the model before me, I could always correct my own work. After two months' practice, I felt able to venture an article on European politics for the *Daily Advocate,* the local Republican paper. I took it to the editor myself, explaining that it was my first attempt at writing in English, and that I expected no compensation for it if he thought it fit to be published. He looked it over, detected only one error, and promised to publish not only that but any other matter in the same line that I might bring him. I wrote thereafter one or two articles a week for the paper, with constantly increasing facility.

After the New Year, 1857, I had frequent occasion to interrupt my labors for days at a time. I learned by chance that some leading Germans in Milwaukee had formed a project similar to my Chicago land scheme, and would apply to the Wisconsin Legislature for a special act incorporating a land company with powers to acquire real estate in any part of the United States and to issue stock and bonds against it. The information revived so strongly my former faith that such an organization could make no end of money, that I went to Milwaukee to confer with the parties in question. I found that, though having no definite plans, they were very enthusiastic about the matter. The idea again got such complete possession of me that I made up my mind to try for a charter myself, alone. I went to Madison, the capital of the State, where the Legislature was holding its biennial session, and interested the Senator and member from Racine County in the scheme. They framed the charter for me, and in due time it was passed by both houses; but, to achieve this success, it was necessary to make several visits to the capital. During my stay there, I renewed my acquaintance with Hermann Goll, whom I had met the year before at Chicago, a man of thorough scholarship and great literary capacity, who was fulfilling the uncongenial duties of editor of the weekly German newspaper. He was thoroughly disgusted with his vocation and surroundings, for he was withal an extreme radical (politically) as well as a most entertaining man. He did not endure his situation long, but returned to his native land of Baden, where he died a few years ago, being at the time the editor of the conservative official journal of the Government of the Grand Duchy. I also became acquainted with Dr. Fuchs, another German scholar and thorough gentleman, and his bright, amiable wife. He held a professorship at the State University. These pleasant acquaintances were the only actual fruits of my repeated visits to Madison, for subsequent efforts in Milwaukee to utilize the charter by forming a land company conjointly with the parties referred to proved unavailing, so that I gave up the attempt in disgust and the act remained a dead letter.

In the course of the winter, I had my first insight into American domestic life and society as it then existed in a comparatively new Western town. My recollections in this connection are of the most agreeable nature. I saw then, for the first time, the neatness, order, comfort, peace, and quiet that, as a rule, characterize the American home; and made the observation, which is confirmed every day of my life, that American women of any social position have not their equals in any other country for brightness, tact, and true womanhood, and that they are as intelligent as American men and superior to them in all other respects —except, of course, knowledge of practical life. The richest men were persons who began life as mechanics or small tradesmen. Their whole bearing showed their origin, but their wives and daughters looked like ladies, and in most cases were really such. Yet those uncouth-mannered men had given, or were giving, the very best education to their children that money could command. The professors of the college imparted a somewhat higher tone to social life than prevailed in other Western towns. Some of them were really learned and ardently devoted to their calling. The older college students and a goodly number of attractive young ladies rendered the social circles very animated and pleasant, at least for one of my age.

What with my past savings and current earnings, I was able to remain in Racine till early in May. I had had such a pleasant and at the same time useful experience there that I found it really hard to make up my mind to leave for good. It was true, too, that my departure was regretted by many of my acquaintances. But it was clear that my aim had to be pursued elsewhere, and, thinking that such pursuit would be more promising in the intellectual centres of the East, I set out once more for New York. I arrived there with a slender purse and half a dozen long articles on miscellaneous subjects, three in German and three in English, prepared in advance, as a means of further introduction to the metropolitan press.

With the acquaintances I had made the year before in the Empire City, I had no trouble in obtaining proper introductions to the editors of the principal American and German dailies—namely, the *Tribune, Times, Herald*, and the *Staats-Zeitung,* the Democratic paper. It was far more difficult to obtain personal interviews with several people, whom, however, I managed to see after more or less antechambering—Charles A. Dana, the editorial manager of the *Tribune,* and also Henry J. Raymond and Frederic Hudson, who filled like positions on the *Times* and *Herald.* The first-mentioned I found quite talkative and affable. He began the conversation in German, which he spoke very fluently, and, after a few keen questions, he soon took my measure, and made me confess that I was a new hand at the journalist's trade and had nothing to offer but a willingness to work and ambitious aspirations. He showed a disposition to sneer at the latter. Still, the ardor with which I pressed my application for employment seemed to impress him. He took down my address, saying that he would perhaps try me as a general reporter of the doings of the Germans in the city. I offered him one of my English articles on "German Life in the Northwest," and he promised to read it. Mr. Raymond also received me kindly, but gave me no encouragement at all, and declined to receive and examine one of my English productions. He intimated that the *Times* had more editorial contributions than it could print, that it was always ready to pay liberally for what it published, and for valuable news. He was perfectly polite, but brief and decided. His whole manner, indeed, revealed the vigorous, resolute mind that characterized his career as a journalist. Mr. Hudson's response to my application was substantially the same. "What do you think that you can do for us?" he asked me, when I got through with my explanation of my wishes; and I found it hard, of course, to reply. "Anything in the way of news that you bring us, I will read, and use if acceptable." He merely cast a glance at the samples of my ability to write, and turned me off, saying, "It would have to be a matter of the highest value to induce the *Herald* to print anything so long."

The *Staats-Zeitung* was then and is now one of the most prosperous newspapers in the world, and, as such, entirely able, but willing only to a moderate degree, to pay for extra contributions. Mrs. Uhl, the widow of its founder, was the active business-manager. She was a woman of commanding and pleasing presence, and superintended the whole concern, including the editorial and business departments, with untiring industry (she was at her post at eight o'clock every morning), excellent judgment, and great success. The politics of the paper were abominable, but it had a Sunday issue on neutral ground, and to it I sought admission. Mrs. Uhl had a very kindly nature, which blossomed out in after years in the shape of private and public charity on the largest practical scale. On her death, in 1884 (she died Mrs. Oswald Ottendorfer), her worth was recognized by one of the greatest public demonstrations ever witnessed in New York. I understood that she was beset all the time with requests like mine, and hence hardly expected the friendly hearing which she granted me. She agreed to have my literary articles read by her literary editor and to advise me promptly of the result. My call at the office of the *New-Yorker Demokrat* bore no fruit, as I had anticipated from what I had heard of its limited pecuniary resources.

In a few days I received my manuscript from Mr. Dana,

with a brief note saying that he could not use it. The *Staats-Zeitung*, on the other hand, informed me that two of my articles had been accepted, and that they would be paid for, when published, at the rate of four dollars a column. They brought actually twenty-one dollars to me in all. This was rather a humiliating compensation for what represented more than a week's hard work, and did not augur well for the rapid acquisition of wealth by means of my pen; but I took the money and worked on. If I remember correctly, my contributions to the *Staats-Zeitung* earned me only four dollars a week. The *Neue Zeit* also continued to accept about a column every fortnight, for which I received five dollars, and I managed, too, to get something to do for the German edition of *Frank Leslie's Illustrated Weekly*, which was started at that time. As regarded the American press, my dream of an editorial connection had been rudely dispelled; but, nothing daunted, I resolved to get *en rapport* with them as a chance reporter or penny-a-liner. I tried all the three dailies named with brief accounts of special occurrences among the German population, such as public festivals, military parades, proceedings of societies, etc., and succeeded fairly well. At least half of what I offered was accepted, but the work was hard and discouraging, owing to the uncertainty of the pay. I do not believe that my income from this source ever exceeded eight dollars a week.

This was literally scraping a precarious livelihood. I continued it for nearly three months and gradually grew very weary of it. I had neither sufficient income nor leisure for social enjoyments, and led a very lonesome life. I began to long for a change and to consider my leaving the West a great mistake. I was already thinking of ways and means of returning there when a chance to do so was suddenly presented to me. A contest had broken out between the Republicans and Democrats of Minnesota in the political convention called under an act of Congress to frame a State Constitution, that attracted a good deal of attention. It flashed upon me that I might induce one of the American dailies to send me as a special correspondent to the scene of action. I proposed this without delay to the three managing editors. Mr. Dana alone was willing to consider it. He would not, however, act upon my bold suggestion to allow me a regular salary and expenses, but agreed, after much parleying, only to let me write not less than twenty columns from St. Paul, and to allow me twelve dollars a column for the work. I figured up the travelling expenses to St. Paul at fifty dollars—more money than I had at my command. I was about to give up the plan, on account of this apparently insuperable obstacle, when an American fellow-reporter, with whom I had struck up a close acquaintance, helped me out with a good piece of advice. He recommended that I should go to Albany and ask Thurlow Weed, the famous editor of the Albany *Journal,* to obtain passes for me. My adviser had himself tried the same thing successfully.

I packed up and took the first evening boat for the capital of the State. On landing in the morning, I made directly for the *Journal* office, and ascertained that the renowned personage I went to see was fortunately in town. I had the desired interview with him before noon. His exterior was the index of a remarkable man. His tall form, beardless face, set in a frame of gray, bushy hair, heavy eyebrows, and a large mouth made a strong combination of features. His kindly eyes and pleasant smile were in contrast to the rest of his face. He gave me a friendly welcome and listened to my request. After questioning me as to the object of my Western trip, he said promptly, "I think I can help you," sat down, and wrote a letter of introduction for me to a local railroad official, requesting him to obtain passes for me as far westward in the direction of St. Paul as possible. The thanks that I expressed were sincere, for I certainly had no claim upon him. The letters had the desired effect. I was given a pass from Albany to Buffalo, orders for transportation thence to Detroit by

Lake Erie, and from Detroit to Grand Haven, Milwaukee, and Prairie du Chien, the terminus of the only railroad at that time crossing the State of Wisconsin to the Mississippi River. I started at once and had a most interesting and enjoyable, but uneventful, trip of four and a half days to Prairie du Chien. There I took a passenger steamer up the Mississippi to my destination. I found the scenery formed by the banks of the river very picturesque. Going upstream and making many landings, we were over twenty-four hours on the boat. I believe that we reached St. Paul on the 15th of August.

The town had not over seven thousand inhabitants. I was struck with the beauty and other advantages of its situation and was at once satisfied it had a great future. At the levee there was a long line of steamboats, showing already an extensive local commerce. The Territory of Minnesota being then on the eve of admission to the Union as a State, the tide of immigration from the Eastern States had set strongly in that direction. Several boats arrived daily from below with crowds of seekers of political and other fortunes. The place was thronged with a floating population far beyond its residential. It consisted of two straggling business streets parallel to the river, gradually ascending to a plateau bordered by wooded hills, which had already been reached by the residence portion of the town and was considerably developed. From the plateau there was a magnificent prospect over the Mississippi valley and a large expanse of country to the west of it. There were two main centres of life in the community—the large brick hotel, at which I stopped, and the Territorial capitol. There was stir enough, to be sure, but who would have dared to prophesy that in a little over thirty years the small town would grow into a city of two hundred thousand people?

The complication in the constitutional convention that led to my journey was this: The Democrats were charged with having perpetrated frauds in the election and sent up five members from Pembina County (now part of North

Dakota), who were rejected as coming from outside territory. The Republicans numbered fifty-nine and the Democrats fifty-four. Upon the rejection of the Pembina delegates, the Democrats seceded and sat in a separate hall. Each party proceeded to make a constitution, denounced the other violently, and the bitterest war was raging between them when I arrived. For a week, there was plenty of material for letters, but wiser counsels prevailed, and a committee of conference was appointed to harmonize the two constitutions and submit only one to the people. The conference was successful, and the committee's report was made to both bodies and adopted on August 30. Thereupon, the "double-headed" convention adjourned and my mission was ended, much sooner than I wished.

Being thus deprived of political material for correspondence, I sought to obtain other by visiting various parts of the Territory. For this purpose, I joined a party of young fellows who set out for a fortnight's hunting-trip to the northwest of St. Paul. We started in an ordinary farmer's wagon, drawn by two horses. After travelling some hours, the road came to an end, and we continued our way at a venture across the wild prairie. We struck a tamarack swamp in the afternoon, and, thinking that it was of no great extent, tried to cross it. We struggled on, but had not reached the end of it when the sun set and we felt obliged to stop for the night in a comparatively dry spot. From the time we entered the swamp, men and animals struggled desperately to protect themselves from the swarms of mosquitoes, but, in spite of the most vigorous resistance, we were quickly stung all over. We walked alongside of the horses, which, although we brushed them incessantly with twigs, were constantly covered and driven almost wild by the insects. Their ears and nostrils suffered especially. On halting for the night, we made a narrow circle of branches strewn with green grass about our camp, and fired it, so as to surround ourselves with a dense smoke. It did but little good, and, owing to our efforts to protect ourselves and the horses, no one of us got any rest. We started again at daybreak, and it took us nearly the whole forenoon to reach dry prairie. The mosquito plague, however, diminished but little, so that we decided to make for St. Paul again as quickly as possible. We arrived there late in the evening of the third day. I was a sight to behold. My face was really disfigured, and I was so exhausted that I stayed in bed for a whole day.

In spite of this experience, I set out on another wagon-trip to the town of Faribault, on the Minnesota River, forty miles southwest of St. Paul. My motive was to see James F. Shields, formerly United States Senator from Illinois, and a resident of Belleville, where I had become acquainted with him. He had distinguished himself in the Mexican War, but belonged to the class of political adventurers, so numerous in the West in those days, who tried their fortunes in one new State after another. Not being reelected to the United States Senate in Illinois, he migrated to Minnesota, whence he managed to be sent as Senator for a short term. Subsequently, on her admission into the Union, he served on the Northern side in the war against the Southern Rebellion, and succeeded in being elected United States Senator from Missouri. The newspapers had announced that Speaker Orr of South Carolina and several other leading Democratic politicians were visiting him, and this fact prompted my journey.

I had another sore trial from the mosquitoes in crossing the so-called Big Woods, a strip of timber, many miles wide, extending from south to north across the State. But otherwise the drive through the rolling prairie country, dotted with lakes fringed by oak groves, to the picturesque valley of the Minnesota was quite interesting. Faribault I found to be an embryo village of a few dozen brick, frame, and log houses, for which a large growth was expected. It never became more than a small country town, however. Under the pre-emption law, General Shields had acquired a quarter-section of land immediately adjoining the town. I found him living upon it, on an eminence commanding a beautiful view of the surrounding country, in a one-story log house of the most primitive description, divided into three rooms. He was sitting in front of it, with his visitors, on rude chairs; smoking a "corn-cob" and looking altogether like a true pioneer. He received me very cordially, and introduced me to the rest of the company, and I spent several hours listening to their varied talk. They were all supplied with a good stock of funny stories, which they dispensed with great liberality. Altogether, I gathered ample material for some descriptive letters, and bitter, therefore, was my disappointment when I found, on my return to St. Paul, a letter from the editor of the *Tribune,* declining to authorize me to write any more, thus leaving me once more without employment. While thinking over my situation, the idea came to me that I had better return to New York and offer my services to the *Tribune,* or any other paper there that might be willing to accept them, as a regular correspondent from the seat of the Sepoy Mutiny in India, which at that time absorbed the anxious attention of the whole world.

I arrived in New York about the middle of September, and immediately entered upon the pursuit of my objects. As no one of the great dailies had, up to that time, published special correspondence from the seat of the Mutiny, I felt very confident of success, and visions of prospective honors and profits cheered me on; but I had not taken one important factor into consideration. The country was fast plunging into the severe financial crisis of 1857. The suspension of the Ohio Life and Trust Company, which ushered in that era of long and general distress, had already occurred and was being daily followed by failures of banks and commercial houses in the city. General distrust prevailed, and trade of every sort had come almost to a standstill. The newspaper business, like every other, was being seriously affected, and publishers and editors necessarily were bent upon reducing rather than enlarging their current expenditures. My successive applications to the editors of the *Tribune, Times,* and *Herald* resulted in nothing, although I saw them more than once. The sole encouragement I received was from the editor of the *Evening Post,* John Bigelow, afterwards Consul-General and Minister to France, but he only offered to pay me twenty dollars a letter for what I wrote.

I was very loath to give up my plan, and for weeks taxed my wits for means to raise the needed funds.[1] The only result was that, in the latter half of October, I found myself penniless and without any prospect of work in the great city, which was swarming with tens of thousands of idle men and women, the victims of the crisis. I was finally obliged to put up in a German boarding-house in Jersey City, and to appeal for help to a former female servant of my parents, whom I accidentally found to be living there. Her husband, whom I had also known in my youth, was a skilful journeyman stone-cutter, and had saved a little money from his earnings. These good people gladly provided for my wants, which did not exceed five dollars a week. In my subsequent prosperity I had the satisfaction of being able to manifest to them my grateful appreciation of their kindness.

I prepared a number of articles, both in German and in English, on various subjects, and every few days went to New York and visited the newspaper offices to find a market for them. But all through October I managed to sell only two German articles, for which I received ten dollars! While in a German office one day, I accidentally picked up the Reading (Pa.) *Adler,* the well-known principal paper of the Pennsylvania Germans in the eastern counties of the State, printed in the singular jargon spoken in those parts. Glancing over the advertising columns, I noticed quite a number of short advertisements for teachers in Berks and Bucks and Lebanon Counties. Being very much discour-

[1] One illusive opening was the Government's military expedition against the Mormons in the autumn of 1857.

aged as to my ability to earn a living by literary work, and anxious to be relieved from my pecuniary straits, it occurred to me that there lay the possibility of regular employment. To be sure, I had not the slightest knowledge of teaching, but, from what I had seen of the country schools in different places, I was persuaded that I could manage to fill the prescribed requirements. Accordingly, I left Jersey City for Reading on the last of October. On reaching it, I called on the County School Commissioner, to whom I explained my aspirations. He informed me that there was no suitable opening for me in his county, but that he had just received a letter from his colleague in the adjoining county of Lebanon, asking for a teacher for one of the district schools under his administration. I took the next train for Lebanon, and presented myself without delay to the School Commissioner. He was a very kindly, elderly man, speaking very good German, who interested himself at once in my case. He asked me whether I had a teacher's certificate, and, when I replied that I had not, suggested that I should submit to an examination at once, or prepare myself for one, as I could not be accepted as a teacher without a certificate. I declared my willingness to be examined on the spot, though doubting my ability to pass, whereupon he assured me that I need have no fears. He made me sit down, and, for an hour and a half, put me through a series of questions in arithmetic, grammar, history, and geography, three-fourths of which, under his kind leading, I answered correctly. Then, on payment of one dollar, I received a certificate pronouncing me duly qualified to teach any district school in the State of Pennsylvania; also a letter of introduction to the Board of School Directors for Swatara Township, the chairman of which resided in the village of Jonestown, six miles from Lebanon, whither I went on foot the next morning.

 I found Jonestown to be a neat, clean place, consisting of a public square from the four sides of which as many streets extended at right angles. The buildings around the square, which contained some fine elms, consisted of three hotels with old-fashioned swinging signs, two stores for general retail trade, and some mechanics' shops. The hamlet had a most sleepy look, which on closer acquaintance proved to be in accordance with its true character. Its population, with the exception of a single family, was entirely made up of Pennsylvania Germans, and their peculiar language was used exclusively. I made my way to the most attractive hotel, the landlord of which, a fine-looking, white-haired man, was watching the goings-on from a chair on the main veranda. He gave me a hearty welcome, and, like a genuine village Boniface, immediately tried to find out who I was and what I wanted. On learning my object in being there, he made himself known as one of the school board, and offered to take me at once to the chairman of it. This proved to be the village doctor, a native of New York State, and an intelligent, well-educated man. He received me very kindly, and, after an hour's talk, we were on the best possible footing.

Having taken my intellectual measure, he told me frankly that I was altogether too well educated for the class of people I was to come in contact with, and for the common-school work I wished to undertake. But, on being informed that I sought the latter not from choice but from necessity, he offered to make it as pleasant as possible for me. He called a meeting of the school directors for the same evening, at which I was formally assigned to the vacant school for the two terms of three months each (the common schools in the county were not kept open longer), and my compensation fixed at thirty dollars a month and board —more than had ever been allowed for the same service. I was but too glad to accept, but was rather taken aback when the doctor explained to me that I was not to have an allowance for board, but would have to "board around" among the farmers whose children were to be my pupils— that is, to change my eating- and sleeping-place once a week. There was nothing to be done, however, but to submit.

The first school-term was not to begin for a week, so I remained at the tavern I had first selected during that time. I went back to Lebanon for the valise that contained all my belongings. I was reduced to the suit I wore, a fall overcoat, and a limited supply of linen and underwear. I bought the prescribed text-books, to the study of which I devoted myself diligently. During the week I also made myself acquainted with the leading villagers and the surrounding country. I found the latter most attractive every way. The Swatara River, that flowed through the village, coursed through a most picturesque valley from the beautiful Blue Mountains, the main ridge of which was but a few miles distant. The rolling country was finely diversified and highly improved, and dotted with prosperous farms. Fine public roads extended in every direction—a feature especially pleasing to a passionate pedestrian like myself. Assuredly, I did not fail to visit at once the scene of my future labors. The school-house was an ordinary building, decidedly neglected, and too small for the number of children entitled to use it, but well-lighted and well-situated on an elevation close to a by-road, about three-quarters of an hour from the village.

I duly entered upon my duties at the appointed time. Only thirty-five pupils out of sixty reported, and the attendance was always meagre, never exceeding forty, and sinking in bad weather often below thirty. The ages of my pupils ranged from eighteen to five, the majority being perhaps twelve, with the sexes about equally divided. Most of them were healthy and comely, but shabbily dressed and anything but cleanly in appearance. The majority of them were evidently intelligent, but the examination with which I began my teaching, in order to find out how they had been taught before and how much they knew, proved that they had received very irregular and limited teaching. Their spelling was very defective, their writing awkward, and their pronunciation of English very incorrect. It became clear that I should be equal to my task, as far as necessary knowledge was concerned, in all the branches except that of writing, in which I was disqualified by my own bad hand. I graded my pupils as best I could under the circumstances, and then proceeded regularly with the prescribed instruction.

The law required five hours' teaching daily. The morning session opened at nine and continued till noon, with ten minutes' recess at half-past ten, followed by an intermission till half-past one, and then two hours more of recitations. Saturday was a holiday. Thus I could not complain of excessive work, nor were my duties irksome to me, as the pupils were well-behaved and I soon got on a good footing with them. During my stay I had but few occasions to administer admonition or punishment, the latter only of a light sort. The main trouble was not bad conduct so much as laziness, especially on the part of the older girls. The general ignorance of my flock was amazing, and I seemed to be among veritable German peasant children. They saw very little of the outside world, and I readily attached them to me by reading and talking to them of it. Though they were the offspring of families that had been settled in Pennsylvania for generations, only a few of them could converse or understand English, so I spoke German to them. At first they found it difficult to understand me, accustomed as they were to the dialect. This very fact made them look upon the "schoolmaster," as they all called me, with awe, as a sort of superior being. Within a few weeks, the whole school was ready to do anything for me, obviously feeling honored by being allowed to talk or walk with me.

I certainly could not boast of great achievements in my experience as a district teacher, but when I contrasted my freedom from care with my last experiences in New York, I felt very content with my temporary lot. This feeling was strengthened when I read in the New York daily *Tribune*, which I had subscribed for, of the progress of the general distress in the large cities. But there was a feature in my new life that was most distasteful to me from the start. As already mentioned, the terms of my engagement included "free board," which was to be furnished in rotation at the homes of my pupils. Each family was bound to keep me only one week, so every Saturday I had to pick up my traps and move to new quarters. As a rule, my hosts were kindly disposed and treated me to the best they had; but their coarse fare, crude manners, and primitive domestic arrangements were hard to put up with. The people I stayed with were all descended from the poorest and most degraded class of peasants, who had emigrated under labor-contracts from my native province a century previous. They brought with them their domestic habits and had stuck to them ever since. I was surprised to find that their table-fare, beverages, furniture, utensils, and domestic practices generally were all but identical with those of the peasantry of the Palatinate at that very time. I found dishes on their tables that are not known in any other part of Germany. They slept on and under featherbeds,—and, alas! I had to submit to these too,—just as the peasants of the Palatinate do to-day. The very bench at the back of the stores for lounging purposes and smoking was not wanting. Of course, these people had been elevated above the level of a hundred years before, as their parents had had the advantage of the generally civilizing results of life in America, but my hosts were, almost without exception, sadly ignorant, narrow, and low. To be obliged to eat at table and to spend the evening hours and free days with these people, and to be obliged to sleep in the same room with the male farm help, was anything but an agreeable necessity. Yet I made the most of my predicament and got along without friction.

I was, however, immensely relieved when my friend the doctor, at Christmas, in response to my earnest and constant entreaties, persuaded the school board to let him arrange for my board and lodging on a different basis. Accordingly, we succeeded in persuading a family with which I had lived a week, and which I liked better than any other, to board me regularly for the modest sum of three dollars a week, which the school board was to pay. The family bore the name of Umberger, and consisted of two brothers and their wives and four children of the elder pair, two of whom were a boy of eighteen and a girl of seventeen. During the four months that I remained with them, there never was the least jarring between us. I requited their kindness by giving the children extra teaching at night, and entertaining the inquisitive older folks during the long winter evenings by telling them of life in the West, in Germany, and in the great American cities. To show how circumscribed the vision of these people necessarily was, I need but mention that most of the farmers and their wives whom I met during the winter, had never seen a railroad, though they lived within six miles of one!

I spent my evenings, except Saturdays, at home, talking and reading. Saturdays I set out for the school-house after breakfast, and, after starting the fire in the stove, spent all day doing journalistic work. I did not want to get out of practice, and I sought also to add to my modest income by it. Nothing that I offered to American papers in New York was accepted, but the *Staats-Zeitung* published some descriptive sketches and a short tale, if I remember aright. Saturday evenings and Sunday afternoons and evenings, I made calls in Jonestown, or spent some time among the loungers around the office stoves in the several taverns. Of course, I longed for company, and sought what there was of it, poor as it was. One Sunday a month I spent in Lebanon, where I picked up a pleasant acquaintance with the editor of the leading local paper, the *Lebanon County Courier*, through some communications on various subjects which I sent him for gratuitous publication.

Time passed quickly till the end of May, 1858, when my engagement was terminated by the closing of the schools.

MEMOIRS OF HENRY VILLARD

BOOK TWO

IN CIVIL-WAR TIME: BULL RUN

CHAPTER VI

THE LINCOLN–DOUGLAS DEBATES.—1858

MAN is the creature of habit, and though the experiences through which I had passed at Jonestown were anything but congenial, I was almost loath to change my peaceful, careless existence for the more active life I really desired. It was evident that I had made many friends who were sorry at my departure, and I did not part from them without sincere regret. The Umberger family all cried when I took leave. I promised them and others to visit Jonestown again soon; but, alas! though I have all along intended to do so, circumstances have always prevented my revisiting the scene of my first and last attempt at teaching up to this writing—that is, during the thirty-eight years that have elapsed since I left. I suppose I should now hardly find any of my acquaintances among the living.[1]

I departed from Jonestown just twenty-three years old, with a moderately replenished wardrobe, about sixty dollars in my pocket, and fifty more due me from the *Staats-Zeitung*. This was all I had in the world except splendid health, eagerness for work, and fully regained and unbounded confidence in myself. I went directly to New York, determined to try once more for regular journalistic employment. I was more fortunate this time than in the previous fall. On calling at the office of the *Staats-Zeitung* and sending in my name to the publisher, Oswald Ottendorfer, I was at once invited into his private office. He received me very cordially, complimented me on my

---

[1] Jonestown was revisited by Mr. Villard in company with his son Oswald in the spring of 1897. All, in fact, whom he had known had disappeared.

work for the paper, and asked me whether I was a professional journalist. Encouraged by his friendly manner, I spoke out frankly about my past and my aspirations. We talked a long time, and he finally told me he would consult with Mrs. Uhl, the proprietress of the paper, as to giving me steady employment, and let me know something definite the next day.

On reporting to him at the appointed hour, he took me to Mrs. Uhl's room and presented me to her. She received me very kindly, saying that she had read my contributions, and hoped that I might become regularly connected with the paper. Mr. Ottendorfer then stated that their weekly edition had a very large circulation throughout the Western States, to keep up which it was necessary to send out special agents from time to time to look after their customers. He proposed that I should travel for the paper through the middle States of Ohio, Indiana, Michigan, and Illinois, collecting old subscriptions and getting new subscribers, and at the same time writing regular descriptive letters to the paper. Mrs. Uhl was willing to have me engaged on trial for three months, and to allow me fifteen dollars a week and actual expenses. I thought I ought not to hesitate for a moment and accepted at once. I received the necessary detailed instructions, the fifty dollars due me, and one hundred dollars in advance on account, and set out the next day for Ohio.

I commenced my canvass at Steubenville, and in the course of the next five weeks, following the subscription-list, visited about twenty-five larger and smaller towns, including Newark, Canton, Massillon, Columbus, Springfield, and Chillicothe. I wrote regularly one letter a week, making from one and a half to two columns, for publication, and this part of my work gave entire satisfaction. But I was not successful in the other respect. I expected to find more or less educated Germans in the places I visited, who would be glad to give me the benefit of their advice and assistance. But I rarely came across any men of culture.

Those I had to deal with were mainly grocers, saloon-keepers, and small mechanics. It was hard to collect past dues, and much harder to enlist new subscribers. My attempts in the latter direction exposed me to no little rudeness, and the pecuniary results of my efforts were so meagre that my collections were not equal to my current expenditures.

I felt it my duty to write Mr. Ottendorfer frankly, at the expiration of a month, that I was afraid I should not prove a successful canvasser, and to propose a new plan of operations. The public press was filled at the time with references to the approaching contest on the stump for the succession to the United States Senate between Senator Stephen A. Douglas and Abraham Lincoln in Illinois. The eyes of the whole country were fixed upon the former as the champion in the Senate of the wing of the Democratic party which had adopted his fallacious doctrine that the people of the Territories should be left free to regulate their domestic institutions—that is, to establish or to keep out slavery, as they saw fit—against the other wing, having the countenance of President Buchanan, which favored the introduction of slavery in Kansas and the other unsettled parts of the Union. Abraham Lincoln was the representative of the young Republican party. A series of joint debates between the two leaders had been arranged, which it was evident would form the principal political event of the season. I suggested to my employers to let me proceed at once to Illinois and observe the approaching political campaign there as the *Staats-Zeitung's* special correspondent. To my great joy, my proposition was readily accepted, and I proceeded without delay to Chicago.[1]

I reached there just in time to witness the grand ovation given to Senator Douglas on his arrival from Washington.

---

[1] Sympathy with the Douglas Democrats in their opposition to the proslavery followers of Buchanan led him to offer to send letters gratuitously, during his Western engagement with the *Staats-Zeitung*, to John W. Forney's Philadelphia *Press*, a Douglas organ.

He was received and escorted through the streets like a conquering hero, and it was made strikingly apparent that the Illinois Democracy were all but unanimously for him against the National Administration. I called on him the next day at the Tremont House to make known my mission, and to ask his leave to accompany him. I was promptly shown to his parlor, where I found him talking to a few friends. I knew him well by sight from my visit to Washington in 1856. He bid me a hearty welcome, and introduced me to the other visitors and to his private secretary, Mr. Sheridan. On learning the object of my call, he said at once that he should be very happy to have my company during the campaign, and directed the secretary to inform me fully regarding his programme, and make the proper arrangements with me. While we were talking, his newly-wedded second wife came in through a side door, and I was introduced to her. She was at once a most lovely and a queenly apparition. Indeed, it seemed to me that I had never seen a woman more beautiful in every way. Her tall figure was perfectly proportioned, and her every movement and gesture most graceful. She presented a marked contrast, in her youthful, blooming freshness and vivacity, to her small, dark, sombre husband. She appeared to be devoted to him, and certainly helped him no little in his political aspirations.

The first joint debate (in the famous series of seven) between Douglas and Lincoln, which I attended, took place on the afternoon of August 21, 1858, at Ottawa, Illinois. It was the great event of the day, and attracted an immense concourse of people from all parts of the State. Douglas spoke first for an hour, followed by Lincoln for an hour and a half; upon which the former closed in another half hour. The Democratic spokesman commanded a strong, sonorous voice, a rapid, vigorous utterance, a telling play of countenance, impressive gestures, and all the other arts of the practised speaker. As far as all external conditions were concerned, there was nothing in favor of Lincoln. He had a lean, lank, indescribably gawky figure, an odd-featured, wrinkled, inexpressive, and altogether uncomely face. He used singularly awkward, almost absurd, up-and-down and sidewise movements of his body to give emphasis to his arguments. His voice was naturally good, but he frequently raised it to an unnatural pitch. Yet the unprejudiced mind felt at once that, while there was on the one side a skilful dialectician and debater arguing a wrong and weak cause, there was on the other a thoroughly earnest and truthful man, inspired by sound convictions in consonance with the true spirit of American institutions. There was nothing in all Douglas's powerful effort that appealed to the higher instincts of human nature, while Lincoln always touched sympathetic chords. Lincoln's speech excited and sustained the enthusiasm of his audience to the end. When he had finished, two stalwart young farmers rushed on the platform, and, in spite of his remonstrances, seized and put him on their shoulders and carried him in that uncomfortable posture for a considerable distance. It was really a ludicrous sight to see the grotesque figure holding frantically on to the heads of his supporters, with his legs dangling from their shoulders, and his pantaloons pulled up so as to expose his underwear almost to his knees. Douglas made dexterous use of this incident in his next speech, expressing sincere regret that, against his wish, he had used up his old friend Lincoln so completely that he had to be carried off the stage. Lincoln retaliated by saying at the first opportunity that he had known Judge Douglas long and well, but there was nevertheless one thing he could not say of him, and that was that the Judge always told the truth.

I was introduced to Lincoln at Freeport, and met him frequently afterwards in the course of the campaign. I must say frankly that, although I found him most approachable, good-natured, and full of wit and humor, I could not take a real personal liking to the man, owing to an inborn weakness for which he was even then notorious and so remained during his great public career. He was inordinately fond of jokes, anecdotes, and stories. He loved to hear them, and still more to tell them himself out of the inexhaustible supply provided by his good memory and his fertile fancy. There would have been no harm in this but for the fact that, the coarser the joke, the lower the anecdote, and the more risky the story, the more he enjoyed them, especially when they were of his own invention. He possessed, moreover, a singular ingenuity in bringing about occasions in conversation for indulgences of this kind. I have to confess, too, that, aside from the prejudice against him which I felt on this account, I believed, with many prominent leaders of the Republican party, that, with regard to separating more effectively the antislavery Northern from the proslavery Southern wing of the Democracy, it would have been better if the reëlection of Douglas had not been opposed.

The party warfare was hotly continued in all parts of the State from early summer till election day in November. Besides the seven joint debates, both Douglas and Lincoln spoke scores of times separately, and numerous other speakers from Illinois and other States contributed incessantly to the agitation. The two leaders visited almost every county in the State. I heard four of the joint debates, and six other speeches by Lincoln and eight by his competitor. Of course, the later efforts became substantial repetitions of the preceding ones, and to listen to them grew more and more tiresome to me. As I had seen something of political campaigns before, this one did not exercise the full charm of novelty upon me. Still, even if I had been a far more callous observer, I could not have helped being struck with the efficient party organizations, the skilful tactics of the managers, the remarkable feats of popular oratory, and the earnestness and enthusiasm of the audiences I witnessed. It was a most instructive object-lesson in practical party politics, and filled me with admiration for the Anglo-American method of working out popular destiny.

In other respects, my experiences were not altogether agreeable. It was a very hot summer, and I was obliged to travel almost continuously. Illinois had then only about a million and a half of inhabitants, poorly-constructed railroads, and bad country roads, over which latter I had to journey quite as much as over the former. The taverns in town and country, as a rule, were wretched; and, as I moved about with the candidates and their followers and encountered crowds everywhere, I fared miserably in many places. Especially in the southern part of the State, then known as "Egypt" and mostly inhabited by settlers from the Southern States, food and lodging were nearly always simply abominable. I still vividly remember the day of semi-starvation and the night with half a dozen roommates I passed at Jonesboro', where the third joint debate took place.

I saw more of Illinois than I have since seen of any other State in the Union, and I acquired a thorough faith, based on the immeasurable fertility of her prairies, in the great growth that she has since attained. I also formed many valuable acquaintances, a number of whom have continued to this day. It was then that I first saw my lifelong friend Horace White, who accompanied Mr. Lincoln as the representative of the Chicago *Tribune*, and R. R. Hitt, the official stenographer of the Republican candidate. He was one of the most skilled shorthand writers in the country, and his success as such led in due time to his appointment as reporter of the United States Supreme Court. This position he resigned for a successful career as diplomat and Congressman.

I firmly believe that, if Stephen A. Douglas had lived, he would have had a brilliant national career. Freed by the Southern rebellion from all identification with pro-slavery interests, the road would have been open to the highest fame and position for which his unusual talents qualified him. As I took final leave of him and Lincoln, doubtless neither of them had any idea that within two years they would be rivals again in the Presidential race. I had it from Lincoln's own lips that the United States Senatorship was the greatest political height he at the time expected to climb. He was full of doubt, too, of his ability to secure the majority of the Legislature against Douglas. These confidences he imparted to me on a special occasion which I must not omit to mention in detail before closing this chapter.

He and I met accidentally, about nine o'clock on a hot, sultry evening, at a flag railroad station about twenty miles west of Springfield, on my return from a great meeting at Petersburg in Menard County. He had been driven to the station in a buggy and left there alone. I was already there. The train that we intended to take for Springfield was about due. After vainly waiting for half an hour for its arrival, a thunderstorm compelled us to take refuge in an empty freight-car standing on a side track, there being no buildings of any sort at the station. We squatted down on the floor of the car and fell to talking on all sorts of subjects. It was then and there he told me that, when he was clerking in a country store, his highest political ambition was to be a member of the State Legislature. "Since then, of course," he said laughingly, "I have grown some, but my friends got me into *this* business [meaning the canvass]. I did not consider myself qualified for the United States Senate, and it took me a long time to persuade myself that I was. Now, to be sure," he continued, with another of his peculiar laughs, "I am convinced that I am good enough for it; but, in spite of it all, I am saying to myself every day: 'It is too big a thing for you; you will never get it.' Mary [his wife] insists, however, that I am going to be Senator and President of the United States, too." These last words he followed with a roar of laughter, with his arms around his knees, and shaking all over with mirth at his wife's ambition. "Just think," he exclaimed, "of such a sucker as me as President!"

He then fell to asking questions regarding my antecedents, and expressed some surprise at my fluent use of English after so short a residence in the United States. Next he wanted to know whether it was true that most of the educated people in Germany were "infidels." I answered that they were not openly professed infidels, but such a conclusion might be drawn from the fact that most of them were not church-goers. "I do not wonder at that," he rejoined; "my own inclination is that way." I ventured to give expression to my own disbelief in the doctrine of the Christian church relative to the existence of God, the divinity of Christ, and immortality. This led him to put other questions to me to draw me out. He did not commit himself, but I received the impression that he was of my own way of thinking. It was no surprise to me, therefore, to find in the writings of his biographers Ward Hill Lamon and W. H. Herndon that I had correctly understood him. Our talk continued till half-past ten, when the belated train arrived. I cherish this accidental rencontre as one of my most precious recollections, since my companion of that night has become one of the greatest figures in history.

I went from Jonesboro' to Chicago, and remained there till after the election. I considered the outcome so uncertain that I did not venture any predictions in my correspondence. Douglas himself, I knew, was much in doubt; Lincoln and his friends were very confident, and therefore bitterly disappointed by the result.

CHAPTER VII

THE PIKE'S PEAK GOLD FEVER.—1858-9

THE real aim of my journalistic efforts was a regular connection with the Anglo-American press. I regarded my work for the *Staats-Zeitung* as only a temporary makeshift, and kept my ulterior object steadily in view. I had given up the idea of securing a position on one of the principal New York papers, and my desires bore upon the Western press. During my sojourn in Ohio, I had daily read the Cincinnati *Daily Commercial* and noticed the ability and enterprise displayed in its columns. At a venture I went to Cincinnati and offered my services to the publisher of the *Commercial*, M. D. Potter. He referred me to the news-editor, Murat Halstead, afterwards the principal proprietor and editor-in-chief of the paper. After a few talks with him, we agreed that I should report the important proceedings at the impending sessions of the Illinois and Indiana Legislatures for the *Commercial*. In the former, I was to look after the reëlection of Douglas. In Indiana, I was to watch the legislative complications that were expected to arise in connection with the claim of each of the two political parties to the rightful control of the majority of the Legislature, which resulted eventually in the election of two sets of United States Senators, by the Republicans and the Democrats respectively.

I spent only a few days early in January, 1859, at Springfield, Illinois, and then went to Indianapolis, where I expected to remain till spring. But my stay was cut short in an unexpected way. In my reports to the *Commercial* I had occasion to criticise rather sharply one of the Democratic State Senators. The next day he rose to a question of privilege, had the report read to the Senate, denounced me in very violent language, and moved that the usual press privileges be withdrawn from me, or, in other words, that I be expelled from the floor. The motion was carried, and it terminated my brief career as a legislative reporter in the Indiana capital, during which I had, however, formed some valuable acquaintances among Indiana politicians. This was my first conflict as a journalist with legislators, but not my last one.

During the fall and winter of 1858, reports of gold discoveries in the easternmost chain of the Rocky Mountains, in the vicinity of Pike's Peak and along the head waters of the Platte River, began to circulate in the press and to attract a great deal of attention throughout the country. The "gold news" had roused my adventurous spirit before my loss of employment, and now suddenly prompted the idea of going to the Rocky Mountains as a correspondent. There was a general hope that the opening of such new sources of national wealth might bring relief to the country from the lingering effects of the crisis of 1857. Its numberless victims—the vast army of the unemployed—began to get excited, and the newspapers to state more and more that great numbers were yielding to the allurements of the new Dorado and preparing to seek it.

On my reaching Cincinnati from Indianapolis, Mr. Halstead, who had vigorously defended me in the editorial columns against the attacks of the Indiana Senator, very readily responded to my suggestion that I should make an investigation of the facts in the Pike's Peak case on the spot for the *Commercial*. We agreed on the conditions of my new engagement, which were to be twenty dollars a week and reasonable travelling expenses. The length of my stay in the Rocky Mountains should depend on the developments there.

It was natural that, at my age and with my sanguine temperament, I should feel the highest elation at this, to my mind, most promising turn of luck. There was no strong evidence that another California had actually been discovered, but I had heard and read much of the quick fortunes made in the gold-mines on the Pacific Coast, and hence my imagination readily got the better of my judgment, and, while reason protested, I indulged in the contemplation of all sorts of fascinating possibilities for myself. I had visions not only of successful gold-hunting, but of fame and fortune as one of the founders of new towns and States. They were not to be realized in the immediate future, but I think I can truly say that to my apprenticeship as a pioneer in the Rocky Mountains I owed the insight into practical life and the enterprise and energy to which my successes later in my career were largely due. In one respect certainly my anticipations rested on reality, and that was in looking forward to extraordinary personal adventures in the pursuit of my mission.

At the time in question, a string of towns had sprung up on the Missouri River, mainly in consequence of the large Free-Soil immigration into the Territory of Kansas as a result of the political events in 1854-5 within its borders. There was a fringe of settlements, too, for from thirty to fifty miles on each side of the river. But the western parts of Missouri and Iowa were still very thinly populated. Excepting these towns and settlements west of the Missouri, the great rising plains between that river and the Rocky Mountains now forming the States of Kansas, Nebraska, Colorado, and Wyoming were, but for a few trading-posts, absolutely uninhabited. There was but one railroad then extending from the Mississippi to the Missouri, from Hannibal to St. Joseph, Missouri. St. Louis was connected with this line by the North Missouri road. Railroad building in Iowa had not yet reached the western part of the State. There was another road extending westward from St. Louis, but it was completed for only about a hundred miles, to Jefferson City, the capital of the

State, on the Missouri River. The only channels of communication for the entire region west of the Missouri River to and beyond the Rocky Mountains to the Pacific States were the Missouri River for steamboats, and the military roads established by the United States Government—that along the Arkansas River to New Mexico, known as the Santa Fé road, and those from Leavenworth and Omaha to Fort Kearny, and thence as a common route along the Platte and North Platte Rivers across the Rocky Mountains to Utah and beyond. Ox- and mule-teams, propelling heavy wagons holding from two to five tons, known as "prairie schooners," were the ordinary means of transportation along these highways.

After reading up in the public Mercantile Library as well as possible regarding the region to be visited, in Government reports upon the explorations of Long, Pike, Frémont, and others, I started from Cincinnati at the end of February. I went to St. Louis and Jefferson City by rail, and at the latter point took a boat up the Missouri to Leavenworth, my immediate destination, as the best starting-point, according to common report, for "Pike's Peak." As we made many landings, we were nearly thirty hours in making the trip. The boat was crowded with "Pike's-Peakers" (mostly young Western men) and their outfits. The river scenery was rather picturesque, though without any striking features, and much like that along the upper Mississippi. We stopped an hour at Kansas City, which was then nothing but a scattering village of a few dozen buildings, including some brick warehouses along the bank. It was the river landing for Westport, five miles inland, right on the boundary of Missouri and Kansas, a town of several thousand people, and famous throughout the West as the principal outfitting and receiving point for the Santa Fé or New Mexico trade. Every spring, large caravans of "prairie schooners," consisting of from forty to eighty wagons, each hauled by ten to twelve oxen or as many mules, set out from that point laden with American goods, returning in the fall with full loads of Mexican wool, hides, and silver bullion. The site of Kansas City was formed by high and steep bluffs between which the streets extended. More unfavorable ground for the development of a town, not to speak of a city, could hardly be imagined; and if anybody had then tried to make me believe that within thirty years a city of 130,000 people would rise upon it, I should have considered him a ridiculous phantast. Yet this actually came to pass.

From Kansas City to Leavenworth the right bank of the river became more animated. Every few miles an embryo town appeared, beginning with Wyandotte at the mouth of the Kansas River and followed by Sumner, Doniphan, and several others whose names I do not remember. Most of them had but a brief, mushroom growth. Leavenworth presented a surprisingly imposing sight. A dozen steamboats were at the landing discharging and receiving passengers and goods, and making a scene of bustling activity. Above the levee, on a gradually ascending plateau, rose the town amphitheatrically. Though but five years old, its resident population was already between six and seven thousand, with a floating one of several thousand more. The main business street was solidly built up with brick and frame structures. The private residences spread out widely over the beautiful parklike rolling prairie with scattered natural groves of trees. The town was swarming with new-comers, and I found it hard to get lodgings anywhere. Over a thousand would-be "Pike's-Peakers" had already arrived, and hundreds were added daily to the number. All seemed as busy as they could be, and I had never seen so much activity in a place of the same size. Leavenworth seemed bound to become an important commercial centre, and the pretensions of Kansas City as a rival looked as absurd to me as they did to the denizens of Leavenworth. Yet Leavenworth soon stagnated, and even to-day hardly exceeds 20,000 in population.

I was well provided with letters of introduction, and quickly made numerous acquaintances. I found also an old one in John C. Vaughan, formerly one of the editors of the Chicago *Tribune,* a most cultivated and polished gentleman, but much addicted to drink. He, with his son Champion, who afterwards had a most erratic career, was in charge of the daily paper. As was natural, there was an extraordinarily large proportion of active, bright young fellows among the inhabitants, and they included an unusual percentage of professional men from the older Western and the Eastern States, with many Harvard and Yale graduates among them. All were eager to make their fortunes and confident of making them quickly. Every one was full of hope that plenty of gold would be found at "Pike's Peak," which would surely lead to the rapid growth of their town into a large city. The large outfitting business already done with intending gold-seekers by the merchants justified this theory. Many were getting ready to go and see for themselves what promise of the precious metals the Rocky Mountains really held out.

I made it at once my special object to gather whatever information was obtainable as to past and present developments at Pike's Peak, and for that purpose not only canvassed Leavenworth, but also visited other river towns to the north of it, like Atchison and St. Joseph, which could be easily reached by boat. It was difficult to glean a few grains of fact from the piles of chaff of exaggeration and outright fiction that I found everywhere. All the river points, from Kansas City to Omaha, which had suffered more than other parts of the country from the subsidence of the speculative fever of 1855–7, saw a chance for a rapid revival in the Pike's Peak excitement, and all were working with might and main to feed it, through their local papers and by every other means. The recklessness with which these systematic efforts for enticing the public were carried on bore bitter fruit, as I shall presently have to relate.

The following is the substance of what I ascertained and reported to the *Commercial*. The first evidence of mineral wealth in the South Platte country was obtained in 1848 by a party of civilized Cherokee Indians, who reached it on a hunting expedition from the Indian Territory, and brought home with them some specimens of quartz-bearing gold. In due course of time, the news of their discovery reached some members of the tribe in Georgia, their old home. One Green Russell, who had been a gold-miner in Georgia as well as in California, heard the story on his return from the latter State, and in the spring of 1857 set out from Georgia with a party of experienced miners to investigate it on the ground. Untoward circumstances compelled the expedition to winter in Western Missouri. It resumed its march in February, 1858, up the Arkansas, over the Santa Fé route. It reached the base of the Rocky Mountains in May, and immediately commenced prospecting for gold. Indications of it were found along the South Platte and its tributaries, but nothing to justify regular mining operations, in consequence of which the expedition dissolved, only nine of the original hundred remaining with the leader. This remnant continued their explorations without satisfactory results, and finally camped on Cherry Creek for the winter. In the spring of 1858, Fall-Leaf, a Delaware Indian, appeared in Lawrence, Kansas, with a small quantity of scale gold which he claimed to have found at the head waters of the Arkansas. This led to the formation of a party of young men who set out in June, reached the base of Pike's Peak, explored the country north and south of it without finding more than the "color" of gold, and wintered also on Cherry Creek.

These expeditions led to the passage of an act by the Kansas Legislature organizing the "County of Arapahoe," comprising the entire western part of the State to the Rocky Mountains; the State limits in that direction never having been defined. Later on, the Governor appointed the officials of this vast county, which included territory enough for a State. Early in the fall of 1858, a public meeting was held at Leavenworth to organize emigration to the gold region. In the first week of October, a large company of residents of Leavenworth commenced the pilgrimage across the Plains. They took the Arkansas route, reaching the base of the mountains by the middle of November. There they came up with the officers for Arapahoe County, and persuaded them to push on with them to the mouth of Cherry Creek.

Here they found the other parties already mentioned, as well as about one hundred and fifty former residents of Eastern Nebraska and Western Iowa, making several hundred people, including two families. To this white population there were added during the winter fluctuating numbers of New Mexicans of Spanish-Indian extraction, and bands of Arapahoe Indians, who fortunately did not molest the new settlers beyond begging victuals of them. With true Western instinct, the first comers lost no time in starting the business of town-making. Their camps were spread over the bottom-land in the two angles formed by Cherry Creek and the South Platte and the low bluffs bordering them. On the left of Cherry Creek, a town site was taken up and called Auraria, and on the right bank another called Denver after the then Territorial Governor of Kansas. On both sides all went to work with a will, and during the winter about one hundred and twenty-five habitations of all sorts and of the rudest description—"dugouts," "adobes," log houses, and frame shanties, made with axe and saw alone—were put up, while many continued to occupy tents. The winter proved unexpectedly mild, with but light snowfalls. Enterprising tradesmen were among the settlers, and a few stores with limited supplies, and mechanics' shops, and, of course, some saloons also, were opened.

In spite of the most diligent search, I collected very little direct proof of the existence of gold at Pike's Peak. I felt warranted in saying through the columns of the *Com-*

mercial that not over a thousand dollars' worth of wash-gold had reached the Missouri River towns from the Rocky Mountains. Green Russell arrived in Leavenworth during the winter, and brought with him about seventy ounces— the fruits of the prospecting of himself and companions during an entire summer. He was beset by eager questioners, but stated candidly that he found no conclusive evidence of really rich diggings, and that the gold he had with him paid him and his followers very poorly for the time and trouble spent in gathering it. He frankly advised against emigration on a large scale, but his warnings had very little effect.

I learned that the enterprising firm of Russell, Majors & Waddell, who did all the freight-carrying for the Government to the military posts on the Plains, had some time before received, from an agent they had sent to the Rocky Mountains to ascertain the facts, a report of so favorable a character that they had decided to start a stage line to Cherry Creek, and had already sent out mules to stock it. I called on the firm, and was told by the manager that I was correctly informed, and that they expected to be able to start the first stage within a fortnight. From all the information I had gathered, it was clear that, in the absence of all settlements for six-sevenths of the distance to the foot of the Rocky Mountains, I had only the choice between the stage and joining a party provided with wagons carrying camping equipage and supplies for a journey of from five to seven weeks. The danger from the numerous tribes of Indians roaming over the Plains had also to be considered. To spend so much time on the way did not suit me, and I decided to engage a seat in the first stage, for which the firm, out of compliment to me as a newspaper man, charged only half price. The travelling time to Cherry Creek was to be only one week.

Having worked up for the *Commercial* all the material procurable at Leavenworth, I decided to avail myself of an opportunity for a trip to Southern Kansas offered me by the kind invitation of the United States District Attorney, Alonzo G. Davis, a native of New York, to accompany him on an official mission to Fort Scott. As we were to go on horseback and camp by the way, I thought it would be a good preparation for the trip across the Plains. We were gone a week, during which I rode about one hundred and eighty miles in the saddle. Not having been on a horse in years, the first day's trip made me very sore, so that I had no enjoyment, but constant discomfort and pain all the way. Still, I stood it to the end without any suspicion of my sufferings on the part of my companions. We travelled over an unbroken stretch of rolling prairie of obviously extraordinary fertility. Sometimes we did not see a house for twenty miles, and we were guided most of the way by the compass. We passed only two or three small clusters of frame shanties, styled towns. Fort Scott proved to be an old trading post with a score of houses around it. The United States District Judge held court on two days, and I had a chance to see justice administered under the most primitive circumstances. There was no court-house, but the Judge sat in a school-house equipped with the rudest furniture. Both criminal and civil cases were tried. There being no place to confine prisoners, the United States marshal and his deputies had to keep them under constant watch at the only wretched hotel in the place. The effort to secure a jury failed entirely, owing to the scarcity of settlers.

On my return I learned that, for various reasons, the first stage of the "Leavenworth and Pike's Peak Express Co.," as the new enterprise was called, would start a week later than I had been told. There was, however, no further postponement, and at the appointed time I got off, early in the morning, amid the cheers of a crowd of at least a thousand spectators, in one of the red-painted, canvas-covered vehicles, with three inside seats for three passengers each, known as "Concord coaches," with four fine Kentucky mules attached that started on a full run. Strange to say, I was the only passenger, owing, no doubt, to the high charges (two hundred dollars), the untried nature of the line, the fear of Indian hostility, and, above all, to the prevailing uncertainty as to the actual state of things at Pike's Peak.

The first day, we followed the military road from Fort Leavenworth to Fort Riley, reaching the valley of the Kansas River after two hours' travel, and keeping in it right along to the last-named point at the junction of the Kansas and its main branch, the Republican River. We rolled on, with many ups and downs, all day over a good dirt road at the rate of eight to ten miles an hour, fresh animals being taken on at regular stations from fifteen to twenty miles apart. The warm spring day could not have been finer. The undulating prairies looked beautiful in their fresh verdure. Even twenty-five miles west from Leavenworth, farms became few and far between. We passed a few new towns of very small dimensions, of which Manhattan, at the mouth of the "Blue" Fork, seemed the most promising. We continued on till we reached Junction City between nine and ten o'clock, where we stopped for the night. We had made one hundred and thirty miles in thirteen hours' actual driving—a splendid record for the first day. Fort Riley was within half a mile. It was garrisoned by several companies of cavalry and infantry, and all the officers and at least a hundred men had turned out to receive the first stage. The opening of the line was quite an event in their monotonous life, especially as it promised a daily instead of a weekly mail. I was invited to the officers' quarters, where I was regaled with eatables and drinkables, and lodged for the night in a very comfortable room. It was my last enjoyment of the luxury of a bed for a long time.

We started again at six in the morning, escorted by half a dozen cavalry officers, who kept us faithful and jolly company to the next stage station, where they took a hearty leave. Several of them I met again a few years later under circumstances that nobody dreamt of then, viz., in the field during the Civil War. We at once left the Kansas River and turned in a northwesterly direction. There was a sort of road for about two hundred miles further up the Kansas, but the stage company had preferred to locate a new route of its own, forming as direct a line as practicable to the settlements at Cherry Creek, and crossing the head waters of the various streams feeding Solomon Fork of the Kansas River, flowing southwardly, and (towards the end of the route) some of the tributaries of the North Platte, flowing northwardly. As the road passed from one divide to another, and as the great Plains rose steadily some five thousand feet from the Missouri River to the Rocky Mountains, there were frequent and steep ascents and descents.

The stage stations had been necessarily selected with reference to water and grazing. They were simply small camps of one large and several small tents manned by three persons—the station-keeper and an assistant, who took care of the twelve mules with which each station was provided for relays, and a male cook, who provided the meals for the two others and the stage passengers. The large tent served as sleeping- and dining-room for the latter, who were expected, as all travellers on the Plains did, to carry with them their bedding—that is, buffalo robes or blankets, rolled up in a waterproof sheet. The mules were grazed under guard in the daytime and picketed at night, when they proved very annoying fellow-campers, as the invariable close approach of prowling prairie-wolves kept them in a panicky state.

The distance from Fort Riley to our destination was about five hundred miles, which it took us six and one-half days to make. There were twenty stations, and we made from three to four a day. We set out at daylight, and it took till dark to complete the prescribed daily run. There was a travelled road for only the first twenty-five miles, and for the rest of the long way we had to trust for guidance over the virgin ground to stakes and piles of stone and buffalo bones and dung erected by the locating party, and the mule tracks left in stocking the stations. The stage had no springs, and hence there was altogether too much jolting. I got out at every ascent, but none the less became sore and stiff, and was glad to stretch out on my blankets at the end of each day's journey. My fatigue ensured the soundest sleep, notwithstanding the hardness of my couch. The bracing prairie air, too, gave me an eager appetite for the two meals a day to which we were limited from want of time. The most magnificent weather favored us all the way.

The first two days from Fort Riley we saw nothing but a monotonous succession of plateaus, frequently broken by ridges, with fringes of cottonwood trees indicating water-courses. We knew that we were in a wilderness inhabited only by Indians and wild beasts. Of the presence of the latter, we had formal notice in the howling of wolves all around us at night. On the third day, we observed that the ordinary prairie grass had given way to the short, early species known as buffalo grass, which had already attained full growth. In the afternoon, the driver, as we came upon a new, long-stretched-out plateau, suddenly shouted, "Here they are," and pointed with his whip at a long black line ahead of us. We were, indeed, in sight of buffaloes. We approached them apace, and, as we came nearer, one line after another appeared before us, and we perceived that we were going right among a large herd of the wild cattle of the Plains. Soon their clumsy, shaggy bodies could be seen in every direction, aggregating thousands of head, bulls and cows, and hundreds of calves. They were not mixed up in a common and great mass, but formed innumerable files, as it were, each headed by a powerful bull. They grazed very quietly, and our passage right through them did not disturb them in the least, though we came within twenty to thirty steps of several files. Only here and there some of the calves took alarm and broke into their clumsy gallop. We had rifles with us, and could have brought down numbers of them, but we forbore, as it would have been a useless slaughter, the stations being well provided with fresh meat. I had read of the steady pursuit of buffalo herds by wolves, and now saw confirmation of it. We counted scores of a large light-gray species hovering singly, like a chain of cowherd dogs, about the rear of the herd, ready to swoop down upon any unlucky laggard.

It took an hour to get through the herd. In the course of the afternoon, we passed another, and enjoyed the same spectacle repeatedly on the two following days. Some of the drivers, who had passed a long time on the Plains, asserted that we had struck the advance-guards of the millions starting early in the year from Texas and following the well-defined "buffalo range" to the British dominions during the spring and summer, returning in the fall and early winter. It was no exaggeration to say that we travelled for days amid buffaloes. At the end of the fifth day, we had passed beyond the belt of buffalo grass, and had gradually reached an altitude of nearly four thousand feet, the air steadily growing drier. Signs appeared that we had entered a more arid stretch of country. The soil turned gravelly. A species of short cactus began to prevail. The streams became mere streaks of red sand, so that water could be had only by digging for it. Willow bushes took the place of the belts of cottonwood trees along them, and finally even the willows disappeared. Prairie-dog villages, guarded by their comical barking occupants, abounded. Swarms of antelope came in sight, some of which scampered off as soon as they saw the coach, but others fell under the charm, as the drivers said, of its red color, and stood motionless while we came quite close to them. It was a delight to breathe the dry, fresh, and bracing air. The transparency of the atmosphere greatly widened the range of vision, and brought forth one mirage after another. Lakes lined with timber and dotted with islands appeared to right and left, while inverted mountain chains inspired us with awe. The illusive effects were truly wonderful.

Towards noon on the sixth day from Leavenworth, I noticed afar off to the southwest what seemed to be at first a cloud in a clear sky. I soon recognized it as a mountain peak, and judged, from the direction, that it could be no other than that named after Pike, the explorer. So it was, the great landmark thus showing itself in the rare atmosphere at a distance of not less than one hundred and fifty miles. I felt quite exalted by the sight. Within a few hours, another peak became visible to the northwest, which I took to be the twin of the other, named after Pike's associate Long. Before dark, many more summits directly to the west loomed up, indicating the outlines of the main chain of the Rocky Mountains.

An extraordinary incident occurred at the last night-station. The man in charge related to us that five days before, while hunting antelopes, he had suddenly discovered, a few miles from the station, five bodies of white men, four of them with broken skulls and otherwise mutilated. On closer examination, he found that there was still life in the uninjured one. He hurried back to the station for a wagon and fetched him into camp. It was evident that want of food and drink had brought the survivor, who was a very skeleton, to the point of death. Careful nursing revived him so far that he was able to relate how he got into his sad plight. He and twenty others, all from Northern Illinois, had left Kansas City six weeks before for Pike's Peak. They had, like so many others, foolishly concluded, on the recommendations of some reckless newspapers, to follow the example of the Mormon emigrants to Utah in crossing the Plains with small carts moved by hand. Thus equipped, they travelled up the Kansas River, and got along rapidly and without mishap to the point, two hundred miles west of Fort Riley, where the road ended. Thence they undertook to cut across the country for Cherry

Creek, pulling and pushing their carts and trusting to a compass for guidance. After a few days they were caught in a snowstorm lasting two days. They suffered intensely from the exposure, became bewildered, and wandered at random. Their provisions gave out, and, exhausted from fatigue, hunger, and thirst, one after another dropped down and was left to die alone in the wilderness. When the survivors were reduced to twelve, brutalized by their sufferings, they entered into a horrible compact that they would live on each other, selected by lot. Some of the victims shot themselves, while others were deliberately killed by the remaining cannibals. The rescued man had three brothers in the party, and admitted that he had sustained himself on their bodies. Subsequent investigation by myself and others proved that his story was true. He was brought into Denver ten days later, physically recovered, but his mind was affected. He insisted that his name was Blue, while an inquiry at his home showed it to be Green.

During our last day's drive, the view of the mountains grew more and more imposing, as we gradually ascended the last and highest plateau of the Plains, forming the dividing ridge between the waters of the Kansas and of the South Platte Rivers. At noon we had reached its very crest, and there to the west and north and south one of the grandest sights to be beheld anywhere in the world was spread out before me. Between my standpoint and the great range lay the basin of the South Platte, which was clearly discernible with its half a dozen tributaries from the west and east. The valley seemed from fifty to seventy miles wide, though broken by many intervening ridges. For three hundred miles, the mighty mountains extended to the right and left, flanked on the south by the great cones of Pike's Peak and the Spanish Peaks, and to the north by the buttress-like form of Long's Peak. They seemed to form an immense wall dividing the continent as if by an impassable barrier. From their summits half-way down, they were all covered with snow, and thence to their base with unbroken forests.

The last fifty miles of our way formed a steady decline, and we spun along at the rate of eight to ten miles an hour. Just as the setting sun was gorgeously illuminating the range, the stage made a final halt in front of the loghouse in Denver that represented the headquarters of the stage company. Our coming was not expected, but the glad intelligence that the first overland stage was arriving spread instantly on both banks of Cherry Creek, and the whole population quickly turned out to see it. We brought a mail of several hundred letters and newspapers, the announcement of which fact drew three cheers for the Express Company. It was a great boon, the last news from the Missouri River being nearly five weeks old. Of course, I was the centre of attraction and overwhelmed with questions. Some one proposed that I should tell the news from the "States" to them all, and I was made to mount a log and entertain the audience for half an hour with what had happened during the four weeks before my departure, for which I got a vote of thanks, and which secured me at once the good will of all the settlers.

CHAPTER VIII

AT CHERRY CREEK.—1859

MY credentials from the company to their local representative, Dr. J. M. Fox, solved at once the important question where I should be able to secure satisfactory board and lodging. The doctor offered to provide both for me in the office-building at a low charge, and there I lodged and took my meals during the next three months. My host was a Missourian, about thirty years old, formerly a medical practitioner, but for some years in the employ of Russell, Majors & Waddell. He was a very intelligent and resolute man, though somewhat inclined to lethargy. He never failed in attentive kindness to me. More than twenty years later, it was in my power to show him my gratitude by taking him into my employ in various positions in California, Oregon, and Montana, one of which he fills at this writing.

Let me describe our abode. It had a splendid position on the edge of a high bluff rising abruptly from the bed of Cherry Creek, and commanding a grand view of the mountains. It was the rudest sort of one-story cabin, built of cottonwood logs, thirty feet long and fifteen wide, and divided by a log partition into two equal compartments, the front one being devoted to office purposes, and the rear one used for cooking, eating, and sleeping. Its roof consisted of logs covered with dirt and gravel. Ingress was had through two doors without locks. It had no windows of any sort; indeed, there was no window-glass then or for months afterwards to be had on Cherry Creek. If the outer light was wanted, the doors had to be left open. Mother Earth furnished the floors, as no lumber of any sort was to be had. Nor had we any other resting-place. Every night buffalo robes were spread on the ground in the rear room, on which, with saddles and (later on) hay for head-rests, we made ourselves comfortable. The furniture consisted of a crude table made out of a packing-box, with small casks serving as seats. Our cook was a half-breed from New Mexico, speaking only Spanish. His knowledge of the culinary art was not great, but, even if it had been greater, it would not have done us much good, inasmuch as his material to work with was very limited at first. Buffalo and antelope meat, bacon, canned fruit, "flapjacks," and bread were for weeks our uniform fare. Later, coffee, tea, canned vegetables, and potatoes from New Mexico were added to it. The express messengers and stage drivers shared our table and sleeping quarters. A "corral" with the stages and mules was immediately behind the building, the "long-ears" regularly disturbing our rest by their plaintive outcries.

The hearsay description of Denver and Auraria proved to be substantially correct; but Auraria, which occupied the left bank of Cherry Creek down to the South Platte River, was far ahead of Denver, which was laid out on the right bank. It contained several dozen scattered habitations of every sort, one- and two-story structures of rough-hewn logs, combinations of dugouts and tents, "adobes," and log walls with canvas roofs, interspersed with wigwams. In Denver not over a dozen structures were up. It seemed as though Auraria would surely get a permanent start of its rival, but it turned out just the other way. Auraria contained all the business places, including some stores with very limited stocks, a tailor's, a shoemaker's, and even a watchmaker's shop, and last, not least, a printing-office, brought from Omaha, and started but a few days before my arrival. From it a readable weekly, the *Rocky Mountain News*, was already being issued, that subsequently grew into a very flourishing and influential concern and exists to this day under the same title. Its then editor, William N. Byers, became a prominent political character in the Territory and State of Colorado.

As was natural, the people of the two towns consisted almost exclusively of males from the several Western States; the five women and seven children, all told, among them were looked upon as curiosities. Very few, apparently, were used to toil with their hands for a living, while the others relied on their wits in the struggle for existence as tradesmen, town speculators, and mining promoters, with a sprinkling of followers of the professions of law and medicine.

It took me but a few days to get acquainted with everybody, and to collect and write up all the "gold" news there was. There was not much of it, in fact; no additional evidence of the existence of mineral wealth in the neighboring mountains had turned up for some months. Unmistakable and general discouragement consequently prevailed. Dr. Fox had exerted himself to the utmost to secure some placer and nugget gold for shipment by the first return stage, but succeeded in getting only a score or so of ounces, which was all there was in the two places. There was shaking of heads and confidential admissions on the part of the most intelligent men that the outlook was almost hopeless. Still, the influx of gold-seekers continued. Every day, and at all hours of the day, they came in from the East over the Platte route and from the South over the Arkansas route, in trains of from three to twenty wagons. The arrivals increased to several hundred a day, and the unoccupied parts of the town sites were dotted with the tents of the new-comers. Quite a number of "hand-carters" were brought in by the wagon-trains, having been picked up at various points on the Plains in the direst distress.

The month of May came without any signs of improvement. Hopelessness took possession more and more of people's minds, and the general abandonment of the country became the subject of frequent discussion. This dispelling of all my confident and high-flown personal expectations gave me also the "blues." In this mood of mind, on the second Sunday in May, I was sitting in the Express Office, in company with Dr. Fox and Joseph Heywood, a well-known Californian, formerly of Cincinnati. We were just discussing the unpromising aspect of affairs when a short, slender, heavily-bearded individual, in miner's garb, entered the room and inquired for letters. He was invited to a seat, and soon got to talking about the resources of the country. Contrary to expectation, he seemed to believe firmly in its mineral wealth. Being asked for his experience in the mountains, from which he claimed to have just arrived, he stated, after a few moments of apparent hesitation, that a little more than a week before, while following up the north fork of Clear Creek, a tributary of the South Platte, in company with John H. Gregory and several others, he had discovered gold-bearing dirt in the vicinity of streaks of quartz rock, that ran over the mountains, in a ravine adjoining the valley of the creek. The dirt, he asserted, had yielded him as much as a dollar's worth of gold to the pan. Perceiving a manifestation of incredulity on the part of his listeners, he produced, in corroboration of his statement, a bottle containing about forty dollars' worth of flour gold, and also several fragments of a hard substance which he designated as decomposed gold-bearing quartz. Mr. Heywood stepped out-doors with one of the pieces for the purpose of examining it with a magnifying-glass. He soon called out Dr. Fox, whom he told that the specimen he held in his hand was as fine quartz as he had seen in the richest quartz veins in California. Several persons having, in the meantime, entered the office and shown, upon hearing the miner's tale, a disposition to doubt its truthfulness, the latter grew rather excited, repeated what he had said, and asserted most emphatically that he would warrant one dollar to the pan of dirt to any number of men who would follow him to the locality in question; adding that they might bring a rope along and swing him up in case he should be found to be a liar.

This was the first news of the discovery of gold-bearing quartz veins in the mountains to reach the Cherry Creek towns. The gulch where the discovery was made took the name of "Gregory Mine." The miner returned the next day to the mountains, accompanied by several Auraria men anxious to obtain confirmation of his story. Nothing more was heard for several days, but, on the fifth, one of the party, one Bates, formerly of Dubuque, Iowa, returned, bringing with him a vial full of scale or placer gold, equal to about five ounces, which he claimed to have washed himself from thirty-nine pans of dirt obtained not far from the spot where Gregory had found a "paying" lode. Bates being known as a reliable man, his story found general credence as he was taken from door to door to repeat it. Exuberant hope took at once the place of the prevailing despondency. Persons on the streets shouted to each other: "We are all right now," "The stuff is here, after all," "The country is safe," etc.

On the following day, a general exodus took place in the direction of North Clear Creek. Whoever could secure provisions enough for a stay in the mountains started off without delay. Traders locked their stores, barkeepers set out with their stock of whiskey, the few mechanics that were engaged in building houses dropped their work. The county judge and sheriff, lawyers and doctors, and even the editor of the *Rocky Mountain News*, joined in the rush. Naturally, I did not stay behind, but started out on a fine mule, borrowed from the Express Company, with my bedding strapped on behind, and with three days' supply of hard bread and bacon, and ground roasted corn, which, mixed with water, furnished a very cooling and nourishing beverage, much used in New Mexico.

The Gregory Gulch was, in an air line, not more than thirty miles from Cherry Creek, but the only practicable route at the time was a roundabout one, measuring fully fifty miles. The first sixteen miles were very easy. The ground rose gradually for twelve miles to the so-called foothills. I could keep my mule steadily on a trot over the intervening natural meadows in their bright spring garb of fresh grass and the greatest variety of high-colored wild flowers. The foot-hills I found a range of elevations to the height of ten hundred to fifteen hundred feet above the prairie, covered with tuft grass and scattering pine, and separated from the main range by a beautiful valley about a mile wide. Riding up this valley for a couple of miles, I reached Clear Creek, a turbulent mountain stream, about fifty feet wide and four to six feet deep, with a powerful current. My animal proved averse to trying the ice-cold water, and I got him across only with great difficulty and after swimming him down-stream for several hundred feet and getting wet to the hips. A mile from the crossing, the trail turned abruptly up a very steep mountain side, rising to a height of at least two thousand feet above the valley, to climb which my mule found a most arduous task, taking several hours to accomplish. At least a hundred other prospectors were toiling up at the same time, some even trying to bring up wagons drawn by oxen. Once up, the rest of the journey proved comparatively easy over broad mountain tops, rich in grass and pine woods, and I managed to reach my destination the same day just about dark. I had a severe sick-headache during the whole afternoon, and was obliged to stop several times because of nausea. This was the effect of the high altitude—between nine thousand and ten thousand feet above the level of the sea—which I felt several times afterwards on trips through the mountains; but I finally got over it. I asked my way to Gregory's camp, introduced myself, and begged a place to lie down for the night. He complied at once, and assigned me a corner of his tent. My animal required no care, as he had had plenty of grass and water on the way, and, after picketing him, I spread my blankets and was asleep in a moment.

In the morning, I took in the situation in a few hours. The "Gregory Mine" was located at an altitude of about nine thousand feet, on the steep southern slope of a narrow ravine, grass-grown and pine-covered, like all of the Rocky Mountain world except the highest peaks. It was washed by the head waters of the north fork of Clear Creek, forming a brook not over six feet wide and two deep. Although but two weeks had elapsed since Gregory had washed out the first "pay dirt" in his pan, there were already many scores of men busily engaged in ripping open the mountain sides with pick and shovel. Dozens of huts of pine branches had been erected and tents pitched. Sluices, "long toms," and "rockers" were in full operation, ditches crossed the gulch, and slides were being constructed—in short, the very picture of a busy, promising mining camp was before me. One of the first things I did was to induce Gregory—a slight, wiry, red-haired, and full-whiskered Georgian—to relate to me his own experience as a gold-seeker. As he deserves to be remembered as the Sutter of the Rocky Mountains, I will preserve his statement as an original contribution to the history of the State of Colorado by reproducing it here.

I left my former home in Gordon County, Ga., in August of last year, for the purpose of going overland to the Frazer River mines in British Columbia. Various untoward circumstances detained me *en route*, and I felt obliged to winter at Fort Laramie [a military post about 250 miles to the northwest of Cherry Creek]. While there, the news of the discovery of gold on the South Platte reached me. I thereupon determined not to go further West, but to make for Pike's Peak. I set out from Fort Laramie early in February, and prospected extensively as I travelled along the base of the mountains. Not finding any trace of gold, I pushed on till I reached the mouth of Clear Creek where the town of Arapahoe was springing up. Here I made up a party of fifteen, and we started up Clear Creek. After toiling for several days up the cañon, we left the main stream and followed a branch coming in from the north. Near its sources we found indications of quartz veins streaking the sides of the gulch down which it flowed. We speedily uncovered and opened one of them with our picks and shovels.

After removing the surface rock to the depth of several feet, we came upon a 'pocket' containing a dirt-like, decayed rock, which on being taken to the creek and washed, yielded four dollars to the pan. We were sure then that we had found what we were after. All our party at once staked off and opened claims on the same lead, and commenced work in dead earnest. We were first prevented by ice and snow from working regularly, but for a week the weather has been warm enough. A great many, as you see, have tracked us to the gulch and taken up claims on other veins and are working them.

I spent nearly a week in Gregory Gulch, enjoying the hospitality of the miners. I visited every "lead" and "claim" then opened, witnessed the digging, hauling, and washing of "pay-dirt," washed out many a pan myself, saw the gold in the riffles of the sluices, and was daily present when the workers caught the quicksilver used to gather the fine gold from the sluices and heated it in retorts into gold-charged cakes. Thoroughly convinced by all this ocular evidence that the new Dorado had really been discovered, I returned to Denver, and felt justified in spreading this great news with all the faith and emphasis of conviction.

A perceptible change had already taken place in the Cherry Creek towns. Building was being resumed. Tradesmen and mechanics were busy. Gold from Clear Creek began to circulate. The caravans of new-comers from the East made direct for the mountains. Several large trains loaded with miscellaneous provisions and merchandise had arrived and reduced somewhat the ruling enormous prices for necessaries, as, twenty-five cents a pound for flour, forty to fifty cents for sugar, five dollars a bushel for corn, etc. In short, a general stir and bustle had taken the place of stagnation.

About a week after my return from the mountains, a notable event occurred in the arrival of Horace Greeley, the famous editor of the New York *Tribune,* accompanied by Albert D. Richardson, a well-known correspondent of the Boston *Journal*. They came in one of the express stages, and had met with a singular and perilous accident. In driving through a herd of buffaloes, the animals, probably maddened at the sight of the red color of the coach, had attacked and upset it. Greeley had received a severe cut below his right knee, crippling him for several weeks, and both journalists were bruised all over. They found quarters in the Denver House, the only "hotel" in Denver, that had been got ready for the reception of guests just before their arrival.

This establishment was about sixty feet long and thirty wide. Its four sides consisted of rough-hewn logs. It had a slanting, skeleton roof covered with canvas. In the interior were neither floors, nor ceilings, nor walls, nor solid partitions to divide the space; but canvas nailed on frames served to set it off for different purposes to the height of seven feet. The front part was occupied by a bar for the sale of strong drinks only, and a dozen gambling-tables, at which various games were conducted by experts in the profession. Several individuals who had been hanging about the towns, and whom I had taken to be men of means awaiting their chances for a respectable use of their money, appeared in this part. Next to the bar-room came another space, enclosed by canvas partitions, where the meals were served. Immediately behind it, six apartments for sleeping-purposes, divided only by the same light material, were set off on each side of a passage. Outside, at the end of the building, the kitchen, presided over by a white male cook, was carried on under canvas. There was no furniture but the gambling- and other tables and benches and chairs, made out of rough boards. Bedsteads were provided of the same material, without mattress or pillows, and also tin wash-basins, which the guests themselves filled out of barrels of water standing in the passageway, and emptied, after use, on the dirt floor.

Altogether, that hotel was a unique institution, and, of course, without comfort or quiet. In the absence of ceilings and with the thin partitions, a sound in any part of the building was heard all over it. Greeley was carried into this hostelry—he could not use his wounded leg—and put into one of the sleeping-chambers described. The *"Tribune* philosopher," as he was known to the entire American public, had naturally a most gentle temper, which he lost only on rare occasions and under the greatest provocation. His benign countenance, indeed, usually wore an expression typical of resignation and forbearance. But, what with the pain of his wound and the endless racket in the place during the entire twenty-four hours, and the special irritation produced upon the apostle of strict temperance and good morals generally by the drinking and gambling going on day and night within a few feet of him, those Christian virtues gradually lost their control over him. I called on him several times a day, and noticed this change of temper distinctly. It gradually expressed itself in swearing at his disturbers so violently that I dared not believe my ears. His wrath culminated on the third night of his tortures. I was fortunate enough to be with him, and thus became an eye- and ear-witness of what happened. About ten o'clock he got up, and insisted on limping to the bar-room. His appearance, though his presence in the building was generally known, created surprise and instant silence. He begged for a chair, and, "Friends," said he, "I have been in pain and without sleep for almost a week, and I am well-nigh worn out. Now I am a guest at this hotel, I pay a high price for my board and lodging, and am entitled to rest during the night. But how can I get it with all this noise going on in this place?" Then he addressed one of the most pathetic appeals I ever heard to those around him to abandon their vicious ways and become sober and industrious. He spoke for nearly an hour, and was listened to with rapt interest and the most perfect respect. He succeeded, too, in his object. The gambling stopped, and the bar was closed every night at eleven o'clock as long as he remained.

Another anecdote connected with Greeley's stay in Denver occurs to me. A German barber, plying his art there, who styled himself Murat, and claimed to be a descendant of the King of Naples, was called in to shave Greeley, and, when he had finished the job and was asked for his charge, coolly named two dollars and a half as the regular price for shaving outside of his shop. Greeley gave him a bland look, pulled out his purse, and handed him the money, saying: "Well, I guess I can afford to pay something for the privilege of getting scraped by royal hands."

After resting a few days longer, Mr. Greeley felt strong enough to undertake a trip to the Gregory mines, and I volunteered to conduct him and his companion there. He had not ridden an animal in twenty-five years, and dreaded the necessity of doing so, but finally made up his mind to it. We drove in a wagon as far as Clear Creek, and there mounted three mules. I led the file into the creek, my companions following me without hesitation. The water was at least a foot higher than when I last crossed, and my animal began swimming at once, wetting me up to the waist. The other beasts imitated mine. Greeley was a sight to behold. Alarmed by the sudden immersion of his mule, he had first raised his legs in order to avoid getting wet. This movement made him lose his balance, and, to steady himself, he threw his arms around the animal's neck. The mule did not like the embrace, and commenced struggling against it and taking his rider down-stream. I took in the situation on reaching the other side, galloped down the creek, and, reëntering it, managed to seize Greeley's bridle and pull him along the bank. The rider's face bore an indescribable expression of fear mingled with mirth at himself. As he came up on the bank, dripping all over, a number of gold-seekers who had watched us gave him three rousing cheers, which brought back the characteristic smile to his countenance.

On reaching Clear Creek on our return trip, Greeley

positively refused to swim across it again on his mule. As he said of himself, "The starch was completely taken out of me by my three days' rough experience, and I had neither strength nor heart for the passage." It turned out that he was very wise in his refusal, for, as his mule was being led across, the saddle-girth broke, and everything it bore, including sleeping-blankets, dropped into the water and was lost. The following passage from a letter of his to the *Tribune* refers to an accident that befell me suddenly between Clear Creek and Denver:

An accident, which might have proved serious, happened to a member of our party, Mr. Villard of the Cincinnati *Commercial*. Riding some distance ahead of us, he was thrown by his mule's saddle slipping forward and turning him so that he fell heavily on his left arm, which was badly bruised, and thence dragged a rod with his heel fast in the stirrup. His mule then stopped, but, when I rode up behind him, I dared not approach him, lest I should start his animal, and waited for the friend who, having heard his call for help, was coming up in front. Mr. Villard was released without further injury, but his arm is temporarily useless.

I had, in fact, to carry the injured arm in a sling for several weeks.

Greeley, Richardson, and I united in a statement to the public regarding the then actual mining developments. It was prepared in perfect good faith, and based strictly on facts observed by the signers themselves. Greeley's political opponents, nevertheless, made it the subject of ridicule and abuse of him for a long time. His inveterate enemy, the senior James Gordon Bennett, especially attacked him for it in the New York *Herald*. The assertions that we had allowed ourselves to be misled and swindled, became so persistent that the leading miners subsequently published sworn statements testifying to the correctness of our account. The steadily growing proof of the existence of great mineral wealth in the Rocky Mountains triumphantly sustained us in the end.

CHAPTER IX

FROM THE ROCKIES TO THE MIDDLE WEST.—1859–60

MY personal prospects were now assured, at least to the extent of a continuance of my engagement on the *Commercial* during the summer and fall. "Pike's Peak" was the all-absorbing topic in the press throughout the United States, and news from there was eagerly sought by editors and publishers. Several other correspondents appeared successively on the field, but I had a great advantage over them through my early advent and my knowledge of the country.

The influx of wanderers across the Plains in search of riches grew steadily greater as the summer advanced. Not less than fifty to sixty thousand fortune-hunters reached the Rocky Mountains before the first of September. Within a few weeks, from four to five thousand had crowded into the Gregory and adjoining gulches. The overflow then found its way along other water-courses to the north and south, and even up to and over the highest range, to the region watered by the Grand and Green Rivers. Thousands followed the South Platte to its sources, and thence reached the western slope through the Ute Pass. In fact, before the next winter set in, the greater part of the territory now included in the boundaries of the State of Colorado had been journeyed and worked over, and in many places permanent mining-camps established. Almost every day, reports of new "strikes" in various parts of the mountains reached the Cherry Creek towns. As soon as they were sufficiently confirmed to warrant it, I set out to verify them on the spot. Thus I was "on the go" the greater part of the time. I usually joined prospectors who had made original discoveries and come to Cherry Creek to obtain supplies and implements for developing them. But several times also I started out with exploring parties without any definite destination. I likewise revisited established mining-camps, like Gregory's, at intervals. In this way the range of my observations extended from Long's Peak to Pike's Peak on the eastern as well as on the western slope of the mountains. I crossed and recrossed the main crest of the mountains repeatedly. I visited those beautiful, all but circular valleys, consisting of mountain meadows dotted with pines singly and in groups, traversed by rushing mountain-streams and surrounded by snow-capped mountains, known as the South, Middle, and North Parks. These trips, while involving sometimes great hardships, never failed to be enjoyable from beginning to end. I think of them even now with rekindled enthusiasm. The contact with primitive nature in its sublimest forms had something inspiring. We travelled every day just as long and as far as we liked. We took ample time for everything—for admiring natural wonders, for enjoying the scenery, for fishing and hunting, and for prospecting. The streams were full of trout and the valleys of elk and deer. We frequently met great herds of elk. We always slept on the ground—and such restful sleep we had, from ten to twelve hours every night! I could name half a dozen flourishing Colorado towns on the sites of which I camped before they were even "taken up." We did our cooking by turns, and rich feasts we had on trout and game. Altogether, I was always sorry when my journalistic duties compelled me to return to Cherry Creek to work up new material into my regular reports.

Yet, in Denver and Auraria, life was also growing from day to day more active, varied, and interesting. They both made astonishing strides. A number of portable saw-mills had arrived, and were furnishing an ample supply of building-material. Hardware for buildings and ready-made windows and doors were also landed by the wagon-load. Skilled mechanics became numerous. The quick means of transit from the Missouri by the stage company—the time had been reduced to six days—also brought a considerable accession of capitalists. In every direction the business of pushing the towns forward was pursued with remarkable energy by midsummer. New buildings were started every day, and their character steadily improved. The original site of Auraria had been taken up by Nebraska men, that of Denver by the party which had come out in consequence of the Leavenworth meeting already mentioned. No Government survey having ever been made, this "taking up" was really squatting at random. The "squatters" had no little trouble in protecting their claims from "jumpers." As was to be expected, the moment the future of the country seemed assured, "additions" to the town site were staked off for miles from its boundaries to the four points of the compass. The Denver Company originally consisted of twelve members, each holding an equal undivided interest. "General" Larimer, originally from Pittsburg and afterwards a resident of Leavenworth, was the leading spirit. In consideration of my having written up the country so assiduously, I was given a one-forty-eighth interest in the association. (It may as well be mentioned here that I helped to locate and became part owner of other town sites in different parts of the country.)

By the end of August, there were fully five thousand people settled on Cherry Creek, including at least one hundred families. Long before that time, the necessity of protecting the real and personal property of the inhabitants had led to the formation of town governments. Although the population was drawn from every part of the United States—it would not be too much to say from every quarter of the globe—it was remarkably respectable and orderly. I do not hesitate to assert that the percentage of vicious elements, gamblers, thieves, murderers, and bad women, was never so large there as in other mining towns in California, Nevada, and Montana. Interference with property and injuries to persons were not frequent, but it was practically impossible to bring offences against either to punishment, owing to the total lack of courts and jails. It was therefore not surprising that Judge Lynch had to be finally appealed to for order and safety. Banishment and hanging were about the only practicable punishments. Yet, during the summer and fall, only fifteen men and women were given notice to leave the country, and only two men hung for murders committed in gambling- and bawdy-house brawls. I witnessed one of the executions. The subject was a fine-looking young man, not over twenty-three, of respectable parentage, great intelligence, and fine education, but brought to this terrible end by drink and other bad habits. He admitted that he deserved to die, and met his doom very bravely.

By the latter part of the summer, the two towns contained several hotels with more or less "modern" improvements, two scores of stores, numerous mechanics' shops, at least one hundred doctors' and lawyers' offices, and other evidences of advancing civilization, besides great numbers of drinking- and gambling-saloons. Several excellent eating-houses were also opened, in which very good meals without lodging could be had at moderate prices—that is, at seventy-five cents a meal (instead of from one and a half to two and a half dollars). The Express Company had moved into a new building some time before, and I had found board and lodging elsewhere. I must not forget to relate an exciting experience we had before the removal of the Express Office from the original log-building. The company made a business of bringing letters from the East, for carrying which they charged twenty-five cents each, following in this a practice common in California and other mining States. At first the charge was willingly paid, but, as the population grew larger, grumblings began to be heard that gradually swelled into general and loud dissatisfaction and violent attacks in the press on the "extortion" of the Express Company. The agitation culminated in indignation meetings and the passage of resolutions denouncing the Company and threatening the use of force to compel a more reasonable charge. For several days crowds gathered in front of and inside the Express Office on the arrival of stages, demanding their letters without offering to pay anything. I stood by my friend, the Express Agent, behind the counter, and it looked twice as though he would have occasion to defend himself against violence. Fortunately, a compromise was reached, in pursuance of which the charge was reduced to ten cents. It was done away with altogether when, before the end of the summer, the Government entered into a contract with the Company for the transportation of the mails.

Late in the summer, the arrivals from the East almost ceased and a return tide set in—that is, a homeward migration which steadily gained in numbers, so that, in the early fall, it looked as though the country would rapidly lose most of its population. This was not surprising, for four out of every five of the immigrants had come without means, and in the expectation that, by the simple use of their hands and ordinary implements, they could quickly gather fortunes from placer diggings. But the truth was, that the alluvial auriferous deposits were very limited and quickly exhausted, and that the precious metals in the Rocky Mountains were buried in veins of quartz and galena, the successful working of which required capital and costly mechanical appliances that had to be brought from the East. Only a few small quartz-mills had been hauled across the Plains and set up in the mountains. Unavoidably, under the circumstances, the bulk of the gold-seekers were doomed to disappointment, and sought their way back to the States as best they could. It turned out that the entire yield in gold and silver in 1859 from the Pike's Peak region did not exceed three-quarters of a million, while many millions had been sunk in outfits and wasted labor to secure this meagre result.

My faith in the future of the country remained unshaken, but, with the advance of the fall, I was obliged to consider the question whether I should remain during the winter or return to the East. It was evident that, whenever snowfall and the freezing up of the streams should compel the cessation of mining operations in the mountains, general dulness would set in and with it a great dearth of news, so that I could hardly expect the *Commercial* to continue my allowance for services. On the other hand, I liked the climate and the pioneer life; and then, too, I had some property interests, as explained. After some weeks of doubt, I was helped to a decision in favor of passing the winter east of the Missouri by a scheme that suddenly dawned upon me and that could be carried out only there. It was to embody my observations and experiences in a book that should be also a guide to the Pike's Peak region for the new tide of gold-seekers that I felt sure would set in again with the coming spring. I submitted the idea to my friends among the leading business men, who thought very highly of it and promised me their support by subscribing for numbers of copies and otherwise.

Accordingly, I made up my mind to start back, taking the Platte route in the last week of October. A short time before my departure, I received an offer for my interest in the Denver town company, viz., twelve hundred dollars in money, a gold watch, a wagon with two horses, and a rifle! The proposal was very tempting, for the town lots had cost me nothing, and the amount of cash seemed imposingly large to me, who had never had more than one-tenth of it at my disposal at one time. I had had no experience in such matters, and lacked all speculative instinct, and, being young and very self-confident, did not really care much for money beyond my current requirements. The wagon and team were just then an especially attractive consideration, as their ownership would solve for me the problem how to travel across the Plains. Hence I accepted after brief hesitation. The outfit for the journey was quickly completed. I secured two passengers, who paid thirty dollars each for the ride of six hundred and fifty miles in the ordinary farmer's wagon. It was just enough to pay for the provisions of the party, and for a few bushels of corn which I took along by way of precaution for the horses. We left Denver early on the morning of October 29. My fixed determination at the time was to return early in the spring, but it was only after the lapse of fully seventeen years that I saw the place again, and then only in consequence of a most extraordinary turn in the wheel of my personal fortunes.

We followed what had become the great highway for the Pike's Peak travel, down the South Platte to its junction with the North Platte, and thence along the main river as far as Fort Kearny, where we left it, going in a southeasterly direction over the military road leading to Fort Leavenworth. With the exception of some sandy stretches of several miles each, the road was hard and level nearly the whole distance to Fort Kearny, so that we could make from twenty-five to thirty miles a day without over-fatiguing the horses, which proved excellent roadsters. The vast numbers of animals that had passed over the same route during the summer, had left not a spear of green or dry grass in the Platte valley, but happily a number of "ranches" had sprung up where hay could be had, though at a high price. There was also an absolute scarcity of firewood, and we had to cook our meals by the use of "buffalo chips" (dry dung) that we collected in bags some distance from the river. My companions were very helpful in taking care of the horses and preparing our morning and evening repasts, and altogether we got along capitally. We slept in and under the wagon, wrapped in our buffalo robes and blankets, with the horses picketed next to it. Splendid weather favored us until we were within a day's travel of Fort Kearny, when a snowstorm came upon us in the night that compelled us to lie still for thirty hours. Of course, cooking was out of the question, and we were reduced to bacon and "hardtack." The horses were kept well blanketed, and fed with corn. When the storm ceased, there was eighteen inches of snow on the ground, but the warm sun made it melt rapidly.

We replenished our supplies, as far as necessary, at Fort Kearny—a trading and military post with three companies of cavalry—and pushed on as fast as possible (forewarned, as we had been by the snowstorm, of the season of blizzards) over the remaining one hundred and eighty miles to St. Joseph on the Missouri, our destination. We reached the first settlements at Marysville, an embryo town eighty miles from Fort Kearny, on the Blue River, after a three days' drive. Here we found decent hotel accommodations and good stabling for the horses, at moderate Eastern prices. From this point on, our hardships were at an end, nice roadside inns being situated at convenient distances all the way. About thirty miles from St. Joseph an extraordinary incident occurred. A buggy with two occupants was coming towards us over the open prairie. As it approached, I thought I recognized one of them, and, sure enough, it turned out to be no less a person than Abraham Lincoln! I stopped the wagon, called him by name, and jumped off to shake hands. He did not recognize me with my full beard and pioneer's costume. When I said, "Don't you know me?" and gave my name, he looked at me, most amazed, and then burst out laughing. "Why, good gracious! you look like a real Pike's-Peaker." His surprise at this unexpected meeting was as great as mine. He was on a lecturing tour through Kansas. It was a cold morning, and the wind blew cuttingly from the northwest. He was shivering in the open buggy, without even a roof over it, in a short overcoat, and without any covering for his legs. I offered him one of my buffalo robes, which he gratefully accepted. He undertook, of course, to return it to me, but I never saw it again. After ten minutes' chat, we separated. The next time I saw him he was the Republican candidate for the Presidency.

We reached St. Joseph the next day, having been only twenty-four days from Denver—a very quick trip under the circumstances. I concluded not to place my team in winter quarters, but to sell it, though I obtained only a very low price for it, and then I took the first train for St. Louis and Cincinnati. In both places I was a sort of attraction, and received a good deal of attention, especially in business and newspaper circles, and spent some weeks very agreeably.

Towards the close of the year, I commenced work upon my proposed book upon the Pike's Peak region. The bulk of the material I needed was already in my possession, but the collection of additional data to give it a reliable character as a "guide" was necessary. Moreover, in order to ensure pecuniary success, I decided to make a regular canvass for subscriptions among the business men of St. Louis and Chicago and the Missouri River towns. Accordingly, I visited all those places, and had reason to be satisfied with the result. I secured not only subscriptions for about ten thousand copies, but a good many advertisements to be printed on fly-leaves at the end of the book. This preliminary work being accomplished, I settled down at a St. Louis hotel for the preparation of the manuscript early in February, and by the middle of March it was ready for the printer.

My venture was indisputably a legitimate one from every point of view, and it really promised very satisfactory results. Indeed, the aid already secured justified the expectation of a profit of at least several thousand dollars, and this prospect filled me with great buoyancy of spirit. But all my fond hopes were to remain unfulfilled. In an evil hour, I was led to contract for printing the book and lithographing the accompanying maps with a firm whose business it was to publish city and town directories all over the West. The firm seemed to have a good standing, and certainly had all the requisite printing facilities. When the book was about half done, however, the firm failed, and all their assets were seized upon by their creditors, including the plates for my book. A complicated contention over the assets ensued. In spite of my unceasing efforts, I succeeded only in the latter part of May in getting control of my manuscript and the finished plates, and it was late in June before the book was ready. My agreement with the subscribers and advertisers had been to deliver it on May 1. The spring emigration to Pike's Peak, for which the book was intended, being over, they refused to accept it. The upshot of it all was, that barely enough copies were sold to cover the cost of the first edition of twenty-five hundred. In other words, instead of the expected financial success, the undertaking proved a failure, leaving me without any compensation for the months of time and trouble I had devoted to it, and, besides, very much reducing my limited means. I did not get over the pang of that disappointment for a long time.

Instead of finding myself an independent capitalist, able to do thereafter only such literary work as suited me—a blissful state to which I had confidently looked forward—I was again obliged to seek regular journalistic employment. Fortunately for me, we were in a "Presidential year," the exciting forerunner of the dreadful crisis through which the country was to pass during the following years. I had been asked by the Cincinnati *Commercial* to attend the memorable Republican National Convention that met at Chicago on May 16, on its behalf, and gladly obeyed the summons. What I saw and heard on that great occasion will always form one of my most cherished and stirring reminiscences. I have attended a number of national gatherings of the great political parties since, but none that even remotely compared with the attendance at the Chicago convention in point of intelligence, character, earnestness, and enthusiasm. It contained the very flower of the leaders of the young Republican party: Horace Greeley, William M. Evarts, Thaddeus Stevens, Preston King, David Wilmot, Andrew G. Curtin, Henry J. Raymond, Thurlow Weed, General James Watson Webb, George William Curtis, George S. Boutwell, George Ashmun, Joshua R. Giddings, William Dennison, "Tom" Corwin, Henry S. Lane, N. B. Judd, Lyman Trumbull, and Carl Schurz. It was undeniably what all the opposition parties—the Douglas Democracy, the Buchanan or Breckinridge Democracy, and the Bell and Everett "American" party—charged it with being: a sectional convention, made up exclusively of representatives of the free States, excepting the five border Slave States. The Proceedings were of absorbing interest, and, upon the whole, harmonious. Still, two divergent tendencies upon the slavery question, one radical and the other conservative, were noticeable, which led to the most dramatic incident of the Convention. It was when the motion of Joshua R. Giddings to embody the preamble to the Declaration of Independence, "That all men are created equal," etc., etc., was voted down, and George William Curtis, then only thirty-six years old, rose to renew it with a matchless burst of eloquence which at once carried away the audience.

In one respect the Convention proved a great disappointment to me. I was enthusiastically for the nomination of William H. Seward, who seemed to me the proper and natural leader of the Republican party ever since his great "irrepressible conflict" speech in 1858. The noisy demonstrations of his followers, and especially of the New York delegation in his favor, had made me sure, too, that his candidacy would be irresistible. I therefore shared fully the intense chagrin of the New York and other State delegations when, on the third ballot, Abraham Lincoln received a larger vote than Seward, and the former's unanimous nomination followed. I had not got over the prejudice against Lincoln with which my personal contact with him in 1858 imbued me. It seemed to me incomprehensible and outrageous that the uncouth, common Illinois politician, whose only experience in public life had been service as a member of the State legislature and in Congress for one term, should carry the day over the eminent and tried statesman, the foremost figure, indeed, in the country.

I devoted my entire time for the remainder of the summer, as well as during the fall till the Presidential election in November, to getting up reports of notable political meetings for the Cincinnati *Commercial,* the *Missouri Democrat,* with whose well-known chief editor, B. Gratz Brown, I had become well acquainted during my stay in St. Louis, and for the New York *Tribune,* connection with which I secured through my acquaintance with Horace Greeley. I was constantly on the wing, and travelled over Illinois, Indiana, Ohio, and Michigan, with occasional incursions into Kentucky, Wisconsin, and Missouri—in sum, from four to five thousand miles. I do not think I exaggerate in saying that I must have attended at least fifty important meetings in the course of four months. While a high order of popular oratory was rare, there was a great deal of very good speaking. I heard Lincoln, Douglas, S. P. Chase, J. C. Breckinridge, Carl Schurz, Schuyler Colfax, Tom Corwin, and a host of lesser lights. I met hundreds of old political acquaintances, and made literally thousands of new ones. It was a singular opportunity to observe and study human nature in general, and the game of practical politics in particular. Upon the whole, I had a very good time, being the recipient of hearty hospitality everywhere. Still, I was very glad when my labors came to an end.

I was in Chicago on the day of the election. Though no great admirer of the Republican standard-bearer, I desired, of course, his success, and felt greatly gratified by it. It was clear to my mind that the triumph of the Republican party would lead to a national crisis. I believed, indeed, that the country was on the threshold of most serious events, and it looked to me as though a violent solution of the slavery question might be rapidly approaching. But I had as little idea as anybody else that the greatest and bloodiest civil war known to history was to break out in the immediate future.

CHAPTER X

WITH LINCOLN AT SPRINGFIELD.—1860-1

I WENT from Chicago to New York partly for a few weeks' rest and enjoyment, to which I was certainly entitled after my arduous labors during the summer and fall, and partly to renew my former efforts to secure a permanent connection with the metropolitan press.[1] The thorough practical training as a reporter I had acquired since my last attempts in the same direction, promised to make the attainment of my object much easier. An offer came to me in the last days of November in an entirely unexpected form. The New York Associated Press proposed to me [2] that I should go to Springfield, Illinois, and remain there till the departure of the President-elect for Washington, supplying it with regular despatches about current events in that place, which was to become for a time the centre of political gravitation. As a fair remuneration was offered, and my condition that I should be permitted to correspond by mail with Western papers was agreed to, I accepted this novel and important mission.

I started at once for Springfield. Having frequently visited the place in 1858 and during the Presidential campaign, I had a good many local acquaintances, including Lincoln; his law-partner, Judge Logan; Richard Yates, the

---

[1] He brought with him a long article on the development of mining in the Rocky Mountains in 1860, which was finally accepted by the *Herald*. This renewed his acquaintance with Frederic Hudson, the managing editor.

[2] Or, rather, the *Herald*, through Mr. Hudson, on hearing of his experience in the Lincoln-Douglas campaign and his acquaintance with Lincoln. By the rules of the Associated Press, his despatches had to be shared by the *Herald* with the other members of the Association.

Governor-elect; Jesse K. Dubois, the State Auditor; and other politicians, and the writers on the two daily papers. Among the latter was William M. Springer, who afterwards attained considerable prominence as a member of Congress of many years' service. Later on, R. R. Hitt turned up as a shorthand reporter of the proceedings of the Legislature. Springfield was then a small but attractive town of some nine thousand inhabitants. The business part centred in the square in which stood the State-house, with the offices of the Governor and of the heads of departments and the legislative chambers. The residence streets extended at right angles from the square. None of the streets were paved, and in wet weather, of which a good deal prevailed during that winter, they were simply impassable. There was but one decent hotel, where I put up, and this became the principal stopping-place of thousands of visitors, who, from curiosity or for political consultation and place-hunting, made a pilgrimage to this transient Mecca during the succeeding months.

When I made the object of my stay known to Mr. Lincoln, he gave me a very friendly welcome, and authorized me to come to him at any time for any information I needed. He introduced me to his private secretary, John G. Nicolay, who owes a very successful career to him. Mr. Lincoln had engaged him only after his election, previous to which he had been a simple clerk on a small salary in one of the State offices. I also then met John Hay for the first time. I do not remember whether he was already in the employ of Mr. Lincoln as assistant private secretary when I arrived or not. But he became such before Mr. Lincoln left Springfield. He was very young—barely twenty-two—handsome and of engaging manners. He had been acting as a correspondent of the St. Louis *Missouri Democrat* for some time. He wrote with much fluency and in a florid style. His career as littérateur and diplomat is well known. He has borne the title of Colonel, though he never saw any actual service. Nicolay and he have shown their gratitude to Abraham Lincoln in their voluminous Life of him, which is certainly a most valuable source of original information, but which cannot be said to be a model of historical justice.

Mr. Lincoln soon found, after his election, that his modest two-story frame dwelling was altogether inadequate for the throng of local callers and of visitors from a distance, and, accordingly, he gladly availed himself of the offer of the use of the Governor's room in the Capitol building. On my arrival, he had already commenced spending a good part of each day in it. He appeared daily, except Sundays, between nine and ten o'clock, and held a reception till noon, to which all comers were admitted, without even the formality of first sending in cards. Whoever chose to call, received the same hearty greeting. At noon, he went home to dinner and reappeared at about two. Then his correspondence was given proper attention, and visitors of distinction were seen by special appointment at either the State-house or the hotel. Occasionally, but very rarely, he passed some time in his law office. In the evening, old friends called at his home for the exchange of news and political views. At times, when important news was expected, he would go to the telegraph or newspaper offices after supper, and stay there till late. Altogether, probably no other President-elect was as approachable for everybody, at least during the first weeks of my stay. But he found in the end, as was to be expected, that this popular practice involved a good deal of fatigue, and that he needed more time for himself; and the hours he gave up to the public were gradually restricted.

I was present almost daily for more or less time during his morning receptions. I generally remained a silent listener, as I could get at him at other hours when I was in need of information. It was a most interesting study to watch the manner of his intercourse with callers. As a rule, he showed remarkable tact in dealing with each of them, whether they were rough-looking Sangamon County farmers still addressing him familiarly as "Abe," sleek and pert commercial travellers, staid merchants, sharp politicians, or preachers, lawyers, or other professional men. He showed a very quick and shrewd perception of and adaptation to individual characteristics and peculiarities. He never evaded a proper question, or failed to give a fit answer. He was ever ready for an argument, which always had an original flavor, and, as a rule, he got the better in the discussion. There was, however, one limitation to the freedom of his talks with his visitors. A great many of them naturally tried to draw him out as to his future policy as President regarding the secession movement in the South, but he would not commit himself. The most remarkable and attractive feature of those daily "levees," however, was his constant indulgence of his story-telling propensity. Of course, all the visitors had heard of it and were eager for the privilege of listening to a practical illustration of his pre-eminence in that line. He knew this, and took special delight in meeting their wishes. He never was at a loss for a story or an anecdote to explain a meaning or enforce a point, the aptness of which was always perfect. His supply was apparently inexhaustible, and the stories sounded so real that it was hard to determine whether he repeated what he had heard from others, or had invented himself.

None of his hearers enjoyed the wit—and wit was an unfailing ingredient—of his stories half as much as he did himself. It was a joy indeed to see the effect upon him. A high-pitched laughter lighted up his otherwise melancholy countenance with thorough merriment. His body shook all over with gleeful emotion, and when he felt particularly good over his performance, he followed his habit of drawing his knees, with his arms around them, up to his very face, as I had seen him do in 1858. I am sorry to state that he often allowed himself altogether too much license in the concoction of the stories. He seemed to be bent upon making his hit by fair means or foul. In other words, he never hesitated to tell a coarse or even outright nasty story, if it served his purpose. All his personal friends could bear testimony on this point. It was a notorious fact that this fondness for low talk clung to him even in the White House. More than once I heard him "with malice aforethought" get off purposely some repulsive fiction in order to rid himself of an uncomfortable caller. Again and again I felt disgust and humiliation that such a person should have been called upon to direct the destinies of a great nation in the direst period of its history. Yet his achievements during the next few years proved him to be one of the great leaders of mankind in adversity, in whom low leanings only set off more strikingly his better qualities. At the time of which I speak, I could not have persuaded myself that the man might possibly possess true greatness of mind and nobility of heart. I do not wish to convey the idea, however, that he was mainly given to trivialities and vulgarities in his conversation; for, in spite of his frequent outbreaks of low humor, his was really a very sober and serious nature, and even inclined to gloominess to such an extent that all his biographers have attributed a strongly melancholic disposition to him.

I often availed myself of his authorization to come to him at any time for information. There were two questions in which the public, of course, felt the deepest interest, and upon which I was expected to supply light, viz., the composition of his Cabinet, and his views upon the secession movement that was daily growing in extent and strength. As to the former, he gave me to understand early, by indirection, that, as everybody expected, William H. Seward and S. P. Chase, his competitors for the Presidential nomination, would be among his constitutional advisers. It was hardly possible for him not to recognize them, and he steadily turned a deaf ear to the remonstrances that were made against them as "extreme men" by leading politicians from the Border States, particularly from Kentucky and Missouri. As to the remaining members of his Cabinet, they were definitely selected much later, and after a protracted and wearisome tussle with the delegations of various States that came to Springfield to urge the claims of their "favorite sons." I shall refer again to this subject.

No one who heard him talk upon the other question could fail to discover his "other side," and to be impressed with his deep earnestness, his anxious contemplation of public affairs, and his thorough sense of the extraordinary responsibilities that were coming upon him. He never refused to talk with me about secession, but generally evaded answers to specific interrogatories, and confined himself to generalizations. I was present at a number of conversations which he had with leading public men upon the same subject, when he showed the same reserve. He did not hesitate to say that the Union ought to, and in his opinion would, be preserved, and to go into long arguments in support of the proposition, based upon the history of the republic, the homogeneity of the population, the natural features of the country, such as the common coast, the rivers and mountains, that compelled political and commercial unity. But he could not be got to say what he would do in the face of Southern secession, except that as President he should be sworn to maintain the Constitution of the United States, and that he was therefore bound to fulfil that duty. He met in the same general way the frequent questions whether he should consider it his duty to resort to coercion by force of arms against the States engaged in attempts to secede. In connection therewith I understood him, however, several times to express doubts as to the practicability of holding the Slave States in the Union by main force, if they were all determined to break it up. He was often embarrassed by efforts of radical antislavery men to get something out of him in encouragement of their hopes that the crisis would result in the abolition of slavery. He did not respond as they wished, and made it clear that he did not desire to be considered an "abolitionist," and that he still held the opinion that property in slaves was entitled to protection under the Constitution, and that its owners could not be deprived of it without due compensation. Consciously or unconsciously, he, like everybody else, must have been influenced in his views by current events. As political passion in the South rose higher and higher, and actual defiance of Federal authority by deeds of violence occurred almost daily after his election, culminating in the formal secession of seven States and the establishment of the Southern Confederacy under Jefferson Davis at Montgomery, Alabama, the belief, which he doubtless had originally, that by a conciliatory course as President he could pacify the rebellious States, must have become shaken. Still, I think I interpret his views up to the time of his departure for Washington correctly in saying that he had not lost faith in the preservation of peace between the North and the South, and he certainly did not dream that his principal duty would be to raise great armies and fleets, and the means to maintain them, for the suppression of the most determined and sanguinary rebellion, in defence of slavery, that our planet ever witnessed.

The Jacksonian "doctrine" that to the "victors belong the spoils," was still so universally the creed of all politicians that it was taken for granted there would be a change not only in all the principal, but also in all the minor, Federal offices. It was also expected that the other time-honored party practice of a division of executive patronage among the several States would be carried out. Accordingly, there appeared deputations from all the Northern and Border States at Springfield to put in their respective claims for recognition. Some of them came not only once, but several times. From a number of States several delegations turned up, representing rival factions in the Republican ranks, each pretending to be the rightful claimant. Almost every State presented candidates for the

Cabinet and for the principal diplomatic and departmental offices. The hotel was the principal haunt of the place-hunters. The tricks, the intrigues, and the manœuvres that were practised by them in pursuit of their aims, came nearly all within the range of my observation, as it was my duty to furnish the earliest possible news of their success or failure. As a rule, the various sets of spoilsmen were very willing to take me into their confidence, but it was not always easy to distinguish what was true in their communications from what they wished me to say to the press purely in furtherance of their interests. Among the political visitors, the most prominent I met were: Simon Cameron, S. P. Chase, Thurlow Weed, Lyman Trumbull, N. B. Judd, Richard J. Oglesby, Francis P. Blair, Sr. and Jr., B. Gratz Brown, William Dennison, D. C. Carter of Ohio, Henry J. Winter, and Oliver P. Morton. Thurlow Weed was by far the most interesting figure and the most astute operator among them all.

From what I have said, it will be understood that the President-elect had a hard time of it with the office-seekers. But as he himself was a thorough believer in the doctrine of rotation in office, he felt it his duty to submit to this tribulation. The Cabinet appointments, other than those already named, were especially troublesome to him. There was an intense struggle between Indiana and Illinois, most embarrassing inasmuch as there were several candidates from his own State, all intimate personal friends. Then came the bitter contest between the Border States of Kentucky, Missouri, and Maryland, and the Pennsylvania cabal pro and contra Simon Cameron. Amid all his perplexities, Lincoln displayed a good deal of patience and shrewdness in dealing with these personal problems. His never-failing stories helped many times to heal wounded feelings and mitigate disappointments. But he gradually showed the wear and tear of these continuous visitations, and finally looked so careworn as to excite one's compassion.

Not a little was added to his trials by the early manifestation of the inordinate greed, coupled with an utter lack of sense of propriety, on the part of Mrs. Lincoln, whose local reputation had repressed in me all desire to know her. I could not, however, avoid making her acquaintance towards the end of my stay in Springfield, and subsequently saw much of her in Washington. How the politicians found out Mrs. Lincoln's weakness, I do not know, but it is a sorry fact that she allowed herself to be persuaded, at an early date, to accept presents for the use of her influence with her husband in support of the aspirations of office-seekers.

I must mention a remarkable occurrence in Springfield, of which I was myself an eye-witness. Early in January, the State Legislature met, and, according to custom, the newly elected Republican Governor was to read the inaugural message to that body in person. The lawmakers assembled in the Lower Chamber at the appointed hour, but the Governor failed to appear. Search was made for him, and, after a delay of half an hour, the doorkeeper formally announced him, and he was escorted through the middle aisle to the Speaker's chair. He seemed hardly able to walk. His attempt to read the first sentences of the message disclosed the nature of the trouble. He was too drunk to stand or to read. He fell back into his chair, and the Clerk of the House read the message in his place. Of course, the scandal was great in the Legislature, in the town, and throughout the State.

During the month of January, 1861, there appeared in Springfield one W. S. Wood, a former hotel manager and organizer of pleasure excursions, I believe, from the interior of New York State, who, on the recommendation of Thurlow Weed, was to take charge of all the arrangements for the journey of the President-elect to Washington. He was a man of comely appearance, greatly impressed with the importance of his mission and inclined to assume airs of consequence and condescension. As he showed a disposition to ignore me, I made a direct appeal to Mr.

Lincoln, who instructed him that I was to be one of the Presidential party. In fact, I was the only member of the press forming part of it as far as Cincinnati, although Messrs. Nicolay and Hay, for some unexplained reason, fail to mention me in naming the members of the party.

The start on the memorable journey was made shortly after eight o'clock on the morning of Monday, February 11. It was a clear, crisp winter day. Only about one hundred people, mostly personal friends, were assembled at the station to shake hands for the last time with their distinguished townsman. It was not strange that he yielded to the sad feelings which must have moved him at the thought of what lay behind and what was before him, and gave them utterance in a pathetic formal farewell to the gathering crowd, as follows:

MY FRIENDS: No one not in my position can appreciate the sadness I feel at this parting. To this people I owe all that I am. Here I have lived more than a quarter of a century; here my children were born, and here one of them lies buried. I know not how soon I shall see you again. A duty devolves upon me which is, perhaps, greater than that which has devolved upon any other man since the days of Washington. He never would have succeeded except for the aid of Divine Providence, upon which he at all times relied. I feel that I cannot succeed without the same Divine aid which sustained him, and in the same Almighty Being I place my reliance for support; and I hope you, my friends, will all pray that I may receive that Divine assistance, without which I cannot succeed, but with which success is certain. Again I bid you all an affectionate farewell.

I reproduce this here, as but for me it would not have been preserved in the exact form in which it was delivered. It was entirely extemporized, and, knowing this, I prevailed on Mr. Lincoln, immediately after starting, to write it out for me on a "pad." I sent it over the wires from the first telegraph station. I kept the pencil manuscript for some time, but, unfortunately, lost it in my wanderings in the course of the Civil War.

Our travelling companions at the start were (besides Mr. and Mrs. Lincoln and the three sons) W. S. Wood; J. G. Nicolay and John Hay; two old personal friends of Mr. Lincoln, Judge David Davis, of Bloomington, afterwards Associate Justice of the U. S. Supreme Court, and N. B. Judd, of Chicago, who had the promise of the Secretaryship of the Interior; Dr. W. S. Wallace, a brother-in-law; Lockwood Todd, a relative of Mrs. Lincoln, who was employed on several important political missions during the next few months; and Ward Hill Lamon, a lawyer of Bloomington, who afterwards became United States Marshal for the District of Columbia, and as such a sort of majordomo at the White House, and finally the author of a biography of Abraham Lincoln. For describing him in this as an infidel, Lamon was much and unjustly attacked. He brought a banjo along, and amused us with negro songs. There was also a military escort, consisting of Colonel Edwin Vose Sumner, the white-haired commander of a cavalry regiment of the regular army, and of Major David Hunter, Captain John Pope, and Captain Hazard of the same service. Colonel Sumner, Major Hunter, and Captain Pope became well-known commanding generals during the war. Another "military" character, a sort of pet of Mr. Lincoln, was Colonel E. E. Ellsworth, who, though a mere youth, of small but broad figure, curly black head, and handsome features, had achieved considerable local notoriety as a captain of a crack "Zouave" militia company in Chicago. He was one of the first victims of the Civil War, being shot by a rebel while raising the United States flag at Alexandria, Virginia.

The party had a special train, composed at first only of an ordinary passenger car—there were no parlor or drawing-room or sleeping cars in those days—a baggage-car and engine. The first day's journey took us from the capital of Illinois to that of Indiana. Until we reached the boundary of the latter State, the demonstrations along the route were insignificant, except at Decatur, where a great crowd, headed by Richard J. Oglesby, then a hotel-keeper, but subsequently a general in the war, Governor, and United States Senator, greeted the future Chief Magistrate, who delivered another farewell speech. At the boundary, the train was boarded by a large delegation of leading Indianians, including Schuyler Colfax, Henry S. Lane, Caleb B. Smith, and Thomas H. Nelson. At Lafayette, a great crowd awaited our coming, and the President-elect had to appear and speak to them. At Indianapolis, where the first day's journey ended, he was formally welcomed by Governor Oliver P. Morton, and replied to him at length. His speech was remarkable for the first public intimation that he should consider it his duty as President to retake the properties of the United States, including the forts unlawfully seized by the rebellious States, and otherwise reestablish the authority of the Federal Government.

The next stage of the journey was from Indianapolis to Cincinnati; the third, from Cincinnati to Columbus; the fourth, from Columbus to Pittsburg; the fifth, from Pittsburg to Cleveland; the sixth, from Cleveland to Buffalo, where a rest was taken over Sunday. The eighth day the journey was continued as far as Albany, and on the following day we reached New York. Everywhere there were formal welcomes by the State or municipal authorities and by great crowds of people, with brass bands, and public and private receptions. In different localities pleasant variations were offered in the way of serenades, torchlight processions, and gala theatrical performances. Altogether, the President had every reason to feel flattered and encouraged by the demonstrations in his honor. But the journey was a very great strain upon his physical and mental strength, and he was well-nigh worn out when he reached Buffalo. He must have spoken at least fifty times during the week. In the kindness of his heart—not from any love of adulation, for he really felt very awkward about it—he never refused to respond to a call for his appearance wherever the train stopped. While he thus satisfied the public curiosity, he disappointed, by his appearance, most of those who saw him for the first time. I could see that impression clearly written on the faces of his rustic audiences. Nor was this surprising, for they certainly saw the most unprepossessing features, the gawkiest figure, and the most awkward manners. Lincoln always had an embarrassed air, too, like a country clodhopper appearing in fashionable society, and was nearly always stiff and unhappy in his off-hand remarks. The least creditable performance en route was his attempt to say something on the question of tariff legislation in his Pittsburg speech. What he said was really nothing but crude, ignorant twaddle, without point or meaning. It proved him to be the veriest novice in economic matters, and strengthened my doubts as to his capacity for the high office he was to fill. So poor was his talk that most of the Republican papers, while they printed it, abstained from comment.

After ten days of the wearisome sameness of the "performances" at the several halting-places, I was very sick of the "travelling show," and I therefore asked to be relieved from my duties on reaching New York. My request was granted, and I remained behind. It turned out that I lost only the reception in Independence Hall in Philadelphia, as the journey was cut short by the incognito night run of the President from Harrisburg to Washington. This sudden move on his part created at the time considerable disappointment, even among his warmest political followers, being regarded as an evidence of unwarranted fear. But subsequent events and developments proved his course to have been a wise one.

CHAPTER XI

AT WASHINGTON IN SUMTER DAYS.—1861

I REMAINED in New York till February 26, and then proceeded also to the national capital. I was conscious of now being so thoroughly qualified as a political writer and observer that I could be perfectly sure of constant and well-paid employment, having the special advantage, too, of being well acquainted with the President and his most intimate friends and advisers. I was also convinced that Washington was the proper and most promising field for me. I conceived the plan of trying a new departure in news-reporting from Washington, viz., to gather and furnish the same political and other news by mail and telegraph to a number of papers in different parts of the country, geographically so situated that they would not interfere with each other by the simultaneous publication of the same matter. I telegraphed a proposal to that effect from New York to the Cincinnati *Commercial* and the Chicago *Tribune,* both of which promptly accepted it. The New York *Tribune* and *Times,* having already special correspondents in Washington, would not accept it; but the elder Bennett and Frederic Hudson of the *Herald* offered to engage me as a telegraphic correspondent, and, as they conceded my condition that I should be free to speak through the *Herald* as a sympathizer with the Republican party, I came to an understanding with them. My enterprise was to be a sort of supplement to the Associated Press, whose then Washington correspondent was very inefficient, but was kept in his place on account of his long services. It was, indeed, the beginning in this country of the news syndicates or agencies of which scores now exist in

Washington and New York. I think I am fairly entitled to be considered the pioneer in this business, though the present generation of journalists is not aware of the fact.

I made my advent accordingly in Washington in high spirits. The *Herald* was to pay me twenty-five dollars a week, the *Commercial* and *Tribune* each fifteen dollars, thus bringing my weekly earnings up to fifty-five dollars, or not far from three thousand a year—really a large income for those days, when even Cabinet officers had only six thousand dollars. I hired a finely furnished suite of rooms for only twelve dollars a month, and engaged board at Willard's, the leading hotel, for thirty dollars a month—prices that will seem almost incredibly low when compared with those of the present day. Altogether, I felt quite rich and very independent. What with Congress in session, the hordes of place-seekers from every part of the Union, and the many public men from the North and South who visited the capital from purely patriotic motives in those critical days, Washington presented a very animated appearance. It had then about sixty thousand inhabitants, a number which the transient sojourners swelled by ten thousand. Leaving out the public buildings, the place seemed like a large village, with its preponderance of plain, low brick or wooden structures, wide, mostly unpaved streets, small shops, general lack of business activity, and a distinctly Southern air of indolence and sloth. Of its numerous hotels, some were very spacious, but all were poorly kept. It could not boast a single decent restaurant, but had no end of bar-rooms. There were neither omnibuses nor street-cars, and the shabby public carriages with their ragged black drivers were simply disgusting.

Still, unattractive as Washington was in all these respects, it was the most important place in the Union, and daily growing in importance; to it the eyes of the whole civilized world turned in curious and anxious expectation. Political life centred at the Capitol and at the three principal hotels, Willard's, Brown's, and the National, and especially Willard's, where the President had taken quarters till he moved into the White House. Among Republicans as well as all classes of their opponents, the entire uncertainty of the outlook caused a feeling of vague apprehension. On the one hand, all attempts in Congress to heal the running secession sore in the Federal body through the Crittenden compromise and the measures proposed by Senators Seward, Anthony, and Powell, and Representatives Vallandigham, Clingman, and Corwin, had failed. The so-called Peace Congress had likewise just miscarried. On the other hand, the seven rebellious States showed the boldest defiance, and were striving with the utmost determination to solidify the structure of the Southern Confederacy they had erected during the winter, and to widen and strengthen it by dragging the Border States after them. There was great division of opinion as to the wisest course to be pursued by the incoming Administration, even among its own supporters. Such leading Republicans as Horace Greeley and Thurlow Weed came out openly in favor of peaceful separation rather than the use of force by the Federal Government against the rebels. Other leaders were willing to go to great lengths in conciliating the South through Federal and State legislation concerning the "peculiar institution." The bulk of the Republican party and the majority of its Representatives in Congress were ready and anxious, however, for the utmost use of Federal power for the reduction of the Southern insurrection and the maintenance of the Union; but not a few of their principal guides, including Seward, still thought that the secession fever would run for a time, but gradually lose force and die out under proper treatment by Mr. Lincoln. The latter himself still held this belief. The prospect of the preservation of peace seemed to grow steadily less, yet only the outright secessionists were inclined to contemplate the spectre of a sanguinary struggle with complacency. The doubtfulness of the situation was increased by the open sympathy and readiness to concede all that would be necessary to placate the South shown by the Democrats of the North. Numerous mass meetings, of which those in Philadelphia under the direction of Mayor Henry, and in Albany under that of Governor Seymour, were the most notable, had been held in the Northern States to protest against "coercion," denounce the "Black Republicans," and demand recognition of the "just claims of our Southern brethren." I for one was fully convinced that a most bloody civil war was inevitable, unless the new Government abdicated its powers as far as the rebellious States were concerned; and I freely expressed that conviction in my correspondence.

Truly, the last man to be envied, under the circumstances, was Abraham Lincoln. The formal calls he received and had to return, the consultations with friends, the finishing touches to his inaugural message (which he had written and set up in type before leaving Springfield, but which received much tinkering before its delivery, at the suggestion of Orville H. Browning, Seward, and others), occupied his time from morning till late at night; and the settlement of the appointments to the principal offices left him, to be sure, little time for thought of the future. The pressure of the place-hunters was tremendous. As the necessary decision of their fate drew nearer, their eagerness to gain access to the chief dispenser of patronage became intensified. The situation is graphically described by Nicolay and Hay in their Life of Lincoln.

I saw Mr. Lincoln twice for a few minutes before the inauguration, when, in response to an expression of sympathy with his tribulations, he groaned out: "Yes, it was bad enough in Springfield, but it was child's play compared with this tussle here. I hardly have a chance to eat or sleep. I am fair game for everybody of that hungry lot." His wife again added not least to his worries. She meddled not only with the distribution of minor offices, but even with the assignment of places in the Cabinet. Moreover, she allowed herself to be approached and continuously surrounded by a common set of men and women, who, through her susceptibility to even the most barefaced flattery, easily gained a controlling influence over her. Among the persons who thus won access to her graces was the so-called "Chevalier" Wikoff, whose name figured as much as any other in the press in those days, who made pretension to the rôle of a sort of cosmopolitan knight-errant, and had the entrée of society, but was, in fact, only a salaried social spy or informer of the New York *Herald*. Wikoff was of middle age, an accomplished man of the world, a fine linguist, with graceful presence, elegant manners, and a conscious, condescending way— altogether, just such a man as would be looked upon as a superior being by a woman accustomed only to Western society. Wikoff showed the utmost assurance in his appeals to the vanity of the mistress of the White House. I myself heard him compliment her upon her looks and dress in so fulsome a way that she ought to have blushed and banished the impertinent fellow from her presence. She accepted Wikoff as a majordomo in general and in special, as a guide in matters of social etiquette, domestic arrangements, and personal requirements, including her toilette, and as always welcome company for visitors in her salon and on her drives.

Great efforts were made to render the inauguration an imposing occasion. The city itself indicated, by the scantiness of festive array, that the mass of the inhabitants were hostile to the new rule. But many thousands, including militia and political organizations, had come from the North and helped to give imposing proportions to the traditional procession from the White House to the farther end of Pennsylvania Avenue. The morning was cloudy and raw; nevertheless, at least thirty thousand people listened to the reading of the message from the historical corner of the Capitol. Probably two-thirds of the immense audience caught every word of the clear utterance of the new President. Not the faintest disturbance occurred then or at any time during the day. On the contrary, the chief figure of the occasion was lustily cheered. For some reason or other, offensive demonstrations and even violence to the President had been apprehended, and the small regular force held in readiness for the repression of such attempts. Old General Scott, who rarely left his quarters, owing to his infirmities, made a special effort and was on duty near the Capitol, receiving frequent reports from the army officers in charge of the detachments of regulars distributed over the city; but not the remotest sign of mischief appeared. In the evening, the customary big inauguration ball came off, and, as usual, it was a very crowded, much mixed and, upon the whole, very ordinary affair, though the newspapers the next morning praised it as the most brilliant festivity that had ever taken place in the national capital.

The inaugural message, which its author and those at whose instance it was changed from its original form had expected to act upon the political situation like oil upon a troubled sea, was received with nothing like enthusiasm even by the Republicans, and fell flat as far as the Northern Democrats and Border States were concerned, while the rebellious States spurned it with derisive contempt. This unsatisfactory effect was not surprising. The message was, to characterize it briefly, a heterogeneous compound of assertion, on the one hand, of the duty of the new Federal executive under his oath to obey the Constitution and enforce the laws and preserve the Union; and, on the other, of intimations and assurances that he would avoid action that might lead to a conflict, and that he favored such constitutional amendments as might pacify the South. It deservedly met, therefore, the same fate as the other attempts at conciliation in and out of Congress already referred to. Instead of finding himself relieved, as he had hoped to be, from the necessity of making good his pledges to do his duty against the rebellious States, the President was directly compelled to face that dreaded contingency.

It came in the shape of the question of holding or giving up Fort Sumter. That last of the Federal strongholds in Charleston harbor not in possession of the rebels had been left—unreënforced and unreprovisioned, after a weak effort to succor the garrison by the *Star of the West* expedition—as the most embarrassing legacy of the Buchanan to the new Administration. On the very morning after his inauguration, the President found on his desk at the White House a communication from the War Department, accompanied by official reports, according to which Fort Sumter could hold out, even if not attacked, only a few weeks longer, and Fort Pickens in Pensacola Bay was also in great danger, unless strengthened by men and supplies. From that hour the fate of the two forts formed his most serious anxiety. He called on General Scott and other officers of the army and navy for information and advice. He caused special messengers to be sent to Major Anderson, in command of Fort Sumter, in order to obtain his own judgment as to his ability to hold out. He submitted the subject for consideration to his Cabinet. The Commanding General of the army, forgetting that he was called on only for his military judgment, advised the abandonment of both forts on political grounds. At the first consultation with the Cabinet on March 15, the majority of the members, in written opinions, advised the evacuation of Sumter and the defence of Pickens. At the next one, a fortnight later, a majority favored the holding of both. The President, after weeks of hesitation and uncertainty, had reached the same conclusion, and would have acted on it even without the concurrence of the Cabinet. Orders to fit out relief expeditions were at once given to the War and Navy Departments.

In the meantime, the press and the public in the North, not having a knowledge of these occurrences, were under the impression that the Government was afraid of decisive steps and was simply drifting with the current of events. Beyond the refusal to receive the Commissioners of the Confederacy who came to Washington a week before the inauguration to negotiate for recognition, hardly any action of the Administration bearing upon the Rebellion was "visible." This naturally produced great irritation and discouragement in patriotic hearts, and Washington was full of indignant Northern men, in and out of Congress, giving vent to their wrath at the supposed blindness, incompetency, or cowardice, whichever it might be, of Lincoln and his Cabinet. It was believed, and openly said, that Seward's infatuated belief in the possibility of a peaceful solution and his fear of coercion had prevailed with the President. The Administration, according to appearances, seemed to be absorbed solely in the distribution of the "spoils," in the shape of Federal offices, among the victors. Much demoralization resulted from this among loyal men. Their discouragement was heightened, moreover, by the continuous desertions of army and navy officers, from the highest to the lowest ranks, to the rebel side, by the numerous resignations from Government offices of Southerners or sympathizers with the South, and by the ostentatious daily departures of Southern men of national reputation, members of the Senate and House and others, to join the Montgomery Legislature and Government. In addition to all this, the obvious general lethargy in the loyal States, the widening divisions among Republicans over the Southern question, and the growing clamor of the Northern Democrats for peace on any terms, seemed from day to day to render it more probable that the Rebellion would be successful, and that, even if the Government should decide upon efforts to put it down, it would not have the support of the majority of the Northern people.

In an instant, as it were, all this was changed. Southern folly and frenzy freed President Lincoln from all embarrassment. The expedition for the relief of Sumter, decided upon by him in compliance with his promise in the inaugural message, that "the power confided to me will be used to hold, occupy, and possess the property and places belonging to the Government," gave birth to the storm by which the political atmosphere was cleared at once of all haze, and the true course for the ship of state shown to its helmsman. Ordered on March 29, the expedition was intended to sail on April 6, but was delayed through various obstacles, and failed of its object in consequence. But its very failure worked like another act of Providence for the right cause. For, as its departure was the signal for the rebel attack on Sumter, its miscarriage caused the fort's surrender. But it was the very striking down of the United States flag by rebel guns that led to the bursting of the patriotic hurricane that swept away all dissensions, all partisan enmities, all fear, all apathy, and united the whole North in the determination to preserve the Union at any cost of blood and treasure. It has been claimed that Lincoln deliberately planned the whole move in sure expectation of its marvellous effect, but this may well be doubted.

The President issued the call for 75,000 men on April 15. On the following day I received a despatch from James Gordon Bennett asking me to come at once to New York. I obeyed the summons by the night train. On reaching the *Herald* office, I found an invitation to accompany him in the afternoon to his residence at Washington Heights and to spend the night there. As was my host's regular custom, we drove from the office up Broadway and Fifth Avenue and through Central Park to the Heights. I had seen Bennett only twice before, and then but for a few minutes each time, and the opportunity to learn more of this notorious character was therefore not unwelcome to me. I must say that his shameful record as a journalist, and particularly the sneaking sympathy of his paper for the Rebellion, and its vile abuse of the Republicans for their antislavery sentiments, made me share the general prejudice against him to such an extent that I had been thinking for some time of severing my connection with the

Herald, although the agreement that all I telegraphed should be printed without change or omission had been strictly kept. With his fine tall and slender figure, large intellectual head covered with an abundance of light curly hair, and strong regular features, his exterior would have been impressive but for his strabismus, which gave him a sinister, forbidding look. Intercourse with him, indeed, quickly revealed his hard, cold, utterly selfish nature and incapacity to appreciate high and noble aims.

His residence was a good-sized frame house in parklike grounds, with no great pretensions either outwardly or inwardly. On the drive and during the dinner, at which his one son—a fine-looking, intelligent youth of twenty—was the only other person present, he did nothing but ask questions bearing upon the characteristics and doings of President Lincoln and the circumstances of my acquaintance with him. After dinner he disclosed his true purpose in sending for me. First, he wanted me to carry a message from him to Mr. Lincoln that the *Herald* would hereafter be unconditionally for the radical suppression of the Rebellion by force of arms, and in the shortest possible time, and would advocate and support any "war measures" by the Government and Congress. I was, of course, very glad to hear this, and promised to repeat these assurances by word of mouth to the President. The truth was, that the *Herald* was obliged to make this complete change in its attitude, there having been ominous signs for some days in New York of danger of mob violence to the paper. Secondly, he wanted me to offer to Secretary Chase his son's famous sailing yacht, the *Rebecca,* as a gift to the Government for the revenue service, and to secure in consideration thereof for its owner the appointment of lieutenant in the same service. The last wish I thought rather amusing, but I agreed to lay it before Secretary Chase, to whom I had ready access as the representative of the Cincinnati *Commercial,* his strongest supporter in Ohio. My host retired early, and was ready before me in the morning for the down drive, on which I accompanied him again. Mr. Hudson—the managing editor, a fine-looking man, and one of the most courteous and obliging I ever met, with extraordinary qualifications for newspaper management—told me in the course of the day that Mr. Bennett was very much pleased with me and had increased my weekly allowance to thirty-five dollars.

I started on my return trip to Washington on the night train of the next day. The run now made in five hours then took from ten to twelve. It was most tiresome, especially at night, as it involved no less than five changes of cars, three crossings by ferryboat over the Hudson, Delaware, and Susquehanna Rivers, an hour's street-car ride through the whole length of Philadelphia, and the slow passage through Baltimore on railroad-cars pulled by horses. We reached Perryville, on the east bank of the Susquehanna, from which place passengers were transferred on a ferryboat to Havre de Grace, opposite, at 3 A.M. We got out of the train and walked to the boat. As it remained stationary, an explanation was sought from the captain, who said that he had been directed to remain where he was until further orders. One weary hour after another passed without any light as to the cause of the delay. There was not even a chance to sit down on the boat, except on the deck. At break of day I made my way to the telegraph-office at the station, but no one was there. The operator did not appear till seven o'clock. He said that, during the night, despatches had passed over the line to the managers of the company in Philadelphia, announcing that bridges and trestles had been burned in the night between Havre de Grace and Baltimore, and that accordingly the movement of all trains between those two points had been ordered stopped. The operator did not know who had done the burning, but it was clear to me at once that the rebel sympathizers in Maryland were the perpetrators, in order to stop the transportation of troops from the North to the capital. This had commenced the very day before on a large scale with the Sixth Massachusetts Regiment, which the great War Governor, John A. Andrew, had started from Boston, one thousand strong, within twenty-four hours after the President's call, and with an equal number of Pennsylvania volunteers. My surmise turned out correct, but I was far from suspecting the bloody events of the memorable nineteenth of April in Baltimore.

Here was a predicament for me. On the one hand, the very interruption of communication with Washington made it the more desirable and necessary for me to be there, in order to supply news through extraordinary channels if the ordinary ones failed. On the other, there was the embarrassing question how to get through, the broken railroad being the only line of land communication between the North and the capital. The first thing I did was to beg for a breakfast at one of the few houses in the hamlet of Perryville—there being no hotel—and I got one of bacon, "hoe-cakes," and indescribable coffee. Next, having seen some small boats tied up at the bank, I went in search of their owners. I found one of them who agreed to row me to Havre de Grace for a dollar, and he landed me there in an hour. This place was a village of a few hundred inhabitants, who were gathered in knots on the streets, discussing the stoppage of trains. They confirmed the burning of the superstructures, and not a few showed their rebellious disposition by expressing themselves as rather glad of it. I set about finding some sort of a vehicle to convey me to Baltimore, about thirty-eight miles distant. There was no livery-stable and but few private owners of carriages, all of whom were afraid to undertake the job, not knowing what had actually happened. After wasting a couple of hours with them, I determined to start on foot just as I was—my valise being checked to Washington—and take my chances of finding means of transportation on the way. After walking some six miles, about noon I reached the home of an apparently well-to-do planter on the roadside. My request for a meal was readily acceded to. The planter proved to be a strong anti-secessionist, though a slaveholder. To my great relief, he consented, in response to my offer to pay twenty-five dollars for the accommodation, to send me in a buggy with one of his slaves as a driver to Baltimore. Although I had heard stories at Havre de Grace and all along the road that the country was "swarming with rebel cavalry," we met no armed men, nor any sort of adventure, and arrived at our destination a little before dark. In driving through the city, I saw no sign of disturbance; the street life seemed to be going on as usual. I went to the Eutaw House, the proprietor of which I had known as a New York hotel-keeper. First of all, I gleaned from the morning and evening newspapers the details of the fearful occurrences the day before during the passage of the Massachusetts and Pennsylvania troops. They also contained the alarming announcement that railroad communication with both the North and the South was entirely interrupted. This left the problem how to get to the capital only half solved for me, but I was too tired to consider at once the other half of the solution, and so, after supper, I sought my bed without delay.

I rose early to consult the landlord as to the best means of reaching Washington, which I was resolved to do at all hazards and at the earliest possible moment. As the speedy reopening of the railroad seemed very doubtful, he recommended the hiring of a carriage, and sent for the keeper of the livery-stable attached to the hotel, who declined, however, absolutely to furnish me a conveyance at any price. Other stablemen were sent for, but with the same result. Finally, it occurred to me to try to secure a saddle-horse, and in this I was successful. But I had to put up a hundred dollars with the hotel-keeper as security for the return of the animal, and to pay five dollars a day and all expenses till returned. I was mounted by nine o'clock, and rode leisurely like a pleasure-rider to the suburbs, where I took by-roads instead of the main highway to the Relay House, the junction of the main and Washington lines of the Baltimore & Ohio Railroad, nine miles from the city. Here rider and horse had a repast, and then started on the long ride of over thirty miles to Washington, where I arrived at seven o'clock without having met any one but harmless country folk en route. After putting up the horse and getting a bath and change of clothes, I went to Willard's for supper. I was surprised to find the halls and public sitting-rooms almost empty, and still more so when the office clerk, in answer to my question, "What's the news?" said, "Well, as you have been away, it will be news to you that we are going to shut up this hotel tomorrow, and this meal will be the last you can be served with here." And so it was. The great caravansary was to be closed for an indefinite time.

An extraordinary change had, indeed, taken place at the capital since my departure. What with the proclamation of the President, which was really a declaration of the existence of civil war, with the prospect of Washington becoming the main objective-point of hostilities, with the riot in Baltimore, and the consequent stoppage of all railroad, mail, and telegraph service with the North, a veritable panic had ensued. Between the fifteenth and the nineteenth, the floating population, to the extent of tens of thousands, had dispersed to the North and South, and they were still leaving, notwithstanding the railroad blockade, by every sort of conveyance. Instead of the nearly one thousand guests that were stowed away at Willard's at the inauguration, not two score remained, and that was the reason for closing it. The other hotels were also empty. Walking on Pennsylvania Avenue in the morning, I could almost count the people in sight on my fingers. A great many private houses and a number of stores were also shut up. The whole city had a deserted look.

This exodus had a redeeming feature, as it consisted largely of secessionists, whose departure was, under the circumstances, a direct relief to the Government. But there was otherwise cause for the gravest alarm, which, in my visits to the White House, to the departments and public offices, I found shared by all loyalists, from the President and Cabinet officers down. The telegraph did not work, the mails did not arrive or depart. From the night of the twentieth on, there was practically no intercourse in any form between the national capital and any part of the country, and the Government remained without any intelligence from any quarter for several days. It knew only in a general way that the destruction of the railroad between Perryville and Washington had led to the adoption of the plan to transport the troops from the North by water to the capital. Literally, it was as though the government of a great nation had been suddenly removed to an island in mid-ocean in a state of entire isolation, and with all the inconveniences, uncertainties, and risks incidental thereto. This extraordinary situation naturally made me and all patriotic minds most anxious.

From what I saw myself and learned from others, I was oppressed by the thought that the Government was in a most perilous plight, that this must be known to the rebel authorities through the many willing and eager informants who left Washington daily for the South, and that, with the audacity they had so far shown, they would without fail take advantage of this, their great opportunity, and gain possession of the capital by a *coup de main*. The circumstances were so favorable to an attempt of this kind that I felt sure it would be made, and was prepared to hear at any moment of the appearance of a rebel force in the streets.

I did not understand then, nor could I ever understand, why the rebel hands were not stretched out to seize so easy a prey—a seizure that might have resulted in the immediate triumph of the insurrection. For, notwithstanding the hundreds of resignations from the army, navy, and civil service of the Government and the large migration to the South, Washington was still full of traitors among the residents and remaining officers and officials, who would eagerly have aided an effort to capture the capital for the Confederacy. There were not over two thousand armed and uniformed men available for defence, one-half being a motley of small commands of regulars from different regiments and arms, and the other consisting of the raw recruits of the Sixth Massachusetts Regiment. Efforts were making to organize the loyal residents and Government employees as a volunteer corps, but, although nearly two thousand such volunteers had been enrolled, not much reliance could be placed on them. Moreover, in the highest places, treason had broken out, from which the Government was to be protected. Adjutant-General Cooper of the army, Colonel Robert E. Lee, the principal aide and most trusted adviser of General Scott, and Commodore Buchanan, commandant of the navy-yard, had resigned and joined the enemy. These and many other desertions were rapidly demoralizing and paralyzing the several branches of the public service. The President relied on General Scott as the mainstay of the Government, and yet the fact could not be disguised that the Commander-in-chief was too decrepit in body and mind to be equal to the dire emergency. As the official record shows, he rather added to than allayed the fears of the President and his Cabinet by giving credence to the exaggerated and even fictitious and absurd reports of the gathering of rebel forces in the vicinity of Washington. There were but few officers left that could be trusted, and they were of inferior rank, and none of them had ever commanded more than a full company. I clearly perceived the growing helplessness and fright of the Government, and was haunted by the apprehension that the appearance of a thousand determined rebels would seal the fate of Washington without even a serious struggle.

The city bore the marks of a state of siege. Detachments of regulars guarded all the public buildings. Patrols were seen in the streets. All the approaches to the city were guarded. The White House was under the special protection of the "Clay" and "Frontier" Guards, two bodies of select volunteers formed by Cassius M. Clay, the well-known Kentucky Unionist, and by General James H. Lane, later United States Senator from Kansas, who had achieved considerable notoriety as a determined fighter during the border troubles in that Territory. They literally camped for several days on the lower floor of the Executive Mansion. The Potomac was also patrolled by small armed boats. All stores of provisions and forage were seized by the War Department, and other defensive preparations made as diligently as possible. Material was got ready for barricading the Treasury and Interior Departments on short notice, as their massive character and isolated position rendered a strong defence practicable.

Nothing proved more conclusively the want of capacity of the military authorities than their failure for days to get any accurate information as to the movement of troops from the North for the relief of the capital. When it is considered that it is but forty miles from Washington to Annapolis, which had been selected as the landing-place for the relief forces, and where several regiments had actually disembarked on the 22d and 23d, and that, moreover, the railroad from Washington to Annapolis Junction, forming twenty of the forty miles, had not been disturbed and trains were moving over it, it will seem amazing that no news of the nearness of help was obtained by the Government. All General Scott did was to send out single mounted scouts along the railroad, who regularly brought back nothing but untrustworthy rumors. A company of regular cavalry, under an enterprising officer with absolute orders to secure positive intelligence, would have accomplished the desired object. As it was, our darkness was not broken by a ray of light till the 25th, and, in the meantime, the impatience, gloom, and depression were hourly increasing. No one felt it more than the President.

I saw him repeatedly, and he fairly groaned at the inexplicable delay in the advent of help from the loyal States. I heard him say, too, when he reviewed the men of the Sixth Massachusetts, the very words that Nicolay and Hay quote: "I begin to believe there is no North. The Seventh New York Regiment is a myth. The Rhode Island troops [reported to be on the way up the Potomac] are another. You are the only real thing." But the "myth" proved to be a reality, after all, on Thursday, the 25th. By a very hard march of twenty-four hours from Annapolis, the Seventh New York and Eighth Massachusetts managed to reach Annapolis Junction on the morning of that day. A train was waiting, and in the course of a few hours the whole of the Seventh Regiment reached its destination. I cannot express the revival of hope and confidence, the exultation, that I felt and that filled all loyal hearts as that crack body of New York Volunteers, nearly a thousand strong, marched up Pennsylvania Avenue, preceded by a magnificent band. After being reviewed by the President and Cabinet, it took possession of Willard's Hotel and occupied it till it moved into camp. The Seventh was immediately followed by the Eighth Massachusetts and by two Rhode Island regiments, accompanied by the youthful Governor Sprague. After that, further reënforcements continued to arrive daily from different loyal States, and, within a month, more than the full call of 75,000 men had reached the capital. But it took until the middle of May to restore railroad communication with the North completely.

From that time on, Washington assumed a most animated aspect. Including the regulars and the three months' men, fully eighty thousand soldiers were added to its population. To the north and east an almost unbroken girdle of military camps extended around the city. The pomp and circumstance of actual war were constantly visible in the public thoroughfares in marching columns of infantry, troops of cavalry, and batteries of artillery.

Thousands of visitors to the troops arrived daily from the North and crowded the streets, where swarmed soldiers of every arm and every sort of uniform. In the first stage of the Rebellion, the Government allowed entire liberty as to uniforms to those commissioned to raise regiments. This privilege was freely availed of by a number of organizations in New York City drawn from foreign-born elements. I was surprised one day to see infantry dressed in the genuine Bavarian uniform. There were Prussian uniforms, too; the "Garibaldi Guards," in the legendary red blouses and bersaglieri hats; "Zouaves" and "Turcoes," clothed as in the French army, with some fanciful American features grafted upon them.

Congress not being in session, my principal duties consisted in gathering news through daily visits to the White House and the different departments. I had no difficulty in soon getting on very good terms with all the heads of departments and their chief subordinates. At certain times of the day, mostly immediately after office hours, I could always be sure of gaining admission to the secretaries, if I desired to see them. I found Secretaries Seward, Chase, and Cameron the most accessible and communicative. A brief experience taught me that even the first two, although their great national reputation was so solidly founded, were anything but impervious to newspaper flattery, and very sensitive under journalistic criticism. Seward was afflicted with an outright weakness in that respect. The *Herald* made a regular practice of bestowing on him extravagant eulogies bordering sometimes on ridiculous exaggeration, in order to smooth the way to his confidence for its correspondents, and the recipient did not always succeed in concealing from them his grateful appreciation. Chase was far less affable than Seward, and kept men at a distance by his stately and occasionally pompous ways; but it did not require much penetration to perceive that he had the very highest opinion of himself and was prone to criticise others rather indiscreetly.

Still, I greatly admired his natural ability and solid acquirements, and especially his high and pure political aims. My acquaintance with him gradually assumed a confidential character, so that he expressed himself very freely regarding public men and matters.

Cameron was the typical American politician, with a well-defined purpose in all he said and did. He also held himself a little too freely at the disposal of newspaper men, to whom he was by far the most cordial and talkative of all the secretaries. He made them feel at once as though they had met an old acquaintance and friend. He was certainly the cleverest political manager in the Cabinet, and, though unquestionably as ambitious as any member of it, he never was guilty of the indiscretions which the political records of Seward and Chase reveal. He had a very shrewd way of tempting journalists by implications and insinuations into publishing things about others that he wished to have said without becoming responsible for them.

The Secretary of the Navy, Gideon Welles, was speedily discovered to be a rather difficult subject for newspaper enterprise, and the representatives of the press confined their attention to his assistant secretary, Captain G. V. Fox, formerly a naval officer. Fox had suddenly acquired a well-deserved national reputation for patriotic bravery by the offer of his services in connection with an expedition of a "sink or swim" character for the relief of Fort Sumter, planned by himself and authorized by President Lincoln and actually attempted, but resulting in failure from a succession of untoward accidents. He was a very strong man, endowed with remarkable ingenuity, courage, and energy, but full of personal prejudices that made him hardly a safe conductor of public affairs. He was an unsparing critic, regardless of the rules of discipline, policy, and comity, and astonishingly free in his talk to our fraternity.

His brother-in-law, Montgomery Blair, the Postmaster-

General, was a similarly positive, intolerant, and determined character. He and Fox were the best haters of the Rebellion in the Administration, and for them the Government was far from moving fast and vigorously enough in its suppression. Blair, however, was very much of a practical politician, and no one believed more strongly in the legitimacy of the distribution of offices among the ruling party. I also became acquainted with his father, Francis P. Blair, Sr., and his brother, Francis P. Blair, Jr., of St. Louis, later a Congressman and Federal general. The father and sons formed a most remarkable trio, possessing a common character. There was no more influential family in the United States at the time. They likewise were not averse to being frequently mentioned and well spoken of in the public journals.

The greatest curiosity was naturally felt throughout the North in the doings of the volunteer troops about Washington, and I was therefore instructed by my employers to make them a special feature in my daily reports. For that purpose I paid regular visits to the regimental camps on the outskirts of the city, to facilitate which I was authorized by the *Herald* to buy a saddle-horse. My daily rides were most enjoyable in various ways. Delightful weather was the rule throughout May and June. The several hours I spent every afternoon in the saddle afforded an agreeable and healthful exercise. Then, some of the regimental headquarters, of which I made the rounds, formed uncommon centres of attraction. Among the officers of some of the New York, New England, and Western regiments, the very flower of the youth of the land could be found. They were remarkable for intelligence, patriotism, and devotion to duty. Nor did they lack the qualities from which the lighter joys of early manhood flow. In their canvas abodes, mirth and gaiety ruled during the off-duty part of the day, and visitors were made to join in various frolics. It was also true, however, that not a few of the regiments consisted of a very low order of elements. Some of the New York and Philadelphia organizations had, indeed, been recruited from the vicious strata of population, and were officered by the worst types of local politicians. The Irish New York regiments were notorious in this respect. It was my duty to look them up also, but I performed it reluctantly and as rarely as possible.

The regiments in which the foreign elements preponderated had a particular interest for me as a European. Of these there were four exclusively German regiments, the Seventh, Eighth, Twentieth, and Twenty-ninth New York Volunteer Infantry, and the so-called "Garibaldi Guards," made up of Italians, Frenchmen, Hungarians, Germans, and other nationalities. The Eighth was under command of Louis Blenker, who had had some military experience not only in the rising of 1849 in Rhenish Bavaria, but also in Greece as a volunteer under King Otto. The colonel of the Twentieth was Max Weber, a former army officer in Baden, and landlord of the Hotel Constanz, at which I stopped after landing in 1853. The colonel of the "Garibaldi Guards" was D'Utassy, the romantic assumed name of a Hungarian Jew with a German patronymic. He and Blenker appeared alternately in the regulation and in the fancy foreign uniforms they had adopted for their regiments. Both were fond of parading through the streets in their gorgeous array on horseback, with mounted staffs behind them. Both bore the unmistakable stamp of adventurers. Blenker, who had been a small dairy farmer, had a rather imposing bearing and accomplished manners, and blossomed out into a great swell. D'Utassy was nothing but a swaggering pretender. It seemed amazing that such men should have been entrusted with the organization of whole regiments; but, owing to the then urgent national emergency and the inexperience of the rulers in war matters, any one with a real or well-feigned military record had not much difficulty in securing recognition.

Speaking of these men, another apparition of those days rises before me. Thomas Francis Meagher, the Irish exile, well known for his political martyrdom and his great natural eloquence and literary talent, came to the capital as the captain of a Zouave company attached to the Sixty-ninth Irish New York Regiment. He had devised a most extraordinary uniform for himself, of the Zouave pattern, literally covered with gold lace. It was a sight to see him strut along Pennsylvania Avenue in it, with the airs of a conquering hero.

Among the regular visitors to the camps was Mrs. Lincoln. It would have been, of course, an entirely proper thing for her, as the wife of the Chief Magistrate of the nation, to show her sympathies for the defenders of the Union by going among them. But the truth was, that she had no liking for them at all, being really, as a native of Kentucky, at heart a secessionist. She went to the camps simply to enjoy the adulation and hospitality offered her there. None were more lavish with these than the officers of the Irish New York regiments, and these she favored especially with her calls.

One of the points of attraction was the headquarters of Governor Sprague of Rhode Island, who had recruited three regiments in his State and led them to Washington. He had very limited mental capacity, but had reached political distinction at an early age—he was then but thirty-one—through the influence of real or reputed great wealth. It was at his headquarters that he became acquainted with Kate, the beautiful and gifted daughter of Secretary Chase. The acquaintance quickly ripened into an engagement that was the social sensation of the day. She was far superior to him in every way, and married him for the enjoyment and power of his money. It turned out one of the unhappiest marriages ever known in American society, ending in moral and material wretchedness for both parties.

CHAPTER XII

Formation of the Federal Army.—1861

THE readiness of the loyal States to place at the disposal of the Government all the men, money, and material needed for the suppression of the Rebellion had been clearly manifest ever since the fall of Fort Sumter. But the great problem for President Lincoln and his chief helpers was the proper use of the national resources so freely offered to them. There were in all the North but a few hundred men to be found regularly trained for the soldier's trade, while thousands were wanted as officers for immediate service. Even with nine-tenths of the loyal officers of the regular army, practical experience did not go beyond the command of companies. With such a scarcity of qualified persons, it was unavoidable that the largest number of officers should be taken from among civilians without the knowledge of even the manual of arms. Still, in acting under this necessity, the General Government and the governments of the several States could certainly have applied the strict test of physical, mental, and moral fitness in the selection of officers. But, unfortunately, the Executive saw a welcome and plentiful opportunity to reward political adherents with commissions in the army, and only too willingly used this extensive new patronage without regard to the fitness of the recipients. As a rule, in all the States, the professional politicians secured the new honors and emoluments. It is safe to say that four-fifths of all the field officers of the three months' regiments appearing in Washington represented this class of men, and the same practice prevailed in the vast levies of volunteers raised subsequently, though to a diminished extent.

The Federal authorities did no better. In officering the new regiments for the regular army authorized by Congress, the most extraordinary appointments were made. Instead of filling the higher places from among the officers who had remained true to the flag, the majority of the field officers were appointed from civil life. Most of the appointees were ordinary politicians having no other than party qualifications. I remember distinctly some of the persons thus favored; one of the notorious cases being the appointment to a full colonelcy, by Secretary Cameron, of a devoted political follower, the chief clerk of the War Department, who, up to the inauguration, had been the sickly, dried-up, pedantic principal of a second-rate school in Pennsylvania. Commissions of line officers were also systematically distributed among favorites. I had a curious personal experience in this respect. I was myself offered a commission as captain in the regular army by Secretary Chase by way of compliment to the Cincinnati *Commercial*—an offer which, I am free to say, sorely tempted me. About the same time I was induced to interest myself in the application for a commission as lieutenant of a young German doctor from Buffalo, who was anxious to exchange the scalpel for the sword. I spoke to Mr. Chase regarding him, and a few days later he received, to his intense surprise, a commission as a captain of infantry. I am sorry to say that my protégé did not do honor to my recommendation, being dismissed for cowardice on the battle-field before he had served a year. One of my amusements in those days was to witness the private lessons in the rudiments of military lore of the appointees for field officers in the new regular regiments by old drill-sergeants. The difficulties which these colonels, lieutenant-colonels, and majors experienced at first even in keeping step and wheeling about, and later on in the manual of arms, led to very comical scenes. I believe it is a matter of record that very few of these appointees ever rendered any valuable service to the Government.

The preparations for war around me had gradually matured my determination to abandon peaceful work in Washington, and to devote myself to the more exciting occupation of a correspondent in the field. I thought it very important to qualify myself as well as possible for my expected new duties, and, accordingly, I purchased a number of standard books in English, French, and German on strategy and tactics, as well as histories of Frederick the Great's, Napoleon's, and Wellington's campaigns, and devoted all my spare time to the study of them.

Of all the difficulties that confronted the Government, the greatest was, beyond all question, the selection of the proper commanders of the loyal armies then forming about the national capital and at other points. Lieutenant-General Scott was still virtually Commander-in-chief, under the President, of all the land forces; but, as already stated, there was no disguising the fact that he was in every way incapable of a proper discharge of the duties of that position, which grew from day to day more onerous and more fraught with the gravest responsibility. He was nearly seventy-five years old, and his physical infirmities were such that he could scarcely leave his invalid-chair. His mind, too, clearly showed the effect of old age. He formed plans for the coming offensive movements of the troops, but he vacillated much respecting them, and discussed them with indiscreet garrulousness. He was very accessible to newspaper men, having always been fond of newspaper fame and flattery, and I called regularly on him, as did the other correspondents. It took very little to make him talk freely of his purposes. I can still see the stately figure, with the grand head and face, and the snowy hair and whiskers, seated in an arm-chair before a great wall-map of the United States, upon which he explained his strategic ideas with a long pointer. The necessity of superseding him had been apparent to President Lincoln ever since war had become inevitable, but it sorely perplexed him how to do it. The makeshift was finally resorted to of leaving him nominally in supreme command, but giving the command in the field to others practically independent of him.

In the critical, anxious days in April, the President was persuaded to promote two subordinate officers in the regular army at once to high rank. The alleged object was to give them, as being specially zealous in their loyalty, the necessary authority to insure the protection of the Government from the traitorous designs for its overthrow then being prosecuted at the capital. The fortunate men were Major McDowell, and Captain Meigs of the engineer corps, both of whom received the rank of brigadier-general. Their promotions over the heads of nearly all the regular army officers naturally created much jealousy and dissatisfaction, especially among those who had outranked them, but to whose credit be it said that no resignations resulted from this abnormal action. General Meigs assumed charge as quartermaster-general of the entire supply department—a function inferior in importance only to the command of the field forces—and General McDowell was placed in command of the troops gathered for the defence of the capital. He owed his brigadier's commission mainly to the influence of Secretary Chase, who had long known him as an Ohio man. The Secretary favored me with a warm introduction to the General, which placed me at once on the best terms with him. He was a man of strong character and much intellectual ability. While his practical military experience was necessarily limited by the narrow opportunities offered in the active service of the small regular army, his theoretical knowledge was very extensive. He was well read in war history. But in my frequent intercourse with him I gained the impression that he lacked the resolute determination which alone could insure success in his trying task of organizing an effective army for aggressive war out of the raw material gathering under his command. With his evident want of confidence in himself, he appeared to be full of misgivings from the start. This self-distrust showed itself in his constant talk of the difficulties surrounding him and of the doubts he felt of the possibility of overcoming them. Of course, my opinion of his qualifications as a commander was at that time that of a novice and had no value whatever, but it was decidedly to the effect that, while he might make a very efficient sub-commander, he had not the stuff of a great captain in him.

All hope of a peaceful settlement with the seceded States had long vanished, but no one as yet foresaw the fearful proportions which the Civil War would assume. The belief was still universal that short work would be made by the Federal Government in suppressing the Rebellion. Its great weakness, arising from its Constitutional inability to call out militia in quotas from the several States for more than three months' service, had been cured by the resolute assumption by Congress of the power to authorize the enlistment of volunteers for three years. All coolheaded and competent advisers of the Government, including General Scott, deemed it imprudent and dangerous to attempt any decisive offensive movements with the three months' militia, and urged postponement until the three years' men had been sufficiently trained for field service. But too much confidence had been produced in the North by the theory, preached in the press and by political leaders, that one vigorous onset would suffice to tumble over and destroy the rebel fabric. This popular feeling was intensified by the removal of the capital of the Southern Confederacy from Montgomery, Alabama, to Richmond, Virginia. The head of the hydra of rebellion having been brought so near the Federal capital, the cry was raised that the honor of the nation required a quick and decisive resentment of this insult, and that it was the duty of the Government forthwith to make one great effort to go for the monster and finish it. The editor of the New York *Tribune,* Horace Greeley, began daily to blow the loudest trumpet for "On to Richmond." The personal pressure upon the powers in Washington by members of Congress— in extra session, too—became great, with the result of persuading them that it was necessary on political grounds to begin an offensive campaign from the Potomac without delay. General Scott and other military advisers reluctantly acquiesced after a definite decision to that effect was reached. The Commander-in-chief directed General McDowell to submit a plan of operations, which was considered in detail and agreed upon at a council of war at the White House on June 29, the President, the Cabinet, and the principal military officers participating.

A brief sketch of the plan will be in place. Virginia formally seceded, by popular vote, on May 23, and the State Government immediately took steps to protect its territory from the Northern invasion threatened from two directions —from Washington, mainly, and from Pennsylvania, where a Northern force under General Patterson was gathering in the neighborhood of Harper's Ferry. For this purpose, Manassas Junction (the meeting of the railroads from Richmond, Alexandria, and the Shenandoah Valley, thirty-five miles southwest of Washington) and Harper's Ferry were occupied by rebel troops. General Beauregard had been given command at the former, and General Joseph E. Johnston at the latter point. Gradually the rebel forces were increased, and early in June those at Manassas were estimated at about twenty thousand, and those at Harper's Ferry at about eight thousand. General McDowell's plan was to move against Beauregard with his own army, while General Patterson held Johnston in the Shenandoah Valley, and while General Butler threatened a direct attack on Richmond from Fortress Monroe; and, after crushing the enemy at Manassas and thereby compelling Johnston to abandon the valley, to unite with Patterson's command for a rapid advance on Richmond.

Every effort was made by McDowell to get his army in motion within a week after the adoption of the plan for the campaign, but more than two weeks elapsed before this was possible. He issued his order to march on July 16. His forces were divided into five divisions of unequal strength, ranging from one of nearly 10,000 men down to one of 2,648, commanded respectively by Generals Tyler, Hunter, Heintzelman, Runyon (afterwards ambassador at Berlin), and Dixon S. Miles. The five divisions represented a total of 34,000 effective men. General Runyon's division constituted the reserve and did not come into action, so that only about 28,500 men with forty-nine guns and a single battalion of cavalry actually took part in the events to be described.

I rode every day to Arlington Heights, where McDowell had established his headquarters in the mansion of the future commander-in-chief of the rebel armies, Robert E. Lee, and talked freely with him about the impending movement. He showed anything but confidence in its success, and plainly displayed distrust of himself and of his soldiery. He repeatedly said that his troops were not yet sufficiently drilled and disciplined for an offensive campaign, and that the politicians were responsible for the premature movement, but that he should be the principal victim if it failed, as he feared. At the same time, there could be no doubt that he would do his whole duty to the best of his ability, and to that end he labored day and night.

I had received early warning of the impending crisis through a newly made acquaintance at headquarters, Captain J. B. Fry, an assistant adjutant-general of the regular army, the Commanding General's chief of staff. The friendly relations then formed with him continued over thirty years. I obtained ready permission to accompany the headquarters. I was already well mounted, and my other preparations for the campaign took very little time. I must confess that I did not share McDowell's apprehensions, but believed in the easy triumph of the Union forces over the rebels, and consequently expected a very interesting and satisfactory experience and a prolonged absence from Washington.

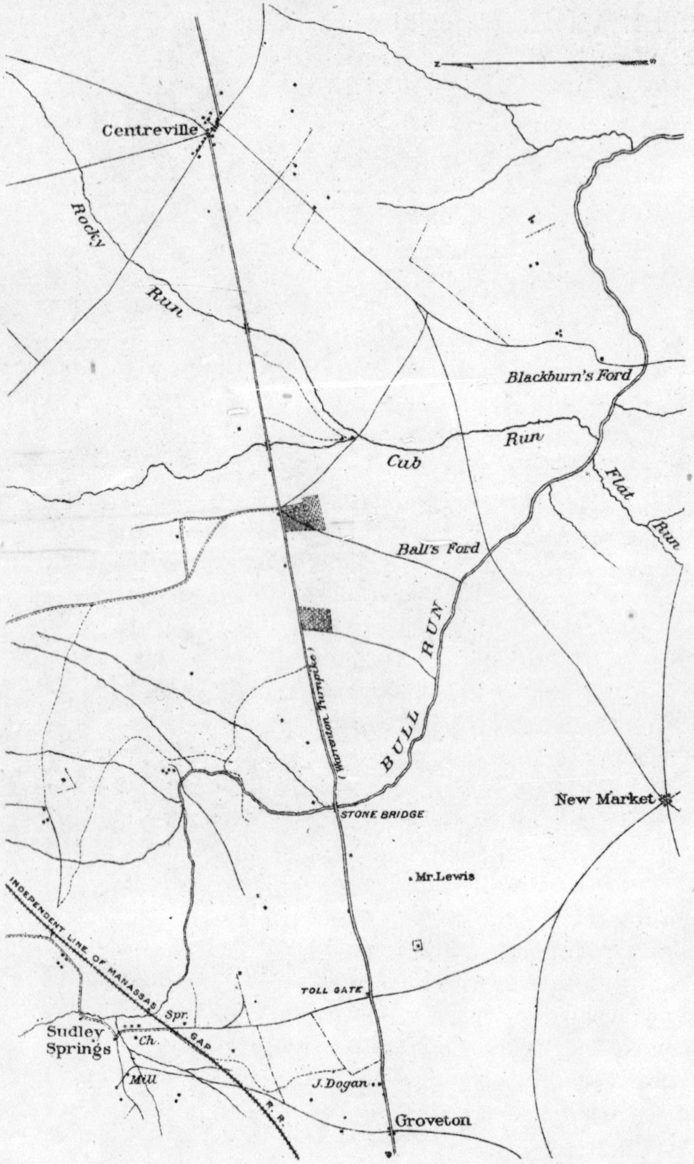

JULIUS BIEN & CO. N.Y.

CHAPTER XIII

BLACKBURN'S FORD AND BULL RUN.—1861

THE advance of the army commenced on July 16. It took so much time to get the several divisions under way from their encampments in the fortifications along Arlington Heights and at Alexandria that only a few miles were accomplished that day. As the headquarters were not to move until the next day, I joined General Tyler and staff, commanding the First Division, which had the lead and had started from near the Georgetown bridge. Coming up with the rear regiment, I had to pass all the troops of the division, as they were following the same road. In passing the brigade commanders and staffs, I rode with them for a time for a chat. Thus I had a short talk with Colonel W. T. Sherman, of the regular army, the future army commander, who had under him the so-called Irish brigade, formed of the Irish New York City regiments. I knew from visits at Fort Corcoran, where the Colonel had had his brigade headquarters, that he was not very proud of his command, which hardly contained a single competent officer, and both the rank and file of which it was especially difficult to discipline properly. But the prospect of active service seemed to have put him into rather good humor. In passing the Sixty-ninth New York regiment, I came up with Captain Thomas Francis Meagher, whose Zouave company formed part of it. He was mounted, but wore a plain undress uniform instead of the gorgeous one already described. As I approached him, I noticed that he was resting his right hand with a cocked revolver on his hip. "Well, Captain," I sang out to him, "you are all ready for the fray?" "Yes," he replied, "there is nothing like being always ready for the 'damned rebs.'" The leer from his eyes and a certain unsteadiness in the saddle indicated plainly that he had braced himself up internally for the fight.

General Tyler went into camp near Fairfax Court-House, and I accepted shelter for the night in a wall-tent offered me by one of his staff. For the first time since my Colorado experience I slept on the ground, with a waterproof sheet under and a blanket over me, and my saddle for a pillow. The reveille was sounded before sunrise, and we were in motion again shortly after five. We expected to have a first encounter with the enemy at Centreville, a small straggling village on the Warrenton turnpike about six miles from Fairfax, but found it evacuated. The few remaining inhabitants reported that the rebel troops had withdrawn behind Bull Run, a small stream some three miles to the west. A halt was made at Centreville, and the division went into camp about the village for the day. General Tyler's orders were "to observe well the roads," under which he felt justified in making a reconnoissance in the direction of the enemy, and, accordingly, he set out for that purpose, escorted by a company of cavalry and two companies of infantry. I was permitted to ride with him. We took a road in a southerly direction towards "Blackburn's Ford" of Bull Run. About noon, we had reached an orchard on a plateau commanding a wide view of the surrounding country, from which clear fields sloped down for about one-third of a mile to the thickly wooded banks of the stream, along which, according to our information, rebel troops were concealed. General Tyler concluded to rouse the game in the woods below by artillery, and sent orders to bring up Captain Ricketts's regular battery, supported by Colonel Richardson's brigade. The battery reached the position with its support about three o'clock, and a section unlimbered directly and commenced shelling the woods. These were the first cannonshots fired against the rebels in front of Washington, and quite excited me. The fire was continued without eliciting any response, when the General ordered it to cease and skirmishers to be thrown out, and advanced down the slope.

Two other newspaper correspondents had appeared on foot with the infantry—E. C. Stedman, the poet and critic, and E. H. House, long connected with the New York *Tribune,* and well known as essayist and critic till he abandoned the profession to become American consul in Japan for many years. As we three felt very hungry, I dismounted and left my horse in charge of an officer's servant, and we followed the skirmishers down the road to a farm-house within a hundred yards of the woods, in the hope of getting something to eat. We found the house locked and apparently deserted. Espying a well-laden cherry-tree, I climbed it in order to supply myself and friends with the fruit. I had just got on a branch when suddenly a terrific roar burst out from the woods seemingly within a few steps of us, followed by a mighty whizzing and clattering all around us. The rebel infantry in the woods had fired a volley against the skirmishers. In less than a minute another volley followed, accompanied by the same great roar and the small noises all around us. It then flashed upon us that the latter were caused by thousands of bullets whistling by us and striking the farm buildings, fences, and trees round about. We were, indeed, right in the line of fire of a whole rebel brigade. With the second volley there came also the deep detonations of artillery fire. Then there was a deafening crash, and I found myself thrown from the tree to the ground. Stedman and House shouted, "Are you hurt?" from their shelter behind the farm-house, to which they had rushed after the second volley. Fortunately, no harm had befallen me.

The rebel fire continued violently, and was answered by our skirmishers and the regiments and two guns that came hurrying down the slope to their support. As the enemy's musketry and artillery swept the entire slope, it was not safe for us to attempt to get out of their reach, and so we remained in our protected position behind the main farm building till the skirmish was over. Our men had entered the woods, but were driven back in confusion by the irresistible fire from the concealed rebel lines. Another regiment having joined them, other attempts to force the rebel line followed, but all failed. It was nearly six o'clock before our troops were withdrawn and we were released from our uncomfortable position.

The outcome of the affair was about sixty killed and wounded on each side. General Tyler was subsequently much criticised for the unnecessary, fruitless loss of life and limb, as he was not authorized to make a reconnoissance in force. But it is an open question whether the demonstration of the presence of the enemy in strong numbers at Blackburn's Ford did not help General McDowell in forming proper plans for the succeeding movements. As for myself, I had certainly had a strong foretaste of actual war. Though not a combatant, I had undergone the formal baptism of fire, and a fire as hot as I was ever under in my varied adventures as a war correspondent. I can truly say that the music of "bullet, ball, and grape-shot" never had much terror for me thereafter.

I was glad to mount my horse again and make my way back to Centreville in search of food for man and beast, and of lodging for the night. On reaching the village, I was hailed from the porch of a spacious dwelling by another newspaper man, who, with some others, had taken possession of it in the absence of the white owners and induced the black servants to cook supper and breakfast for them. I gladly accepted an invitation to share their comforts. My horse was also well taken care of.

The cannonading at Blackburn's Ford had caused the march of the other divisions to be accelerated, as a serious engagement between the First Division and the enemy was supposed to be going on. The whole army was well concentrated in and about Centreville, where General Mc-

Dowell also joined it on the evening of the 18th. It still lay in camp on the two following days, Friday, the 19th, and Saturday, the 20th. General McDowell devoted that time to getting all possible information about the roads to Manassas, the condition of the several crossings of Bull Run by bridges and fords, and the distribution of the enemy's forces, in order to formulate his plans for further operations. What was ascertained regarding the natural and artificial difficulties (abattis, rifle-pits, and batteries in position) of effecting a crossing of Bull Run on the direct line to the Junction, made him abandon his original plan of turning Beauregard's right flank from the south and decide to attempt a flanking movement from the north, concealed by a front attack. He informed his division commanders accordingly on the evening of the 18th; but the engineers, not getting through with the necessary reconnoissances before the afternoon of Saturday, the 20th, the execution of the modified plan was not attempted before the next day.

On Saturday night the division commanders assembled at headquarters to receive their final instructions. The Warrenton turnpike formed the main street of Centreville and ran thence directly southwest to Bull Run, which it crossed on a solid stone bridge of two arches, to which Beauregard's left flank extended. General Tyler was ordered to move with his division over the turnpike to the bridge, a distance of three miles and a half, and there make a feint attack. Hunter and Heintzelman were ordered to make a circuitous night march northward, cross Bull Run at Sudley Springs, between two and three miles above the stone bridge, follow the stream down to the latter, and, taking from the rear the armed fortifications which the enemy were supposed to have at that point, open the way for the crossing of Tyler's division. The three divisions should then jointly attack the rebel left. Miles's division was to remain in reserve at Centreville. Richardson's brigade was to threaten Blackburn's Ford.

The army was aroused at midnight, and, soon after, the three attacking divisions were ready to move. I did not fully know the plan of battle, but supposed that Tyler's division, as it took the lead, would play the principal part and therefore joined its staff. There was unfortunately but the one turnpike for all to march on, so that Hunter and Heintzelman were delayed for hours, and it was nine o'clock when the advance reached Sudley Springs, where it crossed readily without opposition.

Tyler reached the stone bridge shortly after daybreak, but made his feint only after he had learned of the close approach of the other divisions to the ford above. We saw the rebel forces guarding the bridge retreat, but, as the bridge was supposed to be mined, no attempt was made to pass it. General Tyler let the infantry of Sherman's and Keyes's brigades cross the stream half a mile above, the men getting wet to their hips, and march over a mile of level bottom in the direction of the heavy firing that had been heard for some time. A junction was effected with Hunter, and the division made front with Sherman on the right and Keyes on the left, and moved forward in a westerly direction. General Tyler and staff followed in the immediate rear of Keyes's brigade. It soon became evident that, owing either to the nature of the ground or to the fact that Sherman was drawn away by keeping in close touch with the more oblique movement of Hunter's division—I never was able to learn the real cause—Keyes's brigade had become isolated from the rest of the attacking forces. Indeed, it remained after this a separate command, unable to hold communication during the battle either with Sherman or with General McDowell. It thus turned out that my accompanying Tyler was a fatal mistake, as, though we heard the constant rattle of musketry and booming of artillery, we were kept in entire ignorance of the course of events on the field. In fact, all we saw of the battle was the limited part played by Keyes's brigade in it. I realized all this early in the afternoon, and felt very much tempted to strike out alone for the general headquarters, but, being utterly ignorant of their whereabouts, I concluded that a search for them at a venture involved too much risk, and remained. General Tyler and his staff also felt the awkwardness of their position very keenly, and vainly hoped from minute to minute to come again in touch with Sherman or the other divisions. Sherman had, indeed, by his movement come under the direct orders of General McDowell.

Keyes's brigade kept slowly moving to the left of the Warrenton turnpike over broken ground covered with woods and thickets, and gradually reached Young's Branch of Bull Run, crossing which, he came up with the enemy about two o'clock. Two regiments charged up a hill and drove the rebels from about a cluster of farm-buildings, but hostile batteries opened so severely upon them that they could not hold the gained position. During this attack I was again exposed to a heavy fire of small and large guns, but neither as severe nor as sustained as that at Blackburn's Ford. This was the only actual taste I had of the memorable first battle of Bull Run.

After this futile effort, Keyes's brigade rested on its arms along Young's Branch. The firing had steadily continued during the afternoon until after four o'clock, when it gradually died out. Ominous feelings came over us, and our fears that disaster had overtaken our side were soon after confirmed by an aide-de-camp of General Tyler, who had set out nearly two hours before for another effort to reach General McDowell, and returned with the terrible news that the Union forces were in full retreat. The General at once ordered the withdrawal of the brigade in the direction of the stone bridge. Feeling confident that I could find my way back alone, I rode in advance as fast as the ground permitted.

As my object in penning these memoirs is to describe my personal experiences, not to write formal history, I shall not attempt to give a full account of the course of the action in the other parts of the field, or a full analysis of the causes that led to the disastrous defeat of McDowell's army. Even if I undertook to do this, I should no doubt fail in the task, for the official and unofficial accounts of the battle on both sides are extremely confused, fragmentary, and contradictory. It will suffice for me to give, from the most authentic sources, a brief summary of what happened to our right on the ill-starred day, including the personal statements made to me subsequently by General McDowell, the division and brigade commanders, and some of the staff officers.

The skirmishers leading the flanking movement of Hunter and Heintzelman's divisions became engaged with the enemy at about ten o'clock, and soon afterwards the advancing columns were fully exposed to showers of rebel bullets, balls, and shells. The advance came to a stop, and the artillery of the two divisions was brought into play for some time. Only a small force was at first opposed to the divisions, which they would doubtless have easily swept out of their way if they had not halted. The stop of the attacking columns enabled the enemy to bring up reënforcements in the shape of four regiments that had arrived the day before with General Johnston from the Shenandoah Valley. Sherman's brigade having in the meantime joined Hunter on the left, the advance was resumed by our side. The rebels, though much weaker, resisted vigorously, and the severest fighting of the day occurred then, lasting over an hour. The enemy were finally forced back along their whole line for nearly a mile, so that between one and two o'clock victory seemed certain for the Unionists. Jefferson Davis, who had come up from Richmond the day before, and Beauregard and Johnston were thrown into consternation by the stream of demoralized officers and men that came pouring back from the front. But the very success achieved by our troops was to be the cause of their failure. The advance, being on exterior lines, as it were, and spreading the front wider and wider like a fan, resulted in loss of cohesion between the divisions, brigades, and regiments. The advantage of continuous unity of command was also wanting. It cannot be said that the army as a whole had the benefit of intelligent general direction at any time during the day. The division and brigade commanders and even partly the regimental commanders were left to their own devices. Much of this lack of guidance and the consequent confusion was due to the early compulsory retirement of Brigade-Commander Hunter from the field upon receiving a severe wound. Moreover, owing to the fatigue of the troops, who had been on their feet since midnight, and their exhaustion from the intense July heat, more and more men lagged behind as the forward movement proceeded, and the temporary success in the noon hour was probably achieved by less than two-thirds of the effective force that had set out from Centreville. Deducting the killed, wounded, and disabled, the stragglers and skulkers, from the effective number of the two and one-half divisions (Hunter's and Heintzelman's, with Sherman's brigade) at the start, doubtless only about ten thousand Unionists remained confronting the enemy at one o'clock, and they were drawn out on a long, irregular, and barely connected line, and were tired and suffering from hunger and thirst. Nor was there any reserve available to make up for the depletion of their ranks.

Only Beauregard's left flank, with the four regiments from the Shenandoah Valley, had so far been engaged. In falling back before the Union troops, it had reached a strong position on a wooded plateau commanding the lower ground over which the Federals would have to pass in pushing their attack. Here both the rebel commanders, Johnston and Beauregard, themselves took charge. They were now convinced that there the main effort of the Federals was being made, and that no other part of their line was actively endangered. So they ordered regiments from their centre and right to the threatened position. Most luckily for them, too, the remainder of Johnston's command from the Shenandoah Valley arrived by rail during the early afternoon in time to participate in the action. Thus gradually a rebel force was gathered superior to their opponents in numbers and freshness and much better held in hand. When the Unionists resumed their advance, the rebels successfully resisted their rather desultory attacks at different points. With every unsuccessful onward attempt there was a rapid melting away of the assailants. Fewer and fewer officers and men could be rallied for another advance. Towards four o'clock, the rebels felt strong enough to take the offensive. A brigade with a battery under Earle managed to strike the Federal right on the flank and rear and throw it into utter confusion, which spread rapidly along the whole front. Now came the disastrous, disgraceful end. Without any formal orders to retreat, what was left of the several organizations yielded to a general impulse to abandon the field. Officers and men became controlled by the one thought of getting as far as possible from the enemy. Three-fourths were quickly reduced to the condition of a motley, panic-stricken mob. Not that resolute efforts were not made by the General-in-chief and some of the commanders under him to insure an orderly retreat. They were all in vain. The morale of the army was entirely gone, and the instinct of self-preservation alone animated the flying mass.

When I rode away from Keyes's brigade towards the stone bridge, this rearward movement had not yet reached its full dimensions, but the Warrenton turnpike was already swarming with fugitives from the battle-field, going towards Centreville. I made inquiries at the bridge from every passing officer as to the whereabouts of General McDowell's headquarters, but no one could direct me to them. I concluded to wait at the bridge for developments. I had not watched the tide of runaways for more than twenty minutes when one of Hunter's staff officers came dashing down the pike on horseback. I stopped him to repeat my question about McDowell, when he exclaimed excitedly, "You won't find him. All is chaos in front. The battle is lost. Our troops are all giving way and falling back without orders. Get back to Centreville," and galloped on. I waited a while longer till other officers and the increasing flow of retreating soldiery confirmed the news of the general retreat, and then resumed my ride.

A quarter of a mile to the east of the bridge, I found the turnpike blocked by a double line of army wagons, so that my horse could hardly pass them. Half a mile further, I came upon an immovable mass of supply and ammunition wagons, ambulances, and other vehicles, that extended as far as I could see and made further progress on the pike impossible. Fortunately, the persons in charge had already opened a way through the adjacent fields by pulling down the fences. But it occurred to me at once to what further disaster to the Union army this choking up of their main line of retreat might lead. I took it upon myself to call the attention of a passing officer of the quartermaster's department to this danger, and he at once proceeded to try his best to remove the tangle. Time and again, owing to such obstacles, I had to leave the turnpike and proceed through the fields, even having to open a way myself by pulling down fences. I was lucky enough to find no obstruction on the small suspension-bridge over Cob Run. A short distance beyond this I came upon another blockade, in which were involved a number of hackney carriages with members of Congress, some of them known to me, who had driven out from Washington that day and were trying to get to the front to witness the great victory which the favorable course of the action up to the afternoon had led them to expect. They had heard nothing of the defeat, and would not believe me when I told them the bad news.

I passed on, and had not left them more than five minutes when I was startled by the sound of artillery in close proximity behind me. A rebel cavalry detachment with a battery section, sent to cut off our retreat, had suddenly emerged from the woods to the south of the turnpike, and commenced shelling it. A shell hit the horses of a supply-wagon. Shell after shell exploded over and on the roadway, and some of the rebel cavalry dashed up, yelling with all their might. The turnpike and the adjacent fields became instantly the scene of a wild panic. The teamsters jumped off their wagons and ran away as fast as they could. Even ambulances with wounded were deserted. The retreating soldiers all the way from the stone bridge were seized with fright, and started on a full run through the fields in swarms of hundreds and thousands, throwing away their arms and accoutrements, knapsacks, haversacks, and blankets. Within a few minutes after the first rebel gun had been fired, a wild, senseless rabble came rushing by me on foot, horseback, and muleback. A good many soldiers detached animals from wagons and galloped off on them. The members of Congress and other civilians also abandoned their private vehicles, and joined afoot in the race for safety. Among the fugitives there was a well-known newspaper correspondent, who had caught and mounted bareback a badly bleeding artillery horse, and was urging him to extreme speed by merciless cudgelling. The terrified crowds presented a pitiful and humiliating sight. Starting again, filled with greater fears than before for the fate of the army, I rode all the way amid runaways, soldiers and officers of all ranks—I noticed among them fellows with the straps of majors and lieutenant-colonels—and a mixture of civilians, to Centreville, where I arrived shortly before six o'clock, travel-stained, dust-covered, and about as tired, hungry, thirsty, and disgusted with all the world as a human being could well be.

Our nice quarters had fortunately not been occupied, as I had feared, by other "invaders." After securing some food for myself and for my worn-out beast, I started on a hunt for the general headquarters in and about the village, in order to learn what decision had been reached in consequence of the loss of the battle, and thereby govern my own movements. But I could not find any trace of the Commander-in-chief and staff. They had evidently not yet returned from the field, if they had escaped capture. Complete confusion prevailed in the village, nobody being able to find anybody or knowing what to do. While wandering about in search of information, I came up with the head of Colonel Blenker's brigade, which had advanced with the other brigade of the reserve division to near Blackburn's Ford, but was now retreating in obedience to orders from the division commander. Colonel Blenker had not yet heard the full extent of the disaster, but, on learning it from me, formed a line with his command across the main road from Centreville to Fairfax and awaited developments. The other brigade did likewise. Meantime the flow of the stream of demoralized mankind, on foot and mounted, and with no end of vehicles of every sort, poured steadily through the village. There was no attempt to stop or rally the troops by the numerous field and other officers who floated by with the current. I returned to my quarters and sat down on the porch, where I found Messrs. House and Stedman, Mr. Glenn of the Cincinnati *Gazette,* Mr. Painter of the Philadelphia *Inquirer,* and others.

Between eight and nine, the remnants of organizations of Keyes's, Burnside's, and Sherman's brigades reached the place, from whose officers we learned that McDowell was behind them, and that a stand would be made. We watched the street sights till after nine, when my companions determined to seek a night's rest, in the belief that the army would rally about the village. I thought it more prudent to make sure of this, if possible, at headquarters, and set out again in quest of them. I discovered them at the further end of the village. General McDowell was in a building engaged in receiving reports, so that I could not reach him. Captain Fry, however, told me that orders had been first given for a rally of the retreating army at Centreville, but the clear evidences of the hopeless demoralization of the troops which they had observed on the way from the battle-field had shaken the General's determination. He was then, however, informing himself, by consultation with sub-commanders and staff officers, as to whether a rally was still advisable and practicable. Shortly after ten, if I remember the time correctly, I was informed that a retreat to Washington had been determined upon, and would be immediately ordered. It was no surprise to me, as I had become satisfied during the evening that there was nothing else left.

I hurried back to our quarters, and did my duty to my friends by waking and telling them the news and urging them to lose no time in starting back. Two acted promptly and got away, but the other two—Glenn and Painter— could not rouse themselves sufficiently and fell asleep again. They woke late in the morning, and, when they had leisurely dressed themselves and come down for breakfast, found several officers in rebel uniform sitting on the veranda. Fortunately, they were taken by these to belong to the family owning the house, and politely asked whether breakfast could be had. They had presence of mind enough to answer, "Oh, yes, with pleasure"; and, pretending to go in search of the servants, managed to make their escape from the rear of the house by climbing over a fence into an adjacent corn-field, and so safely reaching the woods to which it extended. They arrived in Washington very much elated, of course, at their adventure.

I lost no time in making for the stable, saddled my horse, and in a few minutes was trotting along the Fairfax road. My newspaper instinct was fully aroused. I saw a chance of outstripping the rival correspondents with a report of the battle by reaching Washington as quickly as possible. For that purpose it was essential that I should get in advance of troops retreating in formation, and of supply and other trains. My horse had had three hours' rest and a good meal, and would surely be equal to the eighteen miles' ride. But within a few hundred yards of the east end of the village, I found myself stopped on the highway not only by immense trains of loaded army wagons in the road, but by camps of teamsters and soldiers on both sides of it. I was obliged to dismount and find my way in the dark with the greatest difficulty through and around these impediments. It was nearly one in the morning when I at last was able to go ahead again at a fast trot on a clear road. Still, even for the rest of the way, I frequently passed squads of runaways from the front that must have left the field early in the afternoon and made the best use of their legs ever since. Some were wearily worrying on, others resting on the roadside or cooking meals at camp-fires. Some of those who were halting, being hidden from view by the darkness, amused themselves by sending forth rebel yells so as to frighten the passers-by into the belief that they had fallen upon a rebel ambuscade, and into a dead run for life or rather from imprisonment. The first attempt of the kind deceived me, too, so that I spurred my beast to his greatest possible speed.

About daybreak I passed the camp of a regiment of Pennsylvania three months' men, whose term of service had expired the day before, and who had insisted on marching away from the front to the very sound of the battle. So little martial spirit had been developed in a good portion of the army! A little while later I heard the clatter of hoofs behind me, and, looking back, perceived a mounted officer approaching at full speed. As he came nearer, I saw he wore nothing on his head and was very bald. I soon recognized in him Colonel Ambrose E. Burnside, of the First Regiment of Rhode Island Volunteers, who had commanded a brigade under Heintzelman in the battle. There he was, hatless, swordless, and all alone, making the best of time on his fine black charger. I had made his acquaintance in his camp at Washington, and hence spoke to him as he hastened by. He did not stop to talk, but merely exclaimed, "I am hurrying ahead to get rations for my command." But this struck me as preposterous, as such duties were not performed by regimental commanders, and as it did not account for his being without hat and sword. From this incident, I conceived a natural prejudice against his trustworthiness as a general officer, which my later observations of him as a corps and army commander confirmed.

I reached the fortifications on the Alexandria road, about a mile south of the western end of Long Bridge, near five o'clock. Here I was detained for a while, owing to my semi-military garb and the military accoutrements of my horse, which compelled the guards to apply their orders not to let any officers or men pass on to Washington. The officer on duty was finally called, and let me go on. It was half-past five when I reached the livery-stable where I boarded my horse, and thence sought my rooms. The streets of the capital were as lifeless as usual at that early hour, and most of the inhabitants were doubtless unconscious of the portentous events of the previous day.

It will be readily understood in what state of physical exhaustion I was, after eighteen hours of great fatigue and excitement with but one meal; but I had no right to rest before I had done my duty to the *Herald*. During the night ride I had thought out what seemed to be the best course in reporting the battle. My knowledge of the details of the fighting was very limited, but I had picked up enough information for an intelligible and nearly correct summary of what had occurred. I determined, therefore, to prepare first a succinct report of say six hundred words for transmission by wire when the telegraph-office opened at seven A.M. (In those days the unlimited telegraphing now universally practised by the press was not dreamt of, and I was not free to send more over the wires without special permission of the editor-in-chief, to obtain which would have meant fatal delay.) Next I would allow myself six or seven hours' sleep, and in the afternoon endeavor to collect further material for a fuller account by the last evening mail. It took me only half an hour to write out my despatch, so that before leaving it at the main telegraph-office I had time for an early breakfast at Willard's Hotel. The despatch reached its destination before eight, and was printed at once as an extra. It was the first revelation to the New York public of the extent of the national disaster, and as such created a great sensation, but was not immediately credited.

I slept until two P.M., dined, and then went to the War Department in search of more matter for my mail report. I soon found that they knew less of details than I did, and that General McDowell had reëstablished his headquarters at Arlington Heights. I reluctantly rode there, and was fortunate enough to find Captain Fry, whom I persuaded to dictate to me substantially his recollections and impressions of the battle. What he told me of the orders that had been given by General McDowell, and to what extent they had not been executed, was especially valuable for my purpose. Equally so were his free comments upon the causes of the disaster, chief among which he considered the incapacity of commanding officers, the lack of courage and discipline among the troops, and, above all, the non-fulfilment of General Scott's promise that "if Johnston joined Beauregard, he should have Patterson on his heels."

As I did not get back to Washington before nearly six o'clock, there was no time left to get my full report ready for the last evening mail; hence I wired for leave to transmit it wholly by telegraph, which was granted. I commenced work at half-past six and was through at half-past ten. Two office-boys kept running to the main telegraph-office with the successively finished sheets of the manuscript, so that, within a few minutes after my work was done, the last instalment was being flashed to New York. I felt well satisfied with what I had written and confident that it would prove quite a hit for me. Alas! when it reached me in print, I discovered, to my great disgust, that so much of it had been stricken out or altered that I could no longer feel any pride in the mutilated remnant as my own production. The reason for this treatment was that I had indulged in a good deal of merciless criticism on the lines indicated by Captain Fry, which my employers were afraid to publish. I had been particularly severe on some of the New York regiments and their officers, and the editor did not dare to print my fulminations on my authority alone. The excuse and compliments in the editor's explanatory letter to me were poor compensation for my disappointment.

There was plenty of work for some time in Washington in collecting and verifying more particular information about the battle, correcting first reports in the light of it, and obtaining lists of the casualties. But, by the beginning of August, the Government and Congress had settled down to still more determined endeavors, on a far greater scale than before, for the suppression of the Rebellion. It was evident that a long time would elapse before a new army could be organized and got ready for another offensive movement from Washington, and that nothing would be left for me to do at the capital. It was the general belief, shared by the Government, that Missouri and Kentucky would soon be the scene of active operations. I therefore proposed to the editor of the *Herald* that I be sent to one or other of these States. I was invited to come to New York for a personal consultation, and the result was that I was given a fortnight's vacation, at the end of which I was to go to Louisville, to watch the course of events in Kentucky.

MEMOIRS OF HENRY VILLARD

BOOK THREE

IN CIVIL-WAR TIME: SHILOH

CHAPTER XIV

KENTUCKY IN THE SUMMER AND FALL OF 1861

I REACHED Louisville during the last week of August, 1861, and took a room at the Galt House, the largest and best hotel in the city, kept by Captain Silas Miller, well known throughout the Southwest as a successful commander of Ohio and Mississippi steamboats. He was a staunch and enthusiastic Unionist, owing to which his house was sought by the Kentucky loyalists and shunned by the rebel sympathizers. Louisville could boast of a good deal of commercial activity in ordinary times, but its business was then at a standstill from the stoppage of trade between North and South, and the almost entire cessation of steamboating on the Ohio. Many of the business men and the majority of the young men of the place had gone South to join their fate to that of the Confederacy. Hence, the streets wore a very quiet and even deserted look. The hotel, too, was almost empty. I had a few letters of introduction, one to Mr. Speed, the postmaster, a friend of President Lincoln and brother of the future Attorney-General, and another to a Northern family by the name of Cowan. Both led to very pleasant, though limited, social relations, as four-fifths of the upper class favored the South and showed the utmost animosity towards the loyal element. I also made the acquaintance of George D. Prentice, the poet-journalist, editor of the Louisville *Journal,* and of his principal assistants, with all of whom I was soon on such good terms that their editorial rooms became a familiar resort for me. Mr. Tyler, the agent of the New York Associated Press, a native of Massachusetts, and his wife likewise became my friends.

They were elderly people, and had their peculiarities, but were very intelligent and ardent loyalists. His office was near the hotel, and it soon became my practice to visit it regularly after supper in order to learn and discuss the latest news.

The political situation in the State was stirring and threatening, and furnished ample material for correspondence. Ever since the secession of the cotton States, incessant efforts had been made by the local rebel sympathizers to make Kentucky join the Southern cause. The Governor, Magoffin, did everything in his power to bring this about. All through the winter and spring the outcome remained doubtful. Although secession sentiments prevailed among the upper classes, the majority of the people of the State were doubtless for the maintenance of the Union, but the loyal feeling was not strong enough for immediate, hearty, unconditional support of the Federal Government. There was a general disposition, indeed, even among the leading opponents of secession, to pronounce against the coercion of the rebellious States by force of arms, and to pursue a non-committal, selfish policy of neutrality between North and South, in order to protect the State from the horrors of civil war. Thus, they supported the rebel sympathizer in the gubernatorial chair in his direct refusal, in the name of the State, to furnish its quota of troops under the first call of President Lincoln for 75,000 men. They also approved the action of the Legislature in calling out a force of militia to prevent the "invasion" of its soil by either belligerent.

The Government at Washington was weak enough—mainly owing to Lincoln's tenderness for his native State—to bear with this undutifulness to the Union for a time, but the impracticability of such passiveness became gradually manifest. The incessant endeavors of Magoffin, Simon B. Buckner, the commander of the "State Guards" (the militia called out ostensibly to enforce neutrality, but ready to fight for the South), ex-Vice-President John

C. Breckinridge, George B. Crittenden, Humphrey Marshall, and other conspirators to implicate the State in the Rebellion soon compelled a different course. The Union leaders recognized the necessity of active counter-efforts, and brought about the organization of their followers in clubs and military bodies. The Government had sent General Anderson, of Fort Sumter fame, to Cincinnati in May, on a secret mission for promoting the enlistment of volunteers from Kentucky and Virginia in the United States service. Simultaneously, William Nelson, a lieutenant in the United States Navy, a Kentuckian by birth, of unbounded loyal enthusiasm, to whom President Lincoln's attention had been called, was relieved from naval duty and permitted to go to his native State and take charge of the formal military organization of the Unionists. I had made his acquaintance in Washington through his brother, United States Minister to Chili under President Lincoln. He was thirty-six years old, over six feet high, with a mighty frame, a stentorian voice, a Jove-like head, of tireless, infectious energy, and altogether a remarkable personality. Under his direction, five thousand muskets, sent by the Government, were brought into the State and distributed among the "Home Guards," as the loyalists were designated in distinction from the secessionist "State Guards." Through the influence of General Anderson, nearly two thousand Kentucky Volunteers had been gathered in a camp on the Ohio side a short distance above Cincinnati, and formed into the First and Second Regiments of Kentucky Volunteers. Lovell H. Rousseau, a Louisville lawyer and politician, obtained authority to enlist a brigade of loyal Kentuckians, but likewise deemed it prudent to establish his recruiting camp outside of the State, just opposite Louisville on the Indiana side. These measures had strengthened the Union sentiment greatly and borne fruit in the August State election, which resulted in an overwhelming victory for the loyalists, three-quarters of the new Legislature being of their persuasion. Nelson thereupon immediately established a recruiting camp on his native soil, called Camp Dick Robinson, in the central part of the State, between Danville and Lexington, and soon had gathered several thousand men together.

Meantime, the rebel leaders had not been idle. The "State Guards" had been strengthened. Mass meetings of their sympathizers were to be held during August at different points, at which it was presumed the secession of the State would be openly proclaimed and carried out by simultaneous military movements upon the State capital. Governor Magoffin was to furnish the pretence for the outbreak by making a formal demand upon President Lincoln for a discontinuance of Federal recruiting in the State, which, of course, would be refused. But the growth of the Union feeling brought these schemes to naught, and, when I reached Louisville, it was so greatly in the ascendant that the rebel leaders despaired of their ability to provoke rebellion in the State, and sought to persuade the rebel Government to compel it to share the fate of the Confederacy through invasion.

On September 5, the first news indicating that these efforts had been successful arrived. General Gideon J. Pillow had crossed the Mississippi the day before from the Arkansas side, with six thousand men, and occupied the Kentucky town of Columbus. Two weeks later, the still more startling announcement came that Buckner had invaded the State from the South with a rebel force of five thousand men. He had appeared in Washington in August, where he pretended to be determined to remain neutral, but suddenly disappeared, and made his way to Richmond, where he obtained a commission as brigadier-general, and immediately returned to his State to assume direction of the offensive movement by which it was expected to reach the Ohio and capture Louisville with a rush. He came very near succeeding. He seized the north-bound trains on the Louisville & Nashville Railroad, loaded them with his troops, and pushed on. But for the displacement of a rail by a loyalist, causing the wreck of a south-bound train and obstructing the traffic, he might have reached Louisville. As it was, he stopped at Elizabethtown, thirty-five miles from the city, and, hearing of the approach of Federal troops, became himself alarmed and ordered the railroad bridge over a fork of Salt River, in his front, to be burned. About the same time, intelligence was received of a third invasion from another direction. During the second week of September, General Zollicoffer had started with a division of eight to nine thousand men from Eastern Tennessee for the Cumberland Gap, and reached the Cumberland River about a week later. Thus the neutrality farce—it had been nothing else for months before—came to an end, and Kentucky became one of the theatres of the Civil War, and not the least bloody and devastated.

The rebel offensive against the State naturally led also to a radical change in the attitude of the Federal Government. Just before the occupation of Columbus, General Anderson had visited Washington for consultation, and he returned to Cincinnati with Brigadier-Generals W. T. Sherman and George H. Thomas, who were to serve under him. General Thomas was at once sent to take command of the camp formed by Nelson, and General Sherman to St. Louis to solicit aid for Kentucky from General Frémont. General Anderson himself assumed active command in Kentucky, transferring his headquarters to Louisville. My friend Captain Fry came with him as assistant adjutant-general. General Sherman also reported there to him on his return from the West.

The news of the rebel advances toward the centre of the State produced great excitement and, to tell the truth, consternation and fright in Louisville. Everybody believed that Buckner would make as fast as possible for the Ohio River, and Zollicoffer would lose no time in making for the State capital. There were practically no troops available for contesting such movements but the half-drilled volunteers in Rousseau's and Nelson's camps. I had visited both, and knew that they were very far from being ready to take the field. Indeed, they were not half as efficient as the three-months' men in the Bull Run campaign. Help was telegraphed for and promised by the Federal Government and by the Governors of Ohio and Indiana. But as none could be expected immediately, and as General Anderson fortunately had timely warning of Buckner's contemplated *coup de main,* he at once ordered Sherman to take Rousseau's men and the Louisville Home Guards, numbering in all about twenty-five hundred, and move them by rail to a commanding position known as Muldraugh's Hill, about twenty-eight miles south of the city, on the Louisville & Nashville Railroad. This was promptly done, and that point occupied and fortified as well as possible. Union scouting parties sent out from it ascertained, a few days later, the reassuring fact that Buckner had fallen back to Bowling Green on Green River. Zollicoffer's intended march northward from the Cumberland River to the Blue Grass region, the heart of the State, was also stopped by the counter-movements of General Thomas. Evidently, both sides had exaggerated ideas of each other's strength, and each was afraid of being attacked by the other. Yet I could not help thinking at the time, and still am of the opinion, that, if Buckner and Zollicoffer had really pushed vigorously on, they had a good chance of compelling the at least temporary abandonment of Kentucky by the Federal Government and getting possession of the important city of Louisville and the main railroad artery connecting the Ohio River with the South.

Thus I was thoroughly disappointed in my expectation that active operations would give me plenty of interesting work. The rebels made themselves as secure and comfortable as possible at Bowling Green and in front of the Cumberland Gap, and their opponents no longer looked for the appearance of the enemy "at any moment," but settled down to the work of drilling, disciplining, clothing, and equipping for the winter the Union forces already on the ground, and the reinforcements they steadily received by the arrival of newly-enlisted Ohio and Indiana regiments. By the end of September, nothing was left for me to do but to watch the curious developments in Washington and in Louisville, which I will now describe, in connection with military affairs in Kentucky.

Owing to his age and feeble health, General Anderson found himself unequal to the work and responsibility of his command, and asked to be relieved from duty soon after he had moved his headquarters to Louisville. His wish was reluctantly granted by President Lincoln, and a formal order to that effect issued by the War Department on October 7, and General Sherman directed to take his place. The change was not favorable for me, for, while General Anderson was very accessible and communicative to representatives of the press, General Sherman looked upon them as a nuisance and a danger at headquarters and in the field, and acted toward them accordingly, then as throughout his great war career. I did not, of course, agree with him at that time as to my own calling, but candor constrains me to say that I had to admit in the end that he was entirely right. For what I then observed, on the one hand, of the natural eagerness of volunteer officers of all grades (of whom so many were aspiring politicians at home) to get themselves favorably noticed in the press, even at the cost of indiscretions, and, on the other hand, of the indifference of press-men to military interests in publishing army news, must lead any unprejudiced mind to the conclusion that the harm certain to be done by war correspondents far outweighs any good they can possibly do. If I were a commanding general I would not tolerate any of the tribe within my army lines.

Under the circumstances, it was perfectly useless to approach General Sherman formally as a news-gatherer. I was, however, brought in contact with him in another and more satisfactory way. He appeared every night, like myself, at about nine o'clock, in the office of Mr. Tyler, to learn the news brought in the night Associated Press report. He knew me from the Bull Run campaign as a correspondent of the press. Furthermore, I had been especially commended to him by his brother John (then a member of the House, and subsequently Senator from Ohio and Secretary of the Treasury); and as we met on neutral ground and I asked him no questions, we were soon on very good terms. He was a great talker, and he liked nothing better than to express his mind upon the news as it came. There he sat, smoking a cigar (I hardly ever saw him without one), leaning back in a chair, with his thumbs in the armholes of his vest. Or he was pacing up and down the room, puffing away, with his head bent forward and his arms crossed behind his back. Every piece of military intelligence drew some comment from him, and it was easy to lead him into a long talk if the subject interested him. He expressed himself without any reserve about men and matters, trusting entirely to the good faith of his hearers, who, as a rule, consisted only of Mr. Tyler and myself. As will be readily believed, we found the hours thus spent in his company a great treat, although we did not dream of the celebrity the General was to achieve. I have often wished I had made notes of his sayings. His estimates of military and political leaders particularly would have been worth preserving. Nearly all of them proved to be correct.

In his conversations with us, he discussed also the political and military situation in Kentucky and his own task in connection with it, and I could not help thinking that, in so doing, he said more than was wise and proper. He openly confessed, after he had been assigned to the command of the department, that he had not wished it and was afraid of his new responsibilities. With the vivid imagination inherent to genius, he clearly saw how formidable were the difficulties of the part he was expected to play in the suppression of the Rebellion. They simply appalled him. He found himself in command of raw troops, not exceeding twenty thousand in number. He believed that they should be multiplied many times. He feared the rebel forces in the State largely outnumbered his own, and he could not rid himself of the apprehension that, if he should be attacked, he would have no chance of success. It was not really want of confidence in himself that brought him to this state of mind, but, as it seemed to me, his intense patriotism and despair of the preservation of the Union in view of the fanatical, bloodthirsty hostility to it throughout the South. This dread took such hold of him that, as I was informed by those who were in hourly official intercourse with him, he literally brooded over it day and night. It made him lapse into long, silent moods even outside his headquarters. He lived at the Galt House, occupying rooms on the ground floor. He paced by the hour up and down the corridor leading to them, smoking and obviously absorbed in oppressive thoughts. He did this to such an extent that it was generally noticed and remarked upon by the guests and employees of the hotel. His strange ways led to gossip, and it was soon whispered about that he was suffering from mental depression.

Such was his condition when Secretary Cameron arrived in Louisville for a conference with him. The Secretary had been to St. Louis to remonstrate with General Frémont about his extravagances and arbitrary assumption of power, and came to see General Sherman, who seemed to the Washington authorities to stand very much in need of being brought to reason, in view of his highly exaggerated theories as to the forces required for the extinction of the Rebellion in the Mississippi Valley. Secretary Cameron had with him Samuel Wilkeson, the Washington correspondent of the New York *Tribune*— afterwards for nearly twenty years secretary of the Northern Pacific Railroad Company—whom he allowed to listen to his official and confidential conversations with the General, without, however, disclosing Wilkeson's journalistic character. The conference is fully described in Sherman's Memoirs. The General demonstrated on a map his strategic programme for subduing the Confederacy. He indicated the lines of operation which the several Federal armies in process of formation should follow in the South. He also made an estimate of the numerical strength they should possess, and contended that, to destroy the military power of the Confederacy in the rebel States watered by the Mississippi and its eastern and western tributaries, would require not less than two hundred thousand men. This contention was so contrary to, or rather in advance of, the then still prevailing ideas of the limited power of resistance of the Confederacy and the means necessary to overcome it, that it startled the Secretary and excited doubts as to the state of the General's mind. Wilkeson told me, indeed, immediately after the conference, that Cameron thought the General was unbalanced by exaggerated fears as to the rebel strength, and that it would not do to leave him in command.

This was a great bit of news, but, in the public interest, I did not feel free to use it. My friend Murat Halstead, editor of the Cincinnati *Commercial*, being very much attached to the Sherman family, I communicated it to him in a private letter the same evening. But Halstead could not resist the temptation of utilizing the sensational information for his paper. To my painful surprise and great indignation, he printed, in the first issue after receiving my letter, an editorial paragraph saying in substance that "the country would learn with surprise and regret that Brigadier-General Sherman had become insane." Thus I was the innocent cause of the publication of this cruel misstatement, which resulted in so much annoyance and distress to the General and his friends. But the worst result of the conference was yet to come. In spite of the fact that Cameron had concealed Wilkeson's connection with the press, so that Sherman talked with much more freedom than he would otherwise have done, the Secretary allowed Wilkeson to print every detail of the talk in the *Tribune,* accompanied by sarcastic criticisms of the timorousness of the General and his absurd demands for troops, as evidenced by his requisition for two hundred thousand men, and also by broad insinuations that his mind was upset and that he could not safely be permitted to exercise an important command. This was an abominable outrage, and a striking illustration of the utter unconsciousness at the time, in ruling circles and withal in the public at large, of the detriment to public interests and especially to army discipline wrought by such scandalous improprieties. As was to be foreseen, General Sherman asked to be relieved from his command, and, early in November, his request was readily granted. In fact, it was the general impression that the design of the publication in the *Tribune* was to compel him to retire.

A new military department, "of the Ohio," was formed, and Brigadier-General Don Carlos Buell placed in command, with headquarters at Louisville, where he assumed charge in the second week of November. He held the same views regarding war correspondents as General Sherman, and would not allow them to approach him on any ground. But I continued to enjoy the special advantage of having a friend at court in Captain Fry. General Buell, besides his aversion to members of the press, was by nature reserved, taciturn, and cold in his manners—just the opposite of General Sherman. He repelled rather than attracted not only his subordinates, but all who came in contact with him. He was the choice of General McClellan for the position, and, like him, was destined to prove a failure.

I have referred to the exaggerated estimates of the rebel forces in his front that warped General Sherman's judgment. Together with the unreadiness of the troops under him, it had given rise to his disinclination to think of an early offensive as at all possible. One of the motives of the Government in substituting General Buell for him was its desire that something should be done for the relief of the loyalists in East Tennessee, whose steadfast adherence to the Union, in spite of the merciless persecution and oppression practised toward them by the rebel Government, appealed most strongly to the sympathies of the Northern States, and for whose protection active measures were warmly advocated in the press and in Congress. President Lincoln's interest in their cause was enlisted by the constant pleadings of Andrew Johnson, Horace Maynard, and other leaders on their behalf. He evidenced this by one of the famous documents of the war, the sketch of a plan which he had prepared, in the latter part of September, for an advance into East Tennessee, and sent to the War Department as a positive command, as shown by the first words: "On or about the fifth of October, I wish a movement made to seize and hold a point on the railroad connecting Virginia and Tennessee near the mountain pass called Cumberland Gap." The plan and the ways and means indicated for its execution were unquestionably sound, and proved, like similar emanations at later stages of the war, that Mr. Lincoln's perception of the military situation was a very creditable one.

It was expected that General Buell, upon whom the Commander-in-chief, General McClellan, had himself urged, in his verbal instructions, the necessity of prompt action, with the promise of reinforcements for that purpose, would not be long in starting an expedition for East Tennessee. But it soon turned out that he also was unwilling to take early action. The more his command was swelled by additional troops from the North, the less he apparently became inclined to take the field—this notwithstanding the eagerness of General George H. Thomas to go for Zollicoffer from central Kentucky. On November 25, McClellan repeated his previous oral and written instructions in the strongest language, saying in his letter: "I am still convinced that political and strategical considerations render a prompt movement in force on Eastern Tennessee imperative. . . . I think we owe it to our Union friends in East Tennessee to protect them at all hazards." He followed up this letter two days later with a despatch: "I urge movement at once on Eastern Tennessee unless it is impossible." But Buell did not budge. He pleaded that his troops were anything but ready to take the field. He described them as "little better than a mob." The fact that he was being vainly urged to move became public, and he was attacked in the press and in Congress. But this did not influence him any more than the orders and remonstrances of his superiors. These continued to reach him by mail and wire, but he contrived to find excuses for not complying.

In the latter part of December, the pressure from Washington at last extracted from him the admission that he had never really thought a movement into East Tennessee advisable, and that his programme was a defensive one in an eastern and an offensive one in a western direction. Finally, President Lincoln lost his long-tried patience, and on January 4 wired him: "Please tell me the progress and condition of the movement in the direction of East Tennessee. Answer." Buell, in his reply, amplified his previous admission that the East Tennessee movement had been decidedly against his judgment from the very first, as likely to render doubtful the success of "a movement against the great power of the Rebellion in the west, which is mainly arrayed on the line between Bowling Green and Columbus." President Lincoln replied by mail, commencing his letter thus: "Your despatch of yesterday has been received and disappoints and distresses me," and then argued that, in his judgment, the possession of the railroad between Virginia and East Tennessee seemed to him more important and more to be desired than that of Nashville. Next he lamented the sad fate of the loyalists, if left without help. "But my distress is," he said, "that our friends in East Tennessee are being hanged and driven to despair." "My despatch to you was sent with the knowledge of Senator Johnson and Representative Maynard, and they will be after me to know your answer, which I cannot safely show them." This characteristic wail of the President, with the extraordinary ending, "I do not intend this to be an order in any sense, but merely to show you the grounds of my anxiety," was followed by far more emphatic expressions from General McClellan. "I was extremely sorry," he wrote to Buell, "to learn from your telegram to the President that you had from the beginning attached little or no importance to a movement into East Tennessee. I had not so understood your views, and it develops a radical difference between yours and mine, which I deeply regret." He then gave his reasons for preferring a movement towards East Tennessee to one against Nashville, emphasizing the fact that "the latter would work a prejudicial change in my own plans." On January 13, McClellan wrote again in a way that obliged Buell to promise to comply with the wishes of his superiors. Yet he failed to keep his promise promptly, further excusing himself by reason of want of transportation and the impracticability of the roads.

Meantime, the lack of stirring events and the absolute silence imposed by General Buell's orders upon correspondents in regard to the large army under his command, on penalty of expulsion from the department, made time hang rather heavily on my hands. My social relations were too limited, for the reasons already explained, to relieve the monotony of my daily life. Moreover, no public entertainments of any kind were going on in Louisville, owing to the state of war. But I had a pleasant interruption of my dull existence by spending Christmas week among my friends in Cincinnati. The continual inclemency of the weather added no little to the dreariness of those winter months, during which not a single personal incident worth recording occurred.

My usefulness to my employers would thus not have

been very great but for the accidental discovery and exploitation of a new mine of valuable intelligence. The war having cut off all the former communications between the loyal and rebel States by mail and telegraph, railroad and steamboat, the Northern press was deprived of its regular supply of Southern news. Its scarcity very much increased the demand for and the value of it. The curiosity of the Northern public regarding current events in the South seemed to be even greater than about home affairs. It occurred to me during the fall that, what with the large number of Louisville people who had gone South to help the Confederates and their natural desire to hear from home and to be able to send tidings of themselves, some channel of intelligence might be opened. On close investigation I found out that there were men and women travelling regularly between Louisville and Nashville, who made it their business to carry letters, papers, and other things between the two points—a sort of "underground railroad." By paying liberally for them, I managed to receive through this agency all the leading papers in the South. With clippings from them, which I accompanied by proper comments, I made up regular budgets of Southern news, which became a highly prized feature of the *Herald*. None of its contemporaries was so well served in this respect as long as I remained stationed in Louisville.

CHAPTER XV

THE OCCUPATION OF NASHVILLE.—1862

THE quietude that reigned in Kentucky was suddenly broken in the latter part of January, 1862, by the collision between General Thomas and General Zollicoffer in what is known as the "battle of Mill Springs," though it hardly deserved the name. Zollicoffer, having established himself on the north bank of the Cumberland River, on the road from the Gap to the central part of the State, caused a good deal of annoyance and suffering by sending raiding parties in different directions, as well as by repeated advances and retreats with his main body, which were met by counter-movements by the Federal brigade of General Schoepf, charged by General Thomas to watch the enemy. To put an end to these inflictions, Buell finally authorized Thomas to advance with his division toward the Cumberland. He reached a point ten miles from the rebel encampment on January 18, with part of his forces. The enemy was apprised of his approach, and decided to attack him before all his command had come up. The encounter took place on the following day. Zollicoffer having been killed early in the fight, the rebels lost their cohesion, and were beaten back after a struggle of several hours. They retreated in disorder to their fortified camp at Mill Springs. The Unionists followed them closely and surrounded their position during the night. In the morning it was discovered that the enemy had crossed the Cumberland in the darkness, leaving behind them twelve pieces of artillery, small arms, supplies, and their wounded. It was a very creditable victory for the Union cause, as the rebel strength was one-third greater than General Thomas's; and it had a great moral effect in the loyal States. The principal part in it was borne by the Ninth Ohio Regiment, commanded by Colonel Robert L. McCook. He was a prominent lawyer and partner of John B. Stallo, the well-known German leader at Cincinnati, and was one of the famous family of which no less than ten members, comprising the father and nine sons, bore arms during the war. The regiment had been recruited from among the Germans of Ohio, and was officered in part by ex-officers of the Prussian army, who had brought it up to a high degree of drill and discipline. Colonel McCook himself was wounded. The way to Cumberland Gap and into East Tennessee was now unobstructed, and Thomas was ready to push forward, but he received no orders to that effect, and remained on the Cumberland until the important developments in western Kentucky shortly afterwards changed the entire course of events.

Before speaking of these, it will be proper to describe the composition of Buell's army, whose coming experiences I was to share. It had gradually increased through the fall and winter, by steady reinforcements, until it numbered nearly seventy-two thousand men on the rolls, of whom about three-quarters were effective. They included nearly eighty-four infantry regiments, organized in the States of Kentucky, Ohio, Indiana, Pennsylvania, Illinois, Wisconsin, and Minnesota; half a dozen regiments of cavalry from Kentucky, Indiana, and Ohio; and twenty batteries of six guns each. They first were formed into brigades of four foot regiments and one battery each, numbered consecutively up to twenty-one, and subsequently into six divisions, of four and three brigades, with a cavalry regiment each. The division commanders were, in the order of the numbers of their divisions, Brigadier-Generals George H. Thomas, Alexander McDowell McCook, Ormsby M. Mitchel (a regular-army officer), William Nelson (who had been formally transferred in August from the navy to the army, with the rank of brigadier-general),

Thomas L. Crittenden, and Thomas J. Wood (of the regular army). Among the brigade commanders figured a number who afterwards became well known, such as M. D. Manson, L. H. Rousseau, R. W. Johnson, J. S. Negley, J. B. Turchin, Jacob Ammen, W. B. Hazen, Charles Cruft, M. S. Hascall, and C. G. Harker. During the active operations that followed, I had the opportunity of making the acquaintance of nearly all of these commanders and entering into friendly relations with a number of them, which continued even after the close of the war.

All through November, December, and January there had been, as is shown by the printed official records, correspondence by wire and mail between the Government at Washington and Generals McClellan, Halleck (who had superseded Frémont as commander-in-chief of the military department comprising Missouri and Illinois), and Buell, regarding the future programme for combined action upon the Western theatre of war. As early as the latter half of November, Buell had expressed himself in a general way in favor of using the Cumberland and Tennessee Rivers as offensive lines, with Nashville as the main objective-point. Halleck favored the line of the Tennessee alone, as the movements along two lines would require too much force. But Buell did not urge his general suggestion, nor submit any plans in detail. Hence the protracted discussion had led to no agreement or decision up to the end of January. Buell had, however, slowly crept with his forces nearer the rebel front at Bowling Green, and, at that time, his lines extended from near that place eastwardly to Glasgow, Columbia, and Somerset. He still believed that the rebel forces in his front under Albert Sidney Johnston outnumbered him, and, owing to this illusion, his every forward step was characterized by excessive caution. The truth was, that Johnston's command was only little more than one-third as strong as Buell's army.

The dissensions and hesitations of the commanding generals were brought to an end in an unexpected manner. At the close of January, General Grant, in command at Cairo, and Rear-Admiral Foote, commanding the fleet of river gunboats, succeeded, after several vain attempts, in extracting permission from General Halleck to attack and, if possible, capture Fort Henry, constructed by the rebels for the defence of the Tennessee River near its mouth. On February 6, the loyal public was made joyful by the laconic news from General Grant: "Fort Henry is ours," with the hope-inspiring addition: " I shall take and destroy Fort Donelson on the eighth." The latter fort was erected at a distance of only a day's march from Fort Henry to lock the Cumberland against Northern troops and gunboats. When Grant sent this confident despatch, he had no idea how difficult it would be to make good his word, and how important his success would be in really determining the whole course of the war in the Mississippi and Ohio valleys. The moment he received the news of the fall of Fort Henry, the rebel commander Johnston, at Bowling Green, realizing the danger it involved of the capture of Fort Donelson and of thereby having the centre of the rebel line from Bowling Green to Columbus pierced and his own left flank turned through the opening of the Cumberland and Tennessee Rivers to the Federals, held a council of war, at which, on his recommendation, it was decided to abandon his long-held position in Kentucky for the protection of Tennessee, and to fight for that object at Fort Donelson. This resolution was carried out with admirable promptitude. Fourteen thousand infantry were at once detached, under the command of Generals Buckner and Floyd, for the reinforcement of Donelson, and sent by rail to Clarksville and thence the short distance down the river by boat. The remaining eight thousand of the twenty-two thousand men, all told, that Johnston's army actually consisted of, broke camp and fell back on Nashville. Donelson was further reinforced by four thousand men from General Pillow's command. This throwing of a heavy force into the fort was sound and justified by the circumstances, but it utterly miscarried, owing to the determined offensive of General Grant and the lack of fighting spirit in the garrison. On February 16, the Northern States were electrified by the astonishing tidings of the unconditional surrender of Donelson with fifteen thousand rebels (including General Buckner), twenty thousand stands of arms, forty-eight small and seventeen heavy guns, thousands of horses, and great quantities of commissary and quartermaster's stores.

This great triumph of General Grant not only raised the patriotic enthusiasm of the loyal people to the highest pitch, but instantly broke the spell of apprehension that had kept the Union commanders in the West on the defensive. The force of events carried them irresistibly along. It ended the conflict of their strategic theories by compelling them to take advantage of the unexpected achievement on the Cumberland, which did nothing less than open the way for the Union armies to the very heart of the Confederacy west of the Alleghanies.

Already the fall of Fort Henry had roused Halleck and Buell. They had early information of the abandonment of Bowling Green by the enemy, and correctly divined that Johnston meant to use his forces to save Donelson. Buell was ready enough to take up his former plan of moving up the two rivers. He took the initiative in supporting Grant's operations by ordering Cruft's 13th brigade, stationed at Calhoun on the lower Green River, to join Grant, which it did in time to participate in the attack on Donelson. He started eight additional unassigned regiments by water for the same purpose, and, in response to an appeal from Halleck, he ordered three of his divisions, under Thomas, Nelson, and Crittenden, to make as quickly as possible for Louisville and embark thence on steamboats down the Ohio for the Cumberland. They could not get under way from Louisville, however, until the day of the surrender of Donelson. In consequence of that event, the other three divisions of Buell were at once ordered to move in forced marches upon Nashville. Buell himself joined the advance of General Mitchel's division. The march was made so rapidly that some of the cavalry arrived at Edgefield on the north bank of the Cumberland, opposite Nashville, on the morning of Sunday, the 23d. General Buell himself did not reach the same point with the division, nine thousand strong, till the evening of the following day. He was met there by the mayor of Nashville and a committee of citizens, who reported the evacuation of the city by the Confederate forces, and obtained an appointment for the next morning for the formal surrender. The destruction by the rebels of the suspension bridge for ordinary traffic, as well as of the railroad bridge across the Cumberland, made it impossible for General Buell to enter the city immediately. This deprived him of the satisfaction of being the first Federal commander in the capital of Tennessee, for, early next morning, a fleet of boats, escorted by the gunboat *Conestoga*, came in sight with a large body of his own troops under command of General Nelson, who landed at once and took possession.

The inspiring news of the attack on Fort Donelson caused me much perplexity. I had been at the front a fortnight before the capture of Fort Henry, but returned to Louisville when I learned of the decision to send reinforcements to Grant by the river route, with a view to accompany them. General Nelson, whose division was to take part in that expedition, invited me to come on his boat. I accepted and expected to go on board on the morning of the 16th. But the reports from Donelson in the morning papers of that day indicated such confidence by General Grant in its impending fall that I concluded to wait another day before deciding upon my course, lest, by starting down the Ohio, I might be too late for the capture of the fort, and also miss some important movement by General Buell. I went early in the evening to the Associated Press office, and impatiently awaited, with half a dozen others, the night report. The very first sentence announced the surrender of Donelson, and made all present break out into shouts of delight. I congratulated myself on my wisdom in not going with General Nelson, but in the morning I was obliged to doubt whether I had chosen the better part, on learning that Buell, on hearing of Grant's success, had immediately put his army in motion for Nashville. My quandary was, however, solved on ascertaining later in the day that, in addition to Nelson's division, the divisions of Generals Thomas and Crittenden had been ordered to embark as fast as possible for the Cumberland. Learning that I could not overtake Buell by land, I made up my mind to go by water. Fortunately, a boat started down the river the same evening, with quartermaster's and commissary's stores for Nelson's division. Captain Miller, of the Galt House, knew the captain, and introduced me to him, thanks to which I was very well taken care of on the trip. I left most of my belongings behind, and set out, wearing my campaign army-blue suit and a regulation overcoat.

We reached Fort Donelson the next morning. It lay in a bend of the river on steeply rising bluffs, about a hundred feet above the water. We found a great fleet of boats, including those having on board Nelson's command, which was waiting for telegraphic orders. It took us some hours to make a good landing, owing to the number of craft in the way, and it was nearly dark before I managed to find General Nelson. No orders had yet reached him. He repeated his invitation to come on his boat, but, seeing that it was very crowded, and being assured by him that my boat would follow him wherever he went, I thought it best not to change. We were kept stationary and uncertain as to our final destination for four days. But I found myself in the midst of striking scenes of actual war that made our stay most interesting. There was the Fort itself, a rectangular work, inclosing about one hundred acres, with high ramparts and well-protected water-batteries of heavy guns; its earthen embankments ploughed and torn by our gunboat fire. There were camps of Union soldiers and of rebel prisoners, but few of whom had yet been sent North. The great majority of the latter were only partially uniformed, or were wholly in civilian clothes, and presented a very motley, dirty, and anything but respect-inspiring appearance. I talked much with them, and found them very ready, as defeated soldiers always are, to blame and denounce their officers. There was a chaos of thousands of captured wagons, horses, and mules. Mournful was the sight of long rows of fresh graves containing the killed on both sides, and of the field-hospitals crowded with Federal and Confederate wounded. A striking border to this picture was formed by the score and more of side-wheel and stern-wheel steamboats and grim-looking gunboats, puffing, blowing, and whistling, loaded with human and other freight. Altogether, there was enough to see and describe to keep me fully occupied. In one respect I was, however, disappointed. I failed to see "Unconditional Surrender" Grant, as he did not leave his boat while we remained, and, not knowing anybody on it, I did not feel bold enough to go on board.

At last, on the afternoon of the fourth day, orders reached General Nelson to proceed up the river as far as Clarksville and there await further instructions. We immediately got under way, and reached our destination in a few hours. The banks were well settled and quite attractive. We anchored in the river, not far from the great bridge of the railroad from Louisville to Memphis. Again our patience was tried by lying still for more than twenty-four hours, after which, late in the afternoon of the twenty-fourth, the welcome report came that the way to Nashville was clear, and that we should start for that city at daybreak next morning.

Accordingly, our flotilla of seven boats, convoyed by the gunboat *Conestoga*, got in motion in single file up the river as soon as there was light enough to find the way. The valley proved to be quite picturesque. Bluffs of a very diversified character, now of solid, barren rock, and again heavily timbered, rose close to the banks or bordered wide bottoms forming rich plantations. Half an hour before reaching Nashville, we passed Fort Zollicoffer, an unfinished river-battery with eight guns in position, but deserted. Soon after, we caught sight of the imposing State capitol, standing upon the highest hill within the city limits. A little further, and the ruins of the two bridges connecting the city with the north bank of the river came into view, and in twenty minutes more we were tied to a wharf at the foot of one of the leading streets.

Nashville had then a population of less than twenty thousand. (It had more than eighty thousand in 1890.) It was compactly and regularly built up over an undulating area, rising rather steeply at first and then more gradually from the river to a broken plateau. The lower streets, as in all river-towns the world over, were devoted to business, and the upper ones to residential purposes. The site was crowned by the hill on which the great Statehouse—greater in size than in correct architectural style—occupied a most commanding position. The business buildings, as well as the private residences, were mostly made of brick and stone, and had a solid but unpretentious look, although the style and proportions of a number of the homes gave evidence of wealthy ownership. Altogether, the appearance of the place indicated considerable thrift, and impressed me more as that of a Northern than of a Southern city.

I was among the very first to jump ashore. We supposed General Buell to have taken possession, and were surprised to learn that we were the first "invaders" to enter the city. Having learned also that not a single Confederate soldier remained in it, I did not hesitate to set out alone to see the place and to gather information as to the local events previous to our arrival. In an hour I had walked through all the principal streets. I found the wholesale and retail stores and most of the better class of residences shut up. Very few whites, but plenty of blacks were visible. The State-house presented a curious sight. I discovered only one person—a colored doorkeeper—in the big edifice that had contained, but a few days before, the whole State Government and the State Legislature with all its throng of attendants. They had all "done gone" a week ago, as the sole occupant informed me. Not a door was locked, and a good many stood wide open, indicating a most rapid disappearance of the executive and legislative branches. They had adjourned as far west as was possible within the State limits, viz., to Memphis.

I next sought the American House, the leading hotel, in order to secure board and lodging. The house was open, but seemed utterly deserted. After much ringing of the office bell, a colored man appeared, who, on my inquiry for the proprietor, answered, with a broad grin: "Massa done gone souf." Not a guest had been entertained for several days, and he could not tell what would be done with the hotel. But I boldly ordered him to show me the better rooms and selected the best one, which I told him to reserve against all comers till I returned. I hurried back to the boat, got my saddle-bag and said good-bye to the captain, and within half an hour had taken actual possession of the room. It was well I had acted thus promptly, for, by noon, the hotel swarmed with other correspondents and staff-officers. A quartermaster's clerk with hotel experience was put in charge, the chief cook hunted up, and, with the supplies found in the store-room and meat procured from a butcher, the caravansary was soon in full running order. In a few days the proprietor returned and resumed control.

I lost no time, after securing my quarters, in making for the office of the *Daily American,* the principal paper of the city. I purchased the back numbers for three weeks and found them a mine of interesting information. Especially were the full accounts of what happened in the city after the fall of Donelson of great value to me and to Captain Fry, Buell's chief of staff, to whom I lent them in the evening, as they gave him a clear idea of the rebel military movements throughout the South. I found one of the owners and some of the editors of the paper in the office. I introduced myself as a "Northern colleague," and they were evidently very glad to have some one to consult with as to the course they should pursue. They had continued the publication up to that day, but were in doubt whether it would be safe and profitable for them to go on with it. I advised them to do so by all means, but to print only news from the North and South and local intelligence, without any editorials or biased comments. I assured them that the military authorities would allow this. They followed my suggestion and printed the paper right along. Within a few days, they were able to publish the Northern Associated Press reports, but their Southern news naturally became meagre.

According to appointment, the mayor, B. B. Cheatham, a member of the prominent family of that name, which played a conspicuous part on the Southern side during the Rebellion, called on General Buell, at Edgefield, with a deputation of leading citizens, shortly after our landing. He received assurances that, in view of the surrender of the city at discretion, all law-abiding persons and their property would receive the fullest protection from the Federal troops. Soon after the conference, General Buell crossed over with his staff on a boat, and established his headquarters in a commodious mansion abandoned by its owner. The transfer of the troops he had led also commenced, and on that and the next day about fifteen thousand "Yanks" marched through the streets to encampments selected for them in the suburbs. For ten days, additional arrivals took place to the number of thousands a day, including the divisions that had marched from Bowling Green, as well as those carried up the Cumberland by boats, and before the middle of March the whole of Buell's army was concentrated about Nashville. The only troops quartered in the city, however, were a large provost-marshal's guard, charged with preventing officers and soldiers from entering the city except on duty or with proper permits, which were only sparingly granted.

The mayor at once issued a proclamation announcing the promise of protection and maintenance of order by General Buell, and calling upon all citizens to resume their occupations, and especially to reopen all stores for business, which was gradually done. He also called on the farmers of the vicinity to resume bringing their supplies to the city markets. This was quite in contrast with the bombastic manifesto issued by the Governor of the State, Isham G. Harris, at Memphis, against the ruthless invaders of Tennessee's soil.

A brief account of what happened in Nashville after the fall of Donelson and before the advent of the Federals will be in place here. The rebel commander-in-chief, Johnston, reached Nashville ahead of his troops on February 17, and at once informed the State and city authorities of the impossibility of defending the city, and his direct intention of retreating with his forces beyond it. He expressed his fear at the same time that the Federal gunboats and troops might appear within a few hours. The suddenness and portentousness of this announcement, which immediately became known to the inhabitants, produced at once the deepest consternation among all classes. The measures adopted by the Confederate commander before abandoning the city to its fate intensified the general fright into a regular panic. In order to obstruct and delay the Federal pursuit, the destruction of the railroad and suspension bridges was ordered and carried out—a wanton, useless act, as the height of the river made its use by the largest boats practicable. This only increased the general scare, as indicating want of faith in the re-establishment of Confederate rule. The papers stated that "this brutal outrage upon the city was perpetrated against the earnest and persistent protest of the leading citizens."

Next in folly was the conduct of the officers of the rebel commissary and quartermaster's department, who hastily abandoned their posts, and, before doing so, threw open the magazines holding the immense stores of miscellaneous supplies for the Confederate army, and allowed the public to help themselves to them in order to prevent their falling into the hands of the enemy. Naturally, a wild scramble for this public prey ensued among the lower classes, and, as might have been expected, led to disorder and violence. A lawless, defiant mob had virtual possession of the city. The newspapers reported the street scenes that were enacted for several days as "beggaring description." "The untiring energy of the mayor and city authorities was inadequate to keep down the selfish, grasping spirit from running riot." "Irish laborers and negroes competed with '*gentlemen*' in '*toting*' off '*hog*,' flour, sugar, crackers, clothing, and other things." The Governor at the same time pranced about the streets on horseback, vainly appealing for volunteer help in removing the State records. At a subsequent investigation ordered by the Confederate Congress, it was proved that the loss to the rebel Government from this authorized plundering was over one million dollars, and that it was an entirely unwarranted and culpable waste of public property, as almost a whole week elapsed before the Federals appeared after the retreat of Johnston. The pillage was finally stopped by the energy of the rebel cavalry leader Forrest, who later attained such notoriety as a daring and successful raider. With a command of only forty men, he succeeded in restoring order after several days, and maintained it till our arrival compelled his retirement.

The panic manifested itself in a general effort to run away from the coming "ruthless Northern hordes." The reckless falsehoods that had been circulated by the Southern press about the savage warfare waged by the Northern armies, now bore their natural fruit. Having been constantly told that slaughter, pillage, "booty and beauty" were their insatiate longing, thousands sought safety in instant flight, abandoning homes and business and taking with them only what they could carry on their persons or in vehicles. Even the many sick and wounded soldiers from the hospital swelled the tide. The general fear, in view of the fate of the bridges, that the city would be burned so that the "Yankees" might find another Moscow, had much to do with this needless hegira. There were, indeed, some crazy secessionists who openly proclaimed their purpose to fire every house in the city.

Two days after our landing, I had the satisfaction of getting my first view of "Unconditional Surrender" Grant. He had unexpectedly come up from Clarksville, by boat, for a conference with General Buell. I met him with his staff riding up to the latter's headquarters. I could not help feeling rather disappointed by the commonplace appearance of the man. He stayed only a few hours, but took time to see the city and to pay his respects to the widow of ex-President Polk, who made her home in a stately mansion on the finest residence street, and was one of the few Nashville gentlewomen not scared away by the dread of the Northern vandals. Mrs. Polk, while not concealing her Southern sympathies, received him in a very ladylike manner. Her behavior was very different from that experienced by the Grant party from other women, having the appearance of ladies, in passing through the streets. These "Yankee haters" went so far as to show their venom by spitting contemptuously, sticking out their tongues, and hissing like snakes. I can bear personal testimony that such low manifestations of viragoism were of frequent occurrence during the first weeks after the Federal occupation; but they gradually disappeared.

I am tempted to recall, in this connection, that Grant's visit to Nashville came very near bringing his career as a Federal commander to an early end. He undertook the trip without giving notice, as required by the general field orders, of his intended absence from his command to his immediate superior, General Halleck, who in very strong terms reported this neglect of duty to the War Department, which replied giving him authority to relieve the offender from duty and put him under arrest. Halleck had also wired a severe reprimand to Grant, on receiving which the latter asked to be relieved before the order to the same effect had come by mail from Washington. But the difficulty was made up, most fortunately for the Union cause.

I had plenty to do for a fortnight in writing up the "past and present." Communication by mail and telegraph with the North was opened within forty-eight hours after Buell's advent, and the first week I sent letters daily, and the second every other day. Military and other affairs in and about the city had then, however, settled down to a regular routine, so that material grew very scarce. Not a shot had been fired by either side in occupying and retreating from Nashville, nor was any sound of war heard afterward, so complete had been the disappearance of the rebels from the adjacent portions of Tennessee. Unfortunately for the loyal cause, there was no unity of appreciation among the Federal commanders of the logical strategic consequences of the February victories, or proper recognition of the vital importance of following them up with enterprise and energy. They were engaged for weeks in telegraphing suggestions and counter-suggestions, and, before they had agreed among themselves whether it would be best to advance from Nashville or from middle Tennessee or down the Mississippi, the enemy's movements were again to determine their own. Thus Buell's army remained encamped about Nashville, making good use of the time, however, by assiduous drilling and by completing its field equipment. The Tennessee capital became a new base of operations, and supplies of every kind and of ammunition were accumulated as fast as possible by rail and river.

The monotony into which matters had fallen was relieved

by the advent in Nashville, about the middle of March, of Andrew Johnson. As United States Senator from Tennessee, he had achieved great renown and popularity, upon the outbreak of the Rebellion, by his unswerving, passionate loyalty. On the fall of Nashville, President Lincoln nominated him brigadier-general of volunteers, and, on his immediate confirmation by the Senate, vested him with the special function of Military Governor for the State of Tennessee, which he was to exercise till a regular civil government, faithful to the Union, could be re-established. He took possession, very properly, of the capitol, and at once adopted very vigorous measures for the assertion of his authority and the protection of the loyalists in the State. One of his first acts was to call on the mayor and the city council to take the oath of loyalty to the Federal Government. They refused to do this, by a vote of sixteen to one, whereupon Governor Johnson issued an order removing them and appointing an "acting" mayor, who thenceforth administered the affairs of the city without the control of a council. I saw Johnson almost daily, and watched him closely, in his official and his private relations. My judgment of him was that, while he was doubtless a man of unusual natural parts, he had too violent a temper and was too much addicted to the common Southern habit of free indulgence in strong drink. These failings really unfitted him for his task, and he proved even then as little qualified for the proper fulfilment of high executive responsibilities as he did three years later when a national calamity made him an accidental President of the United States.

Another noted character, popularly known as "Parson Brownlow," appeared about the same time at Nashville. He was a popular preacher in East Tennessee when the Rebellion broke out, and, upon the first active secession movements in the Cotton States, denounced them with extraordinary boldness, energy, and ability, from both the pulpit and the rostrum. He had all the fervor of a regular camp-meeting exhorter, and by his homely, stirring eloquence became the moral mainstay of loyalism in his native section. He defied the rebel sympathizers and authorities there with unflinching bravery, and, in spite of all threats, never ceased to stand up for the Union and denounce secession until he was arrested and imprisoned. After a confinement of several weeks, he was exchanged for a prominent rebel officer, on condition that he should leave East Tennessee. This brought him to Nashville. I was amazed to find in him a tall, thin, beardless, hectic man, who moved about with difficulty and spoke with a husky voice. But, while his bodily weakness was extreme, his strength of spirit seemed unabated. He was a very entertaining talker, and spoke most movingly, with flashing eyes and pointing finger, of the wrongs to himself and his fellow-Tennesseeans. He stayed only a few days in Nashville, and then took a boat for the North in response to pressing invitations to speak in the larger cities, including the national capital, which President Lincoln himself had urged him to visit. Later, he was elected United States Senator by the loyal legislature organized by Andrew Johnson, and was admitted to the Senate.

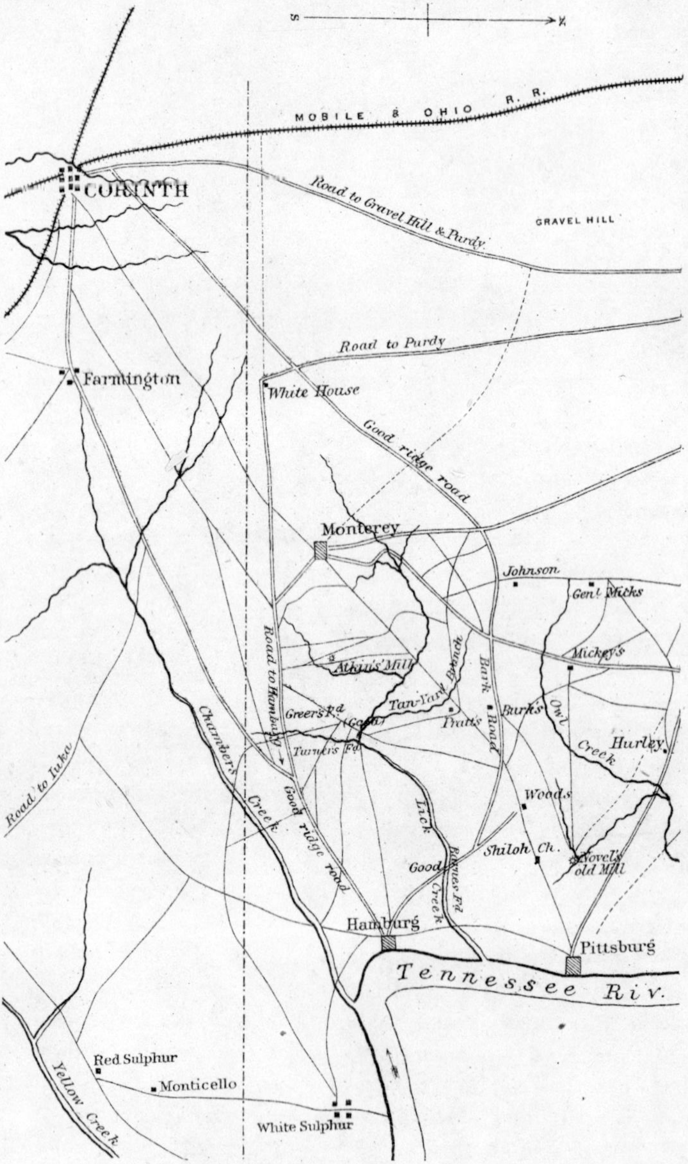

JULIUS BIEN & CO. N.Y.

CHAPTER XVI

The Battle of Shiloh.—1862

GENERAL A. S. JOHNSTON had fallen back at first from Nashville in a southeasterly direction, to Murfreesboro', where he strengthened his force by reinforcements from Kentucky and Tennessee to the number of nineteen thousand, and then moved by rail to the Memphis & Charleston Railroad and over this road to its junction with the Mobile & Ohio Railroad at Corinth, in the northeast corner of Mississippi. This railroad centre was selected as the point of concentration for all the available rebel forces west of the Appalachian Mountains, as from it they could be readily used for the protection of both the middle rebel States and the Mississippi Valley. At Corinth, Johnston found General Beauregard with ten thousand men, and their united command continued to receive accessions. The Union commanders became aware of the proposed rebel concentration early in March, and decided upon their future operations accordingly.

Very strong opinions have been expressed by competent critics, during and since the war, that it was a grave mistake of our military leaders to make for the point chosen by the enemy instead of drawing him away from it by strategic moves and compelling him to meet them upon a field chosen by themselves. It is not for me, however, to discuss the merits or demerits of what was to be known as the Shiloh campaign, but simply to record the fact that Generals Halleck and Buell reached an understanding that the latter's army should join that of General Grant at Savannah on the Tennessee River. The operations of the united armies were to be conducted under the chief command of General Halleck. The railroads being destroyed, there remained for General Buell only the long march from Nashville to Savannah, for which he accordingly prepared.

The orders for the march were issued on March 14. Five divisions—to wit, the First, Second, Fourth, Fifth, and Sixth, under Generals Thomas, McCook, Nelson, Crittenden, and Wood, aggregating thirty-seven thousand effective men—were to move under the direct command of General Buell, while the Third, under General Mitchel, and the newly-formed Seventh, under Brigadier-General G. W. Morgan, were to remain behind to protect Nashville and clear middle Tennessee of rebels, and to take possession of and repair the railroads in that portion of the State. The route to be followed led first in a southerly direction to the considerable towns of Franklin and Columbia, thence turned to the southwest as far as Lawrenceburg, and from this point almost due west through Waynesboro' to Savannah, a total distance of about one hundred and ten miles. On March 15, a cavalry force was sent to save the bridges at the two first-mentioned places, but they had already been destroyed. McCook's division started the next day as the head of the army. The Fourth, Fifth, Sixth, and First divisions followed in the order mentioned, with an interval of a day between them.

I accompanied General McCook by invitation, messing with his division quartermaster. I was well mounted on a fine-looking, strong black horse that I had bought at a low price at Nashville. General Buell had no instructions to hasten, and hence we moved at a moderate pace. The marching, too, was easy at first, over the fine turnpikes from Nashville to Columbia. The country was rolling, picturesque, and well cultivated, the home of large slaveholders living in fine brick mansions on their broad plantations until frightened off by the invaders. The crossing of the stream at Franklin was not difficult, but when we reached Columbia, thirty-five miles from

Nashville, on the third day, we were stopped by the swollen waters of the Duck River, which proved so wide and deep that we had the alternative of bridging it or of waiting for its subsidence. Strange to say, General Buell's army was not provided with any pontoons. The construction of a bridge being decided upon, General R. W. Johnson's brigade of McCook's division was detailed to erect it. The work was mainly performed by the numerous mechanics in the Thirty-second Indiana Regiment, entirely composed of Germans and commanded by Colonel August von Willich. He was descended from the old military family of that name in Prussia, and had been an artillery officer in the Prussian service until he embraced the revolutionary cause in 1848 and 1849. After its failure, he became an exile. He had brought his regiment up to a high point of drill and discipline. It was considered the best in Buell's army in these respects. I made the Colonel's acquaintance on this occasion, and found him a stern and most able and energetic soldier, with astonishingly radical political views for one of his antecedents. The personal relations then formed continued till his death, long after the close of the war.

The bridge construction delayed us ten days on Duck River, and thereby came near entailing disastrous consequences upon the Union cause that might have changed the outcome of the Civil War. As all Buell's advices from Halleck indicated that he (Buell) would meet Grant on the right bank of the Tennessee—that is, with the river between them and the enemy—he felt no apprehension as to Grant's safety before his junction with him. But, unknown to him, it had been decided to transfer Grant's command to the left bank at Pittsburg Landing, some eight miles above Savannah. This transposition, together with the knowledge of Buell's detention at Columbia, had determined A. S. Johnston and Beauregard to strike a blow at Grant before he was reinforced by Buell. The official records make it plain that they would thus have succeeded in overwhelming Grant at Shiloh and destroying his army but for the inspiration or foreboding of Buell's division commanders. The naval soldier, General Nelson, in his ever alert, anxious loyalty, grew fearful that Grant was in great danger from the rebel concentration at Corinth. He urged Buell in the last week of March to hurry to his relief as rapidly as possible, but failed to convince him of the need of any haste. His commander, moreover, pointed out the difficulty of resuming the march before the completion of the bridge over Duck River, which would be finished anyway in a few days. Nelson then offered to get his division over the river by fording it, as the river had rapidly fallen and reached its ordinary stage. Buell yielded to his earnest pleading for permission to try this, and even consented to his forming the advance in place of the Second Division, in case not only his infantry, but also his cavalry and artillery and trains, could be got across. The venturesome mariner immediately commenced his preparations, and on the 28th issued formal orders for the experiment. Reveille was sounded at four A.M. the next day, and in two hours his command was ready to move, with one day's rations in their haversacks.

Having obtained General Nelson's permission to accompany him, I was on the bank at six o'clock, a witness to very exciting and amusing scenes. As each infantry regiment reached the ford, the men, stripping off their pantaloons, rolled them up into small bundles which they carried on the points of their fixed bayonets. The cartridge-boxes were hung around their necks. The men then waded into the river, which was about one hundred and seventy-five feet wide at the ford, and made the passage without any difficulty, the bottom being hard and the greatest depth of water not exceeding three and one-half feet. Approaches having been made down the steep bank, the cavalry, artillery, and wagons effected the crossing also, with but small mishaps, and the whole division was safely encamped on the south bank before dark. The experiment was not repeated by the other troops, as the bridge was completed the next day and McCook's division made use of it on the second day. But the structure was narrow and not strong enough to bear great weight, so that much caution had to be used in moving the army over it. The passage took four days. Nelson's fording exploit was looked upon as an uncalled-for piece of bravado by his fellow-commanders and the rank and file of the army generally. But the two days' start he gained thereby for his division was to be a great boon to the Union cause.

The Fourth Division started early on the 29th en route for Savannah. Instead of hard turnpikes, we found now ordinary dirt roads, which the rain that had set in soon reduced to six and more inches of mud. They were so narrow that the fences on each side had to be thrown down to make room for the troops. The soil deteriorated, too, and the smaller size of the farms and the inferior cultivation indicated plainly that we were no longer in a region where the "peculiar institution" prevailed, but in the domain of the "poor whites." It was very sparsely settled, and we passed only at long intervals a few struggling hamlets consisting of a small number of unpainted, shabby frame buildings. Even the so-called towns we came through—Lawrenceburg, Mount Pleasant, and Waynesboro'—were so small as not to deserve to be called even "villages," and had a very thriftless, decayed appearance. Rain continued to fall and seemed to grow heavier from day to day. It made the march a very dreary and trying one to the troops. In spite of all efforts, no more than an average of ten miles a day could be accomplished, owing to the heaviness of the roads. As the trains followed in the rear of the division, the hardship of bivouacking without tents was imposed on all except the commanders and their staffs, who managed to occupy the few human habitations. I had a roof over me every night, but had to sleep on the bare floor.

Either before or after leaving Columbia, General Buell

decided to make a halt for concentration and rest at Waynesboro', two days' easy march from Savannah, and advised Generals Halleck and Grant, and instructed his division commanders, accordingly. By a fortunate delay of the cavalry detail carrying the order, it failed to reach General Nelson. For some reason or other, the other division commanders also did not receive their orders before passing Waynesboro', so that General Buell's plan (regarding which Halleck wired him as late as April 5, "You are right about concentrating at Waynesboro' ") to stop there for a few days miscarried. Buell notified Grant on April 3 from his camp, seven miles south of Columbia, that he would come right through to Savannah with his leading division. He rode so rapidly with his staff that, on the evening of the following day, he could send a message to Grant three miles west of Waynesboro' (a field-telegraph line had been erected by an advance party), that he desired to meet him in Savannah the next day. He also asked for information about the position and strength of the enemy. Grant answered from Savannah on the 5th: "Your despatch just received. I will be here to meet you to-morrow. The enemy at and near Corinth from sixty to eighty thousand. Information deemed reliable." This message constitutes indisputable proof that its author did not dream of the fearful struggle that burst upon him the next day.

In the meantime, Nelson pushed along with his division as fast as possible. His cavalry advance reached Savannah on the afternoon of April 3; himself and his staff, with whom I rode, and the leading brigade arrived early on the 5th. Savannah turned out to be no better than the villages we had passed. It was situated on elevated ground some distance from the river. As it was already crowded with various headquarters and surrounded by train-camps, camping-grounds for Nelson's division were selected about one and a half miles east of the place. Having hardly a dry thread on me, owing to the incessant rain, I concluded to ride to the river and try for quarters on one of the several boats made fast to the bank. Luckily, I succeeded in this, which meant not only a chance to dry my clothes, but also my first decent meal in almost a week and twelve hours' unbroken sleep in a good bed. General Buell, with his staff and body-guard,[1] also reached Savannah on the evening of the 5th, but so late that he did not try to hunt up General Grant before his appointment with him for the next day, and simply notified him of his arrival.

Early in the morning, the report of musketry and artillery fire was heard from up the river. It was so heavy that General Buell felt sure a serious conflict had commenced. He hastened to Grant's headquarters only to find that he had already started up the river, leaving the following message for him:

SAVANNAH, April 6 [Sunday], 1862.

Heavy firing is heard up the river, indicating plainly that an attack has been made upon our most advanced positions. I have been looking for this, but did not believe that the attack could be made before Monday or Tuesday. This necessitates my joining the forces up the river instead of meeting you to-day as I had contemplated. I have directed Nelson to move to the river with his division.

It must be admitted that, if Grant had really been "looking for this," it was his duty as commander-in-chief to be with his troops and not miles away and separated from them by a river. His absence involved, indeed, the lack of unity of command, the most essential condition of success in battle, and actually compelled his division commanders to take care of themselves as best they could.

---

[1] A select company of young Philadelphians of the better classes, especially recruited for this service and commanded by William J. Palmer, who, after the war, made quite a name for himself as a railroad builder and manager in connection with the Denver & Rio Grande system. The company, I believe, was afterwards increased to a regiment, and Palmer came out of the war with the rank of brigadier-general.

When he reached the scene of the conflict, the worst blows had already been suffered by his forces.

The directions to General Nelson referred to in Grant's message were in the following form:

An attack having been made upon our forces, you will move your entire command to the river opposite Pittsburg Landing. You can easily obtain a guide in the village.

As General Buell had reported his arrival the night before to General Grant, the issue of this order direct to Nelson can be explained only on the theory that Grant failed to hear of Buell's presence. This is confirmed by the following message sent by Grant after he had learned in person the condition of his command at Pittsburg Landing, not to General Buell, but to the "Commanding Officer, Federal forces, near Pittsburg, Tennessee."

GENERAL: The attack upon my forces has been very spirited from early this morning. The appearance of fresh troops on the field now would have a powerful effect, both by inspiring our men and disheartening the enemy. If you will get upon the field, leaving all baggage on the east bank of the river, it will be a move to our advantage and possibly save the day to us. The rebel force is estimated at over one hundred thousand men.

This appeal for help, as well as Grant's first message, fortunately reached Buell and made him alive to the necessity of promptly giving all possible aid to his fellow-commander. He at once sent peremptory orders to all the division commanders still en route (Crittenden was just arriving), to hurry on to the river with the utmost despatch. He next hunted up General Nelson (who, for some never explained reason, did not receive Grant's order till noon), and ordered him to move at once to Pittsburg. There was some delay, too, in finding a guide, so that the division did not get fully under way until after one. The road crossed a bottom partially under water, and was in so bad a condition that the artillery could not be moved over it at all. Even the infantry had to flounder all the way through mire, sometimes over a foot deep. But the officers and men struggled along most willingly, spurred on by the constantly increasing roar of battle, and by the inspiring feeling that they were hurrying to the rescue of their brethren-in-arms. Yet it took them nearly four hours to accomplish the distance of seven miles, and it was nearly five o'clock when the head of Ammen's brigade, which had the lead, reached Pittsburg Landing.

The general belief at Savannah was at first that the firing we heard was incidental to a reconnoissance in force, or to a skirmish of outposts; but, as it grew more violent and continuous, the conviction spread that a general engagement was going on. Grant's second message determined General Buell to go at once to the scene of action with part of his staff, and for that purpose he luckily ordered the very boat on which I had taken up my abode to get up steam. It was, however, only between three and four P.M. that we got under way. We had not proceeded very far when we began to notice numbers of soldiers on the west bank, and became satisfied that they were skulkers from the fight. More and more of them came in sight, and when we were still some distance from our destination they had increased to frequent and thick crowds. But, as our boat turned towards the Landing, we saw before us a dense mass apparently numbering thousands. I was standing with Captain Fry, the chief of staff, on the upper deck, and, appalled at the sight, exclaimed to him: "Oh, heavens! Captain, here is Bull Run all over again!" We heard the unbroken roar of artillery as we steamed up, and, as we neared the scene of the struggle, the sounds of rapid musketry discharges also became distinct, and we could see the flight of shells from the heavy guns of the two Union gunboats in position just above the Landing. We shuddered when we perceived ball after ball from rebel guns fall on the top of the very bluff under which the multitude of fugitives had sought shelter—unmistakable, distressing evidence of the nearness of the enemy. Our first impression could not be other than that the rebels had swept Grant's forces from the field, and that those who had not been killed, wounded, or captured were cowering before us, awaiting their inevitable fate.

On landing, we were met by an overwhelming confirmation of our apprehensions. We found ourselves, indeed, amid an immense, panic-stricken, uncontrollable mob. There were between seven and ten thousand men, of all arms and of all ranks, from field officers downward, all apparently entirely bereft of soldierly spirit, with no sense of obedience left, and animated by the sole impulse of personal safety. A number of officers, mounted and on foot, were making strenuous efforts to re-form the disorganized and demoralized throng; but neither exhortations, orders, adjurations nor threats produced any effect. General Buell brought his authority into play, but was no more obeyed than the others. Nothing availed against the increasing fright caused by the rebel balls and bullets that now began to fall among the crowd, killing several. At this critical moment, hope was revived by the landing of Colonel Ammen's brigade of the Fourth Division, brought over by boat from the opposite bank. It was accompanied by General Nelson himself. With that Jupiter head on his herculean figure, mounted on a heavy charger, he looked the personification of Orlando Furioso, as he rode up through the packed crowds, waving his hat and shouting: "Fall in, boys, fall in and follow me. We shall whip them yet." Finding this did no good, he drew his sword and commenced belaboring the poltroons around him, berating them at the same time with his stentorian voice, in language more forcible than polished. His extraordinary swearing indicated plainly that he had had great practice in that sort of admonition on the quarter-deck. Finding that this method also availed nothing, he applied to General Buell, who had waited for him at the Landing, for permission to drive the stragglers back at the point of the bayonet, and, if they resisted, to fire on them. But he was not allowed to resort to extreme measures.

Buell, without wasting time in trying to find Grant, as immediate action was necessary to prevent the enemy from reaching the river, joined Nelson in leading Ammen's brigade up the bluff. On reaching the plateau, it found itself directly under the fire of the hostile artillery. It was then between five and six o'clock, and the light was fast giving way to darkness. Two regiments of the brigade, the Sixth Ohio and the Thirty-sixth Indiana, were at once deployed and pushed forward. Their vigorous advance caused the rebel guns to retreat. They came close enough to the rebels in front to exchange several volleys with them. Their advance, together with the enfilading fire of the gunboats, checked the enemy. Night put an end to the battle.

I had followed Nelson's men to the top of the bluff, and remained there awaiting developments. I had as little idea of what had really happened to Grant's army as General Buell himself. Nor could I get any connected account out of the runaway officers I met. They had nothing to say except this: "We were surprised at breakfast by rebels four times as strong as ourselves;" "My regiment was cut all to pieces;" "We were ordered to retreat," and such other excuses for knowing nothing. Grant's headquarters were said to be near, but I could not get to them before dark. I made my way back to the Landing, after the firing had ceased, thinking that my best plan would be to find shelter for the night—which threatened to be very trying, as a pouring rain had set in—on the boat on which I had come. But it had been ordered to help bring the remainder of Nelson's division and the other divisions of Buell's army across the river as fast as possible, and I had to wait nearly an hour before it returned from the opposite bank with a huge load of men. It took a long time to discharge them, and then I found to my great chagrin that I could not possibly get my horse on board again, so that I had to choose between abandoning him and passing the night as best I could on the bank. Of course, I faced the latter necessity. After spending some time along the Landing in vain attempts to find something to eat for myself and my animal, I decided to follow the next arrival from Crittenden's division, which followed Nelson's, wherever it might be led, so as to be at any rate at the front in the morning. In so doing, I luckily came by the bivouac of Nelson's headquarters, where I was made welcome by one of the staff to the partial shelter of a rubber blanket hung between two trees near a big log fire, and also to some hard-tack, cold bacon, and brandy and water. My horse was taken charge of by an orderly, but was neither fed nor unsaddled.

None of us attempted to sleep during that memorable, dismal night. Nor would sleep have been possible, as the gunboats sent roaring eight-inch shells over us every ten minutes (in pursuance of the recommendation of General Nelson), in the direction of the enemy, in order at least to deprive the rebels of rest. We sat around the fire, protected as much as possible from the incessant rain by waterproofs, discussing the disaster of the day and the chances for the morrow. Little being known as to the actual condition to which Grant's command had been reduced by its defeat, there was anything but confident expectation. On the contrary, all were very anxious about the outcome of the next twenty-four hours.

The movement of Buell's troops from the right to the left bank continued all night long. The commanders not only managed to get the full infantry force of Nelson and Crittenden's divisions, but also three batteries of artillery, across the river before daybreak. Even General McCook's division reached the front in the morning, after an extraordinary all-night march. Buell and the two first-mentioned division commanders labored as best they could in the darkness, being ignorant of the ground, to get the troops in proper position for an offensive movement as soon as it was light enough for it. With Nelson's staff, I was up and stirring at four on the morning of April 7. The General himself roused his command quietly by riding through the bivouac. At five, he was able to report to General Buell, by an aide-de-camp, that his line of battle with skirmishers in front was ready to move, and received orders to advance on the enemy. Crittenden advanced simultaneously on Nelson's right. I followed in the rear with the ambulances. At half-past five the first shots fell, and, in a few minutes, the musketry-firing was heavy, and presently hostile balls and shells were whizzing over us. Nelson was ordered to stop till Crittenden had closed up on his right and the two field batteries were brought up and put in position to answer effectively the artillery on the other side. Our divisions then moved on again, but were confronted, at about seven, by a strong rebel force that attempted to turn Nelson's left, and, though foiled in this, attacked him so vigorously, supported by a heavy fire from two batteries, that his command began to yield, when the enemy was checked by the well-directed fire of Mendenhall's regular battery. By eight o'clock the musketry and artillery fire from both sides combined into a terrific roar, and hissing and humming missiles flew thickly around us. It seemed as if Crittenden and Nelson were not strong enough to make headway against the bodies opposed to them. But, fortunately, Rousseau's brigade of McCook's division then reached the ground and was immediately formed in line on the right of Crittenden. The other brigades of the same division followed it closely and took up position on its left.

Our line now extended about a mile and a half. The ground in front of it consisted partly of open fields and partly of patches of wood, with thick undergrowth. It was almost level before Nelson, but broken by ravines before Crittenden and McCook. The right wing was not in touch, however, with Grant's command. About nine o'clock we were ready for another advance along the whole line. The battle was speedily raging again with great violence. From one end of the line to the other, the combat lasted for hours, with hardly a lull in the deafening discharge of small arms and guns. Although but a short distance in the rear of the fighting front and actually under fire, it was not possible for me to follow the course of the struggle from my position, owing to the character of the ground and the thickness of the atmosphere from the falling rain mixed with the dense powder-smoke that hung over the field. Nor could I expect to learn anything reliable and connected by remaining in one spot. A sort of field-hospital was established near by, to which the wounded were being brought, in steadily increasing numbers, presenting sights that made me heart-sick, as I had not seen human blood spilled since the battle of Bull Run. But what intelligence the carriers of stretchers, and the surgeons that passed to and fro, brought from the front confused rather than enlightened me. Hence I mounted and set out in search of Buell's and the division headquarters.

I soon found the former, but obtained only very scanty information. Then I tried to discover McCook, in whose direction the heaviest firing was heard. I met the General and staff at a critical moment. Rousseau's brigade, soon after being placed in line, had been vigorously attacked. It repelled the enemy and drove him some distance, capturing a battery. Its advance caused an opening in the line between McCook and Crittenden through which the rebels quickly attempted to push with a very strong force. Perceiving this danger, Colonel von Willich, with his Thirty-second Indiana Regiment, was ordered to strike them, and made a most gallant attack, first delivering several volleys and then charging with the bayonet. Von Willich's was followed by the other regiments of Gibson's brigade, but they were caught in a withering cross-fire and compelled to fall back in considerable confusion. General McCook was doing his best to check this untoward turn when I found him. Kirk's brigade was brought to the relief of Gibson, and stemmed the rebel advance till Rousseau's brigade had replenished its cartridge-boxes and could again take the offensive. Then the whole division once more advanced, and pressed the still vigorously fighting enemy steadily back till his resistance ended in retreat. During the desperate struggle of Gibson's and Kirk's brigades, there was a continuous whistling of bullets above and around us, and it was marvellous that none of the staff were wounded. McCook's part in the conflict was so severe that I felt sure he was bearing the brunt of it, and hence I remained with him till it closed. After the firing had ceased altogether, I hunted up successively Crittenden and Nelson, and only then learned that they, too, had been engaged right along in meeting hostile attacks and following them up with counter ones, resulting in a steady gain of ground. They forced the enemy finally into full retreat by a flank attack by the Fourth and a front one by the Fifth Division, supported by a concentric fire from three batteries. Crittenden's command captured seven field-pieces in this decisive movement. Just before the close of the fighting, two brigades of General Wood's Sixth Division appeared, one of which, Colonel Wagner's, was started in pursuit of the enemy, but stopped by order after following him about a mile.

My recollection is, that it was about four o'clock P.M. when the sound of battle had entirely died away, but, strange to say, no reference whatever to time is made in the official reports of General Buell and his division commanders. I am sure, at any rate, that it was daylight still for nearly two hours after the end of the battle, enabling me to gather many additional details of the contest relating to the engaged portion of the Army of the Ohio. I saw enough killed and wounded Unionists and rebels scattered over the battle-field to indicate heavy losses on both sides, but accurate figures were, of course, unobtainable on that day. The usual suffering of the wounded from thirst was alleviated by the heavy rain that was still falling, yet many moanings and cries for help reached my ears. Buell's troops had recovered the camps from which the rebels had driven Sherman's, McClernand's, Hurlbut's, Prentiss's, and Wallace's divisions of Grant's army the day before, but were not permitted to make themselves comfortable in them, and had to bivouac as best they could for another night. I was so very tired, wet, and hungry— my animal also being in an entirely fagged-out condition —that I made up my mind to find something better for us both than the scanty fare and wet ground that had been our lot for nearly thirty hours, and made for the Landing some time before dark. There were eight boats lying there, and great was my joy when I spied, standing on the bow of one of them, a division quartermaster whom I had become well acquainted with at Louisville. I hailed him, and he responded at once in the heartiest manner to my request for food and shelter for "man and beast." My horse was turned over to a deck-hand. I was shown to a stateroom, and soon I sat down to a generous hot supper, to which I did the amplest justice. I was too exhausted for any brain work that evening, and sought sleep as early as possible.

After ten hours' solid, unconscious rest and a hearty breakfast, I was ready and eager for work. I had but partial material for a complete account of the two days' battle; hence my first object had to be, if there were no more fighting, to secure information regarding the experiences of Grant's army during the two days, and, if possible, also something about the enemy. By eight o'clock I was riding up the bluff again. The swarms of skulkers had almost disappeared, and in their place there was a great jam of ambulances, bringing wounded to the two hospital-boats, and army wagons loading provisions, forage, and ammunition. I proceeded first to Buell's headquarters. There I learned that Wood's two brigades had been ordered to resume the pursuit of the enemy and were already in motion, and that Sherman's division had received orders to the same effect. As I was anxious to obtain Sherman's version of the battle, and feared the pursuit might take him beyond reach, I rode immediately in search of him, and luckily succeeded in finding his camp. He was just ready to mount. On the first day he had been slightly wounded in the right hand, which was bandaged, but he would not allow this to interfere with his duties. He favored me with a succinct, clear, very frank, and strictly truthful account of his own varied fortunes on Sunday and Monday, as well as those of the other division commanders of Grant in their relations to him. These I then tried to hunt up, and to revisit McCook, Crittenden, and Nelson—a harder task than I had supposed, for rain was still pouring down, and the ground fought over everywhere had turned into mire from one to two feet deep. On Grant's line there was still a good deal of confusion. I did not get through with my tour of exploration till nearly three o'clock.

I had spent considerable time in studying—no, this is too strong an expression—in contemplating the "horrors of war," as exemplified by the dreadful sights all over the battle-field. Once only, later in the war, did I behold a spectacle equally grim, shocking, and sickening. There was bloody evidence in every direction that the slaughter had been great. Neither the one side nor the other had removed its dead, and there they were, blue and gray, in their starkness, lying here singly and there literally in rows and heaps. I passed more than a thousand of them. It was morbid, perhaps, on my part, but I lingered to see the effect of sudden violent death on features and limbs. It surprised me that the faces of most of these victims of battle bore a peaceful, contented expression, and that many lay as though they had consciously stretched themselves out to sleep. But there were also many ghastly exceptions, with features repulsively distorted by pain and hatred. There seemed to be but few killed by heavy missiles. Hundreds of severely wounded were likewise still lying about—some in the last agonies, others awaiting quietly their fate, and, alas! many writhing and shrieking in torture from horrible wounds. There was a little frame church near where I had found Sherman, known as the Shiloh meeting-house (it gave its name to the battle), whose interior presented the most woeful scene in all this sadness. The seats for the worshippers had been removed, and on the floor were extended, in two rows, on the bare planks and without any cover over them, twenty-seven dead and dying rebels, officers and men. Not a human being was about to offer them tender mercies. They had been left to their fate, all being obviously beyond relief. Passing the field hospitals, other awful evidences of the bloody work forced themselves upon my observation in the form of piles of amputated limbs. No one as yet knew the extent of the casualties, but I was satisfied that there must have been between eight and ten thousand killed and wounded on our side, which estimate was not far from the actual figures.

I had made some inquiries as to telegraph and mail facilities at the different headquarters, and ascertained that of the former there were as yet none, and that even after they should be secured, newspaper correspondents would not be permitted to use them. As to mails, they would be sent by boats to Cairo, one of which was to start that evening. I stopped again at Buell's headquarters on my way to the Landing, and learned that Wood's pursuit had been continued for eight miles without coming up with the enemy. Sherman had struck the Confederate cavalry rear-guard and driven it back after a lively skirmish. He had obtained positive information that the rebel army was retreating to Corinth. As this rendered it certain that fighting would not occur for some days at least, the thought came to me that it would be a good plan, in order to save time in preparing and sending forward my account of the battle, to go down the river on the first boat, write out my report on the way, and mail it at Cairo on arrival. In pursuance of this, I asked my friend the quartermaster to get me a permit to go on the boat, and to take care of my horse till my return. He agreed to both, and by four o'clock I was properly installed on the sidewheeler that was to leave the same evening for Cairo. I was already congratulating myself on my smartness in hitting upon this scheme, from which I expected a decided advantage in time over other correspondents, when I discovered that two other correspondents had been equally acute and were fellow-passengers. I made their acquaintance, and found them very pleasant companions. One of them was Whitelaw Reid, who achieved a considerable reputation as a war-correspondent, tried cotton-planting unsuccessfully after the war, and then returned to the journalistic profession. He became the regular Washington correspondent and part owner of the Cincinnati *Gazette,* and subsequently editor and owner of the New York *Tribune,* and United States Minister to France. As my colleagues had been with Grant's army and knew very little of Buell's part in the conflict, we helped each other by exchanging notes.

I repeat that I am not trying in these memoirs to write formal history, but to relate personal happenings and observations. Yet in this particular case it seems to me proper, in order to render the foregoing more complete and intelligible, to describe also what happened on the field previous to the appearance of Buell's army. In so doing, I shall not enter into details, but shall merely outline the preceding operations of Grant's command, for the double reason that this will be sufficient for a clearer comprehension of what I have written, and that nothing like accurate particulars have ever been available. With all the official reports before me, I do not hesitate to say that it is impossible to make up from them a lucid, full, and correct description of the battle. I do not believe that the official records of any other battle of the Civil War left so many points in doubt. In order to impart greater accuracy and perhaps some novelty to my sketch, I feel justified in availing myself also of the authoritative rebel accounts, and especially of General Beauregard's official report to the Richmond authorities. I make these references to my sources of information so that I may not be charged with pretending to greater personal knowledge of the battle than I actually acquired.

According to the rebel records, Beauregard, with the approval of his Government, decided and acted on the plan of foiling the supposed purpose of the Northern commanders of cutting the Confederacy in two through the destruction of the railroad lines of communication in southwestern Tennessee and northern Mississippi and Alabama, by rapidly concentrating all the available forces west of the Alleghanies at and about Corinth. He pushed this concentration very energetically, and, by the end of March, the commands of Generals A. S. Johnston, Polk, and Bragg and other troops sent by the governors of the States named were collected in that locality, to the aggregate number of forty thousand fighting men. General Johnston, by virtue of his superior rank, assumed chief command on reaching Corinth. He approved of the previously conceived plan of Beauregard described by the latter in his report on the battle (in which Johnston had been killed), to wit: "to assume the offensive and strike a sudden blow at the enemy in position under General Grant on the west bank of the Tennessee at Pittsburg and in the direction of Savannah, before he was reinforced by the army under General Buell, then known to be advancing for that purpose by rapid marches from Nashville via Columbia. By a rapid and vigorous attack on General Grant, it was expected he would be beaten back into his transports and the river, or captured in time to enable us to profit by the victory and remove to the rear all the stores and munitions that would fall into our hands in such an event before the arrival of General Buell on the scene." The proposed attack was bold and sound strategy, directly invited by General Grant's grave mistake in placing his command on the west bank and thus exposing it to attack, with the river between him and his expected reinforcements. This flagrant blunder, contrary to elementary strategic rules, appears the more inexcusable in view of Grant's belief, as expressed in his dispatches to Buell before quoted, that the rebel forces amounted to one hundred thousand, while he himself had, according to the official returns, not over forty thousand effectives, of which, as will be shown, only about thirty-three thousand became actually engaged.

The rebel commanders worked very industriously in getting ready for the attack, but, to quote again from Beauregard's report, "want of proper officers needful for the proper organization of divisions and brigades, and other difficulties in the way of an effective organization, delayed the movement until the night of the second [of April], when it was heard from a reliable quarter that the junction of the enemy was near at hand. It was then, at a late hour, determined that the attack should be attempted at once, incomplete and imperfect as were our preparations for such a grave and momentous venture, and, accordingly, the same night, at one o'clock on the morning of the third, formal orders to the commanders of corps were issued for the movement."

The starting-points were Corinth and its immediate vicinity, averaging a distance of about twenty miles from the positions of the Federal forces. The rebel chiefs calculated to arrive near the latter on the fourth and assail them early on the fifth. If they had succeeded in this, they would doubtless, as the sequel showed, have accomplished their purpose and destroyed or captured the whole of Grant's command before Buell could have come to its rescue. Happily for the Union cause, the march of the Confederates took a day longer. I am sure these twenty-four hours weighed more decidedly in the balance of events than any other day in the course of the Civil War. It is not too much to say, indeed, that, but for this delay, Grant would not have become a great historical figure and the conqueror of Robert E. Lee, and the Rebellion might have succeeded. The fortunate loss of time was due to the double fact that the rebel troops were unused to marching, and that the roads were too narrow, and were rendered almost impassable by a heavy rainfall on the fourth.

The country between Corinth and Pittsburg Landing consists of an undulating table-land, mainly covered with dense woods and such thick underbrush as to render the passage of troops difficult. It was then little better than a wilderness, broken here and there only by small clearings of from forty to eighty acres, with clusters of log buildings indicating that a few settlers tried to extract a scanty living from the indifferent soil. A main road runs from Corinth due north for about fifteen miles, when it branches off into two roads, one to Pittsburg Landing and the other to Hamburg Landing, four miles above the former. The plateau gradually ascends between the two landings, and, some miles from the river, shows hilly formations. Two streams, Owl and Lick Creeks, rise there, about three miles apart, and flow into the Tennessee. On the ground between them, the battle was fought.

The rebel advance did not reach the intersection of the two roads from Hamburg and Pittsburg, within a short distance of the Federal encampments, till late in the afternoon of Saturday, April 5. General Johnston determined to attack as early as possible the next morning with his army in the following formation: three lines of battle *en échelon*, extending from Owl Creek on the left to Lick Creek on the right. The first line consisted of Hardee's corps, fully deployed with their artillery and cavalry in the rear of the wings. The second line included General Bragg's corps, and was similarly formed, five hundred yards from the first. General Polk's corps formed the third line at a distance of eight hundred yards from the second, in lines of brigades deployed with batteries in rear of each brigade, and the left wing supported by cavalry. Behind all came a reserve under General Breckinridge.

Thus the rebels stood ready, under able, energetic commanders, to fall with concentrated might upon the unsuspecting Union forces. There raged for a long time after the battle an acrimonious controversy in the press and in public forums over the question whether the rebel attack was a surprise to Grant's troops. While it was no doubt true that the Union pickets were on the alert, and that their firing gave a short warning to the Federal camps of the approach of the enemy before the hostile host was actually upon them, it is likewise incontestable that neither General Sherman, whose division held the most advanced position, nor General Grant, had the remotest suspicion that the whole rebel army was within artillery range of the former. Witness Sherman's report by field-telegraph on that very Saturday afternoon to Grant: "All is quiet along my lines now. The enemy has cavalry in our front, and I think there are two regiments and one battery six miles out" (*sic!*). And still later in the day he reported further: "I do not apprehend anything like an attack upon our position." Witness, further, Grant's dispatch to superior authority on the same day: "I have scarcely the faintest idea of an attack being made upon us, but will be prepared, should such a thing take place."

It is hard to reconcile the actual situation of his command with this confident assurance that he "will be prepared." The disconnected location of his six divisions on the west bank surely was not such as a cautious commander should allow if he thought an attack possible. Sherman's separate command had the most advanced position on the main road to Corinth, but his several brigades were spread out over too much ground. McClernand's was some distance in the rear of it; Prentiss's division was on Sherman's left, but not in close touch with it. Hurlbut's and W. H. L. Wallace's divisions were near Pittsburg Landing, from two to three miles from the others. Lew Wallace's division was from five to six miles away, at and about Cramp's Landing, below Pittsburg. It was not only the intervening distance, but also the broken nature of the ground separating the several camps, that made it impracticable to form quickly a connected defensive line. Still worse, the divisions formed entirely independent military units. In other words, no one division commander had authority over the other commanders. They all had to report to, and receive orders from, General Grant, who remained, as we have seen, at Savannah up to almost noon of the first day of battle—an unpardonable error, fraught, as it proved, with the greatest peril. Yet other faults of omission were chargeable to the Federal side. The approaches from Corinth were not properly guarded. No effort was made to protect the front against a sudden hostile offensive by field defences such as were so systematically and effectively used in the subsequent advances on Corinth and in all the later campaigns of the war. Last, not least, there lay special weakness in the fact that the very front divisions contained a number of entirely raw regiments which had had hardly any drilling and but limited knowledge of the use of their arms. Hence it was inevitable that, when the hostile array surged upon the camps like a flood tide, the instant effect was confusion, terror, and all but panic.

The rebel advance began before six A.M. By seven, the front line had reached the Federal advance-guard and firing commenced. Sherman even then did not apprehend a general attack, but sent word of the appearance of the enemy in force in his immediate front to Generals Prentiss, McClernand, and Hurlbut, asking the two latter —he could not "order" them—to get ready to support him and Prentiss respectively with their commands. While a fusillade was uninterruptedly going on between seven and eight along his line, it was only at eight that he became "satisfied for the first time," to quote from his report, "that the enemy designed a determined attack upon our

whole camp." To meet it, he had succeeded in forming his
division, which immediately became heavily engaged, and
within an hour was forced, by the determined onsets of
superior numbers, to give way in great disorder, the
enemy driving it through its camps and far beyond, and
capturing guns and many prisoners.

Meantime, Prentiss fared much worse. The main object
of the rebel attack was to overwhelm the Federal left and
thus open a short way to Grant's base of supplies at Pittsburg Landing. To that end, simultaneously with their
move on Sherman, they threw upon Prentiss an even
heavier mass. His resistance was of no more avail than
Sherman's. His division was soon forced to yield, and
was driven back through its own camp upon McClernand
and Hurlbut. The "Alpine avalanche," as Beauregard
not unfitly calls it, rolled on and next struck McClernand.
He had but two brigades with which to resist, having sent
one early to the support of Sherman. Hurlbut came to
his assistance, and the two, with parts of Prentiss's division, struggled with Sherman on their right through the
forenoon and afternoon to stem the rebel progress. But
they were compelled to retreat from position to position
and fall back over miles of ground, nearer and nearer to
the river. Between five and six o'clock, the rebel right
had arrived within a few thousand feet of the river, and
their shot and shell fell on the bluff rising from the Landing. Some of the rebel cavalry even reached the river
a short distance above Pittsburg and watered their horses.
At this most critical juncture, hope of salvation came with
the appearance of General Nelson's brigade just in time
to fill the unprotected space, on the left of Grant's retreating troops, through which the enemy was pushing for the
Landing.

Assuming that Beauregard tells the truth in his report—
and there is no good reason to doubt it—he did not know
before dark on Sunday that the advance of Buell's army
had actually reached the field, and was made aware of the

fact only by the vigorous attacks on his right early next morning. He records his expectation, up to that discovery, of completing the Federal discomfiture on Monday, but admits that his "officers and men were exhausted by a combat of over twelve hours without food, and jaded by the march of the previous day through mud and water." He adds: "During the night, the rain fell in torrents, adding to the discomfort and harassed condition of the men; the enemy, moreover, had broken their rest by a discharge, at measured intervals, of heavy shells thrown from the gunboats. Therefore, on the following morning, the troops under my command were not in a condition to cope with an equal force of fresh troops, armed and equipped like our adversary." He claims that, notwithstanding this disparity, his troops withstood and repelled all offensive attempts on the second day up to one P.M., when he voluntarily withdrew from so "unequal a conflict."

This claim is flatly contradicted by the official reports of General Buell and his division commanders. Moreover, the rebel archives contain a report from Beauregard's chief aide-de-camp to him, directly affirming that, notwithstanding the General's strenuous personal efforts in seizing and waving regimental flags to make his troops stand, they did not respond, but steadily yielded ground after eleven A.M. on Monday. It is beyond all question just as true that the rebels were compelled to retreat by the attack of the comparatively fresh Federal divisions, as that the latter saved what was left of Grant's army from capture or destruction. Its remnants were re-formed as well as possible, and, with Lew Wallace's division, which turned up at the close of Sunday's fighting, did their share on Monday on Buell's right in making the enemy yield up their encampments. But as they, together, hardly numbered more than fifteen thousand, of which nearly two thirds consisted of odds and ends of four divisions, no decisive offensive power could well be claimed for them.

Besides the physical exhaustion of the rebels on Sunday, other causes worked on their side to bring about their final failure. The most hurtful of these was no doubt the killing of their Commander-in-chief, General A. S. Johnston, between two and three P.M. on Sunday. While riding with the attacking columns, he was struck by several bullets, one of which cut an artery and made him bleed to death in fifteen minutes. His death was probably a greater blow to the Confederacy than the defeat of his purpose, for, according to the testimony of all who knew him personally, on the Southern as well as on the Northern side, there was the stuff for another Robert E. Lee in him, and he might have proved as formidable an antagonist on the western as the latter on the eastern theatre of war. Jefferson Davis fully recognized this in his official lament over the Confederacy's irreparable loss. Perhaps even the result at Shiloh would have been different if Johnston had lived. Leaving his admittedly inferior capacities as a strategist out of consideration, Beauregard was not in bodily condition for an energetic exercise of the chief command, being just convalescent from a severe two months' illness.

Another cause appears from the admission of Beauregard in his report that "officers, non-commissioned officers and men abandoned their colors early in the first day to pillage the captured encampments," and that "others retired shamefully from the field on both days, while the thunder of cannon and the roar and rattle of musketry told them that their brothers were being slaughtered by the fresh legions of the enemy." The General claimed, on a later occasion, that the casualties on the first day and the admitted skulking of a portion of his command had reduced his fighting strength to twenty thousand on the second day, and this number may be accepted as correct. General Braxton Bragg complained as strongly of the straggling and plundering of his men, and ascribes to the weakness and confusion caused by it the failure to finish the battle on the first day.

Shiloh was one of the bloodiest battles of the Civil War. According to the official publications, Grant lost 1437 killed, 5679 wounded, and 2934 missing; Buell, 236 killed, 1816 wounded, and 88 missing—making a total of 1673 killed, 7495 wounded, and 3022 missing—while the rebel loss was 1728 killed, 8012 wounded, and 957 missing. Beauregard overestimated the total Federal loss at 20,000. As shown by some of my quotations, Beauregard's report had the fault of extravagant language, but it was far superior to Grant's in giving an intelligible account of the two days' fighting. In fact, Grant's is about as poor a production as the Rebellion brought forth in that line on the Northern side, and one cannot peruse it without wondering that the author of such a miserable screed ever attained the prominence he did.

CHAPTER XVII

The Siege of Corinth.—1862

THE boat on which I had secured passage for Cairo started down the river some hours after dark, and we reached our destination the following noon. I rose early in the morning and managed to write up my account of the battle completely before arriving, so that I felt free to rest and enjoy myself for two or three days, as far as it was possible, in the small, struggling, rough place which the town at the confluence of the Ohio and Mississippi Rivers then was. A pleasant surprise awaited me at the St. Charles Hotel, where I took quarters. I discovered among the guests A. D. Richardson, whom I had not seen since our parting at Denver in 1859. He had gone there again the following year to engage in newspaper work and "town-site speculations," but, upon the outbreak of the Rebellion, had returned east to take the field as a war correspondent. He shared rooms with three colleagues, to whom he introduced me, and with whom I have kept up a pleasant and intimate acquaintance ever since. One of them was Thomas W. Knox, who had started a weekly paper with Richardson in the town of Golden City that had sprung up at the very point on Clear Creek where Greeley, Richardson, and I crossed. Knox, after the war, became a professional traveller and gatherer of material in various countries for books for young people, which brought him moderate fame and fortune. Another was Junius Henri Browne, the well-known writer, with whom my relations became closest; and the fourth, Richard T. Colburn, who, at the end of the war, followed for many years the well-paid occupation of editor of the publications of banking firms and railroad companies. The four associates had been on duty in Missouri, and were then watching the northern offensive operations on the Mississippi under General Pope. All proved very congenial companions, and I enjoyed my two days with them thoroughly. I then felt it my duty to go back to Pittsburg Landing, upon learning from a St. Louis paper that General Halleck would leave on April 10 for the front, to assume chief direction of the operations of Buell's and Grant's armies in person. After a pleasant trip on a quartermaster's boat, I found myself again with the army on the evening of April 11, my twenty-seventh birthday,[1] which I celebrated, however, only in thought. I was made welcome by Chief-Quartermaster Gamage of McCook's division, and enjoyed his generous hospitality all through the operations against Corinth. General Halleck arrived on the same day with a large staff on a fine Mississippi steamboat.

The appearance of the new General-in-chief naturally excited much anxious curiosity among the commanders under him, and the development of his purposes was awaited with apprehensive expectation. It was generally supposed that he would deal vigorously with the many cases of incompetency and cowardice of officers, from major-generals down, that the battle had brought out. But he confined himself to a very limited weeding out among field and line officers. He perceived, however, at once the great demoralization in which the conflict had left Grant's command, and took drastic measures to improve its condition. On April 14, he issued the following order to General Grant:

Immediate and active measures must be taken to put your command in condition to resist another attack by the enemy. Fractions of batteries will be united temporarily under competent officers,

[1] Really the day before, April 10. See page 1.

supplied with ammunition and placed in position for active service. Divisions and brigades should, where necessary, be reorganized and put in position, and all stragglers returned to their companies and regiments. Your army is not now in condition to resist an attack. It must be made so without delay. Staff officers must be sent out to obtain returns from division commanders and assist in supplying all deficiencies.

When it is considered that Halleck found occasion to issue such an order a whole week after the end of the battle, it must be admitted that the sharp criticism and direct reprimand it contained were well deserved. It constitutes a formal record, never questioned, of the fact, confirmed by Grant's subsequent career, that, while he was a fighting strategist of the highest order, he was not strong either as a disciplinarian or as an organizer. The serious trouble between Halleck and Grant after the fall of Fort Donelson will be remembered. This order naturally produced another great strain in their relations. Halleck manifested his distrust of Grant's capacity as a commander soon afterwards in another striking way, to which I shall refer directly. That the order and what happened subsequently did not move General Grant to ask to be relieved from command, may seem surprising, but the Union cause was saved a second time from that misfortune.

Halleck was conscious that the resumption of the offensive against the enemy at the earliest possible moment was an absolute necessity. Like Grant, he overestimated the rebel strength; and what with this and the condition of Grant's troops, he determined to strengthen himself from every available quarter, and therefore ordered the whole force of General Pope, which was waiting for orders, to embark on boats on the Mississippi after its great success at New Madrid, as well as two divisions from Missouri, to Pittsburg, and, by April 20, he had a great army of fully one hundred thousand men under his immediate orders. By a special field order, the Army of the Tennessee was placed under the orders of General George H. Thomas (whose division was at the same time detached from the Army of the Ohio and made part of his new command), and constituted the right wing; the Army of the Ohio, under General Buell, the centre; and the Army of the Mississippi, under General Pope, the left wing. General Grant was relieved from command of the Army of the Tennessee, and made second in command of the grand army under Halleck. As we shall see, this really meant that Halleck had no use for him.

It continued to rain all through April, so that the roads were reduced to the worst possible condition. Bad enough before the battle, they now consisted of sticky mire so deep that no artillery or loaded wagons could be moved over them. They were only ordinary dirt roads, with nothing but the natural beds of clayish earth. Provisions, forage, and ammunition had to be carried to the camps on horses and mules. Thousands of men were therefore detailed to improve the existing roads by corduroying, ditching, and bridging swampy bottoms and streams, and, where they had become impassable, to make new approaches from Pittsburg Landing to the several camps. A vast amount of work of this kind was accomplished during the three weeks following the battle. The rainfall and the condition of the ground brought great discomfort to all in the camps. It was almost impossible to get dry and keep so. The result was a great deal of sickness, mainly in the form of dysentery. I was told by medical officers that nearly half of the officers and men had it. I had my share of the hardships, but fortunately kept well. Owing to the bad weather and the difficulty of locomotion, those days were very dull ones. There was no news to gather, and all I could do to kill time was to read newspapers and make visits to the army and division headquarters and to the Landing.

By the end of April, the disintegrating effect of the great fight had been repaired, the lost and destroyed equipments and armaments replaced, and the efficiency of the troops considerably increased by constant drilling and strict enforcement of discipline. Still, while there was a decided gain in the latter respect, Halleck's personal observation of the sad plight in which the rebel onslaught had left the Army of the Tennessee, made him distrust the reliability of his forces for either offence or defence. Hence when, for sanitary, strategic, and political reasons, a forward change of position could no longer be put off, he deemed it his duty to act with the utmost caution in approaching the rebel army, which he assumed to be not much, if at all, inferior in numbers to his own. This belief was based on an intercepted despatch from Beauregard to the Richmond War Department, dated Corinth, April 9, in which he stated his effective strength on that day to be thirty-five thousand, which General Van Dorn's command, on the way from Arkansas to join him, would raise to fifty thousand, and urgently asked for reinforcements, as he had eighty-five thousand Federals to confront. Later information received from Halleck led him to believe that Beauregard's appeal for help was being largely responded to. This curious tendency always to overestimate the enemy, that seemed to afflict, like an epidemic mental disease, most Union leaders, now also infected Halleck. He communicated his fears to Assistant Secretary of War Thomas A. Scott, who had arrived with General Pope, and who took it upon himself to recommend, as early as May 6, to the War Department to send, in view of the presumed large reinforcements that were reaching Beauregard, forty to fifty thousand more men to Halleck from the East. As this was not done, he repeated his recommendation several times, and finally induced Governor Morton of Indiana to urge the same measure strongly upon the Government. This led to a characteristic pathetic remonstrance from President Lincoln to Halleck, as follows:

MAY 24, 1862.—Several dispatches from Assistant Secretary Scott and one from Governor Morton, asking for reinforcements for you, have been received. I beg you to be assured we do the best we can.

I mean to cast no blame when I tell you each of our commanders along our line from Richmond to Corinth supposes himself to be confronted by numbers superior to his own.

My dear General, I feel justified in relying very much on you. I believe you and the brave officers and men with you can and will get the victory at Corinth.

Halleck replied disingenuously on the next day:

I have asked for no reinforcements, but only whether any were to be sent to me. If any were to be sent, I would wait for them; if not, I would venture an attack. We are now in immediate presence of the enemy, and the battle may occur at any moment. I have every confidence that we shall succeed, but dislike to run any risk, and therefore have waited to ascertain if any more troops can be hoped for.

This was, of course, tantamount to saying: "I ought to have more troops, but, if I do not get them, the responsibility will not be with me." And yet Beauregard took only 47,000 men away with him from Corinth, according to his official report to his War Department, the correctness of which figure cannot be doubted, while Halleck attributed to him from 85,000 to 120,000, as against 90,000 and 100,000 (or about twice as many as his antagonist) under his own orders. Accordingly, the advance became characterized by a determination to avoid risks as much as possible, by the most vigilant measures against hostile surprises, by a deliberate slowness of movement, and by the most careful selection and protection of the positions successively reached. Halleck was subsequently subjected to a great deal of severe criticism and even ridicule for his deliberateness in moving upon the enemy. But, after properly weighing all the reasons for his course, it is, in my judgment, only just to admit that it involved but little loss of time, and afforded absolute assurance against a repetition of the mishap of April 6.

A first forward movement along the whole line began

on April 29. It brought the entire army about three miles nearer to Corinth—that is, to within an average distance of only twelve miles from the place. Short as the distance was, it required from four to six days to get over the intervening ground. New lines of communication had to be created, including the construction of two bridges over Lick Creek. I saw only the work of this kind done by the Army of the Ohio, but can testify to its extreme laboriousness and to the cheerful spirit with which officers and men accomplished it. Great was the vexation when an extra-heavy downpour on May 3 and 4 made all the water-courses rise, so as to again destroy much of the result of their efforts. The next onward change of location was made on May 7. Rain ceased the day before, and was followed by beautiful, warm, and clear weather, which rapidly dried the ground and roads, and rendered the task of the army much easier. The effect, too, was felt in the rapid reduction of the sick-list and a general revival of spirit and increase of energy. The second advance involved as much road-making as the first. By way of further precaution, in view of the greater nearness to the enemy, the whole front was strengthened, under orders from the Commander-in-chief, by abatis, barricades, rifle-pits, and breastworks. Another advance was ordered and accomplished on the 17th and 18th. The favorable weather reduced the necessary road- and bridge-building, but more work was devoted to the construction of field defences. Indeed, the army was made secure in regularly fortified camps.

 The improved condition of the roads tempted me to extend the range of my observation beyond the lines of the Army of the Ohio. But, in order to do this, a general pass from the Commander-in-chief was indispensable, as otherwise I should have had to risk arrest and punishment within the lines of the other two armies. I rode twice to Halleck's headquarters to obtain such a pass, but met with a rebuff each time. Halleck considered newspaper correspondents with the armies as more dangerous than the enemy, and persistently refused to give them any countenance. Just then, too, he was, as I was told by one of his staff (a Washington acquaintance), very much irritated against the press generally by the tendency of the controversy waged in it over the battle of Shiloh. Nothing daunted by my failure, I bethought myself of the "second in chief command"—that is, of General Grant—and, making my way to his camp, readily succeeded in obtaining the desired *passe-partout* from his chief of staff, Lieutenant-Colonel Rawlins. I observed that a marked stillness prevailed at Grant's headquarters, contrasting greatly with the bustle perceivable about it before Halleck's advent. The fact was, that the "second in command" was confined to a very nominal part. His rôle during the "siege" was, indeed, that of a mere dummy upon a stage—a show, but not a substance. As I ascertained on this and subsequent visits, General Grant's duties were confined to receiving orders from General Halleck for General Thomas, and to transmitting them to him. There was hardly any personal intercourse between the two headquarters. Of course, this embarrassing position was most galling to the victor of Fort Donelson and his whole staff. While Grant said nothing, his staff gave vent to their feelings very freely and vigorously. Grant did not gratify his rival by retiring from the field—Halleck's real object, according to Grant's military household—but wisely bore the humiliation with patience.

The army was not occupied with pick, shovel, and axe alone. Simultaneously with the first advance, an expedition was sent out under General Wallace to destroy the Memphis & Charleston Railroad west of Corinth, in the neighborhood of Purdy, which did not, however, accomplish much. Nearly one-fifth of the troops always performed grand-guard and picket duties. Reconnoissances more or less in force were also regularly made. After the second advance, we began to feel the enemy, and picket-firing and outpost skirmishes became more and more frequent. The first important encounter took place on May 9 between General Paine's division of Pope's army on the extreme left, near the village of Farmington, just south of the Mississippi line. Paine was vigorously attacked by a strong force and compelled to fall back, after several hours' fighting, from his advanced position upon Pope's main line. The same day the rebels made an unsuccessful attempt to capture the advance guard of General McCook in the centre. The advance on May 17 resulted in quite a lively affair between General Sherman and the rebels in front of him. Sherman easily pushed them back. There was a great deal of powder burned in these several collisions, but, owing to the thickly wooded character of the country, the musketry fire was not very effective. The total casualties on our side did not exceed a few hundred, and the rebel loss was probably no greater. Few prisoners were taken by either side.

Under the protection of my general pass within the lines, I made it my object to visit successively the different camps of the Armies of the Tennessee and Mississippi. The region through which the Federal encampments extended was very unattractive and monotonous. Not the least bit of picturesque scenery was to be found within the whole length and breadth of it. The few villages within it, too, consisted of a score or so of ordinary small frame or log houses, mostly deserted by the inhabitants and in wretched condition. My daily rides were, therefore, not very exhilarating, and were often made disagreeable owing to the fact that I knew nobody in Pope's army but the General himself, and only two persons in the Army of the Tennessee, viz., Generals Sherman and Lew Wallace, the latter having been a senator in the Indiana Legislature when I attended that body in the winter of 1858–9. '(Since the war, he has attained fame and fortune as a novel-writer.) I was obliged to introduce myself to everybody, and did not always meet with a friendly reception. The Federal front represented a length of nearly twelve miles, and twice it happened to me that I could not find my way back to my quarters before dark, and had to ask for, and receive, very scant hospitality in the camps where I found myself at nightfall. General Sherman's prejudice against army correspondents had been intensified, owing to the severe press criticisms based upon the published reports that he and his command had been utterly surprised at Shiloh, and he received me rather gruffly. Gen. Lew Wallace was also under a cloud, owing to his failure to get his division up to the front in the first day's battle. He was evidently very much pleased with my call, in the expectation, as he did not hesitate to intimate broadly, that I would publish what he had to say in his own defence. Wallace had the kindness to send an aide-de-camp with me to introduce me to Generals McClernand and Hurlbut, his fellow division commanders, who also received me very graciously, and who likewise complained a good deal of the misrepresentation by the press of their part in the battle. Both claimed that they and their troops fought determinedly all day against overwhelming odds. Both belonged to the class of "political" generals, and sought glory as much through army correspondents as by feats of war—if not more. Nevertheless, they established a fair record as commanders in the later campaigns.

I made bold to recall myself to General Pope as one of the party accompanying President Lincoln from Springfield, and was at once made very welcome at his headquarters, which I visited frequently. He was, no doubt, an able man and good soldier, but, whether from accidental mistakes or a natural incapacity to lead a large force, his performances as an independent commander never equalled his promises. He had two very marked failings—first, he talked too much of himself, of what he could do and of what ought to be done; and, secondly, he indulged, contrary to good discipline and all propriety, in very free comments upon his superiors and fellow-commanders. Through Pope I also made the acquaintance of General Rosecrans, then a division commander in the Army of the Mississippi. He was, outside of the Army of the Ohio, the most affable, frank, and genial general that I had met—a very prize, indeed, for an eager news-gatherer. He invited me to his camp so urgently that I grew suspicious, and thought that he cared more for my pen than my person. My subsequent experience proved that I had judged him correctly.

I had seen General Grant a number of times after the battle, but never had a chance to talk with him before the middle of May. Between that time and the end of the siege, however, I conversed with him on three occasions—twice at his own field-headquarters, and once in passing him accidentally on the main road to Corinth. There was certainly nothing in his outward appearance or in his personal ways or conversation to indicate the great military qualities he possessed. Firmness seemed to me about the only characteristic expressed in his features. Otherwise, he was a very plain, unpretentious, unimposing person, easily approached, reticent as a rule, and yet showing at times a fondness for a chat about all sorts of things. His ordinary exterior, however, made it as difficult for me as in the case of Abraham Lincoln to persuade myself that he was destined to be one of the greatest arbiters of human fortunes.

All officers (excepting army commanders) and men were under strict orders not to pass beyond the encampments of their organizations while in front of the enemy. The effect naturally was that, at any given point of our line, they could not know what was going on along the rest of it. We newspaper correspondents, who had the freedom, so to speak, of the whole army, were generally better informed as to current incidents than even officers as high in rank as division commanders. As collectors and distributors of news we gradually became quite popular. We were the more willing to gratify the general curiosity of the rank and file on our tours through the camps as we could not make use of our knowledge for professional purposes, for our permits to remain with and circulate among the armies had been given on the express pledge on our part not to write anything to our papers, before the occurrence of decisive events, about the number, condition, location, and doings of our troops. I observed this injunction religiously, and hence felt all those weeks as if off duty. I really had a very easy time, and was very well taken care of by my friend, the quartermaster of McCook's division. I shared a large tent with his chief clerk, and was favored with a comfortable camp-bed and very passable meals. A runaway slave—a mulatto—waited on me and attended to my horse. Still, I grew tired of my idleness, and rejoiced when events before Corinth reached a culmination. This came much earlier than was expected by the Federal commanders, and in a surprising form.

What was destined to be the last advance of the Union line took place on May 28 and 29. It was very strongly opposed by rebel skirmishers and outposts, but the enemy was driven back. Later in the day, two attempts were made to regain the lost ground. The new move brought the fronts of Pope's and Buell's lines to the edge of a clearing not more than an average of half a mile from Corinth, and in plain view of the enemy's fortifications covering the town, which appeared to be strong and extensive. Our left, with Sherman's division in advance, did not reach clear ground and did not discover the hostile defences. The 29th was enlivened by a roaring cannonade on the Union side from the heavy Parrott guns that had been brought to the front in anticipation of a regular siege. Pope had planted a battery of four thirty-pounders during the night, from which an enfilading fire was opened in the morning upon the nearest rebel work. As was afterwards ascertained, the fire killed and wounded eighty men and a hundred horses, and destroyed a locomotive and its crew. Sherman also opened with Parrott twenty-pounders upon a building occupied by a rebel outpost, and quickly demolished it. I was with General McCook all day on the 29th. We could see a good portion of the rebel works, but no signs of activity were observable. We heard, however, very distinctly the incessant movement of railroad trains.

The final chapter of the "siege" forms a curious tale, partaking more of the ludicrous than of the horrors of war. In some way the impression prevailed at all the headquarters that the enemy was about to strike a great blow. Halleck issued an order enjoining the greatest caution in feeling the enemy. Sherman was even told, if the risk in holding his new position was too great, to fall back. The apprehension of a rebel attack *en masse* grew stronger in the course of the 29th. The continuous rolling of trains was construed as meaning a concentration of forces at certain points for that purpose. With the night, the anxiety increased, and none of the generals and their staffs on the front line allowed themselves any sleep, and I shared the vigil in McCook's camp. It was all an illusion that was not dispelled till long after midnight. General Halleck issued an order an hour or two after midnight to Buell and Thomas as follows: "There is every indication that the enemy will attack our left this morning, as troops have been moving in that direction for some time. It may be well to make preparations to send as many of the reserves as can be spared in that direction." This order may or may not have been the reflex of the following report from Pope to Halleck, dated May 30, 1:20 A.M.: "The enemy is reënforcing heavily, by trains, in my front and on my left. The cars are running constantly, and the cheering is immense *every time they unload in front of me*. I have no doubt, from all appearances, that I shall be attacked in heavy force at daylight."

General Halleck's feelings may be imagined when at 6 A.M. this unexpected revelation reached him from the same source: "All very quiet since 4 o'clock. Twenty-six trains left during the night. A succession of loud explosions followed by dense black smoke in clouds. Everything indicates evacuation and retreat." Up to that moment, nobody in command seemed to have correctly interpreted the plain signs of the real rebel purpose. Sherman, indeed, early in the morning, asked the general headquarters "how they explained the frequent explosions in Corinth during the night." I need not describe the sensations of our generals when the mortifying truth fully dawned upon them that Beauregard had played most successfully the trick of making a bold offensive show, while really bent upon flight.

The rebel works were almost simultaneously occupied by the picket lines of Pope's and McCook's, Nelson's and Sherman's divisions. A dispute afterward arose as to whom really belonged the honor of having been the first to enter them. McCook and Nelson felt chagrined that Halleck, in his first reports, awarded it to Pope, and later made official reclamation, to which the General-in-chief had, however, the conclusive answer that he had not referred to them because their immediate superior had not reported the facts in their case to him. I lost no time myself in riding into Corinth, and I believe I reached the main street—practically the only one—shortly after 7 A.M. The appearance of the town badly belied its classic name. The principal thoroughfare was lined on both sides, for say a quarter of a mile, with plain frame structures of one or two stories, interspersed with a few brick buildings and one of stone. The private residences, mostly of wood, small and of very simple style, were scattered about. Of the twelve to fifteen hundred or so inhabitants, only a few remained. A number of the buildings were reduced to ashes. The rebels had fired only those that contained Confederate supplies which could not be carried away, but the flames had spread and consumed others. The explosions we had heard arose from abandoned ammunition reached by the fire. The evacuation and destruction had been effected so completely that no spoils of any kind were found. A small number of rebel wounded were found about the town and in the works.

The latter were neither as extensive nor as elaborate as we had supposed them to be. There was an outer and an inner line, the former consisting of rifle-pits with breastworks behind them, the latter of regular field bastions with high parapets, ditches, curtains, and embrasures for artillery. Still, the works afforded proof that it must have been Beauregard's original intention to make a firm stand against Halleck. He does not directly admit this in his official utterances, but it can be read between the lines. He says substantially, in the opening paragraph of his report, dated Tupelo, Miss., June 13:

> The purposes and ends for which I had occupied and held Corinth having been mainly accomplished by the last of May, and, by the 25th of that month, having ascertained definitely that the enemy had received large accessions to his already superior force while ours had been reduced day by day by disease, resulting from bad water and inferior food, I felt it clearly my duty to evacuate that position without delay. I was further induced to this step by the fact that the enemy had declined my offer of battle twice made him outside of my intrenched lines, and sedulously avoided the separation of his corps, which he advanced with uncommon caution, under cover of heavy guns and strong intrenchments, constructed with unusual labor and with singular delay, considering his strength and our relative inferiority in numbers.

The cheap braggadocio of this alleged challenge to his enemy to combat in mediæval style seems to have impressed the rebel Secretary of War and Jefferson Davis more than his silly complaint of Halleck's extreme caution. His superiors no doubt drew from these effusions the just conclusion that he was an arrant humbug, and soon afterward relieved him from the chief command in the West. It must be admitted, however, in face of the facts, that another passage in his report was not unjustified, to wit: "It was then [the morning of May 30th] that the enemy, to his surprise, became satisfied that a large army, approached and invested with such extraordinary preparations, expenses, labor and timidity, had disappeared from his front with all its munitions and heavy guns."

My recollection is very distinct that the singular ending

of the Corinth campaign was a general disappointment to the Union side, from Halleck down. I do not hesitate to say that the latter did not look for the escape of Beauregard from his clutches without a fight. There is absolutely no evidence of such an expectation in his official despatches and reports. I am persuaded, too, that, before it actually happened, such a contingency would have been pronounced a misfortune to the loyal cause. Still, it was natural that, after the event had occurred, Halleck should make the most of the "bloodless victory" in manœuvring his adversary out of so strong a position, chosen and carefully prepared for defence by himself, with forfeiture of the only direct railroad line of communication between the east and west of the Confederacy, exposure of the cotton States to invasion, and abandonment of the middle Mississippi Valley. Nor is it surprising that Halleck's claim to credit for this achievement was, at the time, admitted both by the Government and by the loyal public. Before the end of 1862, the rebel leaders succeeded, however, as we shall see, in largely neutralizing these consequences by a new aggressive campaign in Tennessee and Kentucky, in the light of which their abandonment of Corinth was proved to have been fortunate.

There was no time lost in the pursuit of the vanquished enemy. General Pope, being nearest to the line of retreat, naturally took the lead in it. The task was most arduous, as the roads were narrow and bad, led through a very swampy country, and were obstructed by felled trees and burning bridges. The Union cavalry first caught sight of the rebel rear-guard about eight miles south of Corinth, and kept close at their heels for several days. The enemy was also followed by several columns of infantry and artillery, moving over different roads, commanded by General Rosecrans, under the direction of General Pope. Owing to the natural difficulties, the pursuers accomplished only short distances from day to day, and though they followed the enemy closely, they could not get within striking distance.

On June 4, Rosecrans felt the rebels strongly about two miles north of Baldwin (thirty miles south of Corinth on the Mobile & Ohio Road). He found them in great force and determined to resist his advance. He therefore sent to Pope, his immediate superior, for reënforcements. Pope not only responded, but called on Halleck for more help, whereupon the latter ordered Buell with two divisions to join him. Buell did so, and assumed command as the senior major-general. He issued an order of battle for the 8th, but the same day it turned out that the enemy had retreated further south. Beauregard had, indeed, halted at Baldwin with most of his army, but decided to fall back twenty miles further to Tupelo. Under Halleck's order, no further pursuit was attempted.

Before closing this chapter, I must refer to what was perhaps the strangest incident of the Corinth campaign. On June 4, Halleck telegraphed to Secretary Stanton:

General Pope with 40,000 is thirty miles south of Corinth, pushing the enemy hard. He already reports 10,000 prisoners and deserters from the enemy and 15,000 stands of arms captured. Thousands of the enemy are throwing away their arms. A farmer says that when Beauregard learned that Colonel Elliott had cut the railroad on his line of retreat, he became frantic and told his men to save themselves as best they could. We have captured nine locomotives and a number of cars. The result is all I could possibly desire.

Our impulsive American Carnot replied: "Your glorious dispatch has just been received, and I have sent it into every State. The whole land will soon ring with applause at the achievement of your gallant army and its able and victorious commander." The land was, indeed, soon ringing with patriotic outbursts, as the governors of the loyal States lost no time in congratulating their people on the great reported success and having national salutes fired in its honor.

Again, on June 9, Halleck telegraphed to Stanton:

General Pope estimates rebel loss from casualties, prisoners and desertion at over 20,000, and General Buell at between 20,000 and 30,000. An Englishman employed in the Confederate commissary department says they had 120,000 men in Corinth, and that now they cannot muster more than 80,000.

Some days later, the Northern press published a statement from Beauregard, printed in the Richmond papers, that the dispatch first quoted from Halleck to Stanton "contained almost as many lies as lines," and this charge is also made in his official report. Stanton having called Halleck's attention to this by wire, the latter replied: "In accordance with your instructions, I telegraph to you daily what information I receive of events in this department, stating whether official or unofficial, and, if official, giving the authority. In regard to the number of prisoners and arms taken, I telegraphed the exact language of General Pope. If it was erroneous, the responsibility is his, not mine."

The simple truth was, that Pope's captures of men and arms were only about one-tenth of the number he had reported to Halleck. The whole army was amazed when the newspapers arrived with the correspondence between Stanton and Halleck, and the enthusiastic popular responses it had provoked. I and all knew that a gross deception had been practised. In due time, the Northern press broke out in furious indignation against Pope, who was considered responsible for it. Pope did not defend himself. Singular to relate, it was only in July, 1865, three months after Lee's surrender at Appomattox, that Pope addressed a letter to Halleck calling attention to the subject, disclaiming the authorship of the false report, and asking to have his record set right. Halleck excused himself from complying with the request, on the ground that his papers had been boxed up, as he was about to start for California to take command on the Pacific Coast. Pope thereupon prepared a long letter for publication, in which he denied his responsibility for the report, and criticised Halleck very severely for practically refusing him the satisfaction to which he was entitled. The letter appeared in print and attracted a good deal of attention. I do not remember what Halleck did regarding it.

CHAPTER XVIII

BUELL'S RETREAT TO THE OHIO.—1862

GENERAL McCOOK'S division was ordered to occupy Corinth, and his headquarters were moved within the town limits. For ten days after the evacuation, there was great uncertainty as to the future operations of the army, and, after describing the closing scenes of the "siege," idleness was again my lot. It then became known, however, that General Halleck had determined, with the approval of the Washington authorities, to break up the grand army united under his command. The Army of the Ohio, under Buell, was to enter upon a new campaign through northern Alabama and southeastern Tennessee to East Tennessee, to carry out the long-deferred plan of freeing the loyalists in the latter region from rebel oppression and persecution. The Armies of the Tennessee and Mississippi, under Grant and Pope, were to be employed in holding western Tennessee and northern Mississippi and the adjacent portion of Alabama, and in offensive operations down and west of the Mississippi. In moving eastwardly, Buell's men were to put the Memphis & Charleston Railroad east of Corinth in running order, while the work of repairing the line west of that point was to be undertaken by Grant's troops. The destruction wrought upon it by the rebels between Corinth and Memphis was not very great, as they had to use it up to the evacuation. I received word as early as June 8, if I remember aright, that a construction train that had worked its way from Memphis, which only two days before had fallen into the hands of the Unionists, would reach Corinth and start back the same day. I asked and received permission to go on it. I longed for a change from the monotony of camp life, and especially from the sameness of camp fare, to which I had been subjected for two months. Moreover, the winter clothes which I still was obliged to wear for want of something more suitable, were no longer endurable in the hot weather that had prevailed for a fortnight, and I hoped to be able to buy a summer outfit in the city.

The construction train, consisting of half a dozen freight and flat cars with an ancient locomotive of very shabby and decrepit appearance, arrived towards evening, and, for the sake of greater safety, its return was postponed till the next morning. I was one of a very motley crowd of passengers, numbering several hundred, and consisting of a strong guard, well and sick officers of all ranks, and wounded and ill soldiers. There were no seats, and we all squatted on the floors of the cars, with none too much elbow-room for any of us. We proceeded very slowly from caution, with reference both to the hastily repaired trestles and bridges and to the strong inclination of our engine to refuse to do service. We spent eleven hours in making the distance of only ninety-three miles, thus having plenty of time to observe the region traversed. It seemed even more forbidding than the stretch between Pittsburg and Corinth. Like the rest of my fellow-passengers, I arrived in a very tired, stiff-limbed, dust-covered, and hungry condition, and felt much relieved when I found that the Gayoso House, the principal hostelry of the city, was open for guests. I was pleasantly surprised to discover on the hotel register the names of the four colleagues whom I had met at Cairo. They had arrived the day before from that place. We had a very joyous time together that evening and during the rest of my stay.

Memphis was even then a fine city of about 25,000 inhabitants. The site rises amphitheatrically from the river, from which the city presents an imposing aspect. The buildings on the business streets and the principal private residences were of brick and stone, indicating enterprise and thrift.

The former stood in many solid blocks containing wholesale and retail stores, banks, and offices of every kind. A proper number of the private dwellings were large and elegant abodes of wealth. While a good many of the stores and offices were closed, there was a great deal of life in the streets, and one could not have imagined from their appearance that the place had just been the scene of actual war. There seemed to be as many whites as negroes moving about, and among them hundreds of Union army and navy officers and soldiers and sailors. They formed an entirely peaceful picture, and, indeed, I saw no signs of hostile feeling of any kind during my stay. There was a good deal of suppressed loyalty which showed itself very soon to a surprising extent, and very much facilitated the government of the city under the new rule. The Confederate flag never waved over Memphis again.

The liveliest point was the levee. Some twenty-five steamboats, side- and stern-wheelers, were lying along it. Some of them were commissary and quartermaster boats discharging their loads; others were the regular tenders of the Federal river fleet; while three or four were more or less damaged craft captured from the enemy. Some distance from the long line of ordinary boats lay at anchor in grim blackness six gunboats and four rams. They had performed a most daring and gallant exploit three days before, to which I must make a passing allusion. The fleet, aided by a brigade of Indiana infantry regiments, had been besieging Fort Pillow ever since the reduction of Island No. 10. The fort was constructed by the rebels for the defence of the Mississippi on its left bank at the so-called Chickasaw Bluffs, about sixty-five miles above Memphis. The "siege" consisted altogether of an exchange of heavy shot between the fort and the fleet. On the morning of June 5, it was discovered that the rebels had abandoned the fort; this step being the logical sequence of the rebel retreat from Corinth. It was immediately occupied from the fleet. Commander Davis, flag-officer of the naval force, and Colonel Ellet (commanding the four boats that had been, in an incredibly short time, converted by him, under authority of the War Department, into "rams" of the most formidable character) lost no time in getting under way at noon for Memphis, and anchored for the night a mile and a half above the city. Early next morning, they discovered the rebel fleet of eight gunboats and rams in front of the city. The Federal commanders started for their prey at half-past five. Ellet led the attack with his flagship, the ram *Queen,* followed by the other rams. The fight raged for an hour and a half, with rams against rams, and with gunboats keeping up a tremendous fire at close quarters against gunboats. It was all over at seven, with the nearly complete destruction of the hostile squadron. Seven of its vessels were captured, sunk, or burned, only one escaping down the river. The Federal loss was slight, but included the gallant Ellet, who received a pistol-shot fired by a rebel within a few feet of him when the *Queen* struck the first antagonist. The wound was at first considered slight, but he died from it two weeks later while on the way to his home in Ohio. Ellet was one of the most notable figures of the war. He possessed veritable genius as an engineer, and, being an intense loyalist, offered his special services for "clearing the Mississippi" to Secretary Stanton, who accepted them, commissioned him as colonel, and placed the means at his disposal for carrying out his plans. His untimely death was a great national loss, and was universally lamented.

The terrible spectacle of the naval battle was witnessed by tens of thousands of the inhabitants of the city, whose surrender was demanded by Commander Davis immediately after the cessation of hostilities and conceded by the mayor. Before actual possession was taken, Colonel Ellet's young son landed with a small squad of men, and they boldly made their way through crowds of secession sympathizers to the post-office and custom-house, took down the Confederate flags over those buildings, and hoisted the Stars and Stripes in their place. The Indiana brigade landed by noon and established military rule in the city.

The second day of my stay, my newspaper friends took me on a round of visits to the gunboats and rams. We were rowed successively to the flagship *Benton,* where we saw Commander Davis and Lieutenant Phelps, and then to four others, of whose names I remember only the *Cairo* and the *Carondelet.* They were specially built for the service, and looked to me, who had never seen any men-of-war, quite formidable, with their batteries of heavy guns, uniformed officers and crews, and the perfect order and discipline enforced on them. We were very hospitably received, and found the officers in a high state of elation over their overwhelming triumph, as they had a right to be. We also visited the rams, but were not permitted to see Colonel Ellet, who was said to have a high wound-fever. The rams were Mississippi steamboats cut down to their lower deck, and built up again fore and aft and on both sides with wooden bulwarks from a foot to a foot and a half thick, and covered with iron plates several inches thick. They were roofed over in the same way. Their double, iron-cased prows looked like huge wedges, and formed tremendous instruments of destruction. The illusion prevailed on the fleet, from the highest in command to the simple seamen, that the victory virtually opened the Mississippi down to New Orleans; but alas! it took a great deal more sanguinary work to accomplish that.

My recreation in Memphis was cut short by the news, which I learned early on June 11 from a captain of the commissary department of the Army of the Ohio whom I accidentally met on the street, that General Buell had received formal orders to march, and that General McCook's division had already started from Corinth that very day. Here was a predicament for me, as that doubtless implied that my host, the division quartermaster, and my horse and other belongings were gone also. Bidding a hasty farewell to my colleagues, I managed to catch a train that left at noon for Corinth. We travelled faster than before, but were still nearly eight hours in reaching Corinth. It did not take me long to make the pleasant discovery that, while McCook's division was actually gone, Captain Gamage had stayed behind in charge of the division train, which was to move early the next day. As the programme was that the division should await the train at Iuka, forty-five miles east of Corinth, I concluded to accompany the train, instead of riding ahead and trying to overtake the division, with the risk of capture by rebel guerrillas, who were known to be swarming in northern Mississippi and Alabama.

We were two days in reaching Iuka. It was a hard march for man and beast, the heat being great, the roads covered with deep dust, and the mosquitoes very abundant and aggressive. The route led through a succession of swampy lowlands and hilly stretches covered with poor timber. Only here and there were poverty-stricken farms and clusters of habitations, passing for villages, mostly deserted by the inhabitants. In order to avoid the choking clouds of dust raised by the train, Captain Gamage and I joined the main body of the cavalry escort in front of it. It consisted of the Second Indiana cavalry regiment, commanded by Colonel Edward M. McCook, a first cousin of General A. McD. McCook, and a brother of General Anson G. McCook, who after the war was for many years secretary of the United States Senate, and subsequently chamberlain of the city of New York. Edward McCook was as fine-looking an officer as could be found in the army: tall, graceful in figure and motion, with regular features, brilliant eyes, and black hair and beard. I was soon on very good terms with him, and we subsequently were thrown together a good deal, as will appear hereafter. (He was Territorial Governor of Colorado after the war.) He had a splendid regiment of picked men and horses, well drilled and disciplined by the other field officers, Lieutenant-Colonel Stewart and Major Hill, who had seen long service as non-commissioned officers in a regular cavalry regiment.

Nothing occurred to interrupt our progress, and, on the evening of June 13, I rejoined McCook's division headquarters at Iuka.

Buell's new movement, it will be remembered, was the occupation of the important strategic point, Chattanooga, and the liberation of East Tennessee. But, in addition to general instructions to this effect from Halleck, he also received a specific order to put the line of the Memphis & Charleston Railroad along his route of march in running order, and to maintain it by proper military protection. The distance from Corinth to Chattanooga is 217 miles, and should have been easily traversed by the army in from twenty-five to thirty-five days. General Buell always claimed that, in a personal interview with Halleck on the 11th, he requested to be permitted to choose his own route, his preference being in favor of a line of march through middle Tennessee via McMinnville, but that the order to repair the road and use it as a line of supply was insisted upon. An issue subsequently arose between Buell and Halleck as to the latter's responsibility for this. But, whatever the facts were, it can hardly be disputed that the coming failures of the Army of the Ohio were mainly due to the delays and other injurious effects of the efforts to repair and run the railroad in question. Fully two months were spent by half of the army in opening and holding it to Decatur, only to find that its regular operation could not be maintained, as it ran parallel to the front of the enemy, and hence was peculiarly exposed to interruption. Moreover, it proved impossible to stock it with sufficient motive-power and cars in time to do much good to Buell's forces. The work on the road resulted, too, in scattering the army a good deal, and demoralized the troops by keeping them from their regular military duties. The detention no doubt caused the miscarriage of the general plan for the campaign and the extraordinary turn of events which was to lead the Army of the Ohio, not to East Tennessee, but back to the river whose name it bore.

I left Iuka with McCook's division the day after I joined it. We were closely followed by Crittenden's division that had been pursuing Beauregard and had come on our route at Iuka. Wood's division we found already engaged in road-repairing between Iuka and Florence. Nelson's was similarly occupied between Iuka and Corinth. Our march was again made very trying by the heat and dust and the stinging vermin. But we went into camp on the evening of the 15th, not far from the Tennessee River on the south bank, almost opposite the town of Florence. We lost a whole week here in waiting for the completion of a ferry-boat, without which the river could not be crossed, the bridge over it being destroyed. The army contained plenty of men trained for that and any other sort of mechanical work, but the lack of machine- and hand-tools made the construction of the boat slow and difficult. The week was pleasantly spent, as we had a fine camp, good water, plenty to eat for man and beast, and cool nights free from mosquitoes. The surrounding scenery was quite picturesque. A great enjoyment for me was the daily swim I took in the river. The troops, too, were glad of the chance to clean up. Some diversion was afforded by the arrival of some very light-draught boats from Cairo, with army supplies.

I crossed over to Florence on the 23d, but it took fully three days' and nights' hard work to get the whole division with its artillery and trains over. It did not resume its march on the right bank for several days, owing to an order from Halleck to Buell to hold his command in place, as there were signs of an aggressive movement of the enemy upon Iuka; but this story turned out to have no foundation whatever. Florence was no more worthy of its famous name than Corinth. It looked rather attractive from the south bank, but proved very unclassical upon actual inspection—a straggling combination of brick and frame buildings of very plain style and neglected appearance. It had been occupied for some months by Union troops, and was abandoned by most of the inhabitants. A very brisk trade seemed to be carried on by speculators from the North, provided with permits from the United States Treasury Department, in buying up cotton for cash or in exchange for merchandise. This indulgence on the part of the Federal authorities, which grew into a general practice wherever cotton-producing regions were occupied, was very ill advised, and led everywhere to a regular contraband traffic with the South.

By this time General Buell had made up his mind that his army could not prosecute the campaign into East Tennessee without safe and ample lines of supply, and that, the Memphis & Charleston Road having failed as such, the completion of the two rail lines from Nashville to the Tennessee River, viz., one by way of Franklin, Columbia, Pulaski, and Athens to Decatur, and the other through Murfreesboro', Tullahoma, and Decherd to Stevenson, was imperative. The movements of his command during July were directed accordingly. Generals McCook's and Crittenden's divisions were destined for Stevenson, the farther of the two termini, Nelson's for Athens, Wood's for Decatur. Parts of all these divisions were to work on the railroads mentioned between Stevenson and Decherd and Decatur and Athens and Pulaski. General Thomas's division, which had been finally relieved from duty at and about Corinth, was to replace Wood and Nelson along the Memphis & Charleston. This distribution over a long line made it impracticable for me to observe the doings of any other parts of the army than those under McCook, with whom, as in the advance, I deemed it best to remain; and my narrative will therefore relate solely to his operations up to the re-concentration of the army.

I believe it was on July 2d or 3d that we started from Florence via Athens—an even more unclassical place than Florence—for Huntsville, Alabama, some seventy miles distant. The division made them in four days and a half— very good marching, considering the great heat and suffocating dust in which it was accomplished. The ordinary dirt road led within a few miles of the Tennessee, through a very broken country, and became more and more difficult, owing to many steep ascents and descents, for the troops, artillery, and trains. No signs of the enemy were discovered. Huntsville, a county seat and active trading centre, with a population, I believe, of five to six thousand, presented by its substantial appearance quite a pleasing contrast to the shabby places we had passed before. It was, indeed, one of the most prosperous places in northern Alabama before the war. General O. M. Mitchel, commanding another division, had occupied the town in April, and made it the point from which to clear the country of the rebels as far east as Stevenson and west as Florence; in which he had fully succeeded. General McCook left us at Huntsville on a short leave of absence, but the division resumed its march after a day's rest. We pushed on very steadily for a week and suffered again greatly from heat and dust, making from sixteen to eighteen miles a day, and reached Stevenson on July 14. All through the last day's march, we had heard from time to time the exhilarating sounds of locomotive whistles, and were much rejoiced to learn that the railroad from Nashville to Stevenson had been fully repaired, and that through-trains had arrived over it the day before. We found Louisville papers only two days old— a great treat, as we had heard nothing from the North for fully ten days. We stopped till the return of General McCook on the 17th. On the next day, we moved on to Battle Creek, seven miles, I think, from Stevenson. This brought us within thirty-one miles of Chattanooga, but Buell's army was not destined at that time to get any nearer to that objective-point. Crittenden's division had followed us closely, and General McCook exercised command over it and his own. General Buell, meanwhile, had established his headquarters at Huntsville, being thus separated by a long distance from his advance, consisting of one-third of his army, though in telegraphic communication with it.

There were already at that time more or less telling indications that the withdrawal of the rebels from Corinth had been but the first act in a new strategic programme aiming at a complete shifting of the scene of active operations and the resumption of the offensive by them. It gradually became clear that this programme comprised the transfer of the rebel army from middle Mississippi to Chattanooga, and a flanking movement thence against Buell under the leadership of General Bragg, who had superseded Beauregard. Buell seems to have first grown suspicious of it about the middle of July, when a series of rebel cavalry raids upon his lines of communication in Tennessee and Kentucky began with the sudden appearance of the daring cavalry leader Morgan, in the neighborhood of Bowling Green, and his dash thence through central Kentucky by way of Munfordville, Lebanon, Lexington, and Paris, with a force variously estimated at from one to three thousand mounted men. He captured a number of Federal detachments and inflicted considerable other damage. He recrossed the Cumberland near Mills Springs and safely reached East Tennessee, whence he had started, thus completing a circuit in his rapid movements. The next surprise of the same kind came on July 13, when Forrest, who developed into the most dangerous and successful rebel raider in the West, burst upon the town of Murfreesboro' like a thunderbolt from a clear sky. He utterly surprised and captured the garrison of fourteen hundred cavalry, infantry, and artillery—who, from the brigadier in command down to the rank and file, behaved disgracefully—together with hundreds of animals and wagons and great quantities of supplies, and worked such destruction on the railroad connecting Murfreesboro' with Nashville and Stevenson, between which latter points trains had run through for the first time only the day before, that it took two weeks to repair the damage. We felt the effect of this disaster at once at Battle Creek by the failure of the mails and newspapers, and the orders of the commanding-general to economize as much as possible with food and forage.

But Buell did not at first perceive the true meaning of these raids. He did not interpret them as the precursors, which they really were, of a coming attempt in strong force to compel him to abandon his movement upon Chattanooga and East Tennessee. He thought that his further advance would be disputed in front, and that the raids were merely meant to delay it, and he took measures immediately for the protection of the railroads by ordering Nelson's division to Murfreesboro' and drawing Wood's up to the Nashville & Decatur Road. But he still was confident that he could overcome the enemy in his way, and was far from contemplating the possibility of finding himself obliged before long to abandon his offensive campaign altogether, and to lead his army back to where it had started from early in the year. The arrival of General Bragg at Chattanooga on July 28, which he quickly learned, rather confirmed him in his view of the situation, in accordance with which he hastened the preparations for a resumption of his advance. Supplies were hurried forward to the front, and pontoon bridges for crossing the Tennessee got ready. The army trains were concentrated between Decherd, a railroad junction thirty miles north of Stevenson, and the river. All the troops between Stevenson, Huntsville, and Athens, including General Thomas's division, were ordered to the same vicinity. The army headquarters were also moved to Decherd.

Excepting some scouting excursions to the south and east, McCook's command remained stationary for nearly four weeks at Battle Creek. As I again complied strictly with my pledge not to report anything of the movements of our army, I underwent another involuntary term of idleness. The monotony of camp life was very irksome, yet there was nothing for me to do but to accept it. The division headquarters were kept astir, however, by the accounts of the rebel movements and plans, frequently brought in by spies, refugees, prisoners, and deserters, of which I was informed in confidence. They agreed that a concentration of rebel forces was steadily going on at and about Chattanooga, and that they meant to take the offensive. Reports that Bragg was about to cross the Tennessee, and even that he had actually crossed, commenced coming in early in August, and kept us on the alert, but they all proved to be unfounded. The constant confirmation of the near presence of a hostile army estimated at from fifty to sixty thousand, however, led Buell to give up his belief that Bragg would remain on the defensive and await his own advance upon him, and to act on the presumption that the rebels would cross over the Walden range of hills, rising from the right bank of the Tennessee directly opposite Chattanooga, into the valley of the Sequatchie, and follow that river down to its mouth, debouching near Butte Creek, and turning McCook by recrossing the Tennessee.

He was strengthened in this new theory by the increasing frequency, formidableness, and success of the rebel efforts in Tennessee and Kentucky to obstruct his long channel of supply by the single line of rail from Louisville to Nashville, and the double one from Nashville to his front. More or less numerous bands of mounted guerrillas appeared at many points in both States, annoying or capturing and destroying what came in their way. Reports of encounters with them reached the army headquarters daily. Though defeated in one place, they quickly turned up again in another. A report reached Buell on August 6, that Morgan had reappeared with a large force and was making for Nashville, whereupon orders were immediately issued to fortify that city sufficiently to protect it from surprise. On August 10, the dreaded rebel actually turned up at Gallatin, a town on the Louisville & Nashville line, on the north bank of the Cumberland, only twenty-five miles from Nashville. He surprised and captured the garrison, and then proceeded to destroy culverts and bridges in the direction of the latter city. Moving northwest toward Bowling

Green, he obstructed the tunnel seven miles north of Gallatin, and burned an additional number of wooden superstructures. It was learned about the same time that Forrest had again reached the Cumberland with several thousand cavalry, and was moving toward Nashville. Buell at once sent a cavalry force of seven hundred under Brigadier-General Johnson, an old regular-cavalry man, after Morgan. Johnson overtook him near Gallatin, but, owing to the misbehavior of part of his command, was beaten, and he himself taken prisoner with one hundred and fifty men. The remainder of his men refused to surrender and got away. Johnson was afterward charged with incapacity and cowardice in this affair.

This bad news produced no little anxiety in the army and at our division headquarters. The interruption of rail communication with Louisville, our primary base, was, indeed, a most serious blow, and, if long continued, was bound to frustrate the plan of campaign and compel retrograde movements. General Nelson was therefore detached from his division and ordered to Kentucky to restore our communications and clear that State of Morgan and the guerrillas. The army commander also telegraphed to General Grant, by authority of General Halleck, who had in the meantime been called to Washington as general-in-chief of all troops in the field, for two additional divisions, one to be used for protecting the line north of Nashville, and the other for service on the front in the general advance, which was still believed possible notwithstanding the threatening occurrences in the rear.

To General McCook's command now fell the part of an active corps of observation. On August 19 it received orders, upon the first intelligence of an advance of the enemy along the Sequatchie, to move promptly up that valley to check him and observe his movements. If pressed, he was to fall back over the so-called Therman road, diverging from the Sequatchie to the north, upon the main Union force that was expected to advance from McMinnville. Crittenden's division was also to move up the Sequatchie in the wake of McCook and in his support, and, if necessary, also to fall back over another road upon the column from McMinnville.

We commenced our march up the valley on the 20th, and had been under way some hours when we met two spies with very full and apparently reliable information as to the doings of the enemy. One of them was a non-commissioned officer in an Ohio regiment, a very intelligent man, who had volunteered for this perilous mission. He had spent some days at Chattanooga. He affirmed very positively that Bragg had crossed the river at Chattanooga with seventy regiments and a great deal of artillery, and was moving down the Sequatchie. This intelligence made General McCook fear that he could not reach the Therman road before Bragg, and he decided to fall back with his column to the so-called Higginbottom pike, also leading over the Cumberland Mountains, that bordered the Sequatchie on the north. The General and staff rode in advance up the very steep ascent of the pike to the summit, and I went with them. We ascertained quickly that the road was altogether too steep for artillery and trains, and the General determined to return to Battle Creek and move up its valley by another road over the mountains. He received orders on the 23d to march over the Battle Creek road in one day to Pelham, on the plateau of the Cumberland Mountains, a few miles from Decherd, thence to Altamont, and there to form a junction with Thomas's forces and attack the enemy if he should come over the Therman road. The road proved very difficult and the distance longer than expected, so that we bivouacked on the summit of the mountains seven miles from Pelham, and descended to that point—a wretched-looking, deserted hamlet—early next morning. We found there the first division under temporary command of General Schoepf, a German-Hungarian, who had seen service in the old country and was a thorough soldier. Having ascertained that General

Thomas had left Altamont, we went into camp, awaiting further orders from General Buell, who came over the next day from Decherd and directed us to move on to Altamont.

The plateau and northern outrunners of the Cumberland range that we had traversed from Battle Creek to Altamont, formed a very broken, sterile, and dry stretch of country. With the exception of a little forage of hay and green corn, it was destitute of supplies of every kind; while, owing to the interruption of the Louisville & Nashville Railroad, the troops had subsisted on half-rations for twenty days. The greatest difficulty was the want of water for men and beasts. Our whole division had but one spring to draw from for officers and men, and only pools of stagnant water in a half-dry streamlet several miles away were available for the animals. We were to watch for the supposed approach of the enemy over the Therman road at Altamont (this high-sounding name belonged to as mean a place as Pelham), whence four roads ran in different directions towards middle Tennessee; but the lack of water compelled us to move half a day's march on to Hubbard's Cove on Hickory Creek. Here, orders were received to concentrate with the rest of the army at Murfreesboro' and to make for that point as rapidly as possible.

General Buell had become satisfied some days before that the movement of the enemy down the Sequatchie had been only either a feint or a reconnoissance in force. He next expected an advance of Bragg over the Therman road, and concluded, only after he had been disappointed in this expectation also, that his adversary was moving north over a more easterly route. General Thomas had thought this all along, and urged proper counter-moves upon his superior, without convincing him. Buell now determined upon a rapid concentration of his army at Murfreesboro', upon the theory that Bragg's objective-point was Nashville. Some of his generals did not share this notion, and felt sure that the enemy was not bound for middle Tennessee, but for Kentucky. They were right and Buell wrong, but the general concentrating movement was formally ordered on August 30 and carried out. It was admirably planned, and effected with remarkable precision, considering that it included not only large bodies, but moving detachments, post-garrisons, and railroad guards spread out over a territory of one hundred and fifty by one hundred miles, and that only one week was allowed for completing it.

The day before McCook began his march to Murfreesboro', Edward McCook, the cavalry colonel, unexpectedly appeared with a small mounted escort for a brief visit to his cousin. He had been employed for nearly two months after we parted in escorting supply trains along the Tennessee River, but had followed General Nelson's division when it moved to McMinnville. He had been engaged with his command for some weeks in scouting, hunting, and fighting guerrillas. He invited me to accompany him, and, as I was weary of the monotonous marches, I accepted and rode off with him. For a week, I had an experience that reminded me continually of the song in Schiller's play of the "Robbers"—

"Ein freies Leben führen wir."

The Colonel had a brigade of nominally three mounted regiments, but actually not more than eleven hundred men, under him. They were well armed and relatively well mounted, as their commander had made it his rule to exchange any good horses found in the country for the worn ones of his command. Not having received any new clothing since spring, however, a considerable percentage of the men had substituted civilian garments for parts of their uniforms, and thus presented a rather mixed exterior. More than half had managed to possess themselves of straw and felt hats of various colors. A score or so wore "butternut" or "Confederate gray," being the "scouting squad" in the disguise of rebels for the better performance of their perilous duties.

Altogether, the motley appearance of the brigade was in keeping with the miscellaneous services it had to render. It was literally a "flying column," moving rapidly from point to point, and walking, trotting, and galloping from twenty to forty miles a day. Every morning a number of detachments were sent in advance and to right and left of the main body, scouring the country in search of the enemy, of food and forage, and suitable camping-grounds. The Colonel and I always rode with the advance. Three times we had a chase of rebel game and lively bush-fighting, resulting in some casualties on both sides. We bivouacked every night in the open air, with nothing but waterproofs under, and blankets and roofs of fence rails or branches of trees over us. Saddles served as pillows. A few ambulances and a dozen wagons with ammunition were all our transportation. We literally lived on the country, and, like a swarm of locusts, left nothing eatable behind us. Our men had acquired remarkable skill in making a clean sweep of food and fodder. They were especially smart in discovering the hidden stores and the cattle that had been driven off by the inhabitants, in which they were often helped by the black people, a bevy of whom, mounted on mules, had gradually collected and followed us into "freedom." Our meals were, of course, very irregular, and more remarkable for simplicity than variety; but, while we sometimes went to sleep or started off in the morning without a meal, we got along well enough. I certainly enjoyed the adventurous life, which was to me a repetition of my Colorado days.

One exciting incident impressed itself especially on my mind. While we were riding one afternoon with the advance, a private asked leave to fall out for a certain purpose. He tied his horse to a fence and climbed over the latter into a corn-field. In about five minutes we heard a shot from the direction of the field. Fearing at once that something had happened to the man, we stopped and sent back a platoon for him. Soon afterward one of the latter galloped up with the news that the poor fellow had been found shot dead. It being evidently a case of stealthy murder, we at once returned to the scene, and there the Colonel decided to make an example. We made for the dwelling of the owner of the farm, where only women and children seemed to be. We could get nothing out of them, but a male slave, when threatened, confessed that young "Massa" had fired the shot. Thereupon, all human beings and animals were ordered out of the buildings, which were immediately set on fire and burned down in less than an hour. Stern retribution like this, and even sterner, had become a necessity, owing to the frequent assassinations that had occurred in middle Tennessee during the summer. The worst outrage of this kind was the murder of General Robert L. McCook (whom I mentioned as colonel of the 9th Ohio, in connection with the battle of Mill Springs) while going to a railroad station in an ambulance, on sick-leave. General Buell had issued orders to hang at once every civilian caught as a guerrilla, and Colonel McCook's command had inflicted the death penalty in five cases already.

According to instructions, we had made our way to and beyond McMinnville. Some twelve miles to the east of that place, our scouts brought us the positive intelligence that Bragg's army was moving to the north over the road leading through Spencer and Sparta to Carthage on the Tennessee River, and was already near the latter. We at once started back with this important news, and, on reaching McMinnville—a rather pretty and substantial town of several thousand inhabitants—the Colonel reported it by wire to the army headquarters. Like the rest of the army, we also were ordered to Murfreesboro', and marched there in two days. We passed through a rich agricultural country, one large plantation with fine brick dwellings and out-buildings succeeding another. The road was a well-macadamized highway. As the brigade had met its wagon train at McMinnville and drawn commissary and quartermaster supplies, our "freebooter" days came to an end.

The converging movement to Murfreesboro' of the different parts of the army was substantially completed on September 5. But Colonel McCook's report of Bragg's northward passage, which was confirmed from other sources, and the alarming news, received about the same time, of the bad defeat of General Nelson in eastern Kentucky, had at last brought the real situation home to General Buell, viz., that his adversary was fast executing a bold flanking march into central Kentucky, with Louisville doubtless as the objective-point, and that there was nothing left but to try and beat him in a race for the Ohio River. Hence the army did not tarry at all at Murfreesboro', but, in obedience to general orders, immediately continued on in forced marches to Nashville and thence on to the north. I rejoined McCook's division near Murfreesboro'—which proved to be quite a pleasant, compactly built-up little town—again to share its fortunes for almost two months.

With General Buell's cold, impassive nature and habitual reserve and reticence, any strong expression of feeling could hardly be expected from him, but those who came in contact with him in those days perceived, nevertheless, that he was greatly afflicted by the turn of events. It could not well be otherwise, for what was happening meant nothing less than a forced change from the offensive to the defensive, which, in spite of whatever explanations might be offered by him, would have the appearance of a compulsory retreat, and was sure to be looked upon as such by the Government, the public, and his own army. Furthermore, there was the undeniable discredit and humiliation of the involuntary abandonment of much of the fruit of the great expenditure of life, labor, and money during the summer in occupying rebel territory, incessant fighting on a small scale, repairing railroads, and doing a vast amount of other hard work. The distrust of Buell as an army commander, of which the battle of Shiloh and the siege of Corinth had relieved him, now set in again more strongly than before. The necessity of following Bragg's lead back to where they had started from, naturally had a very dispiriting influence upon the commanders under him. As we shall see, it demoralized also the rank and file to a dangerous extent. Anxiety as to the new campaign about to be entered upon pervaded the whole army. I confess that I shared the general depression.

McCook's division formed the rear of the army. We left Murfreesboro' early on the morning of September 7, with 11,000 infantry, 3000 cavalry, and an enormous train of 750 wagons, forming a column over ten miles long. The heat was great, and we rode nearly all the time in clouds of dust, but had accomplished our severe task of thirty miles at 11 P.M. of the same day, and went into camp within two miles and a half of Nashville. General McCook himself proceeded to General Buell's headquarters, and there at midnight received orders to cross the Cumberland the next day and march as fast as possible toward Franklin in Kentucky. General Buell announced his determination to start at once, with the divisions of McCook, Crittenden, Ammen, Wood, Rousseau, and Mitchel, in pursuit of Bragg, who was reported to be marching from Carthage to Glasgow, fifty miles north of the former place and ninety-five miles from Nashville. General Thomas, with his own, Negley's, and Palmer's divisions, was to be left behind for the defence of Nashville, which was to be held at all hazards. General McCook advised him to abandon the city, and asked as a special favor to be allowed to burn it "as the most treasonable secession nest" in the whole South, but Buell would not entertain this radical suggestion. The Louisville & Nashville Railroad remained broken up from Nashville to within fifty miles of Louisville, so that human legs and animals formed our sole reliance for transportation. As only half-rations could be allowed for the march, it was a question whether the powers of endurance of man and beast would prove equal to the task.

We were in motion again in the morning, passed the river, and had marched some miles to the north of it on the Franklin turnpike, when instructions from Buell overtook us to halt till further orders. In the evening an order came to hurry to Edgefield Junction to the support of the division of General Ammen, who believed the enemy was approaching him in force. Instead of sleeping, we had a night's march of it, reaching the Junction at two in the morning, only to find that there had been a false alarm. During the following forenoon, we again got under way as the head of the army for Franklin and Bowling Green. General Buell and staff overtook us and rode with us all day. He hoped, by forcing the marching of his command to the utmost, to come up with the enemy between Glasgow and Bowling Green, in the direction of which point the rebel cavalry advance was reported to be going from Glasgow, with the bulk of Bragg's army following closely behind it. But there was a difference of thirty-five miles in distance, and apparently two days' time in addition, in Bragg's favor, so that the outcome of the race was uncertain, and everybody felt anxious. It took us three more days' marching to reach Bowling Green, where we stopped for two days in order to give the other divisions time to come up. The last of these joined us on the evening of the 15th. On the 16th, the army started again in three columns over as many different roads toward Glasgow, prepared to attack the enemy whenever encountered. But our advance cavalry reported the same evening that Bragg had left Glasgow and moved directly upon Munfordville. Our route of march was at once changed, and Cave City and Horse Wells, ten miles from Munfordville, made the next day. There we had a most discouraging surprise. The whole garrison of Munfordville, over two thousand infantry, came into our lines disarmed as paroled prisoners of war. They had shamefully surrendered in the morning to Bragg, after some resistance. Though they held a very strong position, their cowardly commanders allowed themselves to be frightened into a capitulation by the threats and display of force of the rebel general.

This scandalous incident produced a thrill of disgust and discouragement in our army. However, we pushed on towards Munfordville the next day, and found that the enemy was still there. Thus we had at least the satisfaction of having overtaken him, owing to his delay at Munfordville, which was some compensation for the surrender. We felt the rebel position on the 19th and 20th. Bragg withdrew the next day, his rear guard being driven out of the town by our advance. Our army followed him closely, and skirmishing was kept up with his rear constantly on the following three days, up to a point within thirty-five miles of Louisville, when he changed his direction to the east towards Bardstown, with a view, as became subsequently known, of effecting a junction with the forces of General Kirby Smith, approaching from eastern Kentucky in the so-called "Blue Grass" region. Bragg's deflection opened the way to Louisville to Buell, and he decided, as part of his command had exhausted its supplies and urgently needed replenishment of clothing and footwear, and as, moreover, a large body of fresh troops was gathered there from which he could fill his depleted ranks, to push as rapidly as posible for that city, and start from it upon a new campaign against Bragg.

McCook's division was continuously in motion, with the exception of two days' halt at Prewitt's Knob, between Bowling Green and Louisville. It made the distance of one hundred and twenty miles in seven marching days, of which the last three were the hardest; twenty-four, twenty-three, and twenty-one miles respectively being made. The division not having the lead of the army, nothing noteworthy happened during that week, and I do not deem it worth my while to give the uninteresting details of our marching experience. Two nights we slept on the floor in farm-houses, but the rest of the week we had to bivouac. As the rebels had stripped the country ahead of us, we were limited to the scanty army fare we brought along. Notwithstanding the insufficient food, the troops bore the hardships of the long march—there was an average of about one hundred and eighty-five miles made by them between Nashville and Louisville—remarkably well. There was considerable straggling in search of food, but the percentage of footsore and sick was low. We were favored by magnificent fall weather, moderately warm during the day and not too cool at night. When within ten miles of Louisville, I rode ahead of the division over the familiar highway and drew up in front of the Galt House at 10 P.M. on September 27. The old night clerk was at his post, but he did not recognize me with my dust-begrimed countenance and full-grown beard, and, evidently distrusting my general vagabondish appearance, replied to my application for a room: "We are all full." But he changed his tone at once when I mentioned my name, and had me escorted to a good bedroom on the top floor. My trunks were sent up—nearly eight months had gone by since I had locked them—and I once more enjoyed the long-missed luxury of a choice of under- and upperwear. It was high time that I did, for my Memphis outfit was fast giving out, and I had not been out of my dust-crusted clothes for ten days. My first indulgence was a hot bath, and the next a hearty supper, followed by eleven hours' sleep.

CHAPTER XIX

THE PERRYVILLE CAMPAIGN.—1862

NEXT morning I wrote up my notes made during the march, and, after noon, set out in search of McCook's division, which I found encamped near the Jefferson ferry. I also called on my Louisville friends and received a hearty welcome from them. They expressed the intense anxiety which the loyalists had undergone for a fortnight, owing to the steady approach of Bragg's army. Nor did they feel at ease after our arrival, for they had lost all faith in General Buell, and believed that he had been entirely outgeneralled by the rebel commander. In the course of the evening, I learned from the chief of staff, Colonel Fry, that the army was expected to move anew against Bragg within a few days, which put an end to my plan of visiting Cincinnati.

The invasion of Kentucky by Bragg's army had been preceded in the middle of August by the advance from eastern Tennessee into the State of a rebel force of about fifteen thousand men under General Kirby Smith. Crossing the Cumberland Mountains through two passes to the east of Cumberland Gap, he had turned the Federal force of about 10,000 men under General Morgan at the latter point and moved unopposed toward the "Blue Grass" country. About the same time, another rebel body, of about four thousand, under General Humphrey Marshall (a member of the prominent Kentucky family of the same name, who, in spite of his very fat body, displayed great physical energy and mobility), had entered the State from western Virginia, seeking a junction with Kirby Smith. John Morgan, the notorious rebel raider, was also coursing again through central Kentucky.

General Nelson, detached from his division by General Buell and ordered to Kentucky to clear it of guerrillas and raiders before Kirby Smith's appearance on the scene, reported to Major-General Wright at Louisville, and was sent by him at once to Lexington to take command of all the troops in that vicinity. They consisted of about ten infantry regiments from Indiana and Ohio and a Kentucky cavalry regiment, most of them just organized, with perfectly raw officers and men, a large portion of whom were going through their first drill. They numbered between seven and eight thousand men. Kirby Smith reached their advanced posts on August 29, and drove them and their supports steadily before him upon the main body at Richmond, some twenty miles south of Lexington. He attacked the Unionists there with his whole force the next day, and, after driving them from position to position, completely overwhelmed them. The routed Federals lost nearly half their number in killed, wounded, and prisoners, the remainder fleeing in the greatest disorder, and without stopping, through Lexington to Louisville. This victory gave Kirby Smith the choice of an unobstructed advance, either upon Louisville or Cincinnati. He marched toward the latter city, and came within six miles of the Ohio River. His approach caused the greatest consternation, not only in Cincinnati, but throughout Ohio and Indiana. Martial law was proclaimed in the Queen City, and preparations pushed night and day for her defence.

The indignation and rage of the Kentucky loyalists and the authorities and people of the two other States over the new rebel invasion was intense, and centred upon General Buell. In the press and at public meetings he was denounced, not only for his incapacity to cope with his rebel adversaries, but for his alleged sympathy for the South and consequent half-heartedness in waging war against it. Hot demands for his removal were made upon the President and Secretary of War by the Governors and members of Congress from the threatened States. The President resisted till Buell was obliged to follow Bragg back to the Ohio River, when he finally yielded to the rising pressure. An order was delivered to General Buell, on the morning after his arrival at Louisville, by a staff officer of General Halleck sent especially for that purpose, requiring him to turn his command over to General Thomas. General Thomas simultaneously received an order to assume command, but immediately telegraphed a request to Washington that the orders be countermanded and that General Buell be retained, to which the President assented. I learned this portentous news about noon on the 29th, but, secrecy being enjoined, I made no use of it. It became known, of course, to the general officers under Buell, and brought out divided opinions as to the justice and propriety, in the then situation, of his removal. It naturally had the effect of weakening his authority, and led, as I personally had occasion to observe, to still louder criticism of him.

Owing not only to this surprise, but to a terrible tragedy enacted almost under my eyes, September 29th will always be literally a red-letter day in my recollection. I was just finishing breakfast in the hotel dining-room on the ground floor when I heard the sound of a shot coming from the large entrance hall directly in front. I hurried out, and learned to my horror that General Jefferson C. Davis had shot General Nelson with a revolver, and that the victim was being led to his room, toward which I hastened. He was just able to reach it with the support of two friends, only to sink on the bed with life fast ebbing away. The bullet had penetrated the left breast near the heart. There he lay, bodily a giant among men, reminding one of a dying lion. A clerical friend of the General, who happened to be in the hotel, appearing, I retired. In ten minutes death ensued. This dreadful end was caused by Nelson's violent temper. After the disaster at Lexington, he had been ordered by Major-General Wright to take charge of the defence of Louisville. General Davis, who commanded one of the divisions sent by General Grant to General Buell but had been at home on sick-leave, on finding himself unable to join it, owing to the interruption of communications, had reported a week before for duty to Nelson, who placed him over a body of militia known as the "home guards." Nelson was not satisfied with the way he filled this function, relieved him from duty after a violent scene, and ordered him to report to General Wright at Cincinnati. The latter sent him back to Louisville, where he had arrived the day before. At the fatal moment, General Nelson was standing with Governor Morton of Indiana in front of the office counter, when General Davis approached and asked him to apologize for his rude behavior when he removed him from command. General Nelson refused to listen and turned away. Davis, who was a small, frail-looking man, followed him and insisted upon an apology. Nelson thereupon called him a puppy and struck him in the face. Davis at once went for a revolver, re-approached Nelson, and fired it at a distance of only a few feet. That Nelson's conduct was utterly unjustified and brutal, admits of no doubt. Indeed, his excitable temper made him too often play the part of a bully, although he was really good-natured and kind-hearted. The awful event made a sensation in the army and throughout the country, but Davis was released from arrest without a trial.

General Buell found a motley mass of about twenty thousand officers and men at Louisville, consisting of newly organized regiments from several Western States, of men discharged from hospitals or returning from furloughs and trying to reach their commands. There was great need of this accession of force. For, in truth, not a single regiment in his army had more than half of the officers and men on its muster-rolls present for duty, while a number had not more than one-third. The causes of this depletion were disease, straggling, desertion (very few to the enemy, but many to Northern homes), and the furloughing which was practised to a most reprehensible extent by regimental and company commanders. Aspiring local politicians, as so many of them were, they were afraid to refuse strongly backed applications for leave. Moreover, incredible as it may sound, thousands of furloughs were granted, at the instance of political leaders and with the approval of the Washington authorities, in order to assure satisfactory results in State, Congressional, and county elections. Heavy drafts for voting purposes had been especially made on the Army of the Ohio in order to defeat the dangerous and rising "copperheadism" (the telling generic term applied to disloyalty throughout the North) in Indiana and Ohio. The aggregate effect of these several sappings of the strength of the army was, that General Buell reached Louisville with only between 37,000 and 40,000 effectives. Under the circumstances, it was the part of prudence not to attempt to form new organizations out of the new troops he found gathered in the city, but to strengthen existing ones with them. Nor was any other course practicable. They were mostly raw, undrilled, undisciplined, and not even all armed, and there were not enough experienced officers to command them.

For once, not a moment of time was lost in preparing for the new offensive campaign. Under the spur of threatened removal and disgrace, General Buell devoted night and day to the arduous work of reorganizing the army and supplying it with food, forage, and ammunition, and re-clothing the older troops. He allowed only the last three days of the month for this heavy task. Three army corps were formed, consisting of three divisions each: the first commanded by General McCook, the second by General Crittenden, and the third by General Gilbert, a newcomer, the singular circumstances of whose appearance will be told later on. The new regiments were distributed among the three corps, bringing their aggregate strength up to 58,000 effectives of all arms. The march from Louisville was commenced on October 1. Owing to the shortness of time,

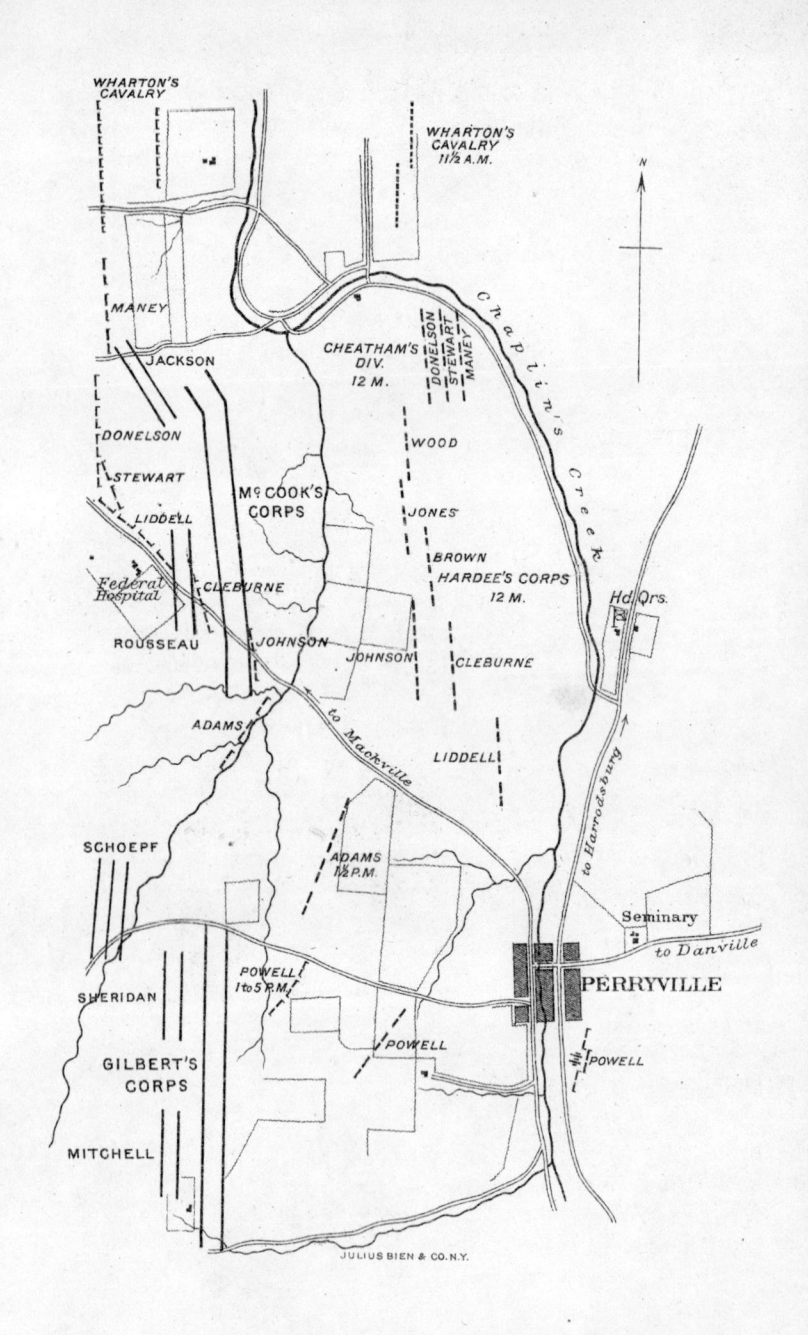
WHARTON'S CAVALRY
WHARTON'S CAVALRY 11/2 A.M.
N
MANEY
JACKSON
CHEATHAM'S DIV. 12 M.
DONELSON
STEWART
MANEY
Chaplin's Creek
DONELSON
STEWART
WOOD
McCOOK'S CORPS
LIDDELL
JONES
BROWN
HARDEE'S CORPS 12 M.
Federal Hospital
CLEBURNE
Hd.Qrs.
ROUSSEAU
JOHNSON
JOHNSON
CLEBURNE
ADAMS
to Mackville
LIDDELL
to Harrodsburg
SCHOEPF
ADAMS 1½ P.M.
Seminary
to Danville
POWELL 1 to 5 P.M.
SHERIDAN
PERRYVILLE
POWELL
POWELL
GILBERT'S CORPS
MITCHELL
JULIUS BIEN & CO. N.Y.

it had been impossible, notwithstanding the most strenuous efforts, to issue a full supply of clothing and footwear and canteens and haversacks to all the troops that needed them. The army moved in the lightest marching order. No baggage was allowed to be taken along, for either officers or men, and I set out with a roll of blankets strapped to my horse and one change of underclothing and toilet utensils in my saddle-bags. Only one wagon per regiment was allowed for officers' blankets and rations, and one other for cooking-utensils for the rank and file.

I obtained leave to accompany General McCook and staff again. I naturally felt most at home there, and should have better facilities for my work than before, owing to the higher command of the General. Our corps formed the left wing of the army. On leaving Louisville it divided. The second division, now commanded by General Sill, took the road to Frankfort, while the third, under General Rousseau, and the tenth, under General Jackson, consisting mainly of new regiments, with the corps headquarters, took the road to Bardstown. After following this for six miles, we took another, bearing to the left toward Taylorsville. We camped for the night, after marching about twenty miles. The next day we reached Taylorsville on the Salt River. Despite the fall season, a July heat prevailed, the roads were dusty, and water was scarce, owing to the extremely dry summer. We rested at Taylorsville on the 3d, and the next continued on to the town of Bloomfield, where we bivouacked for two days. On the 6th, we made a short march of seven miles to the Chaplin River, and on the 7th we pushed a few miles further on to Mackville. Thanks to the kindness of my friends of General McCook's staff, I slept in houses every night but one, and had enough to eat. The unseasonable heat and constant dust on the road were as trying to me as to everybody else.

We knew we were nearing the enemy, Bragg's main force, and advanced cautiously, with flankers and skirmishers thrown out. From the 2d, the latter came in touch with detachments of rebel cavalry and artillery, and frequently exchanged shots with them as they fell back. About two in the morning of the 8th, our headquarters were roused by an order from General Buell to move the corps at 3 A.M. to a position near Perryville. The Commander-in-chief had discovered, through a reconnoissance in force, that the enemy was in great strength between him and Perryville and evidently forming for battle, and he took his measures accordingly to get the three corps into a strong connected line during the night. Owing to the darkness, it was impossible to get the order distributed and the divisions under way before 5 A.M. Shortly afterward, we heard the continuous booming of artillery, which electrified the troops—being the first real sound of battle we had heard since Corinth—and quickened our movements. The ground on which the two divisions (the third had not yet rejoined the corps) were to form a line, about three miles northeast of Perryville, was reached between 10 and 11 A.M. We found troops of Gilbert's corps already there, and proceeded to select a line starting from its left. Everybody expected hard fighting. The day was to be, indeed, a most bloody one for McCook's command. The troops could not be said to be in good fighting condition. For several days men and animals had suffered severely from heat and dust, and, most of all, from the scarcity of water; on the 7th, hardly any was obtained. The line of battle crossed Doctor's Creek, a tributary of Chaplin River, but it contained water only in pools, access to which the rebels were evidently bent on preventing.

It appears from the official rebel reports that Bragg's reason for turning, as already mentioned, from the direct route to Louisville towards Bardstown, in an easterly direction, was that Kirby Smith's corps was unable to join him for a direct movement on the city, and that he did not feel strong enough alone to attempt its capture with Buell at his heels. Smith's force had been sent off for a vain effort to intercept the command of the Union General Morgan, in its retreat from Cumberland Gap to the Ohio River through eastern Kentucky. Bragg moved leisurely into the Blue Grass region with the triple object of feeding his hungry troops on the abundance of that fat land, of awaiting the return of Kirby Smith's command, and of installing at Frankfort, the capital, the so-called "provisional government" for the State that had been organized by local rebels since his appearance in it. The inauguration proved a great farce. It took place at the State capitol in the presence of Bragg and many rebel generals and other officers, on October 4, but the new Governor sought safety in retreat immediately after the ceremony, in company with Bragg, on learning of the rapid approach of the Union army. According to Bragg's account, one of the leading motives of his movement into Kentucky was the strong assurance of leading rebel sympathizers that the people would rise in a body to welcome their Southern brethren as liberators from the Northern yoke. Utter disappointment awaited him in this respect. As he said in his report to the Richmond War Department: "The campaign here was predicated on a belief and the most positive assurances that the people of Kentucky would rise in mass and assert their independence. No people ever had so favorable an opportunity, but I am distressed to add there was little or no disposition to avail of it."

Bragg was evidently surprised by Buell's early start from Louisville against him, of which he claims to have had information on October 2. On that day he sent orders to General Polk to move from Bardstown toward Frankfort and strike Buell in flank and rear, and General Kirby Smith was ordered at the same time to make a front attack. General Polk submitted his orders to a council of generals, who agreed with him that they could not be executed, and, accordingly, they were not. On being informed of this, Bragg countermanded his order to General Smith, and decided to effect a concentration of his forces further south. The action of General Polk led subsequently to an angry controversy between him and the generals who had supported him, and General Bragg; the latter contending that, but for this disobedience of his orders, Buell's whole army would surely have been beaten in detail. Having been informed in the meantime that the Union army was still advancing in three separate columns over as many different roads, he thought there was another opportunity to try the same game that Polk had failed to carry out. On October 6 he issued orders to Polk to attack the Union right, and, after overwhelming it, to join Smith in disposing of the hostile centre and left. Thus was brought on the collision known as the battle of "Perryville" or "Chaplin Hills."

The field of action lay mainly in the angle formed by Chaplin River and Doctor's Creek. It consisted of rolling ground, with undulations here and there, high enough to be called "hills," the summits of which commanded wide views. On one of these, McCook's corps headquarters were established. In the clear sunlight we looked upon an attractive and diversified scene of numerous farm-houses rising from large fields of ripe corn, alternating with more or less extensive patches of timber. The sight was literally one of peace and plenty—alas! to be instantly exchanged for the roar and carnage of battle.

As mentioned, we heard the sounds of fighting as we moved towards our position on the morning of the 8th. They were due to a lively skirmish between Colonel Daniel McCook's (a brother of General McCook) brigade of General Sheridan's division of Gilbert's corps and the advance of the enemy. Sheridan had reached the ground late on the preceding evening and had ordered Colonel McCook to occupy the height on the east side of Doctor's Creek, so as to command what water there was in it. The hill was in possession of the rebels, who resisted stubbornly, but finally yielded after a lively exchange of musketry and artillery fire. During the early forenoon the reënforced enemy tried to retake the position, but gave it up after a protracted artillery practice.

On reaching the ground, General McCook assigned General Rousseau's division to a position connecting with Gilbert's left, and ordered a line of skirmishers to be thrown forward to examine the woods on his left and front. He also sent an aide to General Jackson, and, in compliance with orders, galloped off to report in person to General Buell, whose headquarters were about two and a half miles to the rear, near Gilbert's left. The Commander-in-chief had had a severe fall from his horse two days before and could not move about, and this circumstance had an unfortunate bearing upon the fate of the day. McCook was verbally directed to make a reconnoissance towards the Chaplin River, and rode back at once to execute it. As Buell himself says, in his official report, he had rather expected an attack on Gilbert's corps early in the morning, when it was still alone on the ground; but, none having been made and McCook being now also in position, he did not believe that the enemy would make an offensive attempt during the remainder of the day.

I remained with General Rousseau during the absence of General McCook. The "feeling" for the enemy not having discovered him in front, Rousseau decided to move his line forward nearer to the Chaplin River, so as to procure water for the parched throats of his men. After moving about half a mile, we stopped, as there were renewed indications of the appearance of the enemy in the woods in front of us. Rousseau rode forward some distance to reconnoitre; I followed him and shared his experience during the following dreadful hours. We saw directly a moving rebel force. In a few minutes its approach was signalled by the sudden opening of a rain of shells, apparently from several massed batteries, upon us. The General at once ordered two of his batteries to return the fire. Thereupon, at least twenty-four guns sent whizzing and exploding missiles at each other by and over us as a roaring prelude to the sanguinary battle that was thus begun at about 1:30 P.M.

Messengers from our cavalry pickets and skirmish line now reported the approach of heavy columns of rebel infantry and artillery. Rousseau at once rode back to prepare for the shock. To his right brigade, Colonel Lytle's, he sent orders by an aide. The centre and left brigades, under Colonels Harris and Starkweather, he put in position himself. He caused two batteries to be so stationed on adjacent heights as to give a cross fire upon the advancing enemy. These dispositions having been made, we hurried back from the left to the centre of the division, which, we could clearly see, a mighty rebel column was about to strike.

Meantime, General McCook, finding Rousseau's line advanced when he reached the front again, had ordered part of the 33d Ohio regiment of Harris's brigade as skirmishers into the woods before its line, and then hastened to find General Jackson, his other division commander, to direct him to make his line conform to Rousseau's. Hearing musketry fire from the woods mentioned, he galloped back to Harris's front, and ordered the remainder of the 33d Ohio and the 2d Ohio to the support of the skirmishers. Thus Rousseau found part of his centre engaged on his return from the left. The formidable proportions of the rebel attack being now fully developed, he led another of Harris's regiments, the 24th Illinois, forward in person, in line of battle, till it reached the left of the 33d Ohio. I followed him and soon heard the whistling of bullets, first scatteringly and then continuously about us. Just then we were shocked by an ill-boding sight on our left. Another rebel column had pushed obliquely, like a wedge, against the right of Jackson's division, consisting of a brigade of raw men. The sheets of fire and hail of lead which rapidly burst forth from it on coming within firing distance were too much for the Federals. We plainly saw the brigade break and fly rearward in utter confusion, drawing the other brigade with them. The panic was due in part to the killing of General Jackson by the first rebel volley. Here was another striking reminder of Bull Run and Pittsburg Landing. The direction from which this terrible assault had come, made it clear that the enemy's plan was to roll up our line from left to right, and he had certainly begun its execution most threateningly.

Leaving Colonel Harris to lead his two remaining regiments, the 38th Indiana and 94th Illinois, to the support of the three already under fire, Rousseau galloped once more to his left, now imperilled by Jackson's disaster. Colonel Starkweather was ordered to open an enfilading fire with his two batteries, which was done promptly, but did not at first check the advancing enemy, who, despite the gaps torn through their ranks by our shot and shell, approached steadily, loading and discharging volley after volley from their small arms while advancing. At this stage of the combat, an incident happened that has always remained fresh in my mind. The 1st Wisconsin Infantry, although already within range of the rebel musketry and losing officers and men, when they recognized General Rousseau stuck their caps on their swords and bayonets, and, waving their arms over their heads, broke out into rousing cheers for him and shouts of defiance at the enemy. Rousseau, feeling that he was defending the key of our position and that the fate of the corps, and even of the army, would turn upon his successful resistance, remained close to the scene of this struggle. I dismounted and watched the course of the fighting for over an hour. The atmosphere was so clear and the sun shone so brightly that, barring momentary obscuration by the powder smoke, every move of assailants and assailed could be clearly perceived with the naked eye or the field-glass from the commanding point where we stood. We could see the victims drop, seemingly by the scores, on both sides, under the effect of the rapid exchange of volleys by regiments. Soon the flow of wounded to the rear indicated the severity of our losses. We could trace distinctly our shot and shells as they tore gaps through the rebel ranks, while the hostile missiles whirled past or burst above us. We were so near that we heard the peculiar pattering noise of falling bullets. We were all struck with the desperate valor of the rebels. Led by mounted officers, their broad columns came to the attack in quick movement and with death-defying steadiness, uttering wild yells, till, staggered by the sweeping cross-fire of our artillery and the volleys from Starkweather's regiments, they fell back to the shelter of corn-fields and breaks of the ground. But again and again, with revived pluck, they returned to the charge, to be again checked by our batteries and steadfast infantry. Gradually they gained ground, however, and the fire of their guns and musketry grew hotter and hotter. Still our line stood, and every once in a while a cheer arose from it above the din of battle. Towards four o'clock, the report came that the ammunition of our men was giving out, and that they were reduced to what they took from the cartridge-boxes of their dead and wounded comrades. When this was exhausted, they stood receiving fire without being able to return it. Then, owing to what had happened to the centre and right of the division, an order reached them to fall back to the position first assigned to them in the morning by General McCook. The brigade left one-third of their number in killed and wounded on the field. Its two batteries were brought off, although one of them had had nearly all its horses killed.

About the hour named, a message reached Rousseau asking him to meet General McCook at a farm-house in the rear of the centre of the corps. Being anxious to learn the course of the action in other parts of the field, and feeling very hungry and thirsty, and hoping to find something to eat and drink—not a swallow of water or anything else had passed my lips all day—I galloped there with him. On reaching the house, we discovered that General McCook had left, as the enemy, having worked around our right, had planted a battery directly in line of the house and was shelling it furiously. We had instant proof that it was a most dangerous place, since four shells exploded at once above us as we halted in front of it. The location of this hostile battery made Rousseau anxious for the safety of his right and centre, and he determined to return at once to his front, and sent word to that effect to General McCook by an orderly, whom I concluded to accompany.

We found the corps commander some distance further to the rear, in a very excited and perturbed state of mind, as he well might be in the awful predicament of finding himself on the verge of a complete rout of his corps. His chief-of-staff told me hurriedly that the whole corps had been assailed by overwhelming numbers, that the centre was being forced back and the right turned, that appeals for aid had been made more than an hour before through staff officers to the nearest division commander of General Gilbert's corps, but that no reinforcements had yet appeared, and that there was imminent danger of a disaster. I further learned that the General and staff had been separated from the corps headquarters since his visit to Buell. It turned out that, owing to the general retrograde movement of the corps, the vehicles attached to it had fallen into the hands of the enemy, including the mess-wagon and the field-carriage with the general's and staff's papers and baggage, and my own saddle-bags containing my toilet utensils and changes of underclothing. Owing to this mishap, I got no food, but only a mouthful of brandy and water from the flask of an aide-de-camp.

I have told in the foregoing what I saw myself of the action. The following narrative of the other occurrences of the day is taken mainly from my report of the battle to the New York *Tribune*, which was made up at the time from accounts of eye and ear witnesses.

The enemy, intent upon rolling up the line of McCook's corps from left to right, and having made no further progress against the left after their first success in driving Jackson's division from its position, next tried to break the centre. But Harris's brigade, as well as Starkweather's, withstood their repeated, determined onsets in great force. They also held their ground firmly until after all the cartridge-boxes of the living and dead and wounded had been emptied, and withdrew only when the rest of our line fell back. The brigade on the right, under Colonel Lytle, was assailed at the same time and as vigorously as the centre. It succeeded, however, in repulsing every front attack up to between four and five o'clock, when a strong column of the enemy, concealed by the undulations of the ground, managed to pass around its right, and suddenly, almost without warning, fell upon the flank and rear of the brigade and drove it before them in much disorder. Colonel Lytle was severely wounded and taken prisoner. This turning movement would not have been possible if General Gilbert had not ordered General Sheridan to fall back for half a mile from the position Colonel David McCook's brigade had wrested from the enemy in the morning, in which it had connected with Lytle's right. The rebel success involved the gravest peril to McCook's whole corps—indeed, threatened it with utter defeat and destruction. This calamity would surely have befallen it had not, at the critical moment, the rebel move against Lytle been arrested by counter-attacks from Gilbert's corps. How this came about will best appear from the following extract from my account of the battle in the *Tribune:*

General McCook states that at 3 P.M. he dispatched Captain Horace W. Fisher of his staff to the nearest commander of troops for assistance. He first met General Schoepf marching at the head of his division, and reported his condition to him. General Schoepf expressed a desire to act at once, as he was moving to the front under orders for that same purpose. He requested Captain Fisher to see General Gilbert, the commander of the corps, who was riding with the column. Gilbert said that he was very sorry to learn that General McCook was in so pressed a condition, but that he could not send him reinforcements without special orders from General Buell. Owing to the delay in first hunting for General Gilbert and next in finding General Buell, the aide-de-camp did not succeed in reporting the precarious plight of the first corps to the latter until nearly four o'clock. General Buell stepped out of his tent, held his ear towards the scene of action, listened for a few moments, and then, turning sharply to Captain Fisher, exclaimed: "Captain, you must be mistaken. I cannot hear any sound of musketry. There cannot be any serious engagement."

Captain Fisher thus returned without any assurance of reinforcements. Shortly after he had left the army headquarters, however, General Buell concluded, after all, to inquire into the alleged "serious engagement," and sent Major Wright of his staff to ascertain whether General McCook really needed assistance and to direct General Gilbert to furnish it. But the latter had already acted before the Major reached him, in response to another and more urgent appeal from McCook through another staff officer, and ordered Colonel Gooding's brigade of General Mitchell's division with the Fifth Wisconsin battery to the relief of Rousseau. When he received Buell's order, he sent another brigade of Schoepf's division forward for the same purpose. Gooding's brigade tried to come in touch with Rousseau's retreating right, but failed to do so owing to the remnants of Lytle's brigade having fallen back nearly a mile before rallying, and became hotly engaged with the enemy. It was assailed by far superior numbers, but withstood until nearly dark, when, finding itself unsupported on either side, it fell back upon the corps line after losing over five hundred in killed and wounded out of a total of only 1423 engaged. Its commander had his horse shot under him and fell into the hands of the enemy.

The reinforcing brigade under General Steedman from Schoepf's division arrived on the field at dark, too late to do any good.

Simultaneously with the turning movement around Lytle's right, part of the rebel forces again attacked Colonel McCook's brigade, on Sheridan's left, in order to dislodge Hiscock's large battery of Parrott guns that was directing an effective enfilading fire from a very advantageous position upon the hostile infantry and batteries. But McCook's men repelled the two onsets. General Sheridan and Colonel McCook from their standpoint clearly observed the course of the rebel flanking column, and understood the danger it brought to McCook's corps. As it passed along their front, they were eager to strike it in the flank, which they could have done most effectively, but they were held back by orders from General Gilbert, and chafed in vain at the loss of this fine chance of changing the fortunes of the day. It is easy to comprehend the bitterness and pain that Colonel McCook and his younger brother John felt, as they saw their brother's command apparently doomed, without being permitted to help him. The older brother did not hesitate, during and after the battle, to proclaim loudly that the flanking operation was invited and made practicable by their change of position under the orders of Gilbert.

The rebel wave that had swept away Lytle and struck Gooding was, however, stayed and forced back during the last hour of daylight. Having passed by Sheridan and reached Mitchell's front with their left and rear fully exposed, the latter division commander, not being under restraining orders, seized the opportunity and ordered Colonel Carlin to attack the enemy with his brigade. Carlin (a regular-army officer, who subsequently distinguished himself as a cavalry commander) immediately moved forward, and, reaching the brow of a hill, discovered the rebels directly before him. He formed his brigade and led a charge at the double quick with enthusiastic cheers, and succeeded, after a short resistance of the enemy, in breaking through his line. The rebels broke and fled in confusion, Carlin following them for nearly two miles to and through the town of Perryville, and then, retracing his steps to the field of action, captured close to the town a heavy ammunition train with its guard of 150 officers and men. This was the last incident of the sanguinary day. Nightfall put an end to hostilities on both sides.

The result of the day was unquestionably a decided rebel success. The enemy had driven McCook's whole line back from a mile and a half to two miles, and inflicted a loss of 39 officers and 806 men killed, 94 officers and 2757 men wounded, and 515 missing—a total of 4211, of which the First Corps alone lost 29 officers and 643 men killed, 66 officers and 2136 men wounded, and 425 missing—a total of 3299, or more than three-quarters of the entire loss. Eleven guns and much booty were also taken by the rebels from the corps. This is sufficient proof that McCook's command bore the brunt of the fight. In fact, it fought the battle. Rousseau's division had 7000, Jackson's 5500 effectives. The greater portion of the latter were stampeded, as we have seen, at the beginning of the battle, so that hardly more than 9000 men remained fighting in line, to which, towards the close, Gooding's 1400 and Carlin's 2000 were added. As usual, both the Union and Confederate commanders, in their official reports, claim to have been attacked by from two to three and four times the number of their troops. Bragg's official account proves that the rebels had only three divisions of infantry with about 14,500 effectives engaged. But, as their attacks were made in massed bodies of two or three brigades against certain points of our line, there was good ground for saying that the assailants attacked with greatly superior numbers.

It is the simple truth that to the "daring charges" of his infantry, as General Bragg justly calls them, the triumph of the rebel arms was due. But it is equally true that their commanders ran the greatest risk in acting on the assumption that only one Federal corps was confronting them, and that they owed their escape from the severest punishment for this hardihood to faults of omission and commission on our side. The enemy rushed, in unconscious recklessness, into the trap which the convergence of our three corps upon Perryville really formed for him, and he owed it partly to accident and partly to our mistakes and blunders that it was not sprung on him. It is enough to state the astounding fact that not far from forty thousand muskets and some eighty pieces of artillery of our army never fired a shot during the whole day. We had, indeed, such an abundance of forces gathered so near to Perryville that, had there been but a proper perception of our opportunity and promptness and energy in availing of it, the enemy would have been entirely enveloped and crushed. We had five-sixths of Gilbert's and the whole of Crittenden's corps intact for that purpose. That, instead, we were badly beaten in part was clearly attributable, first, to the fall and hurt of General Buell, which prevented him from having personal cognizance of the situation at the front and taking prompt action accordingly; second, to his unwillingness to accept the assurance of General McCook's aide-de-camp that a serious engagement was in progress, and consequent delay in ordering support to the First Corps; third, to the inexperience and incapacity of General Gilbert. This officer, a captain in the regular army, appeared in the part of a corps commander literally without ever having led any troops—not as much as a company—under fire, and, strangest of all, without the shadow of a real title to his rank, as is shown by another quotation from my reports to the *Tribune:*

I must record a singular discovery regarding General Gilbert. Soon after the battle, General Rousseau heard some rumors of doubts relative to the former's actual rank, and addressed a letter of inquiry upon the subject to General Buell, who sent it to General Gilbert. The latter wrote on the back of it: "I am a major-general by the appointment of Major-General Wright." General Wright, the military Department Commander for Ohio and Kentucky previous to the return of General Buell to Louisville, of course had not the remotest authority to issue commissions or confer rank. Here was the startling revelation, which excited the utmost astonishment in Buell himself, that a mere pretender or impostor had exercised the next highest function of command, to the all but fatal detriment of the whole army. Naturally, the disclosure greatly intensified the indignation and disgust of the commanders under him and under McCook at his failure to relieve the First Corps and to seize the chance, plainly within his grasp, to turn our defeat into a rout of the enemy.

The command of the corps was soon after taken from him. Brief as his career had been, he succeeded not only in proving his incompetency to command, but in incurring the hatred of his subordinates generally, for he lowered himself by abusing officers, whipping teamsters and soldiers, and by other brutal interferences in matters beneath his station.

In closing my description of the battle, I deem it my duty to state that, while I was writing it in the spring of 1896—nearly thirty-four years after the event—the curious fact was discovered that General Buell was informed, by signal message, as early as 2 P. M., of the rebel attack in force upon General McCook's division. The discovery rests on the evidence of the signal-officer who received the message.

I have to own that, before the firing had ceased altogether, my appetite got the better of my sense of duty and my interest in the battle, and I set out in search of food and drink for myself and horse. Knowing that Buell's headquarters had been stationary all day, I felt sure that my needs could be satisfied there. I found them, after some wandering, at about seven o'clock. Colonel Fry, on my supplication, readily agreed to take care of me, and I was soon devouring a cold supper. My own and my animal's condition may be judged from the fact that I had been in the saddle since three in the morning, less two hours at the most, and had had nothing but a cup of coffee and some hard-tack at that hour. The horse had had no food or water for a whole day, and an orderly had to take him a quarter of a mile for a chance to drink. The Colonel secured me a nook in a tent occupied by staff officers for a resting-place, and a blanket to wrap up in. An almost full moon had arisen and lighted up the field very brightly, but my own and my quadruped's fatigue was too great for another effort, and I remained at headquarters.

General Buell now clearly understood the situation in which the events of the day had left his army, and decided to make a general attack on the enemy at daylight. Dispositions for that purpose were made during the night. The corps commanders were sent for to receive their instructions, and remained in consultation with the General-in-chief till after midnight. The army hardly got any sleep. All the troops at the front were kept moving into proper positions for the onset in the morning. The gathering of our wounded was also continued all night. Being fully informed as to the programme for the morrow, and having arranged to be called at four, I sought sleep early.

When I was aroused at four, I found that nobody else at headquarters had slept. A light breakfast was ready, at which I learned from the staff that, since one o'clock, several reports had come in from our picket-lines that continuous noises had been heard, indicating the movement of artillery and trains and a general retreat of the enemy. Naturally, this was not considered satisfactory news. It was confirmed between six and seven by the forward movement of the corps of Crittenden and Gilbert, which were to attack the enemy's front and left, while McCook remained in reserve. They met no resistance, and fully developed the fact that the whole rebel army had disappeared from our front. They left behind all their dead and severely wounded, and all the captured pieces of artillery but two, and about fifteen hundred of our small arms which they had collected.

General Buell was greatly disappointed, as he had confidently held to the opinion, based on his overestimate of the rebel strength and on the theory that Bragg had to await the approach of Kirby Smith's force, that the rebels would stand and fight. He was so satisfied of this that he would not entertain a suggestion made by General Crittenden to swing his corps around on its left during the night, so as to bring it across Bragg's only line of retreat. Buell did not think, however, that the rebel move meant an abandonment of Kentucky, but simply a falling back to another position with a view to facilitating the junction with Smith. This wrong supposition led him, after crossing the Chaplin River, instead of undertaking at once an energetic pursuit, to get his army into a favorable position just beyond Perryville and there await the arrival of General Sill's division, which took place only on the third day after the battle.

I spent the morning of the 9th in writing my first account of the battle, which a surgeon in charge of an ambulance train of wounded bound for Louisville promised to mail at the first railroad station, and devoted the afternoon to a ride over the entire battle-field. I could easily trace the course of the action by the ghastly lines of dead and severely wounded from the points of the first rebel attacks to where they stopped in the evening. On our side, most of the victims lay in rows along our front, where the most vigorous defence was made. Along Jackson's line, the casualties had obviously been few, showing that most of his division had sought safety in flight. The number of the fallen was greatest along Starkweather's brigade, while Harris's and Lytle's losses appeared to be about even. Nearly all our wounded had been removed either during the action or at night. The direction of the rebel advances was literally marked by trails of blood from a quarter to half a mile long. I counted over five hundred of their dead. Most of them appeared to have been killed instantly by bullets and artillery fire; but many showed by their distorted features that they had passed through more or less prolonged agonies. I found some two score that had been struck and mutilated by cannon-balls and shells—some with upper and lower limbs torn off, others with chest and abdomen laid open, and one with his entire and another with half his head gone. Our sanitary corps was at work gathering up the hundreds of wounded the enemy had mercilessly left on the field. These had suffered indescribably since they fell, from pain, cold, and want of food and water. The hopeless cases were left to die where they lay, and I passed dozens of them writhing in the last agony. The track of slaughter formed awful proof of the blind heroism, born of fanatical devotion to their bad cause, with which the rebels faced—yea, courted—death. At three points I found, in spaces not over five hundred feet long and wide, successive swaths of from twenty to fifty bodies, cut down by our small arms and batteries, showing that the most murderous fire did not stop them. Altogether, the sights formed as horrifying a spectacle as those on the field of Shiloh.

I devoted the 10th to visits to General Rousseau and the headquarters of General Crittenden and his division commanders. All the generals I saw expressed their great disappointment and humiliation at the unsatisfactory results, so far, of the operations of the army since it turned north from Nashville. Several of them charged Bragg's escape without severe punishment directly to mismanagement. The belief was very general that he would not fight again in Kentucky. One of the bitterest talkers was General Rousseau. He denounced General Gilbert without stint for failing to support McCook in the battle. Rousseau, a lawyer and politician at Louisville when the war broke out, an ardent loyalist, and one of the first to raise volunteers in Kentucky for the Union cause, was considered at first a "political" general and did not stand very high with trained military men. But active service in the field had rapidly made him a true soldier and able commander. He manifested great courage at Shiloh, and his conduct in this battle was certainly admirable. His fearlessness under fire shone out all the afternoon. He was middle-aged, of tall, full stature, with fine manly face, and presented a commanding, martial appearance, especially on horseback.

I also had an hour with Colonel Daniel McCook, whose acquaintance I had made during my stay at Leavenworth in the spring of 1859, where he was practising law. Like all the McCooks, he was of a very genial, frank, and yet resolute nature. Like his father and his eldest brother, he was doomed to lose his life in the service of his country.

He fell in Sherman's Atlanta campaign. In his anxiety for the reputation of his brother, the General, he fairly boiled with indignation at the derelictions of Buell and Gilbert. He conducted me to the several positions occupied during the conflict, and demonstrated how, on the one hand, the falling back from the position taken from the rebels early in the morning had left Rousseau's right unprotected, and how, on the other, the rebel turning movement might have been used to our advantage by falling upon their flank and rear. He took me to the headquarters of General Sheridan, with whom I had a long talk. I had met him casually more than once during the Corinth campaign as Colonel of the 2d Michigan Cavalry. Up to that time, his army record did not indicate the brilliant future before him. Nor did he impress me as a man of more than ordinary intellectual ability. His exterior was anything but prepossessing. Of hardly middle height, with a round head, low brow, and decidedly coarse Irish features, a disproportionately broad and long body on short legs, he did not make a very imposing personality. He looked like a bold *sabreur*, but nothing more.

The arrival of General Sill's division being assured for the evening of the 11th, Buell, on the same day, sent out three brigades from Crittenden's and Gilbert's corps, headed by my friend Colonel Edward McCook's and Colonel Gray's mounted commands. Having learned this, I made my way at once to McCook, who was very willing to have me accompany him again. He had been incessantly engaged in outpost and advance-guard duty during the march from Nashville to Louisville and thence to Perryville, and there had been but few days on which his command had not rubbed against the enemy. We followed the pike from Perryville to Harrodsburg, and encountered and skirmished with rebel cavalry, apparently supported by a strong infantry force. But they fell back before evening, and we entered Harrodsburg unopposed, where we found more than a thousand rebel sick and wounded. The next day we moved on toward Dix River, a tributary of the Kentucky, and discovered that the whole rebel army had crossed it. Buell, being uncertain whether the enemy would retreat further or would avail himself of the strong positions which the country between the two rivers afforded and await attack, had ordered his whole army to advance on the same day from a line extending from Harrodsburg to Danville. On the 13th, our movement was continued in a southeasterly direction upon the last-mentioned place. There we ascertained definitely that Bragg was really in full retreat towards the Cumberland River. Even Buell now had to believe this, and he decided upon an energetic pursuit in force. At midnight General Wood's division marched from Danville and came up with and engaged the enemy's rear-guard of cavalry and artillery in the morning at Stanford. But it became evident during the day that the enemy's object was only to obstruct our advance, which he did by destroying bridges and blocking the road by felled trees. I rode with McCook's cavalry brigade in advance of Gilbert's corps through Lancaster to Crab Orchard, but we did not collide again with the rebels. At the last-named point, the several roads followed by the army converged into one, of a very rugged and difficult character, so that the army could have followed the enemy only in one column twenty miles long, which would have been useless and absurd. McCook's and Gilbert's corps were therefore halted on the 15th.

All the reports from the pursuing column confirmed the general impression that Bragg and Kirby Smith were making for Cumberland Gap and would not stop short of East Tennessee. This meant the end of the Kentucky campaign for Buell's army. In view of this, and the destitute condition in which the loss of my travelling-bag had left me, I resolved to return to Louisville, and set out on the return journey on the afternoon of the 15th, bound for Bardstown, the nearest railroad station to which trains were known to be running. My route was via Stanford,

Danville, Perryville, and Springfield, and I reached the railroad late on the 17th. While riding along the turnpike that intersected the battle-field about two miles west of Perryville, I smelled a sickening stench, obviously arising from a spot close to the highway. Suspecting an effect of the battle, I turned into a field to discover the cause of it. Not more than a hundred yards from the road, a terrible sight shocked me. In a clear space of not over an acre, there were more than fifty dead rebels, off whom at least a hundred hogs were making a sickening feast. The fallen Confederates had evidently been overlooked by our burying parties. Decomposition had swelled the bodies into awful monstrosities, and the nasty beasts were hard at work disembowelling them and gnawing into the skulls for their brains. Such is war!

I reached Louisville on the 18th. I wired immediately to the *Tribune* that the campaign was ended, and that no important events were likely to occur for some time, and asked for instructions. The next morning the answer came to report in person in New York as soon as possible, which obviously meant a change of my field of duty. The order was very welcome, and I started for the East on the 20th.

General Buell was relieved from the command of the Army of the Cumberland soon afterwards, and General Rosecrans put in his place. The change was inevitable. The Government, it will be remembered, had already tried to replace him with General Thomas, and was now determined upon removing him. The loyal public and the governments of the Western States again demanded his displacement, more vehemently than before. The greater portion of his army also wished for a new commander, and Buell himself was conscious that his prestige was gone, and intimated to the Government that he expected to be relieved. He never was given another active command, and takes his place in history as one of the failures of the war, beside Frémont, McClellan, Burnside, Hooker, Pope, and Halleck. The main cause of his downfall being the delay in his march to East Tennessee in consequence of Halleck's order to repair the Memphis & Charleston Railroad as he advanced, Buell may be considered a victim of circumstances as well as of his own personal defects. He possessed much natural ability, and probably more theoretical knowledge of the science of war than any other Union commander. But the latter acquirement proved more of a detriment than an advantage to him, for it made him too prone, in preparing his army for active operations, to require a greater degree of readiness than the known worse condition of his adversaries called for. And again, he was too much inclined to base his deductions as to the purposes of the enemy on what, according to the theory of strategy, leaders of armies ought to do under certain circumstances. The rebel commanders regularly set his calculations at naught by defying theory and rule in taking the offensive, whether their troops were well clad or shod, or well supplied with provisions and transportation or not, and passing over mountains and rivers and through sterile regions that he assumed to be insurmountable obstacles. The subsequent publications in his defence show this shortcoming clearly, and also bring out his excessive caution very distinctly. He was incapable of bold resolution and daring action, contrasting strikingly in this respect with the Confederate generals. Notwithstanding the uniform superiority of his army in numbers, armament, equipment and supplies, he was (with the exception of the second day at Shiloh, when he acted under orders) always on the defensive. If the conditions had been reversed and his antagonists had enjoyed such superiority, they would doubtless have made short work of him. General Buell is entitled to full credit, however, for always faithfully and tirelessly discharging his duties to the best of his ability. The charges made in the press and otherwise at the time, that he was at heart not loyal to the Union, and even sympathized with the Southern cause, were utterly unfounded and calumnious.

MEMOIRS OF HENRY VILLARD

BOOK FOUR

IN CIVIL-WAR TIME: FREDERICKSBURG

CHAPTER XX

IN WASHINGTON ONCE MORE.—1862

I WAS very kindly received by my employers of the *Tribune*, and, according to their liberal practice, was given a week's leave of absence, which I spent in New York. On reporting again for duty, I offered to write a full review of the operations of the Army of the Ohio under Buell, and the managing editor authorized me to prepare it. Hearing from friends on McCook's staff that the official reports of the Perryville campaign had been forwarded to Washington, I asked permission to go there in order to get a sight of them, if possible. My application led to the discussion of my future duties. George W. Smalley had been the chief correspondent of the *Tribune* with the Army of the Potomac until after the battle of Antietam, of which he wrote a remarkable description— the best piece of work of the kind produced during the Civil War, in my opinion. (He subsequently served as the London correspondent of the *Tribune* for nearly thirty years, and since the summer of 1896 has represented the London *Times* in the United States.) A regular editorial writer on war subjects being needed, it had been decided to keep him, as such, in New York. It was determined that I should fill the vacancy, and, with that understanding, I started for the national capital early in November. My departure was hastened by the momentous announcement of the second removal of General George B. McClellan from the command of the Army of the Potomac, and the appointment of General Ambrose E. Burnside in his place, by direct order of the President of the United States.

The disastrous end of the humiliating Peninsular campaign under McClellan in the early part of the summer had produced such deep and angry dissatisfaction in the loyal States, that President Lincoln felt compelled to change his forbearing course towards the commander of the Army of the Potomac, and to entrust another with the conduct of the operations in Virginia. His choice fell upon General John Pope, who, in the last days of June, was placed in command of the Army of Virginia, then consisting of only three army corps, but which was to be strengthened by transfers from McClellan's forces. The hopes entertained of General Pope were grievously disappointed by his utter defeat by General Lee in the second battle of Bull Run. The vanquished General pleaded in extenuation of his total failure the insufficiency of his army, owing to the slowness of McClellan in reinforcing him and to the deliberate and malevolent disregard of his orders during the battle by General Fitz-John Porter. The story that McClellan and the commanders under him, among whom Porter was his strongest partisan, were determined not to allow Pope to achieve a victory, was spread by the press and found general credence. Great, therefore, was the astonishment and indignation of the loyal public when the President again placed McClellan at the head of the remnants of the armies of the Potomac and of Virginia. This feeling was greatly intensified when it became known that his restoration had been opposed and, indeed, formally protested against by a majority of the Cabinet. The battle of Antietam reconciled the North to the President's action, but the passiveness into which McClellan relapsed after that success rekindled the general impatience and distrust of him. Again the President exercised altogether too much forbearance under the greatest provocation. He resisted all pressure for McClellan's removal until the latter failed to meet the final test of his ability as a strategist which the Commander-in-chief had resolved to apply to him, by allowing Lee to appear once more with his whole force to the east of the Blue Mountains.

The removal formed the all-absorbing topic in Washington. I soon satisfied myself that the bulk of the army under McClellan and a majority of the general officers disapproved and were, contrary to all discipline, loud in their denunciations of it. In the Capitol, as well as throughout the loyal States, there were signs of a tendency to make a national political issue of it. The President's proclamation of the abolition of slavery of September 22 had met with strong opposition in the border States and among the Democrats of the free States, especially in New York, Ohio, and Indiana. It was known that McClellan, and the generals nearest to him, were also opposed to this portentous act. It was proclaimed by the Democratic press that his relief from active command was due to his hostility to it, and a concession to the "Abolitionists," who then, as I could personally confirm, still seemed to many Union generals no better than the rebels. General McClellan did nothing to disclaim this pseudo-political martyrdom, which was certainly a convenient cloak for the real cause of his dismissal—his military shortcomings. I even heard talk in the hotel lobbies and bar-rooms about the intention of the deposed commander to lead the army to Washington and take possession of the Government; but that impious wish of not a few never became a real purpose. McClellan quietly obeyed the Presidential order to repair to, and report from, Trenton, New Jersey.

Since my encounter with General Burnside in the memorable night of the retreat from Centreville after the first battle of Bull Run, he had achieved creditable successes in the North Carolina expedition, and risen from a brigade to a corps command, and was apparently held in high esteem by the Government, the press, and the public. But I had not got over the feeling of prejudice caused by his behavior on that occasion, and hence the news that he had been selected as the successor of McClellan did not inspire me with confidence in a change for the better from the continuous defeats of the national forces in the Eastern theatre of war. Nor was my apprehension modified by the chorus of rejoicing among loyalists in Washington and the North over the definitive retirement of McClellan and the substitution of Burnside in his place; for it was not based wholly upon the incident referred to, but on my personal knowledge of his limited mental capacities, acquired during my intercourse with him in the spring and summer of 1861. My fears were heightened when I learned, soon after his elevation was made known, that he had at first declined the promotion, on the ground that he was not qualified for the highest command and that McClellan was the only proper man to lead the Eastern army. This admission of incapacity and want of confidence in himself made his appointment in spite of it an inexcusable mistake. Thus to force the gravest responsibilities upon a reluctant man was almost to invite the further disaster that came. I know of but one other similar instance—the ordering of Field Marshal Benedek to the chief command of the Austrian army in the war of 1866.

Washington had changed greatly since I last saw it in August, 1861. Owing to the increase of the regular Government officials by many thousands, because of the vast growth of the public business in connection with the war, the population had nearly doubled. At the time of my departure, dozens of stores on the business thoroughfares and hundreds of residences were to rent for a mere song. Now, not a building of either class was unoccupied, and high rents were asked and readily obtained. New hotels had been opened, and were, like the old ones, well filled. What with the constant presence of tens of thousands of troops in the barracks and camps in and about the capital, and the thousands of wounded in the hospitals, and the multitude of visitors from the North to relatives and friends in the army, the principal streets always presented a very lively appearance. There was also a good deal of building going on—the best evidence of faith in the ultimate triumph of the Government.

I devoted myself first to the elaboration of the review of the campaigns of the Army of the Ohio above mentioned. It was not easy to obtain access to the official reports relating to them in the War Department, but I managed to secure copies of the more important ones. The review was completed in time for its publication in the *Tribune* of November 12. It filled more than an entire page of the paper.

The Washington office of the *Tribune* was then in a small, one-story brick building on F Street between 13th and 14th, directly opposite Willard's Hotel. Samuel Wilkeson, who had accompanied Secretary Cameron to Louisville, was principal correspondent in charge. As a co-laborer, he had Adams S. Hill, a graduate of Harvard College, twenty-nine years old, a sharp-witted and indefatigable collector of news, who had previously been connected with the editorial department of the paper. I was entirely independent of Wilkeson, and had only to make the office the medium for transmitting, with a view to greater safety and despatch, my war news to New York while I was in the field. I naturally made much use of it, however, during my stay. It was the resort of politicians, officials, and army officers, who frequented it, especially in the evening, to bring news or to hear and discuss it. This made it a very interesting place.

I made special efforts to renew former acquaintances in higher circles in order to learn the inside workings of the Government and its intentions regarding the army. In common with the public, I was aware that the President was not in harmony with the strongest members of his Cabinet. Edwin M. Stanton had succeeded Simon Cameron as Secretary of War. This change, while of immeasurable benefit to the country, proved a decided disadvantage to my profession; for whereas Cameron was always accessible and communicative—no doubt, too much so for the public good—his successor had the doors of the War Department closed to newspaper men. Seward, Blair, and Chase still practised their affable ways towards them. I saw and had a long talk with each of the first two. Secretary Chase I saw frequently, as of old. He spoke very freely of the past and present, and in confidence criticised without stint the mistakes that had been made in the civil administration and the conduct of the war. It was very evident that he was too confident of his own superiority, mental and otherwise, to get along smoothly with the head of the Government, and that sooner or later there would be an open breach. The emancipation proclamation had temporarily improved the relations between him and the President, as the treatment of the slavery question had been one of the principal subjects of disagreement, but their characters were too radically different to get along without further friction.

I also had a long conversation with Mr. Lincoln. It took place after the publication of my review of Buell's campaigns, a reference to which by the President made it the exclusive subject discussed. He asked my opinion of the principal commanders under Buell, which I expressed with entire frankness. He surprised me by his familiarity with details of movements and battles which I did not suppose had come to his knowledge. As he kept me talking for over half an hour, I flattered myself that what I had to say interested him. This impression was confirmed by his intimation that he should be glad to see me again, after I had told him, in response to his question as to my future movements, that I should be with the Army of the Potomac.

My inquiries soon satisfied me that the army would not be allowed to go into winter quarters, but that the President, the Secretary of War, and Halleck, as General-in-chief, would insist, notwithstanding the near approach of winter, upon an immediate resumption of active operations, and accordingly I made my preparations to take the field at the earliest necessary moment. I anticipated a good deal of embarrassment at first, from the fact that my acquaintance with superior officers in the Army of the Potomac was very limited, and that the *Tribune* had severely attacked McClellan and some of his corps commanders in connection with both the Peninsular and Pope's campaigns. I hoped, however, to overcome this hindrance to a successful discharge of my duties. Under the régime of Stanton and Halleck, it was anything but easy for correspondents to obtain permits to go to, and remain at, the front, as the Secretary fully shared the opinion of the General-in-chief that newspaper men were a pest. It had been arranged that I was to have three assistants, who were to be directly under my orders, and whose reports were to be revised by me before being forwarded to the New York office. We were all allowed horses, camp equipments, and a servant.

To overcome McClellan's slowness, the President issued, on October 6, a peremptory order requiring him to cross the Potomac with his army and "give battle to the enemy or drive him South." As it produced no effect, the President, a week later, addressed a long letter to him explaining the plan of operations the General was expected to follow and the reasons therefor. It began: "You remember my speaking to you of what I called your over-cautiousness. Are you not over-cautious when you assume that you cannot do what the enemy is constantly doing? Should you not claim to be at least his equal in prowess and act upon that claim?" The letter was altogether a very remarkable production, and proved that the author had acquired a clear and sound judgment upon strategic questions. The prescribed plan was well conceived and perfectly feasible. The very fact, however, that the President found it necessary to address such an implied censure to McClellan and to tell him what to do, was conclusive proof of the grievous error he committed in re-appointing him.

According to the Presidential order for the new campaign, the army was to follow Lee by a flank march on the interior line to Richmond, keeping close to the base of the Blue Ridge, so as to prevent debouchments from its passes upon the Federal right and rear, and to force the enemy into battle whenever and wherever practicable. McClellan's tardiness in carrying it out had enabled Lee to obstruct its execution by passing through the Ridge and moving on the same line as the Union army, but ahead of it, towards Richmond. This led, as mentioned, to the final dismissal of the Federal commander.

After assuming command, General Burnside proposed, instead of following Lee directly, to move down the Rappahannock on the north side to Falmouth, opposite the town of Fredericksburg, and to establish a new base of supplies on the estuary of the Potomac, fifteen miles to the north of it, known as Acquia Creek. Neither the President nor General Halleck approved of this change of programme, and the latter paid a visit to General Burnside at Warrenton in order to persuade him to adhere to the President's plan. But he did not succeed in this, and the result was an understanding that he should submit to the President a modification of it, in pursuance of which the army was to cross the Rappahannock by the upper fords and to move down the south side and seize the heights of Fredericksburg; this movement to be accompanied by repairing and reopening the railroad opposite Washington as a line of communication between Alexandria and Fredericksburg. Until this could be accomplished, the Acquia Creek route was to be used as a line of supplies. On November 14, Halleck telegraphed the "assent" of the President, who would not permit the use of the word "approval." Thus the brief and fatal Fredericksburg campaign was inaugurated.

General Burnside had made himself responsible for the outcome by insisting upon the deviation from the Presidential plan. But, unfortunately, he assumed still graver responsibility. Instead of crossing the river by the upper fords, he marched down the north side to Falmouth. General Halleck makes the point-blank charge, in a report to the President, that the movement on the north side was never approved or authorized. It was the cause of Burnside's failure to occupy the Fredericksburg heights ahead of the enemy, and of the subsequent terrible defeat of his army. Our forces moved from Warrenton on November 15 and reached Falmouth on the 20th. Lee, on discovering the direction of our march, started Longstreet's corps for Fredericksburg, but it did not arrive there till the 21st; hence there was ample time to anticipate the rebels in taking possession of the commanding heights. General Sumner, commanding the corps, asked permission to cross a few miles above the town, where the river was fordable, but did not obtain it. Thus the position, in the vain attempt to secure which so much loyal blood was afterwards shed, was left to the enemy.

This neglect became the subject of one of the most virulent controversies engendered by the shortcomings of the Federal commanders during the war. The Congressional Committee on the Conduct of the War inquired into it, and the testimony taken before it fills several hundred pages. It was attempted to be shown, in defence of General Burnside, that his plan of marching to Falmouth had been approved by his superiors in Washington, and that he was led to expect, on his arrival there, to find supplies, pontoons for bridges, and gunboats to protect them. General Halleck not only absolutely denied that he authorized the move to Falmouth, but also insisted that Burnside could not expect supplies at points held by the rebels until he reached these, and that he was repeatedly informed that gunboats could not at that time ascend the river to Fredericksburg. But the truth was confessed by General Burnside himself in this passage in his brief and only report of the coming battle to General Halleck: "The fact that I decided to move from Warrenton on this line rather against the opinion of the President, the Secretary of War, and yourself, and that you left the whole movement in my hands without giving me orders, makes me the only one responsible."

CHAPTER XXI

With Burnside before Fredericksburg.—1862

HAVING, after a good deal of effort, received permission to proceed to the front, I secured an order for transportation on one of the Government boats from Quartermaster-General Meigs. I managed to get myself and belongings, including my horse, on one of the many craft loading with army supplies, on the morning of November 29. We steamed off in the afternoon, but, Acquia Creek being sixty-five miles from Washington, and the boat making only six and seven miles an hour, we did not reach our destination before midnight. The captain let me share his supper, but there were sleeping accommodations only for the officers and crew, so that I was obliged to seek rest on the floor of the small mess-room. I was up at daybreak. In the estuary were several score of vessels at anchor—gunboats, steamboats of all kinds, schooners, scows, barges, and canal-boats—all awaiting their turn to discharge at the one available wharf. It looked as if I might have to wait for days before I could get my horse ashore. The captain was rowed to the landing early, and I accompanied him to ascertain the prospect before me. Fortunately, we had some railroad material aboard that was urgently needed in repairing the section between Acquia and Falmouth of the road from Alexandria to Fredericksburg, which had been utterly destroyed at an earlier stage of the war, and we were made fast to the wharf by noon and my luggage and animal safely transferred to it shortly afterward.

The railroad was near the wharf, and a locomotive and an old passenger coach and a dozen freight cars stood upon the track, but I was told that the section to the front would not be opened for traffic for several days. Accordingly, I saddled my horse, and, with my valise in front and my roll of bedding strapped behind me, started for Falmouth. There had been a severe frost followed by a thaw, and the thousands of army wagons that had passed over the road for several days had reduced it to a very bad condition, so that I could only walk my horse. It took me over four hours to reach the first camps, about a mile from the Rappahannock. The ravages of war were visible all the way. The country seemed to have been burned over. The scrub timber was coal-black, and, in the frequent clearings where farming had been carried on, there was nothing to be seen but half-destroyed fences and the ruins of dwellings and outhouses without any inhabitants.

I had letters of introduction to General John G. Parke, the chief-of-staff, from a regular-army friend in Washington, and to General Hooker from Mr. Smalley, who had been with the General in the Antietam campaign. I also knew General E. V. Sumner, and General Daniel Butterfield, who had set out from New York as colonel of the 12th New York Militia, a three months' regiment. As night was approaching, and it was evident that I should not be likely to find any of these officers except with difficulty in the dark, it occurred to me to ask a division sutler, whose tent showed a large display of goods, whether he could not accommodate me for the night. I told him who I was, and he readily consented to do the best he could for me and my beast. I had a really luxurious supper and a good night's sleep on a camp-bed, for which my generous host, whose name I have forgotten, would not accept any compensation.

The next day was brisk and clear—just right for my first sight of the Army of the Potomac. A short ride brought me to an elevated point commanding a wide view of the surroundings. There was a large plateau, forming several plantations with commodious brick mansions—one of which had been burned—standing amidst groups of the usual outbuildings and stately groves of shade trees. Patches of timber broke the cultivated surface. In every direction vast encampments were visible. The plateau was from 100 to 125 feet above the Rappahannock, whose flow was for several miles almost due east. It seemed like a regular plain, but was really divided by two deep wooded ravines, down which "runs," as small water-courses were called in the local vernacular, made for the river. Through one of these the railroad approached it. The small village of Falmouth appeared some distance above, on the left bank of the Rappahannock. Almost directly before and beneath me, on the right bank, the old town of Fredericksburg was situated. It presented itself as a compact mass of brick buildings extending half a mile along, and a quarter of a mile from, the river. The site of the city rose but slightly near the river, but a mile south of it there were considerable heights, extending like the arc of a circle, with the river as the chord, and forming an amphitheatre, as it were, about a mile wide and two miles long, traversed by several highways, the Richmond railroad, and three streamlets, of which the Massaponax was the farthest to the east, and the most considerable. It was known that the rebels occupied the town, but no signs of them were then discernible. The railroad bridge at the east end was in ruins.

After assuming command, General Burnside reorganized the army into three grand divisions of two army corps each —the right, centre, and left—under the respective commands of Major-Generals Sumner, Hooker, and Franklin. The right Grand Division consisted of the Second and Ninth Army Corps, commanded by Major-General D. N. Couch and Brigadier-General O. B. Willcox; the centre Grand Division, of the Third and Fifth Army Corps, under Brigadier-Generals George Stoneman and Daniel Butterfield; and the left Grand Division, of the First and Sixth Army Corps, under Major-General John F. Reynolds and Brigadier-General William F. Smith. The army and the grand-division and army-corps headquarters were all in prominent positions and were readily recognized by flags and other signs, so that it was easy for me to make my way to them. I first proceeded to General Burnside's headquarters, which consisted of a group of tents next to a large dwelling called, I believe, the Lacy house, the home of a planter of that name. The Commanding-general had shunned it, and was setting the good example of camping. General Parke received me politely and readily countersigned my pass, but put me under strict injunction not to write anything about the position, strength, and condition of the army. I learned that, two days before, a meeting of the President and General Burnside had taken place at Acquia Creek, in the afternoon, on the boat in which the President had come from Washington, and lasted several hours, Mr. Lincoln returning immediately afterwards to Washington. I ascertained the purport of his flying visit after my return to Washington, and may as well mention here that it was to dissuade Burnside from a direct attack on the enemy in his obviously very strong position on the heights of Fredericksburg. But the President found the General stolidly bent on making the attempt to defeat Lee where he was. Nicolay and Hay relate that, on his way back to Washington, Lincoln prepared a memorandum for a flanking movement, which he allowed Halleck and Burnside, however, to overrule.

I next sought General Hooker. I had never met him and was, of course, eager to see and take my own measure of "Fighting Joe," which sobriquet the press had already affixed to him. His exterior was certainly most attractive and commanding. He was fully six feet high, finely proportioned, with a soldierly, erect carriage, handsome and noble features, a slight fringe of side-whiskers, a rosy complexion, abundant blond hair, a fine and expressive mouth, and—most striking of all—great, speaking gray-blue eyes; he looked, indeed, like the ideal soldier and captain, fit for a model of a war-god. There was only one other man in the army, as far as my own observations went, that came near him in these external qualities—General Winfield S. Hancock. My letter of introduction from Mr. Smalley commended me very strongly to the General's confidence, yet he received me rather stiffly and coldly. This I found, however, to be his natural manner, for, after a short general conversation—his voice being most agreeable—he burst forth into unsparing criticism of the general conduct of the war in the East, of the Government, of Halleck, McClellan, Pope, and, last but not least, of his present immediate superior. He had even then an unenviable notoriety for a rash tongue, to which he added lamentably in his subsequent career. His language was so severe and, at the same time, so infused with self-assertion as to give rise immediately to a fear on my part that he might be inclined to make use of me for his own glorification and for the detraction of others. This made it prudent for me not to place myself under more personal obligations to him than I could possibly help. Hence, I abstained from requesting, as I had first intended, permission to stop at his headquarters. After an hour's talk I passed on, with the General's assurance that he should always be glad to see me.

General Sumner, on whom I next called, remembered me very well and gave me a hearty welcome. A colonel of cavalry at the outbreak of the war, he, like all regular-army officers, had had no practical experience up to that time in serving with larger bodies of troops than a regiment. He had been an excellent regimental commander, very strict in the enforcement of discipline and thorough drilling, and withal a model cavalry soldier. But he was almost too old for the proper discharge of the duties of higher command, and also lacked the natural parts for it. Yet the force of circumstances, or, rather, his rank in the regular army and the lack of competent commanders, together with his fervid loyalty and enthusiastic devotion to the flag, had carried him rapidly in a year and a half from the command of a regiment to that of a brigade, a division, an army corps, and an army wing numbering sixty thousand men. He was the very picture of a veteran soldier—tall, slender, erect, with a fine head thickly covered with white hair, and a noble face fringed with a white beard. He was polished in speech and manner, and seemed almost too full of kindliness for his stern profession. Encouraged by his hearty way, I ventured to ask whether I could be provided for at his headquarters, whereupon he sent at once for his son, Captain S. S. Sumner, who served as his aide-de-camp, and instructed him to take care of me, which was quickly done. I was to take my meals with the medical director, Surgeon Dougherty, and his assistants, and to sleep with the latter in a large hospital tent. I had every reason to be grateful for the provision made for me, as I was treated with unvarying courtesy by my mess and tent-mates during the two weeks and a half I was to spend with them. To be at the headquarters of a grand division proved a very great advantage to me.

Having thus come well to anchor, I sought to make further acquaintances among the officers. Everybody understood that an early offensive movement was contemplated, and it was the general belief that it would take place within a few days. But the end of the month came, and the first days of December passed, without the expected stirring events, so that I had more time for familiarizing myself with the army than I anticipated. General Butterfield I saw early and often, and he helped me in every possible way. Starting in a practical life as a business man in New York, he always had a strong penchant for military matters, and entered the militia early, and, by his enthusiasm and aptitude, worked his way up to the command of a regiment when he was but thirty. His regiment was among the first to enlist for three months, at the expiration of which term he was appointed a lieutenant-colonel in the regular army and a brigadier-general of volunteers. He had gone through the Peninsular campaign with credit, and risen to the command of a division. The formation of the grand divisions secured his promotion to the command of the Fifth Corps. He was a very handsome man, of middle stature, with regular, delicate features, jet-black hair and mustache, and very soldierly bearing. He seemed to have a better knowledge of men and matters in the army than any other officer I became acquainted with, and he allowed me to draw liberally on his store.

I met General Burnside twice. He showed to me, as to everybody else, a prepossessing *bonhomie* that made one feel at home with him at once. Indeed, he wore his genial, frank, honest, sincere nature on his sleeve. But there was nothing in his exterior or in his conversation that indicated intellectual eminence or executive ability of a high order. He inspired confidence in his honesty of purpose and ardent loyalty, but it was not possible that any experienced judge of men should be impressed with him as a great man. He talked without reserve of his intention to take the offensive at the earliest possible moment, but, of course, gave no intimation of his plan of operations. As he complained of the delay in the arrival of the pontoon trains for bridging the river, I was satisfied that the purposed blow at Lee would not be struck until that difficulty was removed, and that the risky attempt of a front attack would be made.

Besides the generals named, I had the opportunity to meet General Couch, commanding the Second Corps, and Generals W. S. Hancock, O. O. Howard, and William H. French, division commanders under him; General Willcox, commanding the Ninth Corps, and General S. D. Sturgis, commanding his Second Division; Generals Stoneman and A. A. Humphreys, division commanders under Hooker; General Reynolds, commanding the First Army Corps under Franklin, and the division commanders John Gibbon, George G. Meade, and John Newton; and General Hunt, chief of artillery. Couch, Hancock, Reynolds, Humphreys, Newton, and Hunt impressed me most as thorough soldiers.

Hancock's imposing physique, already spoken of, was sure to attract attention. I also found four more old acquaintances among the general officers—Daniel E. Sickles, division commander under Hooker, well known as a Democratic politician and member of Congress from New York (who afterwards lost a leg at Gettysburg and is still living at this writing); John Cochrane, commanding a brigade, also a New York Congressman of more than local fame; Brigadier-General Sol. Meredith, a popular Indiana politician, remarkable for his great size; and the redoubtable Irish leader and poet, Thomas Francis Meagher, who, *mirabile dictu,* had likewise reached the rank of brigadier-general. At the end of a fortnight, indeed, I already felt very much at home in the Army of the Potomac.

When the army first appeared opposite Fredericksburg on November 20, the rebels occupying the town kept up a fire from small arms upon any Union parties that ventured to go to the river for water. General Sumner thereupon addressed a communication to the mayor, demanding the surrender of the place, under threat of bombardment, on the expiration of sixteen hours allowed for the removal of the population. A compromise was reached under which, on the one side no more acts of hostility were to be committed from the town, and on the other the Federal forces were not to occupy it until further notice. It was well known, however, that the Confederates occupied the buildings along the river for a determined resistance to any attempt to cross, but the established truce was strictly maintained. According to my recollection, not a shot was fired from small arms or artillery within my hearing up to the formal opening of hostilities. This was, of course, mainly due to the fact that the contending forces were separated by the river.

The delay in the arrival of the pontoons was caused by a succession of mishaps and mistakes. During the Antietam campaign, the pontoon trains attached to the army had been ordered to Harper's Ferry and remained there ever since, as no occasion had arisen meanwhile to call for their use elsewhere. They were supposed by Generals Burnside and Halleck to be at Washington, and, of course, the longer time required for their transportation from the other point was not at first taken into account. An order to send them forward was, for some never-explained reason, six days in reaching its destination. When they reached Washington, they were ordered to be hauled overland to the Rappahannock. This was a grave error of judgment, as it took several days to secure the necessary teams, and the roads were found to be so bad that the pontoon wagons could not progress more than five miles a day. The attempt had finally to be abandoned altogether and the water route taken. A whole fortnight was thus lost in getting the bridge material to the front. It was this delay that prevented the earlier occupation of Fredericksburg and its surroundings by our forces, and may have been the principal cause of our eventual defeat. As it was, the full means for bridging the river simultaneously at several points were not at hand until after the first week in December.

The great natural obstacle of the river made it impracticable to discover the position and strength of the enemy by regular reconnoissances. Nor did we seem to obtain much information regarding him from spies. It was chiefly through the Richmond papers, which were as indiscreet in publishing army news as their Northern contemporaries, and which reached headquarters from various directions, that we received intelligence from the other side. But even through them we had only circumstantial evidence that Lee's whole army was distributed over the opposite heights. While an air line to them from the bluffs on the left bank was not much over a mile in length, even with the strongest field-glasses little could be discovered of the rebels beyond the field-works they had immediately undertaken and steadily continued. They probably saw not much more of us than we of them.

JULIUS BIEN & CO. N.Y.

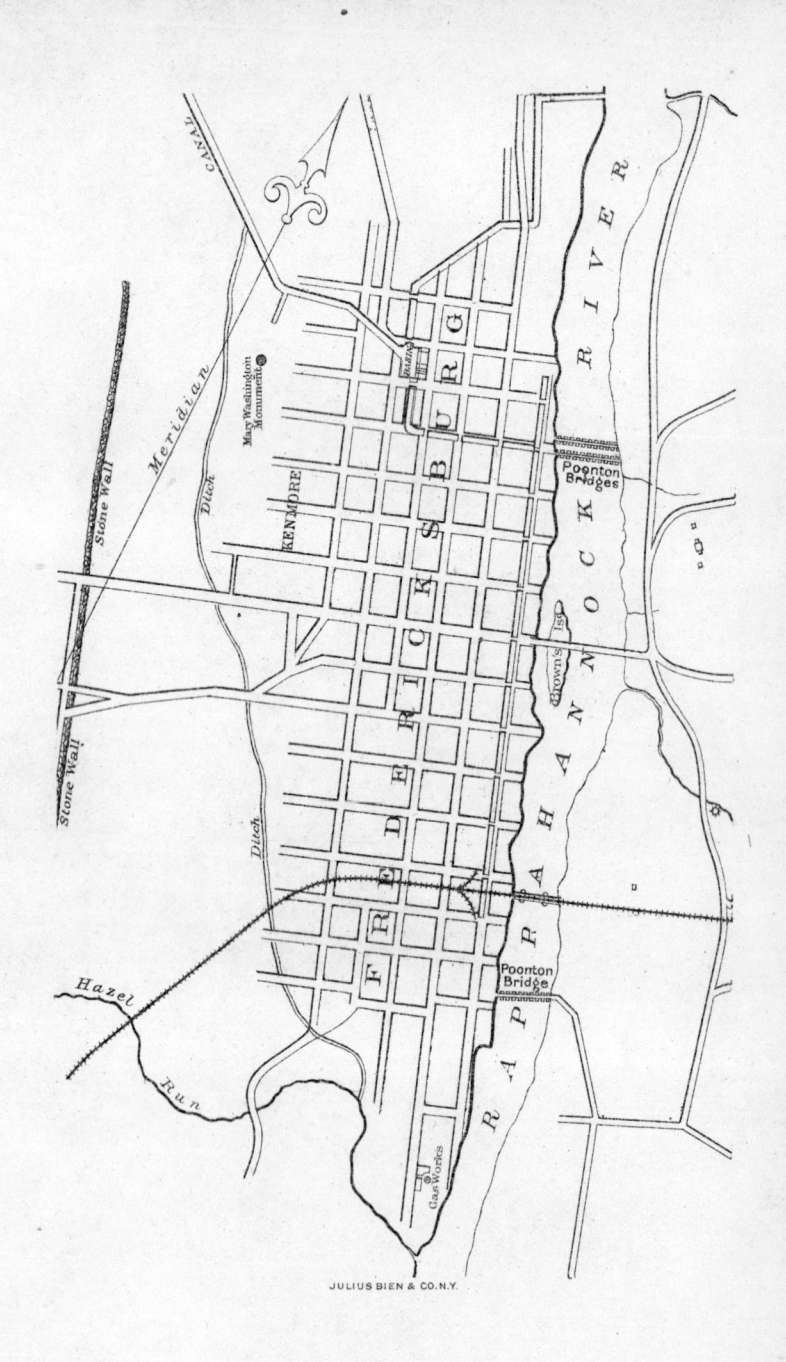

CHAPTER XXII

THE BATTLE OF FREDERICKSBURG.—1862

I ASCERTAINED on December 9 that all the preparations for the proposed active operations were completed, and that they would be undertaken immediately. The plan decided upon by General Burnside, and communicated formally to the Grand Division commanders, was as follows:

To concentrate all the siege and most of the field artillery on the ridge on which the plateau on the left bank abutted, and from which their fire would command the town, the opposite plain, and the encircling hills beyond it.

To throw five bridges across the river during the night of the 10th to the 11th—two at the upper end of Fredericksburg, one at the lower end, and two a mile below the latter; making the total distance between the extreme bridges about two miles.

Immediately after the completion of the bridges, the Right Grand Division was to cross by the upper bridges and move through Fredericksburg and form beyond the town. The Left Grand Division was to cross by the two lower bridges to the plain on the right bank, and the Centre Grand Division to be held in reserve on the north bank, ready to move either to the support of the Right or Left Grand Division.

The Right Grand Division to attack the enemy's left on the Fredericksburg heights with one of Hooker's corps and with a division of the other as reserve.

The Left Grand Division to make a simultaneous and diverting attack on the rebel right, with Stoneman's division in reserve.

On the 10th, the unmistakable signs of impending action were observable on all sides. There were conferences at army-corps and division headquarters, increased home letter-writing, and talk about the expected fighting, throughout the encampments, special inspections of the arms and accoutrements of infantry and artillery, distribution of ammunition, cooking of extra rations, and enlargement of field-hospital accommodations. The artillery was assembled in four groups or divisions at as many convenient points, and the pontoon trucks advanced nearer to the edge of the plateau.

The artillery moved first into position between dusk and midnight. No less than one hundred and seventy-nine guns, nearly all rifled, and ranging from $4\frac{1}{2}$-inch siege and 20-pounder Parrott to 3-inch guns, were arrayed, forming a close chain from Falmouth down the bank for two miles, ready to belch forth death and destruction in terrible concert whenever the signal was given. I believe it was the greatest assemblage of artillery in any battle of the Civil War. I watched the movement in front of the Right Grand Division for several hours, and was much impressed with the regularity, quickness, and noiselessness of it.

The first duty of the artillery was to cover the construction of the five bridges. The line of batteries being established, the Brigade of Volunteer Engineers, under General Woodbury, with a battalion of regular engineers, started with five bridge trains so as to reach the bank of the river at three o'clock in the morning (December 11). The way for the descent of the trains had been carefully prepared; still it was a difficult and risky undertaking, for there were no less than one hundred and fifty boats to be hauled on wagons, each of which required four horses. From the upper plateau with the encampments, a steep road led to a second plateau about one hundred feet below, nearly half a mile wide, which gradually inclined to the bank proper; the last hundred feet to the water being rather abrupt. The movement of the pontoons was to be concealed from the enemy, but, what with the accompanying five hundred engineers, the six hundred animals, and the escort of an infantry regiment to each of the trains, success in this seemed hardly probable. Yet the trains not only reached the bank at the fixed hour, but the engineers, according to orders, began at once unloading the material, and accomplished this without being at all disturbed by the rebels in Fredericksburg until daybreak. Their guards, reliefs, and main bodies must all have slept very soundly, or they would surely have tried some rifle practice, even in the dark. I did not see the creditable night performance of the pontoniers myself, having sought a good night's rest after the artillery had got into position, in view of the fatiguing labors I looked for on the next day. I slept so well that I was not roused by the musketry and artillery fire to which the bridge-throwing led, between six and seven o'clock, and did not stir till called for breakfast at seven. I dressed and ate very hurriedly amidst the roar of artillery, but it was nearly eight o'clock before I got to the line of our fighting batteries.

I quickly learned that the fire had no other object than to cover the completion of the bridges. The pontoons for those at the upper and lower ends of the town not only had been pushed into the water without interference from the enemy, but were half way across when, shortly after six, the bridge-builders received a sharp musketry fire from the other side which compelled them to abandon their work, after having some officers and a number of non-commissioned officers and privates killed and wounded. The infantry supports fired in return, but effected nothing. Thereupon, four batteries on the bluffs above opened a violent fire, with shot and shell from twenty-four guns, upon the other bank, for about fifteen minutes. When they ceased, the engineers tried to resume their work, but were pelted again with rebel bullets. As a thick fog hung over the river, obliging the batteries to fire at random, six light batteries were ordered down to the river bank; four near the upper and two near the middle bridge. The fire from the batteries above and below was then kept up at intervals, and was going on when I reached the scene.

A lull then occurred for another attempt of the engineers to finish the bridges, but again they failed, owing to the increased severity of the rebel fire. At nine another general cannonade was opened upon the rebel cover from over a hundred light and heavy guns. The roar of the discharges, the whizzing of the missiles, the bursting of the shells, and the crashing as they struck the buildings, combined in a deafening and yet inspiring war concert. At ten, our fire ceased, when the engineers once more endeavored to add pontoons to those already in place, only to be again driven back. Our batteries repeated their performance, pouring shot and shell upon the buildings from which the rebels fired. At eleven, the fog had lifted sufficiently to make the houses and streets distinguishable, thus giving surer aim to our artillerists. To a column of rebel infantry seen moving down a street they at once gave attention, making it disappear. The whole forenoon was thus spent in futile efforts for the completion of the upper bridges. It became evident, too, that every new attempt made it harder for the engineer officers to get their men to expose themselves. The latter finally refused to obey orders, or ran away from the pontoons to shelter as soon as the hostile bullets whistled around them. Irritated at this successful defiance of us by a small rebel force, General Burnside, shortly after noon, ordered a general bombardment of the town at large. Some one hundred and fifty guns were accordingly turned upon it, causing, as it seemed to me, twice as furious a roaring as before. Several buildings were soon seen to burn. This terrific cannonade was kept up for nearly two hours, when it was stopped for a further effort to finish the bridges.

At the suggestion of the chief of artillery, General Hunt, it was decided to try and rush troops across the river in bridge boats, to attack and drive away the enemy. This dangerous duty naturally devolved upon, and was accepted with alacrity by, the regiments serving as supports to the several bridge trains. At the upper bridge, the Seventh Michigan was to cross, while the Nineteenth Massachusetts deployed along the bank to cover the boats with their rifles. The daring venture was preceded by another tremendous outburst of our artillery, lasting half an hour. While it continued, boats were to be pushed into the river, manned by officers and men of the regiment named, and rowed over as fast as possible. But the engineers who were to push the boats skulked off again at the first rebel fire. The Michigan men, under Colonel Baxter, promptly assumed their part and shoved and carried the boats into the water. Six started off first, filled with less than one hundred men. Our batteries became silent, and on our side all eyes were anxiously fixed upon the small flotilla. There was great risk of a failure, as there were not enough experienced oarsmen to handle the boats, and as the force in them was small. The rebels sent a shower of bullets, killing one man and seriously wounding the Colonel and several others. But the other bank was reached, and the party formed quickly under it and then rushed up the first street, and in a few minutes had captured some thirty rebels and established themselves in a building after losing another officer and more men. This achievement was one of the bravest feats of the whole war. The remainder of the Michigan regiment and the Nineteenth Massachusetts followed in boats as rapidly as possible. As they forced their way into the town, there was some street fighting, but our men, spreading to right and left, soon had the loopholed buildings along the bank cleared of all rebels. The engineers could not be induced to resume the bridge work until our men had secured a foothold, when they took hold again, and by four o'clock the upper bridge was at last completed.

At the three other bridges to be thrown by the volunteer engineers, a similar experience was had. The enemy foiled successive efforts to lay them by his severe musketry fire, which inflicted, however, but slight losses. The second and third could not be completed until, as at the upper bridge, one of the covering regiments, the Eighty-ninth New York, had secured a lodgment on the other bank by a dash in boats across the river, which was effected without loss and with the capture of a company of rebels. The least resistance was encountered by the regular engineer battalion charged with laying the lowest bridge. Only a small party of rebels confronted them on the south bank, and they were speedily driven off by the fire of the infantry supports. The approach to the water was difficult, and all the material had to be hauled by hand for several hundred yards. Ice in the river also impeded progress, yet the commandant of the battalion could report at 11 A.M. that the bridge was ready for the passage of infantry and artillery.

After the lower bridges were finished to the south bank, the rebels did not disturb the Federal detachments that established themselves upon it for the protection of the structures. In the town, however, the conflict described did not end the fighting. The Seventh Michigan and the Nineteenth Massachusetts had been rapidly followed, partly in boats but mainly over the bridge, by two New York, one Pennsylvania, and another Massachusetts regiment of General O. O. Howard's division. After being formed in the first street parallel to the river, they advanced up the streets crossing it at right angles. When they attempted to pass the second parallel street they were met by a hail of bullets, and it required a hard struggle to force the rebels gradually out of the town. Darkness set in before our troops reached its upper end, and compelled the cessation of firing lest they should fire upon each other. During the night the rebels retired entirely from the place. The remainder of Howard's division and Hawkins's brigade of the Ninth Corps passed over, and by morning the whole town was occupied by our troops. The street fighting cost us nearly a hundred officers and men killed and wounded. I did not myself observe the last-mentioned occurrences. I had watched the bridge-throwing attempts all day, first from the upper and in the afternoon from the lower plateau. But, as it was so near nightfall when it became possible to get over, I concluded not to cross, but proceeded to General Sumner's headquarters.

The result of the day was, of course, very disappointing to General Burnside. He had relied on getting sufficient troops over the river to strike on the next day, and had issued formal orders to that effect, instead of which twenty-four hours were lost and the enemy given a long warning of his purposes and sufficient time for counter-preparations. Moreover, the delay impaired the fitness of his army for the bloody task before it, from the fatigue involved in its being kept massed under arms ready for the movement across the river so long before it could be executed. As all experienced commanders know, lying still under such circumstances is more wearing to troops than activity. Having satisfied myself that nothing was likely to happen during the night, I returned to my quarters for a good rest.

I was ready for duty early in the morning. The weather continued mild, but a heavy fog again prevailed, making it impossible to see more than a hundred yards ahead. I found Hancock's and French's divisions ready to move, and they commenced crossing before 8 A.M. They were followed closely during the forenoon by Burns's, Sturgis's, and Getty's divisions of the Eleventh Army Corps. The five divisions used the three upper bridges. As the day advanced, the fog lifted, and the five heavy, long bodies in motion over the floating structures formed a curious and withal impressive sight. At a distance the men and animals seemed to be stepping on the water itself. Everybody looked for a great effort of the rebel artillery to impede our passage, but, to our general surprise, instead of the anticipated cannonade from the enemy, only scattering shot and shell at intervals were aimed at us, without doing any harm. The rebel official reports state, in explanation of this weak demonstration, that the river lay too low for effective firing; but I can bear personal testimony to the contrary, as I saw some of their projectiles strike the water within a few feet of the upper bridge.

After watching the crossing of the troops for two hours, I rode over the second bridge myself and at once looked the town over. Fredericksburg is not only one of the oldest, but was, up to the outbreak of the Rebellion, one of the most substantial Virginia towns. It was compactly built up, with brick structures of plain but solid appearance. The red brick, white door- and window-sills, and white marble steps, reminded one of Philadelphia. The lower part was devoted to business; the upper consisted of private residences, among them a number of spacious two- and three-story mansions. As the mart of a rich agricultural district, the place was once thriving, but its prosperity had waned since the opening of railroads had to a great extent diverted its trade to Alexandria and Richmond. Along the river front, where formerly steamboat traffic had been carried on, there were marked signs of decay. The population of between four and five thousand included some of the oldest and best-known families in the State. The white inhabitants had nearly all fled. I saw only two, one of whom, in reply to a question, told me that he did not believe there were twenty-five left. Even of negroes not more than a score were in sight, and they seemed to be much cowed and rather afraid to be friendly with their liberators. Our troops had either found the business buildings open, or had forced them and used them for night quarters. As might be supposed, private property in the abandoned shops, especially in the warehouses from which the enemy had fired, such as tobacco, flour, bacon, sugar, and other articles of consumption, was not respected, but was taken without stint. Of tobacco particularly a large quantity was appropriated.

As the built-up portion of the town extended only a dozen blocks along and five blocks from the river, there was not enough street space for the 30,000 men of the two corps and their concomitant animals, batteries, ammunition wagons, ambulances, and all the rest. Howard's division moved from the lowest to an upper street to make room for Hancock and French, and they in turn made room for the divisions of the Ninth Corps. When I got over, the streets were already so densely filled with masses of infantry, mounted staffs and cavalry escorts, guns and vehicles, that I could hardly make my way through them. In the afternoon the overcrowding reached a choking point, and orders had to be sent to stop the crossing of artillery after about two-thirds of the batteries of the two corps had got over. There was nothing to do but to let the troops make themselves as comfortable as they could in the buildings and on the sidewalks and streets, preserving their organizations as much as possible. Much hardship was endured during the night by those bivouacking on the frosty ground in mud ankle-deep. But, as may be supposed, there was a good deal of swarming about by the soldiers, and resultant confusion, with too much opportunity to skulk out of sight. I could not help thinking, and all the officers I talked with about this cramped condition of our force had similar thoughts, that the enemy would surely make use of this tempting opportunity to bombard the town in his turn, after we got jammed and packed into it like sheep in a pen. Had he improved it, there would have been no attack by us, but a desperate struggle to regain the north bank, ending probably in the slaughter and capture of most of our troops. Not only was this reflection shared by the general officers I met, but also the logical deduction from it that it was a grave error to place the Right Grand Division in such a perilous position. The opinion prevailed, too, that even if the much-feared bombardment should not foil the whole movement before it could be made, it would not be possible to debouch from the town for an attack on the enemy, as all the approaches to his front were perpendicular to it, open and swept by his guns. During the whole afternoon I apprehended every moment that there would be an outburst of the rebel artillery, and felt most anxious accordingly. But the enemy happily confined himself to the desultory firing already mentioned. Night came on without a noteworthy incident. I had come prepared to spend it in Fredericksburg, but as I could find nothing better for a resting-place than space to stretch out on the floor of a room in one of the private residences with half a dozen others, I decided to return to my camp, after I had learned positively from General Couch that we should rest on the defensive till the next day.

The Centre Grand Division, being designated as the reserve and support to both the Right and Left Grand Divisions, moved near the three upper bridges, but no part of it crossed the river on the 12th, and the entire body remained in position till the next day. During the night, however, General Hooker received orders to send Sickles's and Birney's divisions, of General Stoneman's corps, to the two lower bridges, ready to cross and support General Franklin. This was promptly done. The river thus separated the main body of the army from its reserve—a strategic risk which all the authorities on the art of war condemn, and which can be explained, but not justified, in this case on the theory that the enemy would not dare to attack us.

General Franklin's two army corps, according to orders, had marched before daybreak on the 11th to near the points fixed upon for the two lower bridges, which were completed during the forenoon, but the General received no orders to cross until 4 P.M., when he was directed to take his whole command over. The movement had commenced when a new order came to remain on the north side, and to send only one brigade over for the protection of the bridges. Devens's brigade, of Newton's division, being on the other side, was assigned for this service. Renewed orders to cross having been received, Smith's corps commenced passing over at daybreak. Brooks's first division led, followed by Howe's second and Newton's third. The first and second divisions immediately formed in line of battle, with the third in reserve. In this formation the corps advanced during the forenoon, concealed by the fog from the enemy, a distance of about one mile to the Richmond road. Here they took up a protected position, in which they remained all day and bivouacked in the night. Towards noon the fog lifted and revealed the corps to the enemy, who, however, did nothing but maintain a feeble and almost harmless artillery fire. Reynolds's First Corps followed immediately in the wake of the Sixth; Gibbon's division leading, with Meade's and Doubleday's next in order. It formed with Gibbon on the left, Meade on the right, and Doubleday in reserve. The corps then advanced so as to connect with Smith's left. With the exception of slight skirmishing in moving forward, the corps was not disturbed during the rest of the day or the night, which it also passed in bivouac.

Hoping to hear something of the programme for the morrow, I went to General Burnside's headquarters about 10 P.M. I found a great assemblage of general and staff officers in conference with the General-in-chief or awaiting orders. The drift of their conversation was such as to warrant the inference that the enemy would be assailed in the morning. I was aware that orders for the action had been issued to the Grand Division commanders during the night of the 10th and 11th, and they appeared to be left standing as originally given. I could not find out, however, the hour for the opening of the conflict. It had not then been fixed, and, indeed, the order to attack was issued only in the morning, so as to observe special caution. I was awake at six and again in Fredericksburg before daylight—too early by several hours.

The day was like the preceding ones—mild, but very foggy at daybreak and until late in the forenoon. General French's division being in the front and certain to lead in the impending fight on our right, I made my way to its commander with some difficulty. The division was ready to move, but the commander was awaiting his orders. They came only at half-past nine, and directed that the division should move out on the telegraph and plank roads and form in column by brigades, led by heavy lines of skirmishers, and be ready to attack, but not to do so without further orders. After drawing in the picket line, the division was accordingly formed in the outskirts of the town (through which the streets, with scattered buildings, still extended), under cover of the fog, by eleven o'clock. Hancock's division supported it immediately in the rear. Extraordinary as it may seem, no attempt had been made during our occupancy of the town to reconnoitre the ground between it and the heights, and therefore nothing was known of its character in detail. A reconnoissance in force to ascertain what natural or artificial obstacles there were to a front attack, and to discover the best line for its delivery, should have, but had not, preceded it. The assailants throughout the impending struggle had to take their chances in this respect; and to this, I was persuaded then, and am so now, after an examination of all the official reports of the corps, division, brigade, and regimental commanders engaged, our fearful failure was largely due.

French received the order to move forward only at noon. I was with his staff when it came, and remained with them, as will appear. The division advanced on and between parallel streets. A strong body of skirmishers led, and was followed at a distance of three hundred yards by the three brigades of General Kimball and Colonels Andrews and Palmer, with intervals of two hundred yards between them. The two streets mentioned led to the so-called plank and telegraph roads, which crossed a canal, or rather mill-race, a short distance beyond. This watercourse was fifteen feet wide and from four to six feet deep, and proved a first serious impediment, as it could be crossed only by bridges, necessitating the contraction of the deployed lines into long, narrow columns, and involving loss of time. Beyond the bridges, the line of battle was quickly re-formed and the advance continued in the described order. The ground for perhaps 1200 feet rose gradually to a low crest and was obstructed considerably by a number of isolated dwellings with outbuildings and board and rail fences and stone walls. The passage of the canal and the deployment beyond led evidently to our first discovery by the enemy, for, immediately, there was a combined outburst upon us of artillery and musketry fire, with a mighty roar and rattle from the front, right, and left. The fire was converging and shook our column by its suddenness and severity, killing and wounding hundreds. Several shells struck right in the lines, tearing wide gaps in them. But they pushed on over the intervening space and reached the crest mentioned, under the shelter of which the formation was restored as much as possible. Then the skirmishers rushed over the crest, followed by Kimball's and the other brigades, on towards the second heights. They found themselves again exposed to a murderous rain of shot, shell, and bullets, from the front and each flank, but continued on with fixed bayonets and without stopping to fire, despite the constant thinning out of their ranks. They made their way for a thousand feet or so over rough and muddy ground and over fences, walls and other obstacles, when they found themselves within a short distance of the enemy's first line, along a ravine from which they received such a hail of bullets from rebel infantry in rifle-pits and behind a high stone wall, covering their front for nearly a mile, and such showers of grape-shot from field-pieces and from guns in position in earthworks on the heights a thousand feet to the rear of the wall, that they staggered and halted and in part lay down for shelter in the unevennesses of the ground. The skirmishers and Kimball's first brigade were the first thus brought to bay; the latter after losing one-fourth of their number, including their commander, who was badly wounded. Some time passed before the other brigades, also rather disordered by the hindrances described and decimated by rebel fire, came up to support. The lines of the three brigades became mixed into one. Numbers sought safety in retreat without orders, the remainder holding the position gained, but making no headway towards that of the enemy. They kept up an irregular fire, which, however, could have but little effect upon the sheltered rebels.

Hancock's first division had followed the third closely, but, unlike it, was not permitted to pass up the streets unopposed. It was exposed to the rebel shot and shell all the way to the canal and beyond it, suffering thereby heavier losses than the third before reaching the front. Colonel Zook's brigade was in the lead. When it reached French's line, an order came from the corps commander to French and Hancock, at about two o'clock, to storm the rebel position. Zook immediately started for it, followed by French's mixed-up line. Hurrying forward at double quick, they came within twenty-five yards of the stone wall, but could not withstand the terrible fire that swept from it against them, and fell back, leaving the ground covered with their dead and wounded. The next brigade of Hancock—the Irish under General Meagher—repeated the attempt, but was also bloodily repulsed, and the last brigade, under General Caldwell, speedily met with the same fate. Its commander received two severe wounds while urging his men forward. To this brigade belonged the 61st and 64th New York regiments that had relieved French's picket line in the morning and rejoined the brigade as it moved to the front. When it had come within a hundred feet of the rebels, Colonel Nelson A. Miles, of the 61st New York, observing that they were on the defensive, asked General Caldwell's leave to lead a rush with his regiment and such other troops as would follow, but was refused. Miles's men then did good work in picking off the rebel cannoneers with their rifled muskets at close range, when he was shot in the neck and obliged to leave the field. I mention this incident because the then Colonel is the present Commander-in-chief of the United States army, and has always been confident that, if permitted, he would have carried the rebel works and turned the fortune of the day.

I had ridden on with the staff of General French behind his division to the first crest. We were exposed to the hostile fire up to that position, but relatively sheltered by it from bullets, while shot and shell continued to fall around us. I remained there, as it enabled me to see the approach of the several bodies of our troops and even watch (while lying down) from the crest the actual onsets. My station also proved very advantageous, owing to the frequent reports that came in from sub-commanders of the progress of the struggle, and to the opportunity it gave me to meet, first, General Hancock, and, later on, other division commanders, and even General Couch, at the base of the crest. After the failure of the assaults described, I began to fear that the day would go against us. The stream of wounded told of heavy losses. Officers and men showed signs of physical exhaustion and demoralization. Some regiments at the front broke and dispersed. Skulking to the rear increased. The officers found it hard and often impossible to get their men up again for new efforts after they had once lain down. Generals French and Hancock themselves were forced to the conclusion, between two and three o'clock, that the rebel position could not be carried by direct assault.

General Couch also no longer believed in the possibility of the success of a front attack, and hence ordered General Howard's division to make an effort to turn the enemy's left. But he had hardly commenced this movement when Couch countermanded it, owing to urgent appeals for support from both French and Hancock, and ordered the division to the front. It advanced with Owen's brigade in the lead, Hall's and Sully's next. The first two brigades came as near to the enemy as French's and Hancock's brigades, and likewise made several onsets on his rifle-pits, but could make no more headway against the rebel fire than the others. The three divisions, however, steadily kept their positions, replying to the enemy's fire as best they could. They held them even after a number of the regiments had exhausted their ammunition and were left with nothing but their bayonets for defence.

Simultaneously with the forward movement of the Second Corps, General Willcox's Ninth Corps had moved into position on Couch's left, with Sturgis's division next to it, Getty's as the centre, and Burns's as the left; each division being in two lines. The line of the corps extended over two small creeks, known as Hazel Run and Deep Run, flowing due north into the river and to Franklin's right. When Couch advanced, Sturgis was ordered to follow in support of his left, and took his command at once to the outskirts of the town. He had just formed his line under heavy fire when the stream of demoralized men from Couch's front reached it. He at once ordered Ferrero's brigade to the front. It soon collided with a rebel column that was coming down from the heights, threatening to turn Couch's left, and succeeded in checking its advance and driving it back to the line of rifle-pits. The brigade became exposed to an intense fire, and Sturgis directed his other (Nagle's) brigade to a position from which he hoped that a flank fire might be opened for Ferrero's relief, but the broken ground made this move a fruitless one. Thereupon, Nagle went to the direct support of the latter. The whole division became thus engaged, and, like Couch's divisions, made several attempts to take the rifle-pits and stone wall, but recoiled before the enemy's furious fire.

Of the two other divisions of the Ninth Corps, Burns's acted in concert with Franklin's Grand Division; Getty's was held in reserve to guard the lower end of the town and observe the roads leading down from the heights between Sumner and Franklin until late in the afternoon, when Willcox ordered it to the relief of Sturgis. Its experience was but a repetition of the other vain efforts against the rebel position. Formed in two lines of brigades, it advanced to and beyond the first crest, only to be stopped by the destructive storm of rebel missiles. Towards noon General Hooker was ordered to send support to Sumner, and, accordingly, Whipple's division crossed over to Fredericksburg. Carroll's brigade was directed to the front for the relief of Sturgis, and Viatt's marched through Fredericksburg and took position to the extreme right of Couch's line for the protection of that flank. Carroll arrived at the front just as part of Sturgis's line was yielding. It rushed forward with a shout to reoccupy the position, and regained and held it.

The unfavorable reports from Sumner's front led General Burnside to direct General Hooker, shortly before 2 P.M., to send his remaining force—Butterfield's Fifth Corps—to the support of the right. General Hooker obeyed, but with a natural reluctance, as this movement tended to deprive him of the opportunity to exercise independent command in the battle, for Whipple's division of Stoneman's corps was already detached and placed under Sumner's orders, and its other two divisions had been ordered, as Hooker bitterly relates in his official report, to the Left Grand Division without his knowledge. While Butterfield was crossing, an order came from the general headquarters to hurry one of his divisions to the relief of Sturgis. Griffin's was selected for that duty and moved to the front as quickly as possible, but it was nearly four o'clock when he reached it. The first brigade, under Colonel James Burns, was directed to relieve Ferrero's, and did so under a murderous fire. A short time before nightfall, Griffin was ordered to make a last attempt to carry the enemy's position. His first and second brigades, aided on the left by Carroll's brigade of Whipple's division, undertook once more the desperate task. The line advanced bravely, losing hundreds by the deadly rebel hail of lead and iron, and pushed up to within a score of yards of the fatal stone wall, only to be stopped and forced to take refuge behind the crest from which they had started. The third brigade was brought up, but, before the attack could be renewed, darkness ended the fighting.

General Butterfield's orders were, to go, with his remaining two divisions, to the relief of Sumner's right by a new attack. Burnside, Sumner, and Hooker had in the morning obtained full information regarding the defences of the enemy from an intelligent and communicative prisoner. This had raised doubts in Hooker's mind as to the possibility of the success of any direct attack, and they were confirmed by his observations after arriving on the ground with Butterfield, and by information from some of the generals who had already been in action. Believing that another attack would result in further waste of blood, he sent an aide to General Burnside with the request for a revocation of his orders. The reply of his superior was that the attack must be made. Hooker thereupon went himself to see and remonstrate with Burnside, but this effort, too, was futile, and Butterfield had also to try what his brother commander had already found to be an absolutely forlorn hope.

I felt sure that to send in division after division, to butt against and recoil from the rebel bulwarks, would be simply seeking defeat in detail, and that our only hope lay in the success of the Left Grand Division, whose aim was to force back the enemy's right and thus compel the withdrawal of his left also. But when no encouraging tidings had come from Franklin up to three o'clock and the advance of Howard's division had also miscarried, I began to be alarmed about the safety of our right. It seemed logical to expect that, after repelling a series of attacks, the enemy would take the offensive in his turn and pour down from the heights in main force upon our beaten, decimated, confused, exhausted, and discouraged troops. This was indeed looked for by Couch and his division commanders. But, fortunately for our side, the rebels proved not as aggressive as expected. They came out of their entrenchments only twice in force, in pursuit of our retreating men, and were readily driven back. One of these attempts I have already mentioned; the other occurred about three o'clock, when a column advanced within 150 yards of Hancock's front, but, its leader being killed, fell back. Still, the danger remained of our being overwhelmed and driven back in confusion upon the town, and of my being caught in the catastrophe, and, therefore, about half-past three, I started for the rear. There was then a lull in the rebel fire, but, when I had traversed half the distance to the mill-race, shot and shell and rifle bullets again went over and by me in showers for a few minutes.

I observed further striking evidence of the rapid disintegration of our troops. I passed at least a thousand officers and privates making for the town; perhaps one-fourth of them were slightly wounded, many of whom were needlessly helped along by skulkers—a very common trick on battle-fields. The remainder simply were tired, hungry, and thirsty, and had no more stomach for fighting. I came upon General Thomas Francis Meagher, who stood mounted in front of some buildings used as hospitals for the Irish brigade, with about three hundred men and officers, both wounded and in good condition, around him. I asked him what he was about, and he answered: "This is all that is left of my 1200 men, and I am going to take them to the other side of the river," which he actually did. I learned afterwards that, after leading his brigade part way on foot to the front under fire, he turned back on the pretence that he could not walk any further, owing to an abscess in his knee, and had to get his horse. During his absence the brigade pushed on, but was driven back, like the rest of Hancock's division, after losing nearly one-third of their force, and retired in disorder. His retreat across the river without orders was nothing but a piece of arrant cowardice, for which, however, he never received punishment on account of his popularity among the Irish.

I carried some eatables for myself in one side of my saddle-bags, and oats for my horse in the other. Passing a fine brick dwelling with a stable attached, and seeing a negro looking out of one of the front windows, it occurred to me to take a rest, as all firing had again ceased. I called the negro, and he reluctantly came out with a very frightened look. I asked him to take my horse to the stable and give him the oats while I ate my lunch inside. He was too scared to refuse, and so I dismounted and entered the house and the parlor on the lower floor. It was elegantly furnished, and the owners had evidently taken sudden flight and left everything in their home undisturbed in charge of the servants. I made myself comfortable in an armchair, and made short work of my hard-tack and bacon. Overcome with fatigue, I fell asleep, but was roused directly by a tremendous crash. A shell had struck the building, entering through the rear of the house and reaching a front chamber on the upper floor, where it exploded and destroyed all the contents. The negro appeared with chattering teeth and scarcely able to speak from terror. I was not inclined to continue my rest under such circumstances, and, as the roar of battle made itself again heard, I got my horse and passed on.

It was then a little after four o'clock. I did not know that Butterfield's corps had been ordered to cross and to join in the attack, but I learned of this movement by coming up with the infantry and artillery of the corps in the streets. Ascertaining the direction which Hooker and Butterfield had taken for the outskirts, I went in search of them and was lucky enough to come up with them in a few minutes. Hooker had determined to precede the attack of the Fifth Corps by a concentrated artillery fire upon the enemy's position. Very little use had been made of artillery on our side up to that hour. Ten batteries, with fourteen rifled 3-inch and forty-two 12-pounder guns, had crossed with Sumner's Grand Division, and nine batteries, with forty-eight light rifles, with Butterfield's corps and Whipple's division. Of the nineteen batteries only seven took part, in any degree, in the battle; the remainder being left in the streets of the town or sent back to the north bank. The limited employment of our guns was due to the rising ground over which our troops had to pass to the attack. It ascended to such a degree that our batteries could not well fire from the rear without the risk of hitting our own troops. Further, the location of the rebel batteries was so high, and they were so well protected by earthworks, that an effective fire could not easily be brought to bear upon them. Moreover, the field afforded hardly any other than greatly exposed positions for our batteries. The outcome of several attempts made before Hooker's to employ them showed this. Dickinson's mounted battery of four 10-pounders was called forward after French's and Hancock's repulse, and opened fire from the outskirts on the left; but its commander and one-fourth of the gunners and horses were killed and disabled in a short time, compelling it to retire. Arnold's battery of six rifled guns was put to use near the same point, but their fire was impeded by our columns coming within range. Two New York batteries also supported our advances as well as possible. This and the prelude to Butterfield's attack constituted the artillery's part in the day's work on our right.

It was Captain Hazard's regular-army battery of six 12-pounders and four pieces of Captain Frank's battery, of the same calibre, to which the perilous duty of leading off in the last effort to storm the enemy's position was assigned. They had already started for the front when I met Hooker and Butterfield. They reached a favorable point for their work within two hundred yards of the death-dealing stone wall. In a few minutes after they had opened a most vigorous fire, the horses of all the officers were shot under them, and such further havoc caused among the gunners and animals that Captain Hazard impressed some of the infantry near him to serve his pieces. The batteries held their ground until they were ordered to withdraw.

The execution of the dread task of the Fifth Corps devolved upon Humphreys's division of two brigades. Allabach's second brigade took the lead, and was formed for the attack under the crest with Tyler's first brigade as support. Making for the front, Allabach, accompanied by Humphreys, came up with the mixed-up remainder of Couch's divisions that were still holding the line from which their attack started. They were lying on the ground. Allabach's regiments, which had been in service only four months and never under fire, at once instinctively followed their example, lay down, and opened fire from the ground. Humphreys saw at once that musketry could have no effect, and ordered a bayonet charge. Allabach's men could, however, be induced only with great difficulty to stop firing and rise and push on. The charge was made but checked, after only about one hundred and fifty feet had been passed over, by the tempest of the rebel fire. Our men broke and ran back. Humphreys at once led up Tyler's brigade to renew the charge. What happened to it had better be told in Humphreys's words:

Riding along the two lines of the brigade, I ordered the men not to fire, saying that it was useless—that the bayonet alone was the weapon to fight with here. Anticipating, too, the serious obstacle they would meet in the masses of men lying along the front, I ordered them to disregard and pass right over them. I ordered the officers to the front, and, with a hurrah, the brigade, led by General Tyler and myself, advanced gallantly over the ground under the heaviest fire. As the brigade reached the masses of our men lying down, they actually tried to stop our advance. They called to our men not to go forward, and some attempted to prevent by force their doing so. The effect upon my command was what I apprehended—the line was somewhat disordered and in part forced to form into a column, but still advanced rapidly. The fire of the enemy's musketry and artillery, furious as it was before, now became still hotter. The stone wall was a sheet of flame that enveloped the head and flanks of the column. Officers and men were falling rapidly, and the head of the column was brought to a stand when close up to the wall. Up to this time, not a shot had been fired by the column, but now some firing began. It lasted but a minute when, in spite of all our efforts, the column turned and retired slowly. I attempted to rally the brigade behind the natural embankment [the crest so often mentioned], but the united efforts of myself, General Tyler, my staff, and the other officers could not arrest the retiring mass.

General Humphreys had two horses shot under him, and all the members of his staff, except one, had their animals killed or disabled. The loss of the division was over a thousand killed and wounded in the ten to fifteen minutes during which the brigades were charging, including five colonels, three lieutenant-colonels, and three majors. Sykes's division of the Fifth Corps moved to the front and relieved Howard's men, but did not get into action.

Night came soon after Humphreys's repulse, and ended the dreadful havoc of the day. On our right, not only was the whole Right Grand and half of the Centre Grand Division completely beaten piecemeal, with the severe average loss in action of nearly fifteen per cent., but one-half of the remainder was reduced to a confused mass, demoralized by the exposure to useless slaughter and by the great hardships suffered for forty-eight hours. Yet greater disaster threatened from the cooping up of our troops in this condition within the narrow space of the town, which, with the pontoon bridges—the only precarious means of escape from this trap—was completely exposed to the rebel fire. I remained with Hooker until the report of Humphreys's failure had reached us, when I rode back into the town a little before five. Riding about the streets to learn something of the condition of our wounded, I saw the extent of the demoralization that had befallen us. It is not too much to say that the town was in possession of a cowed mob, thousands and thousands of officers and men of probably all the regiments that had been engaged filling from roof to cellar every building not used for headquarters and hospital purposes—just the worn-out crowd in the midst of which a stampede was as likely to break out at any moment as in a frightened flock of sheep. I knew that the line from which we attacked was still held, but not one-third of the force that had advanced to it still defended it. What, I asked myself, must not inevitably happen if the almost unharmed and relatively fresh enemy should come upon us by a night or early morning attack? Was Robert E. Lee, with his record of vigorous, daring leadership, likely to let escape him such an opportunity to profit by our incompetent generalship, inflicting a greater disaster than any yet upon the North by forcing the surrender or destruction of forty thousand Unionists? I knew that Hooker, Couch, and Butterfield, and the division commanders likewise, shuddered at the dreadful plight of their commands; and it was, therefore, in the deepest anxiety for the fate of the army that I returned at about six o'clock to the north bank, in order to receive the reports of my assistants at Burnside's headquarters. One was to watch the operations of the Left, another those of the Centre Grand Division, and the third to collect lists of casualties. All three disappointed me grievously. The first turned up only at seven, and had but a very meagre and otherwise unsatisfactory account of the events on the Left. The second did not appear till after nine, and handed in an entirely worthless account of the doings of the Centre. This obliged me to work till nearly midnight in gathering fuller information myself from the general staff officers who came to the general headquarters in the course of the evening.

It seems proper to let an account of what happened on our left come immediately after my story of the experiences of the right. The following summary description is derived not only from my own observations and the statements of others at the time, but from other authentic sources, including the evidence given before the Congressional Committee on the Conduct of the War and the published Official Records.

The position occupied by our left on the eve of the battle, to restate it briefly, was as follows: The line of Smith's corps, forming the right, extended in the plain about a mile from and almost parallel to the river, across Deep Run

Creek. Reynolds's First Corps was in close contact with Smith's left, and continued the line in the same general direction to the small hamlet of Smithfield, where Meade's division, on the extreme left, formed an obtuse angle with the division next to it, in order to guard that flank more effectively. Birney's and Sickles's divisions of Stoneman's corps, intended as the support and reserve of the two corps, remained on the north bank, close to the bridges over which Franklin had crossed.

General Burnside had conferred with General Franklin and his corps commanders during the previous afternoon, at the headquarters of the Left Grand Division, regarding the plan of battle. General Franklin proposed that he should be authorized to attack the enemy from his position with a main strength of 30,000 men. If this were permitted, Hooker's two divisions would have to be ordered across the river during the night and advanced so as to be ready to act as his reserve. Burnside neither consented to, nor dissented from, this recommendation during the conference, but, when he rode away at six P.M., promised, in response to Franklin's urgent request for early instructions, to send his final orders before midnight. Franklin waited anxiously for them all night, but heard nothing until Brigadier-General Hardie of the general headquarters appeared at half-past seven in the morning with an oral message that orders would follow immediately. They arrived at eight, and were to the effect that Franklin should keep his whole command in position for a rapid movement down the old Richmond road (running from Fredericksburg parallel to the river, near our front), and send at least a division to seize the heights below Smithfield.

General Franklin construed these rather indefinite instructions as directing simply a reconnoissance in force, and acted under that impression. He sent corresponding orders to General Reynolds, who designated Meade's division to advance towards the enemy, supported by Gibbon's division on the right and covered by Doubleday's on the left. Meade was under way at 8:30 A.M. The objective point of his advance was near the eastern outrunners of the heights encircling Fredericksburg and the adjacent plain, where they abut upon the valley of the Massaponax. Between the heights and Meade's starting-point there was a depression crossed by the track of the railroad. The ground first sloped and was cleared and cultivated for several hundred yards, and then came thick woods up to and beyond the track and to the very heights. The enemy held the track, the woods, and the heights. The column of attack was, as usual, led by a regiment deployed as skirmishers, followed by a brigade in two lines, with the division artillery and another brigade behind it, and the third brigade in reserve. The movement was slow at first, as the impediments of fences and draining ditches had to be overcome. The column, having moved parallel to the river for a quarter of a mile, turned to the right and crossed the old Richmond highway. The enemy then opened a violent fire upon it. The column was halted, and the division artillery brought into play against the rebel batteries, which ceased firing after twenty minutes, when the advance was resumed. Meantime, Gibbon's division had been ordered to advance and to make a front attack simultaneously with Meade's. This advance was likewise opposed by the rebel artillery and brought Doubleday's into action. Meade's guns, having gained a new position, reopened fire, and some of the batteries belonging to the left of Smith's corps joined in. The furious cannonade lasted for some time, but the enemy's fire finally came to a stop, owing to the blowing up of several of his ammunition-boxes. Our batteries then shelled the woods in our front in order to clear them of rebel infantry. About one o'clock Meade and Gibbon resumed the advance.

Meade's front brigade passed the cleared ground, entered the woods and drove the rebel infantry through them to the railroad track, where they offered a strong resistance but were forced from this position and beyond the woods up the heights and over the crest, with the loss of several flags and three hundred prisoners. Having reached some open ground, the brigade received musketry fire from the front, and shell and grape-shot from the right flank. No support arriving, the brigade, after sustaining this severe fire for a time, fell back. Meade's next brigade, after passing the track, was assailed on both the right and left flanks, and in facing and following the enemy in both directions its regiments got separated, some working to the right and some to the left. One regiment on the right got nearly as far as the leading brigade, but turned back with it. The last brigade of the division was exposed to a destructive fire from the rebel guns that were supposed to be silenced, before it reached the woods in front of the track. General Jackson, the commander, being killed as the brigade was ascending through the woods, it began to waver under the severe fire when only a part had attained the heights, and retreated with the other brigades.

Gibbon's attack was made to the right of Meade in the same formation by three successive lines of brigades. They did not get beyond the track. The leading brigade was brought to a stop at the railroad embankment by an artillery fire from the enemy behind it and in the woods. Its left was at once thrown into confusion. Another brigade, ordered to its support, soon in turn became disordered, and the greater part of it gave way. The division commander now ordered his last brigade to drive the enemy from his position at the point of the bayonet. After unslinging knapsacks and fixing bayonets, the brigade advanced to the attack with three regiments forming a front and two a rear line. It passed over open ground through the confused, retreating throngs of the other brigades of the division. The rebel fire was so galling that the brigade staggered and the men commenced firing without orders. By strenuous efforts of the officers, however, they were made to discontinue firing and resume the advance vigorously, and, as the brigade neared the embankment, the men with a shout and on a run leaped the ditches, rushed over the track and into the woods beyond, killing a number of the enemy with the bayonet and capturing two hundred prisoners. But the further advance of the brigade was stopped by new forces of the enemy assailing it on both flanks. General Gibbon being wounded and obliged to leave the field at 2:30 P.M., his successor in command, General Taylor, on failing to receive support and being advised of Meade's retrograde movement on his left, ordered the brigade to retreat. It was commanded by Colonel Root, of the 94th New York, and composed of that, the 104th and 105th New York, 107th Pennsylvania, and 16th Massachusetts regiments. I have given these details of its performance because it was the most gallant incident of the whole battle.

While Meade's division was engaged, General Birney's division of the Third Corps had advanced to its support with three brigades. It did not relieve Meade on the front, but served as a barrier to the enemy's forces that had started in pursuit of our repulsed divisions. Part of Ward's brigade gave way, but the remainder of it, and the other two brigades, rendered splendid service in checking and driving back the foe that was advancing rapidly with triumphant yells. Not only was Meade protected in his retreat, but two regiments of Berry's brigade went to the aid of Gibbon's retiring division. How little power the latter and Meade's had left to stay the hostile pursuit is shown by what General Stoneman says of their condition: "Every effort was made to rally them [the two divisions], but all to no purpose. Regardless of threats and force and deaf to all entreaties, they sullenly and persistently moved to the rear, and were re-formed near the bank of the river by their officers, many of whom used every endeavor to halt their weary and overpowered troops." It may be added that their retreat left all the artillery that had been in action without any support, so that but for Birney it would have been captured.

Sickles's division of Stoneman's corps did not reach the south bank until nearly 3 P. M., and, being ordered to take position on the right of Birney, did not get into line until after the latter's successful encounter with the enemy was over. One of Sickles's batteries got engaged with a rebel one and silenced it after a score of rounds. His skirmish line, too, had a lively exchange of shots, but the rest of his command did not get into action. But it is not too much to say that, but for the timely intervention of Stoneman's two divisions, the pursuing enemy would have made his way through the gap in our line and to the flanks of the Left Grand Division, and probably overcome them easily.

Doubleday's division of Reynolds's corps had been designated to protect the left flank of the Grand Division by diverting the enemy from the front, and moved forward some two miles for that purpose when Meade set out for his attack along the river, over the plain towards the Massaponax. Its progress was slow, owing to obstructions similar to those encountered by Meade. His skirmishers exchanged fire with the enemy during most of the day, and he was also exposed to the rebel guns, which some of his batteries engaged. But he did not collide with the enemy in force and suffered but little loss. Smith's corps remained passive all day. Its pickets kept up a desultory exchange of shots. It was within the range of the rebel guns, but suffered barely any damage, though some of the corps artillery participated in the cannonading during the forenoon and afternoon. Shortly before dark, Newton's division was ordered to support Stoneman's divisions, but did not become engaged.

Except along the picket lines, the infantry fire ceased on both sides before four o'clock, but the rebels kept up a determined fire upon us from some forty guns, which our batteries answered as vigorously as possible. The cannonade did not cease till nightfall, which found the Left Grand Division substantially occupying the same position from which Reynolds's corps had sallied forth in the morning.

It clearly appears from the foregoing narrative that Franklin's failure on the left was the result of the same causes that brought about our discomfiture on the right. Here, as there, the offensive strength was spent in successive fruitless assaults, with limited forces, upon strong rebel positions. Happily, only three of Franklin's divisions were subjected to this waste of blood, while seven divisions were used up under Sumner and Hooker. But the rebel defences above Fredericksburg were much more formidable and less approachable than those confronting the left, and hence made the attempt to take them by front assaults, *a priori*, a grievous error. With Franklin the case was different. For, while it cannot be absolutely maintained that an attack in main force, such as he had himself recommended to General Burnside, would have been successful, a favorable outcome was possible, whereas the attacks in detail by divisions were foredoomed to repulse. These were the hard facts: only three of the eight divisions at the disposal of Franklin took part in the action; the movement of Doubleday proved useless, the enemy not being in strength in that direction; and not a shot was fired by Smith's infantry, except on the skirmish line.

Franklin's course brought on another of those numerous painful and humiliating controversies that mark the ill-starred career of the Army of the Potomac. No blame can attach to this commander for taking the indefinite orders he received from Burnside in the morning to mean a reconnoissance in force only. But two other orders from the Commander-in-chief were orally delivered to him at about 2 P.M., by Captain Goddard, aide-de-camp, in these words: "Tell General Franklin, with my compliments, that I wish him to make a vigorous attack with his whole force. Our right is hard pressed." This order appears to have been based on the report of another aide-de-camp who had been sent by Burnside to Franklin for information about the doings of the latter's command, and who had reported that General Smith's corps was not engaged. Franklin admitted in the subsequent investigation before the Congressional Committee on the Conduct of the War that he received this order, but that he could not execute it, owing to the unfavorable turn the action had already taken on his front. But, except on the ground that he mistook the bearing of his first orders, it seems impossible to justify and excuse the inaction of the Sixth Corps. Its commander, General Smith, told me himself, at a later stage of the war, that he had been expecting every minute orders to move to the attack, and was puzzled and disappointed that he had to stand still all day. Of course, it cannot be positively claimed that the offensive employment of Smith's corps would have ensured victory on the left, but it is of official record that both Meade and Gibbon ascribe their repulse to the want of support, and, moreover, there can be no doubt that our failure, after the success of Meade's first onset, must be ascribed to our giving the enemy the chance to concentrate all his forces on the left against a little more than one-third of ours.

After learning that we had been discomfited on the left as well as on the right, I felt fully persuaded that our defeat was irretrievable, and that nothing remained to the Commander-in-chief but to solve the seemingly desperate problem of getting the army again over the river without further harm. I was sure, moreover, that if a resumption of the offensive should be recklessly attempted, it would be vehemently opposed by Generals Sumner and Hooker, and by their corps and division commanders. Nor was my conviction shaken by the sneering and contemptuous rebuffs my corresponding expressions met with from certain members of Burnside's staff. They talked as though the day's fighting had been only a prelude to another and greater action. Their swagger was so confident that, stirred up as I was by the grave peril of the army, I came near yielding to an impulse to approach Burnside and tell him the dire truth, which I feared he did not know. But I gave up that design when I heard, at about eight o'clock, that he had made up his mind to see Generals Sumner and Hooker and their corps commanders in person in Fredericksburg, and learn from them the condition of their commands.

I did not think for a moment that the result of Burnside's visit to the other side of the river would be anything else than an immediate withdrawal of the Right and Centre Grand Divisions to the north bank. But I was mistaken in this. For, when Burnside returned to his headquarters, he had made up his mind to repeat the folly of the day before, and to try another direct attack, and he actually telegraphed to General Halleck at 4:30 in the morning: "I have just returned from the field. Our troops are all over the river. We hold the first ridge outside the town and three miles below. We hope to carry the crest to-day. Our loss is heavy—say 5000." The Commander-in-chief had actually formed the desperate resolve of leading, himself, a storming column of his own former Ninth Corps. General Sumner, however, succeeded in dissuading him from the rash venture by telling him that not one general officer approved of it.

In the meantime, confident of the correctness of my judgment that there would be no more fighting, and in pursuance of my regular instructions after every important action to carry, whenever feasible, the account of it in person to New York or Washington, I had made up my mind to set out for the national capital after getting a few hours' sleep. I was confirmed in this intention on being informed that Burnside had interdicted all telegraphic communications to the North regarding the battle, which opened the possibility of achieving a great "beat" for the *Tribune* by exclusive first news.

CHAPTER XXIII

CARRYING THE NEWS TO WASHINGTON.—1862

I SOUGHT my quarters shortly before eleven, and arranged to be called so as to start for Acquia Creek at 3 A.M. I set out on horseback. Never before or since have I had such a terrible ride. It was pitch dark—indeed, I could not make out anything beyond my horse's head. There was no distinct road, but the army trains, in trying to avoid mud and move on solid ground, had made tracks of a seemingly infinite width, but all reduced to a miry state. Hence I travelled most of the way through a sea of mire from one to two feet deep. From time to time I struck stretches of corduroy, but, as the logs were loose, they made riding only more difficult and dangerous. Four times my horse stumbled and fell, throwing me once, so that I landed with a splash in a pool from which I emerged covered with liquid earth. I could not tell in what direction I floundered on, and, not meeting any one, had to trust to my animal's instinct. I was glad enough, therefore, when day dawned and broken-down wagons and débris of all sorts assured me that I had not gone astray. I had calculated on making the distance in from three to four hours, but I did not reach Acquia Creek before nine o'clock.

I proceeded directly to the tent of the quartermaster in charge of the depot of supplies and transportation. He was the same official whom I had met on my way down. He had heard the boom of the artillery the day before and knew that a general action had taken place, but had heard nothing of the result. Hence, he was glad and grateful to get the scanty scraps of news I was inclined to give in exchange for a plentiful breakfast which his cook prepared for me. Naturally I cherished the hope that my night ride would give me the start of my rivals, the correspondents of other Northern papers, and was very much elated on learning that none of them had arrived before me. But imagine my dismay when the quartermaster, in reply to my question as to when the first boat would start for Washington, informed me that he had received orders before daylight from General Burnside not to allow any officer or soldier, or any one else attached to the army, or any civilian, and especially no press correspondents, to go North without a special permit from his headquarters.

This was a knockdown blow, for it looked not only as if I should be disappointed in my hope of getting ahead of my competitors, but as if my coming to Acquia Creek would prove a great blunder, leaving me separated from the army and unable to get back to it for at least a day, owing to my own extreme fatigue and the exhaustion of my animal. To my further disgust, C. C. Coffin, the correspondent of the Boston *Journal* writing under the signature of "Carleton," whom I knew as one of the most intelligent, energetic, and indefatigable reporters in the field, turned up in the quartermaster's tent as I was finishing my breakfast. To be sure, the interdict applied to him as well as to me, and he was always very genial company; but one never likes to discover that other people are as smart as one's self.

My ambition as a correspondent was too strong, however, to make me submit meekly to the situation. On the contrary, with body and spirit refreshed by a solid breakfast, nothing was further from my thoughts, and I resolved to try my best to defy Burnside and circumvent Coffin. But the resolution was easier than its execution, and I wandered up and down the long dock—the only dry spot in sight—for an hour or so, vainly taxing my brain for an escape from the trap I was caught in. It naturally occurred to me first to arrange to slip off secretly on one of the four vessels discharging on the dock, but on inquiry it appeared that only one of them would go directly to Washington after unloading, and that at least twenty-four hours would elapse before the craft started on its return trip. Suddenly, however, I conceived a possible solution of the quandary. I saw two negroes row away from the dock in a small boat and stop a hundred yards or so from it to fish. The idea flashed upon me that I might get them to row me out into the river, about half a mile away, in order to intercept one of the numerous steam-vessels passing up and down between the capital and Hampton Roads. But in executing this plan it was necessary to prevent discovery and imitation by Coffin. Walking back to the quartermaster's, I found to my joy that the Boston *Journal's* correspondent had given way to his fatigue and was fast asleep on a camp-bed. I lost no time in retracing my steps and hailing the negroes. They promptly responded and rowed up to the dock. Not deeming it safe to disclose my real purpose, in case I should be seen and stopped by some one in authority, I offered them a dollar each to let me fish with one of their rods. They accepted with a pleased grin, and I let myself down into the boat. Telling them that I wanted to fish further out, I made them row out to the river proper so as to be beyond recognition from the dock. Then I let them know that I wanted to be put aboard the first steamer from below, and, pulling out two five-dollar greenbacks, told them that they should have them if they did this for me. The size of the reward was evidently overwhelming, and they agreed promptly to my proposal.

We slowly rowed down the river, and in less than an hour a steam-vessel came in sight that proved to be a freight-propeller under Government charter. Getting as near as practicable, I hailed a person standing on the upper deck, who proved to be the captain. Shouting to him that I wished to be taken aboard, he asked whether I had a transportation order, as he was forbidden to carry passengers without one. As he slowed down, I had got hold of a rope hanging from the side of the propeller, and, fearing that the captain would refuse to take me, I pulled the boat up to an opening in the guard railing on the lower deck, jumped aboard, tossed the greenbacks to the oarsmen, and told them to make off as fast as possible, which they did with a vengeance. The captain was at first disposed to be wrathy at my summary proceeding, but became mollified on being shown my general army pass, and on my assurance that I commanded enough influence to protect him in case my performance should get him into trouble. Being now certain of having the start of all my rivals, I felt very jubilant. The only drawback was that the propeller was very slow, making only about eight or nine miles against the stream, so that I could not expect to reach Washington before 7 or 8 P.M. This gave me ample time, however, to clean up, which my night ride had rendered very necessary, to sleep for a couple of hours, and, most important of all, to get an account of the battle ready for instant transmission by mail or telegraph. I had it finished at seven, but we reached the dock on the Eastern Branch only at a quarter-past eight. Before leaving the boat, I thanked the captain warmly for his kindness, and begged him to accept a fifty-dollar bill in recognition of the great service he had rendered me. He was much surprised, and at first declined the present, but yielded when I urged him to accept it for his wife and children.

I made all speed to the *Tribune* office, where I was told there would be no use in trying to send my report by telegraph, as the Government censor at the main telegraph office had been ordered by the Secretary of War not to allow any news from Fredericksburg to be transmitted without previous submission to and special approval by him. But there was time to send it by special messenger on the night train, which was done. It may as well be mentioned here that my account met the same fate as that of the first battle of Bull Run. I had stated in it as strongly as possible that the Army of the Potomac had suffered another great, general defeat; that an inexcusable, murderous blunder had been made in attempting to overcome the enemy by direct attack; and that the Union cause was threatened by the greatest disaster yet suffered, in consequence of the perilous situation in which the defeat left the army. The editor was afraid to let the *Tribune* solely assume the whole responsibility for what would no doubt prove a great shock to the loyal public, lest I might be mistaken in my opinion, and, accordingly, the report was very much modified, but was printed as an extra issue the following morning.

My duty being thus fully discharged, I went to Willard's Hotel for my supper. At the entrance I met Senator Henry Wilson of Massachusetts, known to the local correspondents as the most persistent news-hunter in Washington. He knew I had joined the Army of the Potomac, and at once surmised that I was from the front, and greeted me with the questions: "Have you come from the army? What is the news? Have we won the fight?" I answered: "Senator, you know whatever news I have belongs to my paper, but, for the sake of the cause, I will tell you in strict confidence that Burnside is defeated, and in such a bad plight that I think you can render no greater service to the country than to go at once to the White House and tell the President, if he does not know what has happened on the Rappahannock, to make an immediate demand for the truth. You can state further to him that, as I believe he knows me to be a truthful man, I do not hesitate to say to him, through you, that, in my deliberate judgment, he ought not to wait for information, but instantly order the army back to the north bank." Afer a few more words, the Senator started for the Presidential mansion. After supper I went back to the *Tribune* office, but had hardly entered it when the Senator reappeared, and, taking me aside, told me that he had seen the President, who desired me to come with him to the White House at once. Of course I went, although I was still in my campaign clothes and hardly presentable. It was nearly ten o'clock. The Senator informed me on the way that he had not given my message to the President.

We found Mr. Lincoln in the old reception-room on the second floor, opposite the landing. He greeted me with a hearty hand-shake, saying, "I am much obliged to you for coming, for we are very anxious and have heard very little." He then asked me to give him, as far as my personal knowledge permitted, a general outline of what had happened, which I did as fully as I could in a few minutes. He followed up my account with one question after another for over half an hour. He inquired regarding the defences of the rebels on our right front, their command of the town and river, the physical and moral condition of our troops before and after the fight, the chances of success of another attack from either of our wings, the extent of our losses, and the feeling among the general officers. He was very careful not to ask anything so as to imply criticism of anybody, although I ventured to mingle a good deal of censure with my statements of facts. But his questions and the expression of his face showed that he believed I was aiming to tell the truth, and that he felt growing anxiety. When he ended the interview by repeating his thanks, I made bold to say as earnestly as I could: "Mr. President, it is, of course, not for me to offer advice to you, but I hope my sincere loyalty may be accepted as my excuse for taking the liberty of telling you what is not only my conviction but that of every general officer I saw during and after the fighting, that success is impossible, and that the worst disaster yet suffered by our forces will befall the Army of the Potomac if the attack is renewed, and unless the army is withdrawn at once to the north side. Pardon me, Mr. President, but I cannot help telling you further that you cannot render the country a greater service than by ordering General Burnside to withdraw from the south bank forthwith, if he has not already done so."

The President took no offence, but, with a melancholy smile, remarked, "I hope it is not so bad as all that," whereupon we took our leave. The Senator was fully impressed with the danger of the situation and gratified that I had spoken so frankly. I felt thankful myself that I had been thus permitted to make an effort in the highest quarter for the salvation of the army, and I walked away with a sense of having discharged a patriotic duty. I have always been proud of my action, though it produced no effect. Burnside was, indeed, allowed to dispose of the fate of the army without interference from Washington; but, fortunately, the truth that there was safety only in withdrawal came to him in the end, after two days of floundering and vacillation, and the Army of the Potomac returned unmolested to the north bank during the night of the 15th–16th.

With the official history of the memorable Saturday, from both Union and Confederate sources, before me, I contend unhesitatingly that the escape of the Army of the Potomac from the Fredericksburg trap must be ascribed to the ignorance of the rebel Commander-in-chief of the extent of our losses and of the confusion and demoralization of our right. His despatches, during and immediately after the action, to the Richmond Secretary of War prove that he not only did not know the physical and moral disability wrought among our forces, but believed that there had been only a preliminary trial of arms, and that the battle would be renewed at daylight the next morning. Further proof is furnished by this quotation from his report: "The attack on the 13th had been so easily repulsed, and by so small a part of our army, that it was not supposed the enemy would limit his efforts to an attempt which, in view of the magnitude of his preparations, seemed to be comparatively insignificant. . . . . . But we were necessarily ignorant of the extent to which he had suffered, and only became aware of it when, on the morning of the 16th, it was discovered that he had availed himself of the darkness of night and the prevalence of a violent storm of wind and rain to recross the river." To assume that, with a knowledge of our condition, Lee would not have launched his columns, under the protecting fire of his artillery, down upon our broken, shattered, cowed, huddled-up right, would be simply to deny, as I have already said, his indisputable mastery of the art of war. It is true that the line of the right on the first crest, from which our attacks were started, was held during the night following the battle and during the next day by the organizations that last came into the fight. But, owing to casualties and depletion through skulking, they numbered barely one-third of their strength before the battle, and hence could have offered but a weak resistance.

The discredit to the Federal arms on account of the battle of Fredericksburg is not diminished by the relative strength of the two armies. The Army of Northern Virginia was composed of the First Army Corps under General James Longstreet and the Second under General Thomas J. Jackson; the former opposed to our right and the latter to our left. The First Corps consisted of five divisions with a total of sixteen brigades, varying from two to five regiments. The Second Corps was made up of four divisions with nineteen brigades of from two to seven regiments. The two corps thus represented an aggregate of nine divisions with thirty-five brigades. There was a cavalry force also, but it played as little part in the battle as our own. There appear to have been fifty-one batteries attached to the rebel army. The Army of the Potomac consisted, as set forth, of six army corps of eighteen divisions and fifty-six brigades, with seventy batteries of from four to six guns each. A comparison of the respective organizations shows that our brigades averaged more regiments than those of the enemy. The entire effective force of Lee, according to rebel authority, was, indeed, under fifty thousand, while Burnside's before the battle was more than double that number. Nor is this all. Lee, in his congratulatory order to his army, says that it took less than twenty thousand of his men to repel our attacks both on the right and on the left. This is perfectly credible, considering that our attacks were made by divisions and brigades only, and is borne out by his official list of casualties showing the organizations actually engaged. But it is true, also, as set forth in my narrative, that five divisions on our left and one on our right did not take part in the action.

We lost 124 officers and 1160 men killed, 654 officers and 8946 men wounded, and 20 officers and 1749 men missing or captured (of which, as the rebels claimed only 900 prisoners, one-half were doubtless killed), making a total loss of 12,653. The proportion of officers among the killed and wounded was extraordinary and not equalled in any other battle of the Civil War. The rebel loss is reported only under the general head of killed and wounded, at 458 and 3743 respectively, or a total of 4201. The prisoners we took brought it up to about 5000, or forty per cent. of our loss. Jackson's corps lost three-fifths of the total, namely, 328 killed and 2354 wounded, and more than half of the prisoners taken by us. Our divisions which attacked him lost, together, 4284. Deducting Jackson's and Franklin's losses from the totals, the horrible fact appears that our loss on the right amounted to more than four times that of the enemy, which brings out in gory relief the useless butchery of our soldiers.

With this I gladly close the sickening story of the appalling disaster for which Ambrose E. Burnside will, to the end of time, stand charged with the responsibility.

END OF VOLUME ONE.

The Riverside Press
Electrotyped and printed by H. O. Houghton & Co.
Cambridge, Mass., U. S. A.